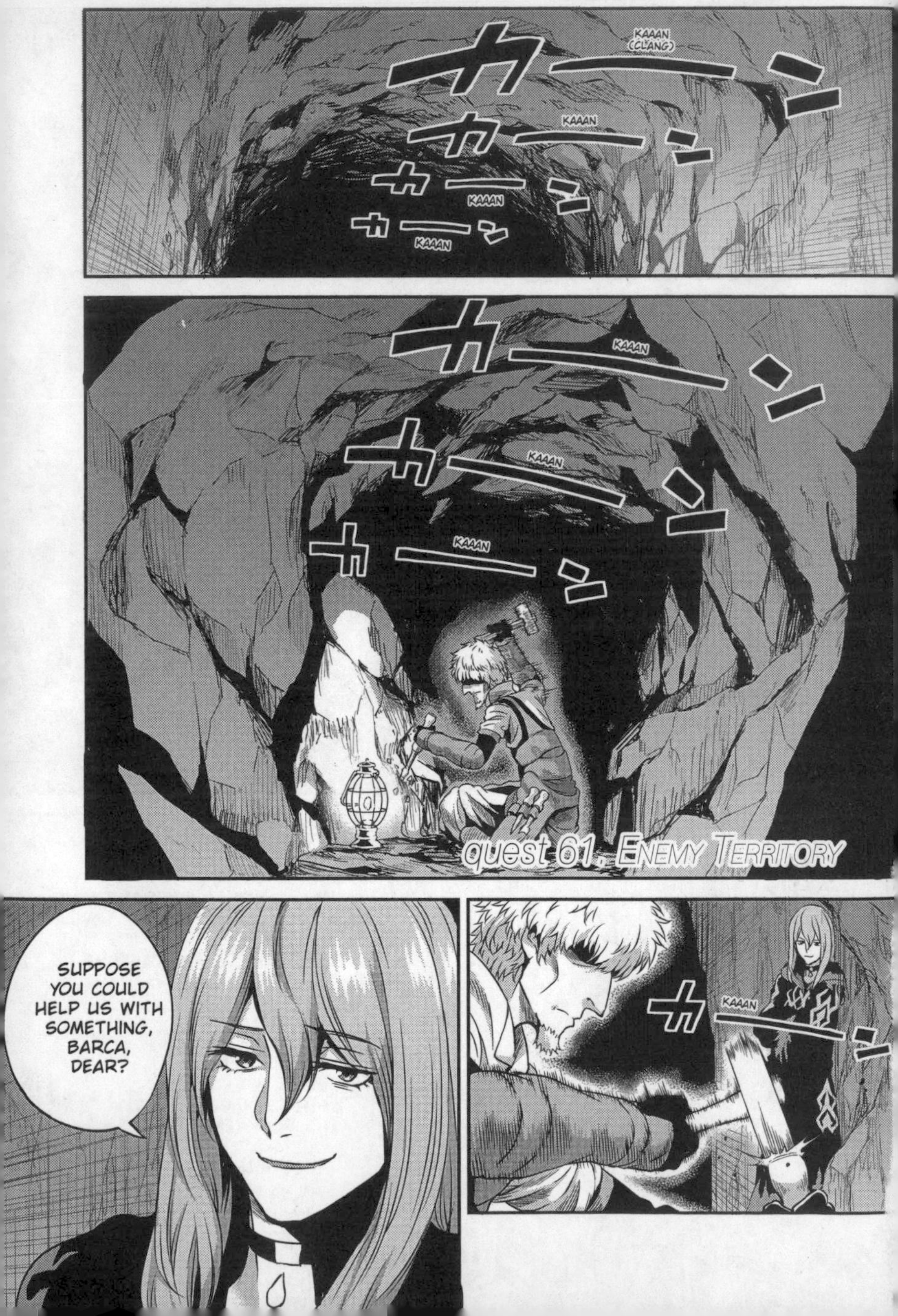
KAAAN (CLANG)
KAAAN
KAAAN
KAAAN
KAAAN
KAAAN
KAAAN
quest 61. Enemy Territory
KAAAN
SUPPOSE YOU COULD HELP US WITH SOMETHING, BARCA, DEAR?

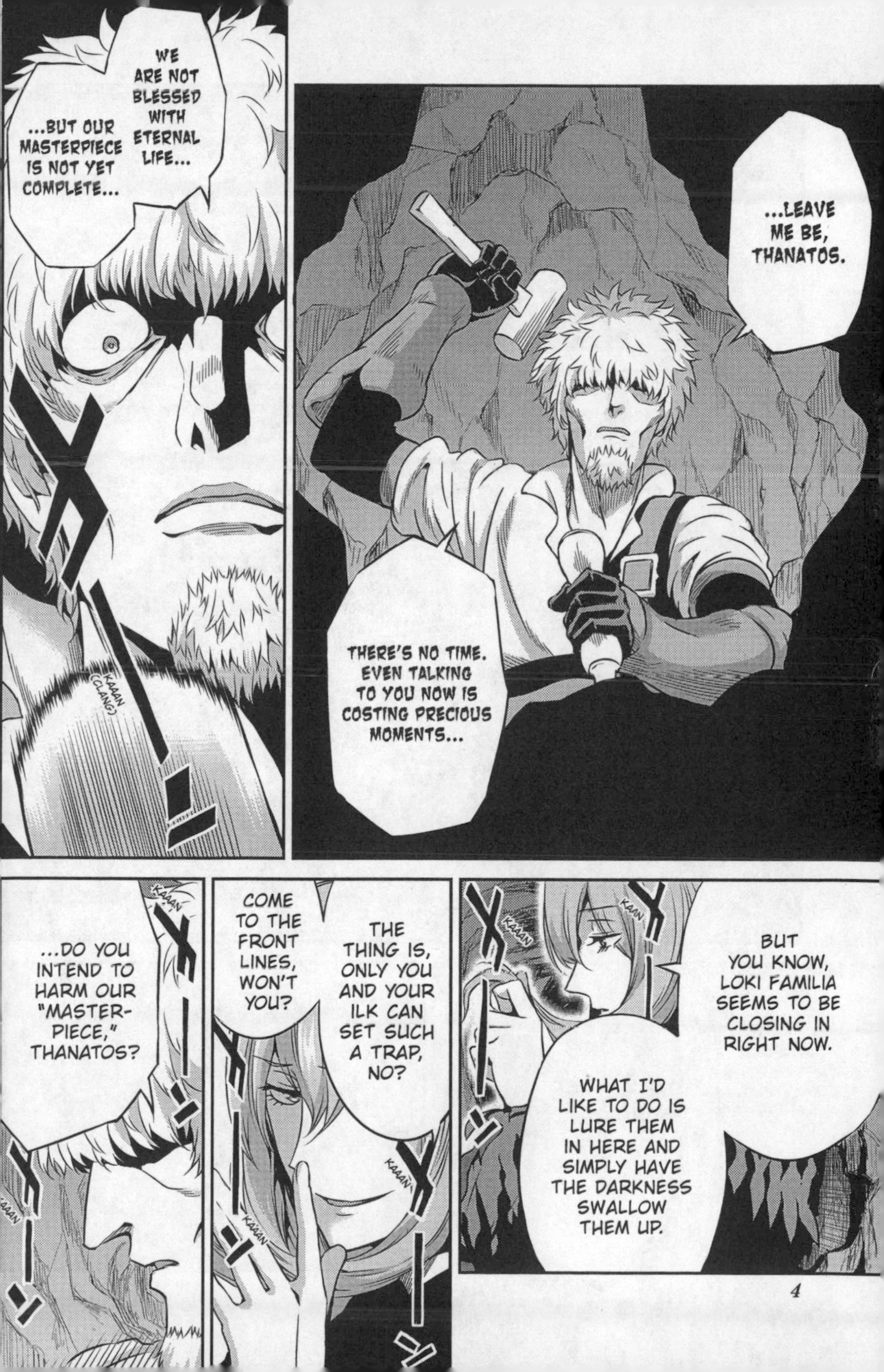
...LEAVE ME BE, THANATOS.
THERE'S NO TIME. EVEN TALKING TO YOU NOW IS COSTING PRECIOUS MOMENTS...
WE ARE NOT BLESSED WITH ETERNAL LIFE...
...BUT OUR MASTERPIECE IS NOT YET COMPLETE...
KAAAN (CLANG)
BUT YOU KNOW, LOKI FAMILIA SEEMS TO BE CLOSING IN RIGHT NOW.
KAAN
KAAAN
WHAT I'D LIKE TO DO IS LURE THEM IN HERE AND SIMPLY HAVE THE DARKNESS SWALLOW THEM UP.
THE THING IS, ONLY YOU AND YOUR ILK CAN SET SUCH A TRAP, NO?
COME TO THE FRONT LINES, WON'T YOU?
KAAAN
KAAAN
KAAAN
...DO YOU INTEND TO HARM OUR "MASTER-PIECE," THANATOS?
KAAAN

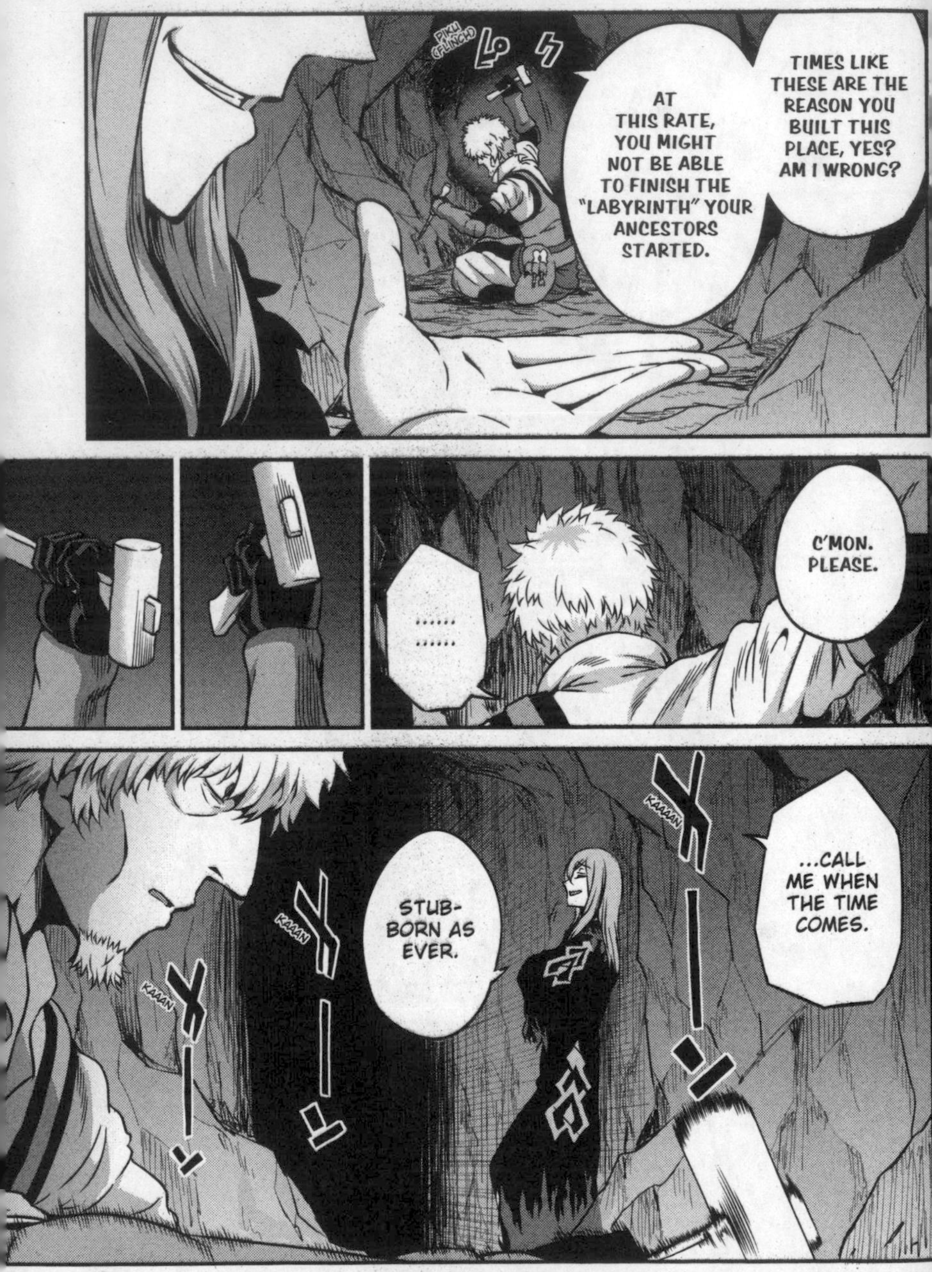
TIMES LIKE THESE ARE THE REASON YOU BUILT THIS PLACE, YES? AM I WRONG?
AT THIS RATE, YOU MIGHT NOT BE ABLE TO FINISH THE "LABYRINTH" YOUR ANCESTORS STARTED.
PIKU (FLINCH)
C'MON. PLEASE.
......
......
...CALL ME WHEN THE TIME COMES.
KAAAAN
STUB-BORN AS EVER.
KAAAN
KAAAN

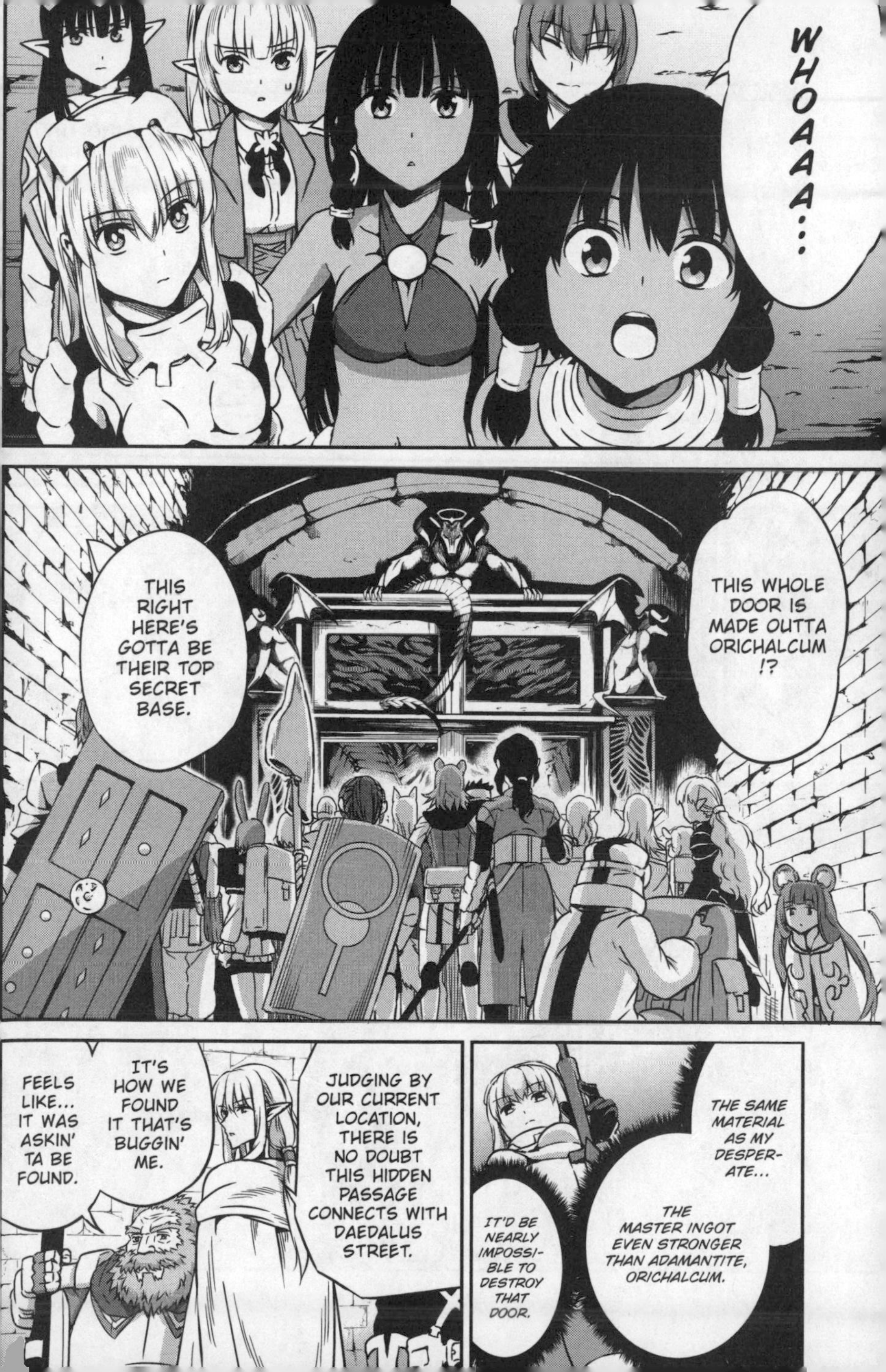
WHOAAA...
THIS WHOLE DOOR IS MADE OUTTA ORICHALCUM!?
THIS RIGHT HERE'S GOTTA BE THEIR TOP SECRET BASE.
THE SAME MATERIAL AS MY DESPERATE...
THE MASTER INGOT EVEN STRONGER THAN ADAMANTITE, ORICHALCUM.
IT'D BE NEARLY IMPOSSIBLE TO DESTROY THAT DOOR.
JUDGING BY OUR CURRENT LOCATION, THERE IS NO DOUBT THIS HIDDEN PASSAGE CONNECTS WITH DAEDALUS STREET.
IT'S HOW WE FOUND IT THAT'S BUGGIN' ME.
FEELS LIKE... IT WAS ASKIN' TA BE FOUND.

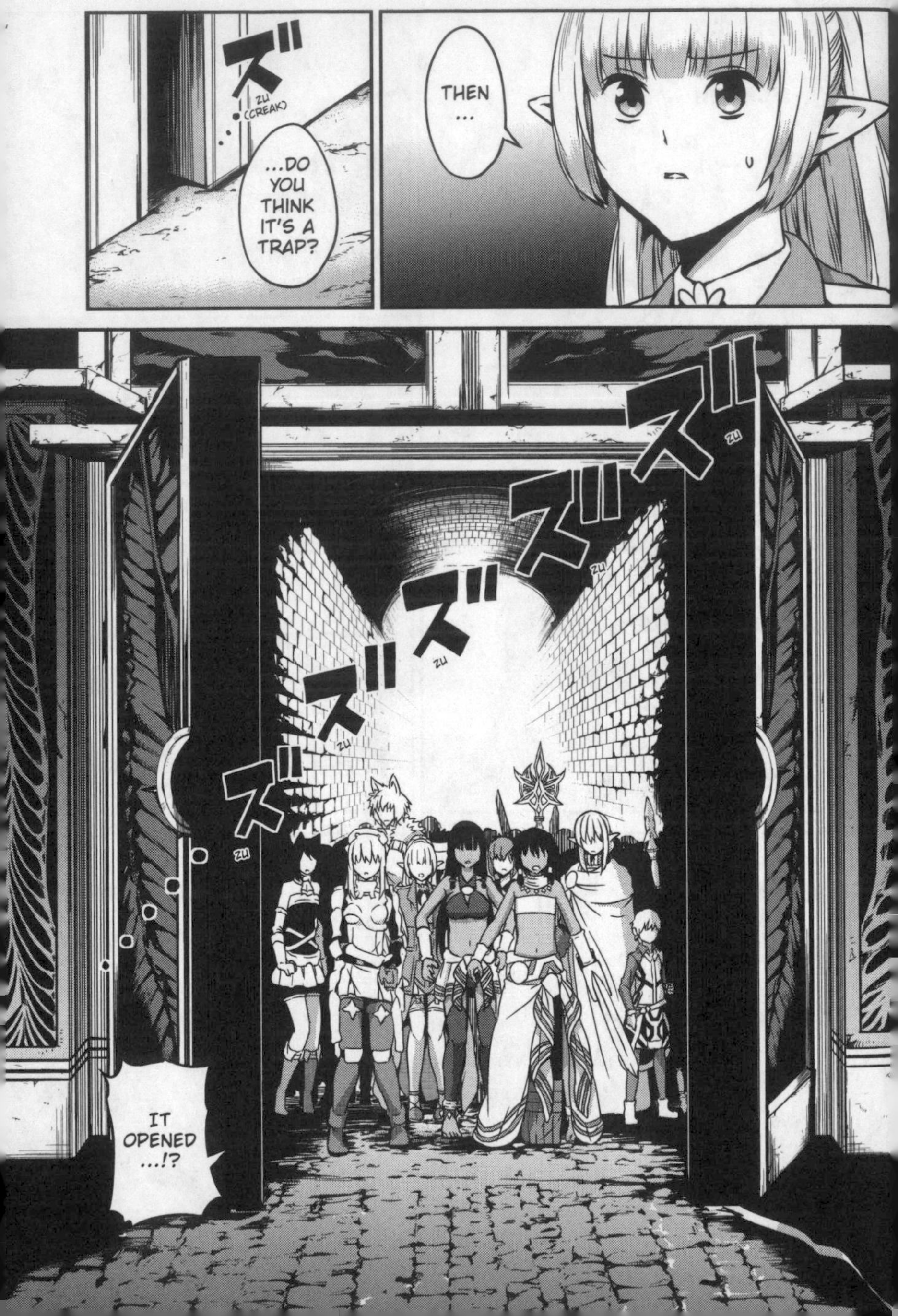
THEN ...
ズ
ZU (CREAK)
...DO YOU THINK IT'S A TRAP?
ズズ
ZU
ズズ
ZU
ズズ
ZU
ズズ
ZU
ズズ
ZU
IT OPENED ...!?

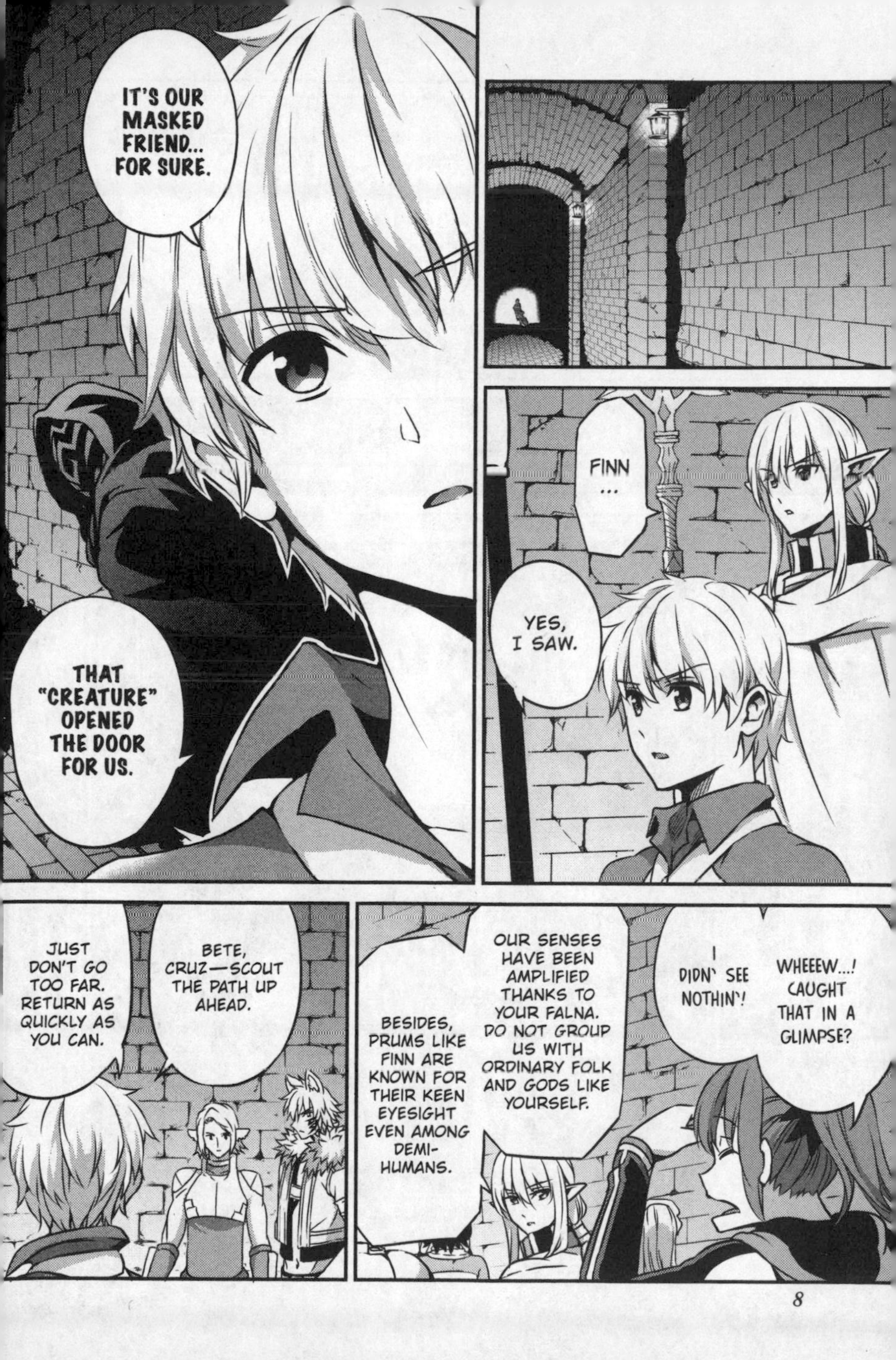
FINN ...
YES, I SAW.
IT'S OUR MASKED FRIEND... FOR SURE.
THAT "CREATURE" OPENED THE DOOR FOR US.
WHEEEW...! CAUGHT THAT IN A GLIMPSE?
I DIDN' SEE NOTHIN'!
OUR SENSES HAVE BEEN AMPLIFIED THANKS TO YOUR FALNA. DO NOT GROUP US WITH ORDINARY FOLK AND GODS LIKE YOURSELF.
BESIDES, PRUMS LIKE FINN ARE KNOWN FOR THEIR KEEN EYESIGHT EVEN AMONG DEMI-HUMANS.
BETE, CRUZ—SCOUT THE PATH UP AHEAD.
JUST DON'T GO TOO FAR. RETURN AS QUICKLY AS YOU CAN.

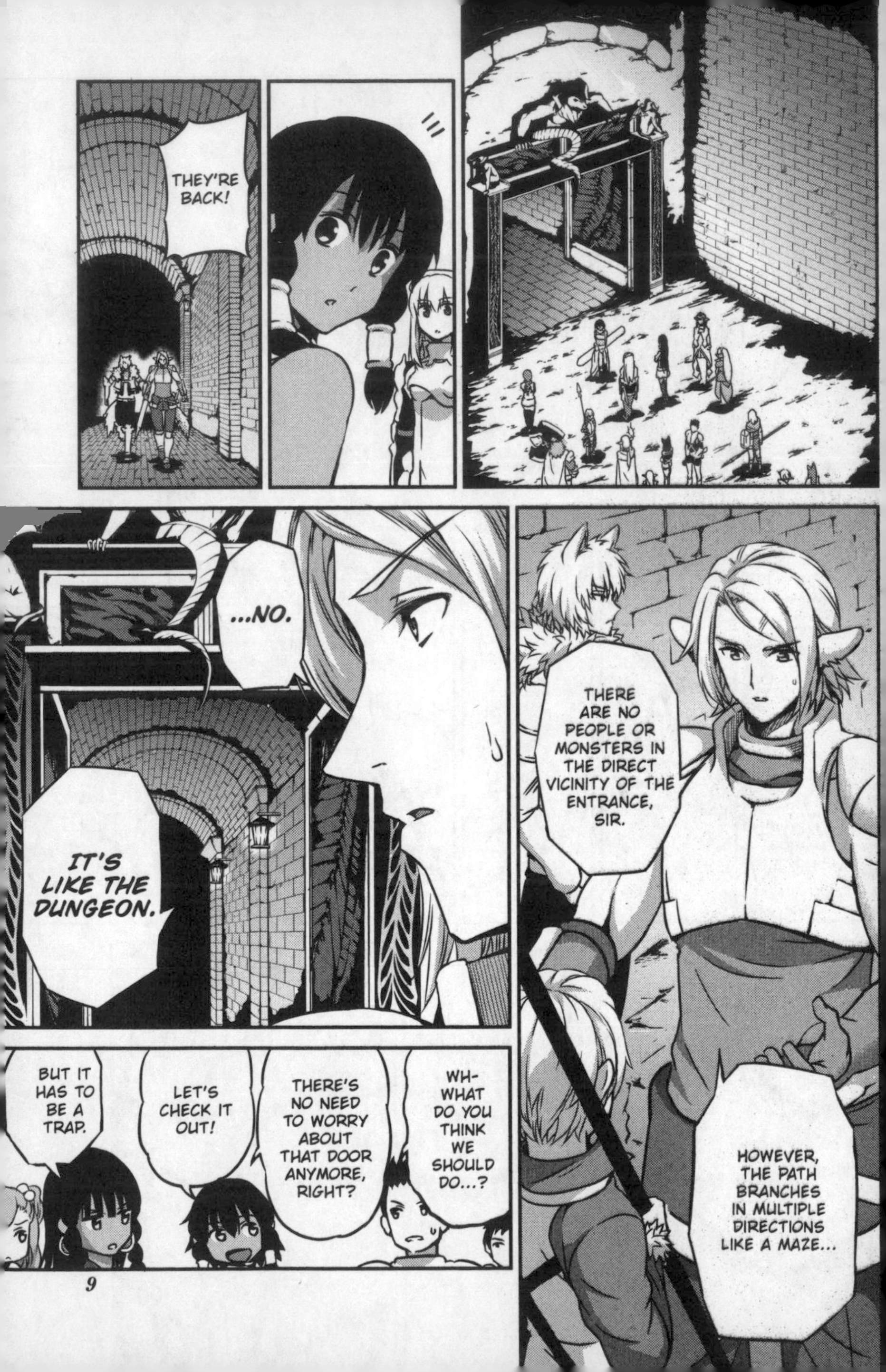
THEY'RE BACK!
THERE ARE NO PEOPLE OR MONSTERS IN THE DIRECT VICINITY OF THE ENTRANCE, SIR.
HOWEVER, THE PATH BRANCHES IN MULTIPLE DIRECTIONS LIKE A MAZE...
...NO.
IT'S LIKE THE DUNGEON.
WH-WHAT DO YOU THINK WE SHOULD DO...?
THERE'S NO NEED TO WORRY ABOUT THAT DOOR ANYMORE, RIGHT?
LET'S CHECK IT OUT!
BUT IT HAS TO BE A TRAP.

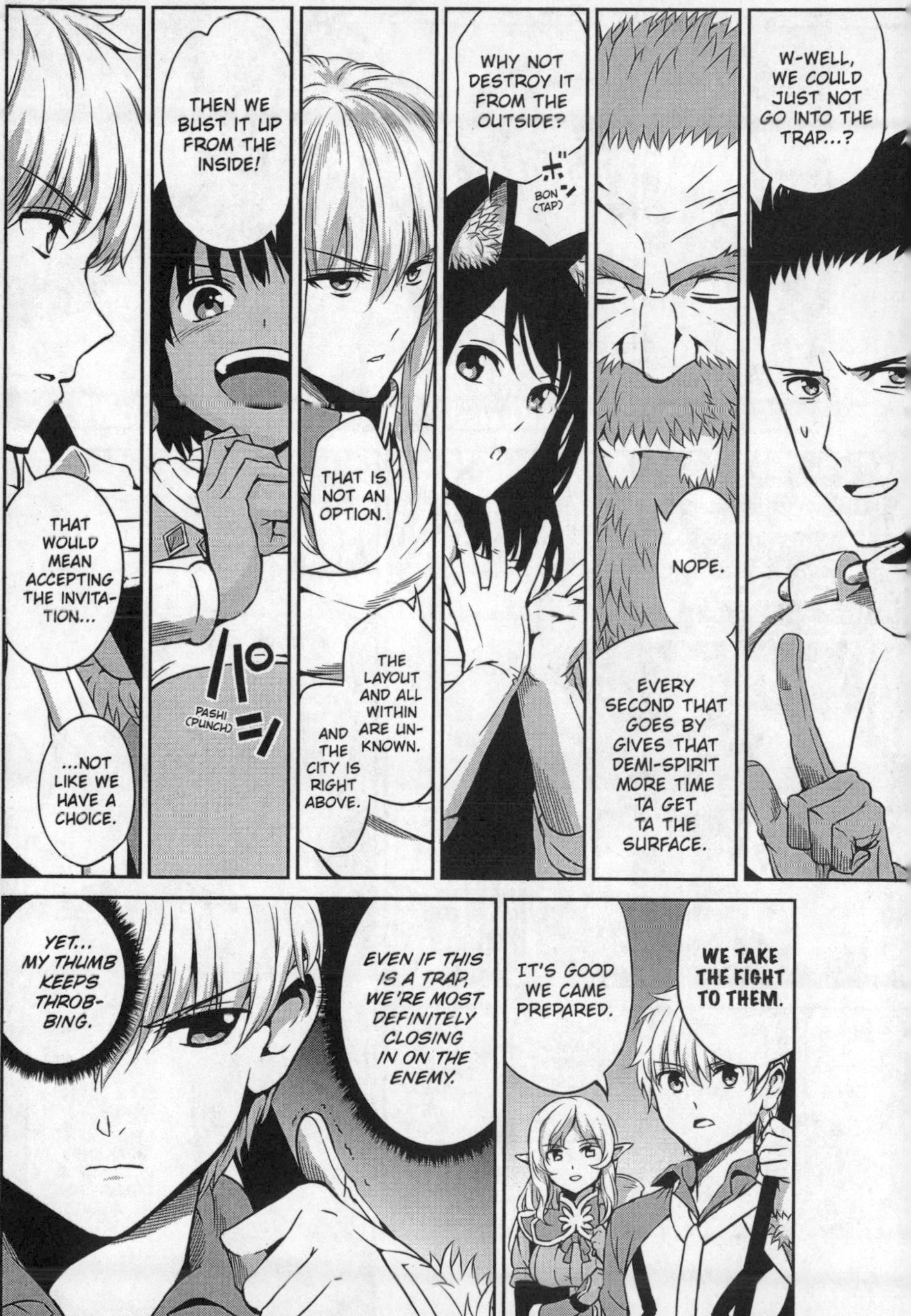
W-WELL, WE COULD JUST NOT GO INTO THE TRAP...?
NOPE.
EVERY SECOND THAT GOES BY GIVES THAT DEMI-SPIRIT MORE TIME TA GET TA THE SURFACE.
WHY NOT DESTROY IT FROM THE OUTSIDE?
BON (TAP)
THAT IS NOT AN OPTION.
THE LAYOUT AND ALL WITHIN ARE UN-KNOWN.
AND THE CITY IS RIGHT ABOVE.
THEN WE BUST IT UP FROM THE INSIDE!
PASHI (PUNCH)
THAT WOULD MEAN ACCEPTING THE INVITA-TION...
...NOT LIKE WE HAVE A CHOICE.
WE TAKE THE FIGHT TO THEM.
IT'S GOOD WE CAME PREPARED.
EVEN IF THIS IS A TRAP, WE'RE MOST DEFINITELY CLOSING IN ON THE ENEMY.
YET... MY THUMB KEEPS THROB-BING.

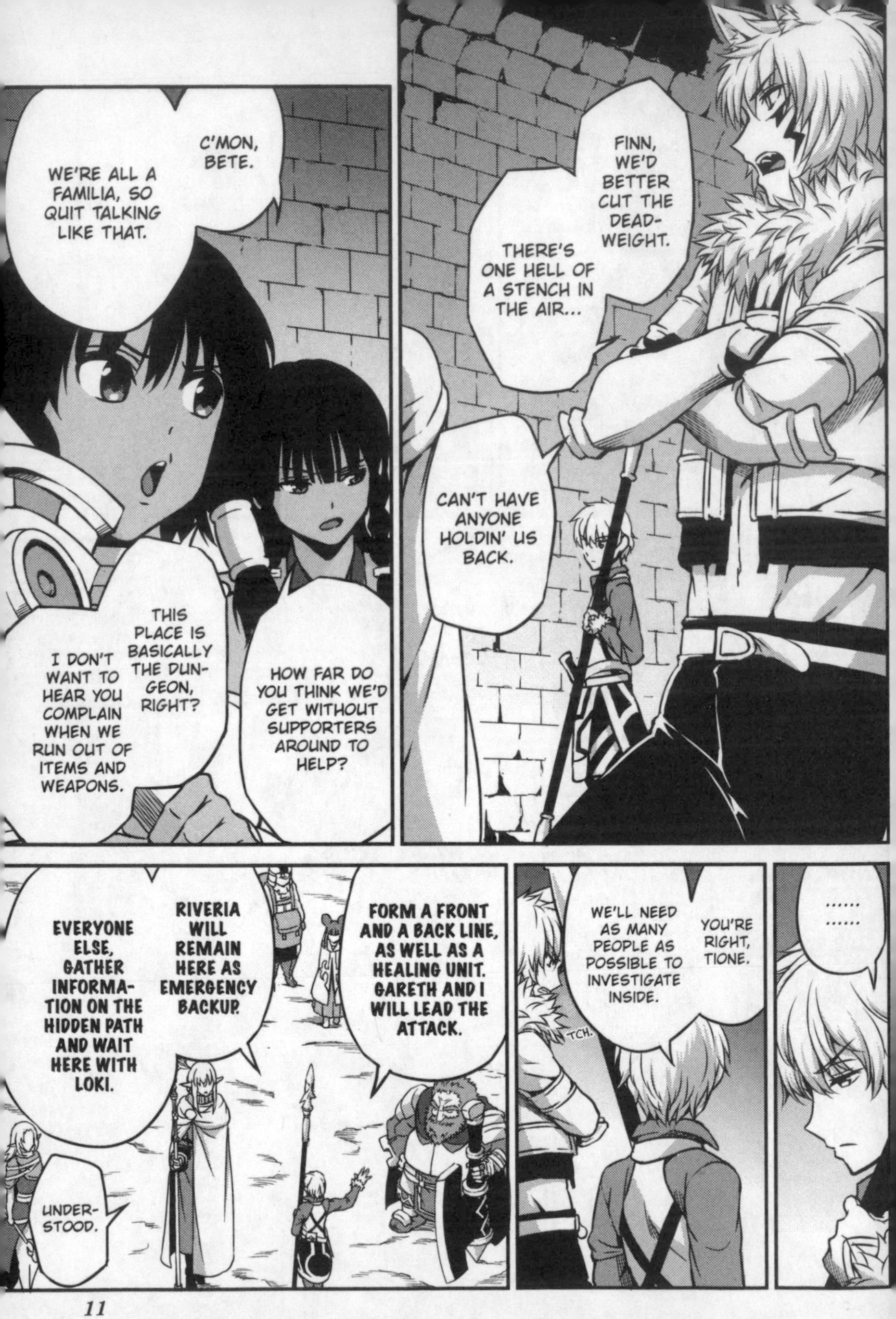
FINN, WE'D BETTER CUT THE DEAD-WEIGHT.
THERE'S ONE HELL OF A STENCH IN THE AIR...
CAN'T HAVE ANYONE HOLDIN' US BACK.
C'MON, BETE.
WE'RE ALL A FAMILIA, SO QUIT TALKING LIKE THAT.
HOW FAR DO YOU THINK WE'D GET WITHOUT SUPPORTERS AROUND TO HELP?
THIS PLACE IS BASICALLY THE DUN-GEON, RIGHT?
I DON'T WANT TO HEAR YOU COMPLAIN WHEN WE RUN OUT OF ITEMS AND WEAPONS.
......
......
YOU'RE RIGHT, TIONE.
WE'LL NEED AS MANY PEOPLE AS POSSIBLE TO INVESTIGATE INSIDE.
TCH.
FORM A FRONT AND A BACK LINE, AS WELL AS A HEALING UNIT. GARETH AND I WILL LEAD THE ATTACK.
RIVERIA WILL REMAIN HERE AS EMERGENCY BACKUP.
EVERYONE ELSE, GATHER INFORMA-TION ON THE HIDDEN PATH AND WAIT HERE WITH LOKI.
UNDER-STOOD.

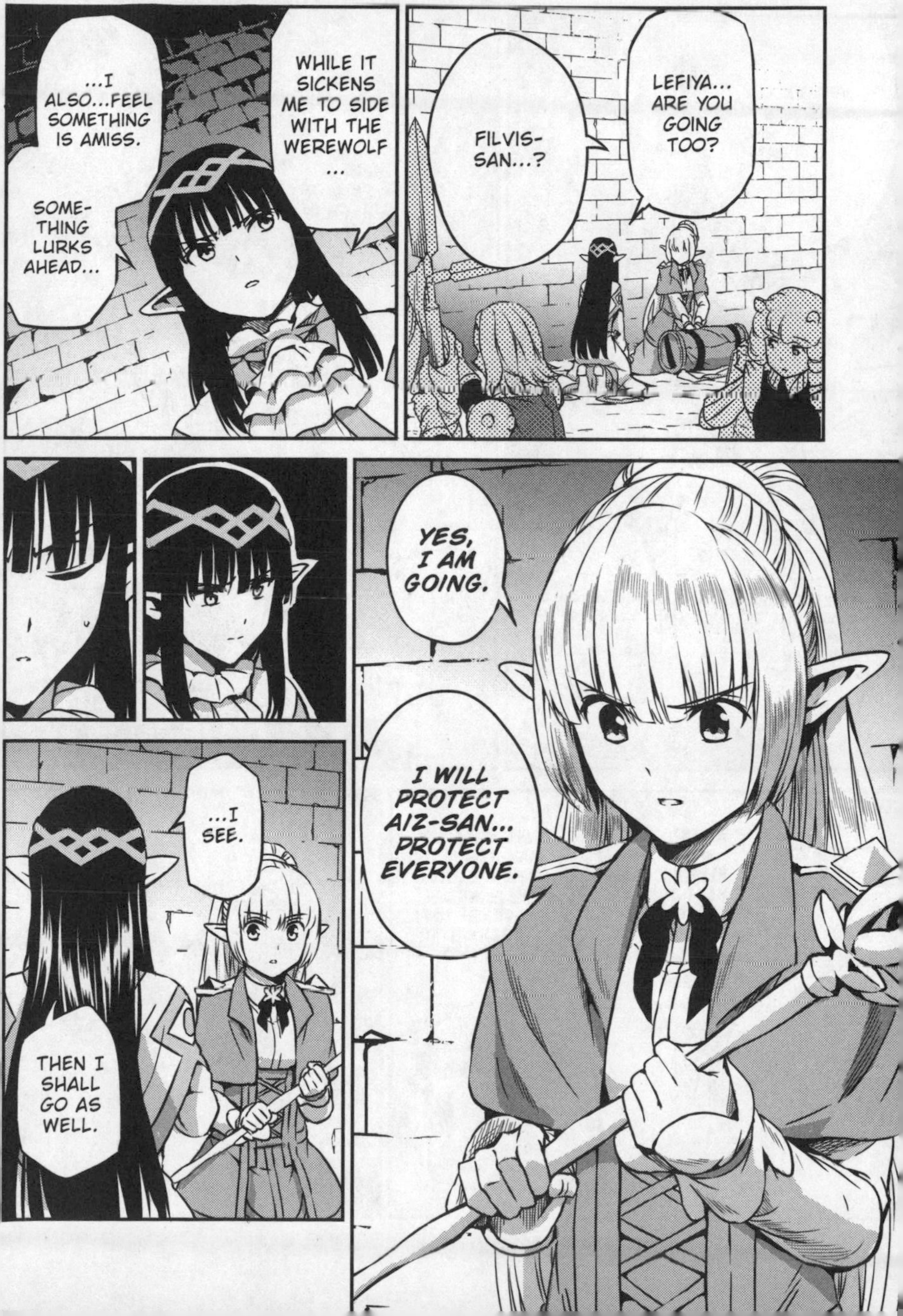
LEFIYA... ARE YOU GOING TOO?
FILVIS-SAN...?
WHILE IT SICKENS ME TO SIDE WITH THE WEREWOLF ...
...I ALSO...FEEL SOMETHING IS AMISS.
SOME-THING LURKS AHEAD...
YES, I AM GOING.
I WILL PROTECT AIZ-SAN... PROTECT EVERYONE.
...I SEE.
THEN I SHALL GO AS WELL.

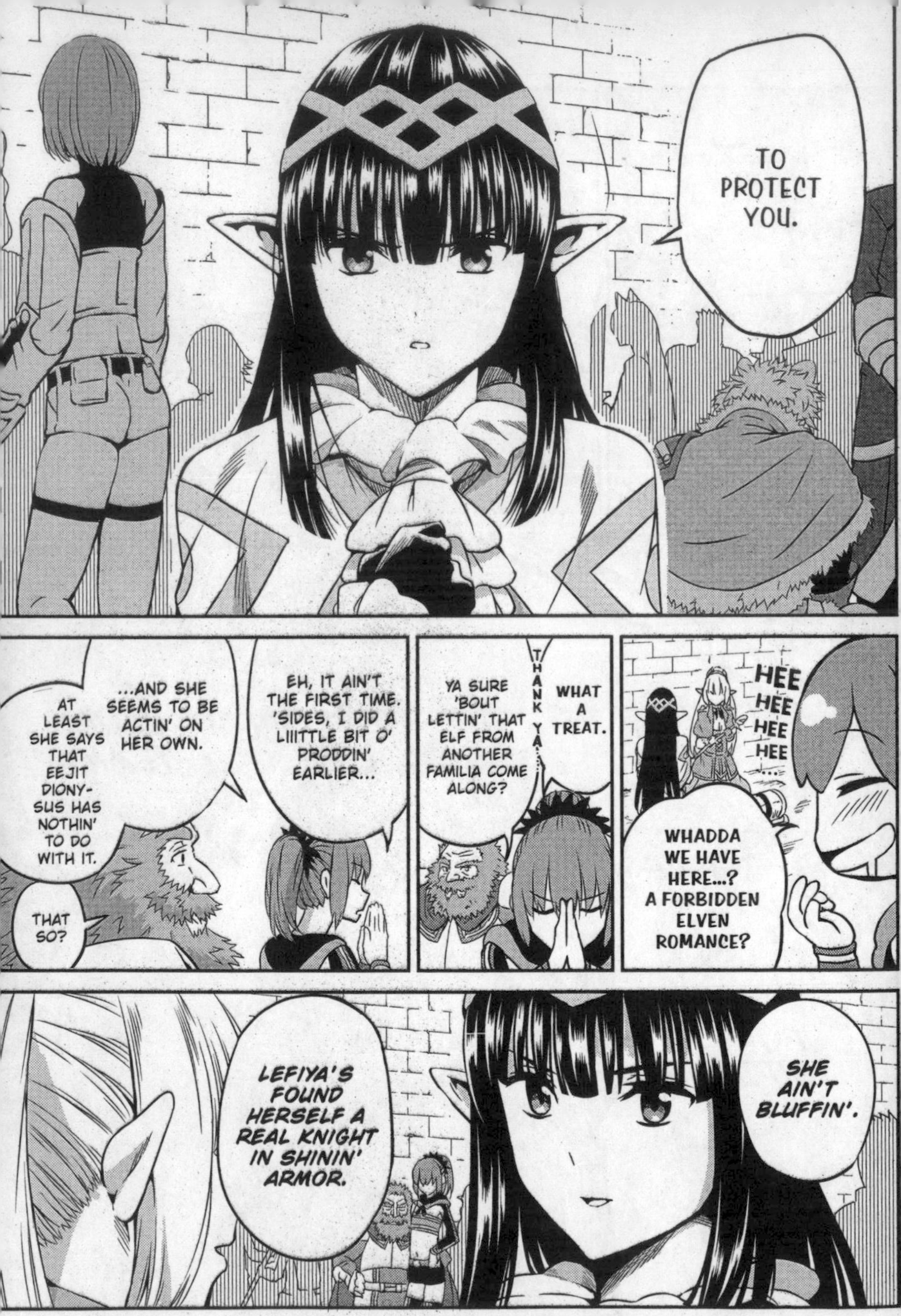
TO PROTECT YOU.
HEE HEE HEE HEE...
WHADDA WE HAVE HERE...? A FORBIDDEN ELVEN ROMANCE?
WHAT A TREAT.
THANK YA...
YA SURE 'BOUT LETTIN' THAT ELF FROM ANOTHER FAMILIA COME ALONG?
EH, IT AIN'T THE FIRST TIME. 'SIDES, I DID A LIIITTLE BIT O' PRODDIN' EARLIER...
...AND SHE SEEMS TO BE ACTIN' ON HER OWN.
AT LEAST SHE SAYS THAT EEJIT DIONYSUS HAS NOTHIN' TO DO WITH IT.
THAT SO?
SHE AIN'T BLUFFIN'.
LEFIYA'S FOUND HERSELF A REAL KNIGHT IN SHININ' ARMOR.

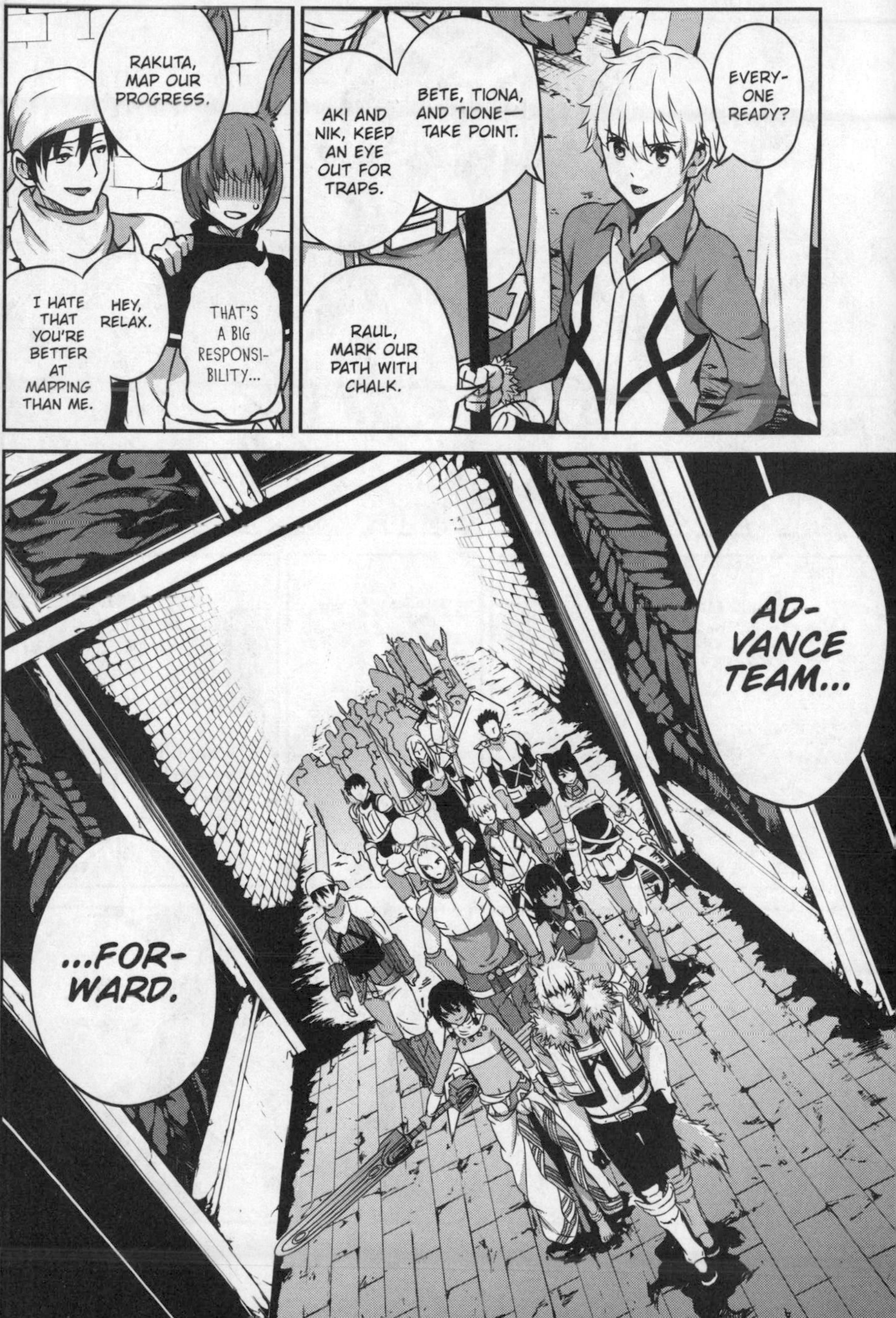
EVERYONE READY?
BETE, TIONA, AND TIONE—TAKE POINT.
AKI AND NIK, KEEP AN EYE OUT FOR TRAPS.
RAUL, MARK OUR PATH WITH CHALK.
RAKUTA, MAP OUR PROGRESS.
THAT'S A BIG RESPONSIBILITY...
HEY, RELAX.
I HATE THAT YOU'RE BETTER AT MAPPING THAN ME.
ADVANCE TEAM...
...FORWARD.

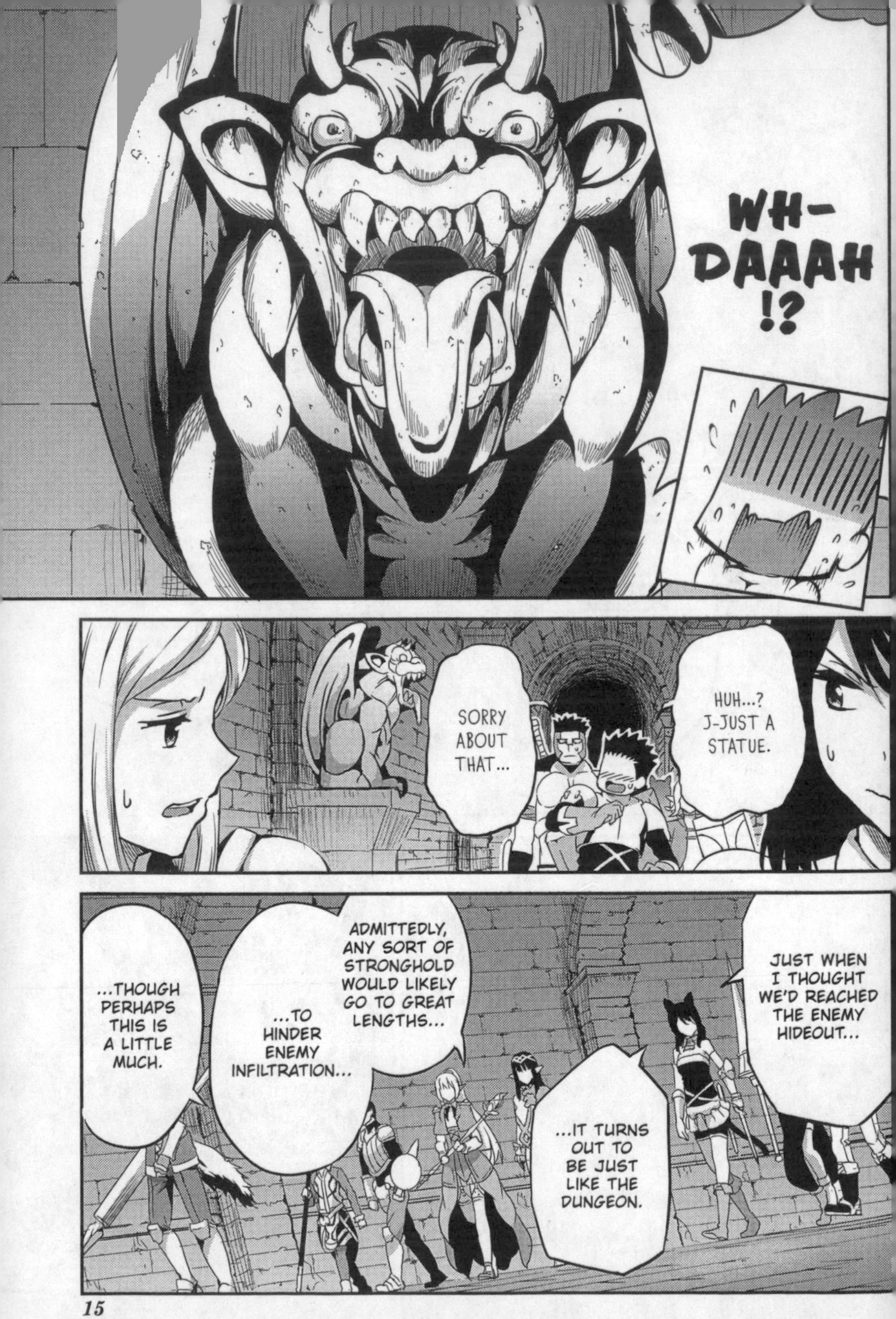
WH-DAAAH!?
HUH...? J-JUST A STATUE.
SORRY ABOUT THAT...
JUST WHEN I THOUGHT WE'D REACHED THE ENEMY HIDEOUT...
...IT TURNS OUT TO BE JUST LIKE THE DUNGEON.
ADMITTEDLY, ANY SORT OF STRONGHOLD WOULD LIKELY GO TO GREAT LENGTHS...
...TO HINDER ENEMY INFILTRATION...
...THOUGH PERHAPS THIS IS A LITTLE MUCH.

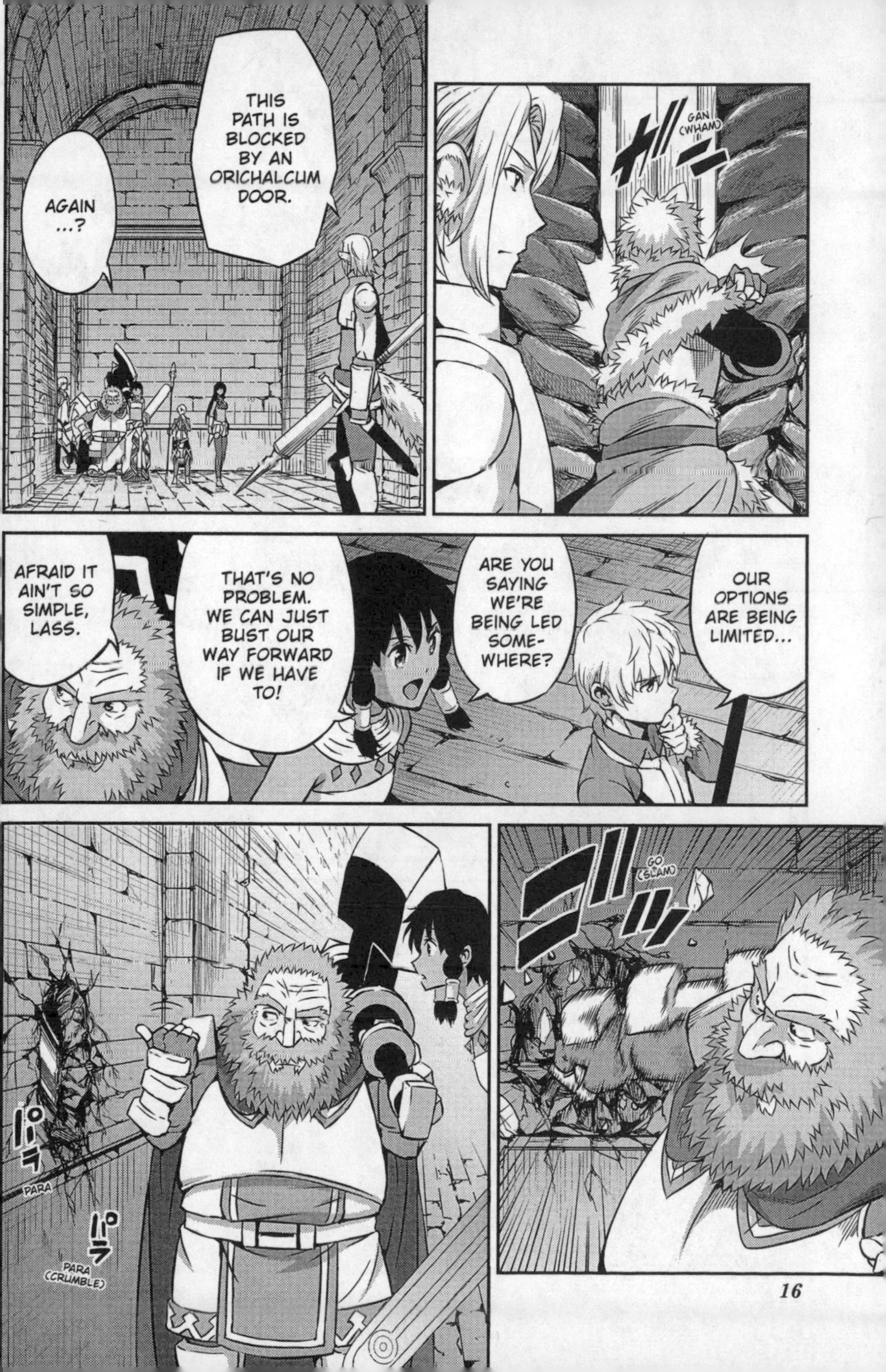

GAN (WHAM)
THIS PATH IS BLOCKED BY AN ORICHALCUM DOOR.
AGAIN ...?
OUR OPTIONS ARE BEING LIMITED...
ARE YOU SAYING WE'RE BEING LED SOME-WHERE?
THAT'S NO PROBLEM. WE CAN JUST BUST OUR WAY FORWARD IF WE HAVE TO!
AFRAID IT AIN'T SO SIMPLE, LASS.
GO (SLAM)
PARA
PARA (CRUMBLE)

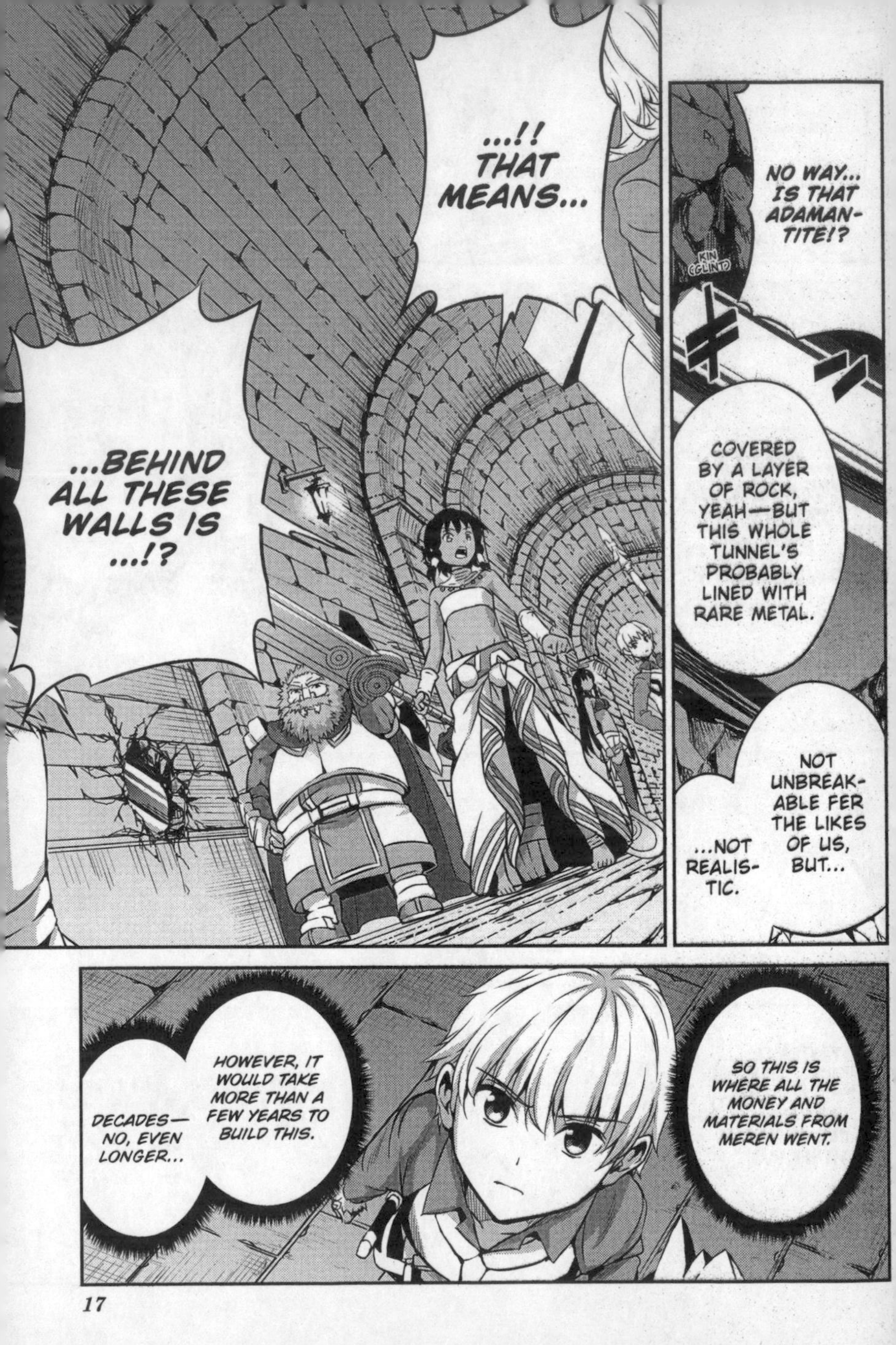
NO WAY... IS THAT ADAMANTITE!?
KIN (GLINT)
COVERED BY A LAYER OF ROCK, YEAH—BUT THIS WHOLE TUNNEL'S PROBABLY LINED WITH RARE METAL.
NOT UNBREAKABLE FER THE LIKES OF US, BUT...
...NOT REALISTIC.
...!! THAT MEANS...
...BEHIND ALL THESE WALLS IS ...!?
SO THIS IS WHERE ALL THE MONEY AND MATERIALS FROM MEREN WENT.
HOWEVER, IT WOULD TAKE MORE THAN A FEW YEARS TO BUILD THIS.
DECADES—NO, EVEN LONGER...

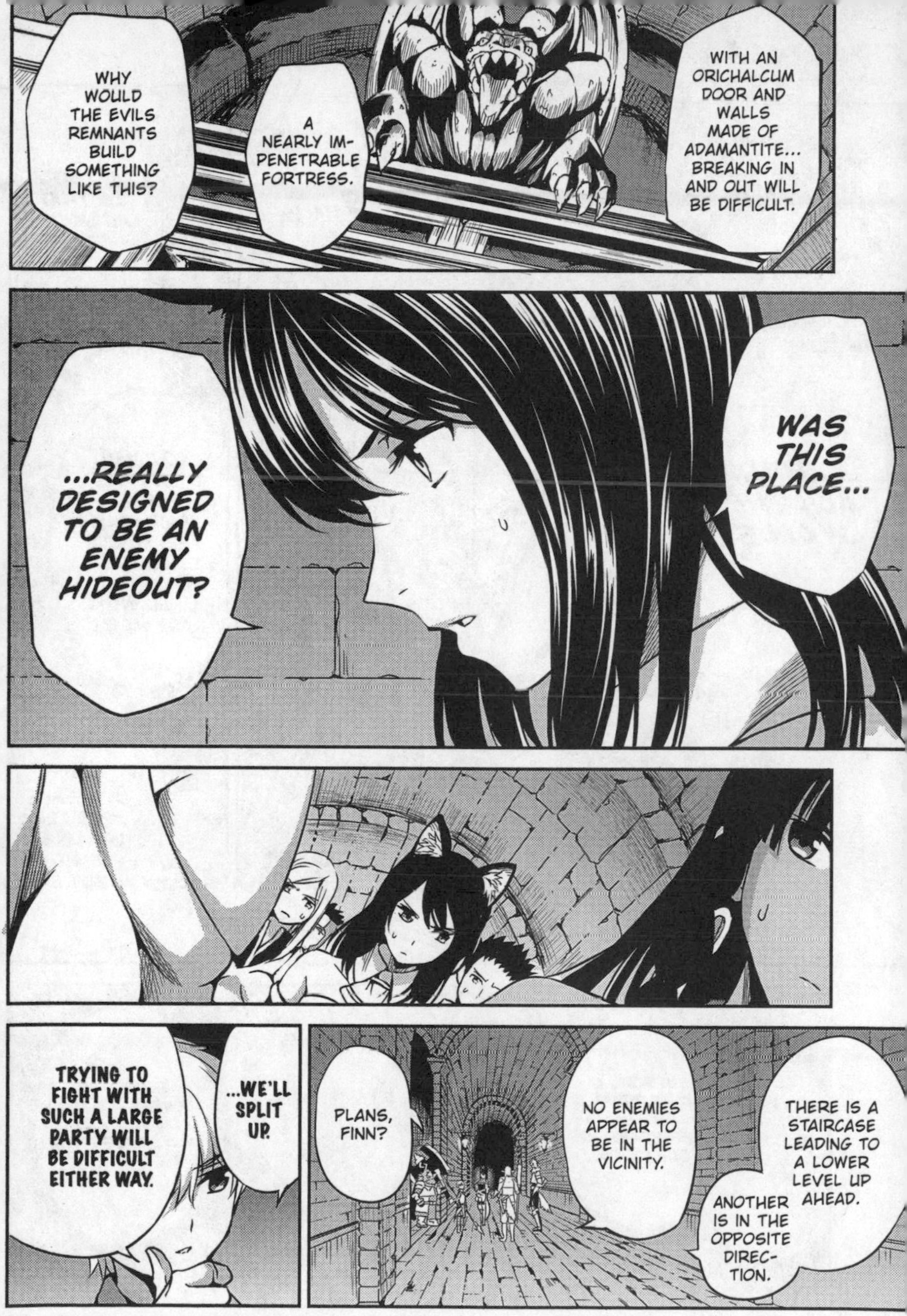
WITH AN ORICHALCUM DOOR AND WALLS MADE OF ADAMANTITE... BREAKING IN AND OUT WILL BE DIFFICULT.
A NEARLY IMPENETRABLE FORTRESS.
WHY WOULD THE EVILS REMNANTS BUILD SOMETHING LIKE THIS?
WAS THIS PLACE...
...REALLY DESIGNED TO BE AN ENEMY HIDEOUT?
THERE IS A STAIRCASE LEADING TO A LOWER LEVEL UP AHEAD.
ANOTHER IS IN THE OPPOSITE DIRECTION.
NO ENEMIES APPEAR TO BE IN THE VICINITY.
PLANS, FINN?
...WE'LL SPLIT UP.
TRYING TO FIGHT WITH SUCH A LARGE PARTY WILL BE DIFFICULT EITHER WAY.

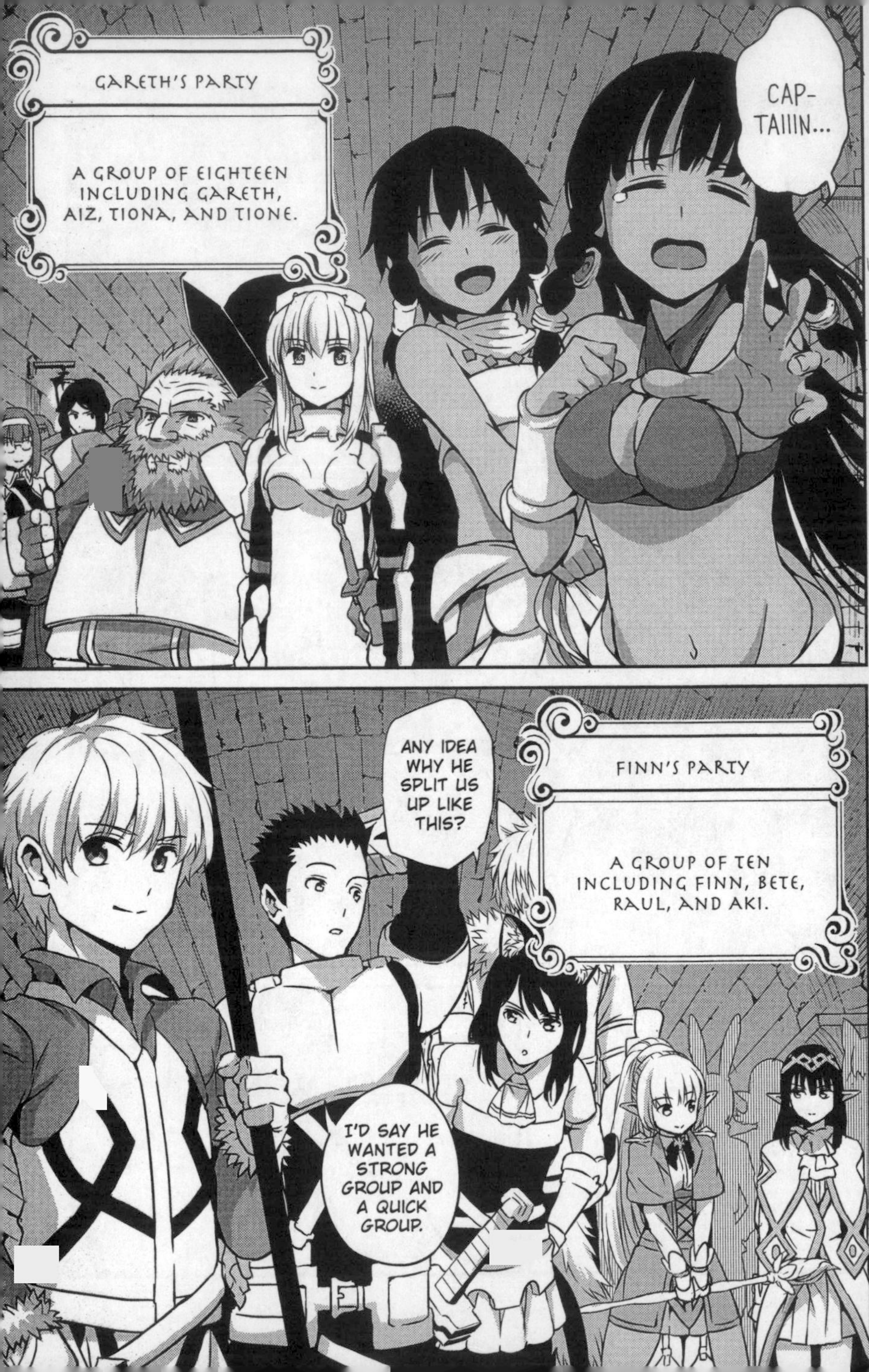
CAP-
TAIIIN...
GARETH'S PARTY
A GROUP OF EIGHTEEN INCLUDING GARETH, AIZ, TIONA, AND TIONE.
FINN'S PARTY
A GROUP OF TEN INCLUDING FINN, BETE, RAUL, AND AKI.
ANY IDEA WHY HE SPLIT US UP LIKE THIS?
I'D SAY HE WANTED A STRONG GROUP AND A QUICK GROUP.

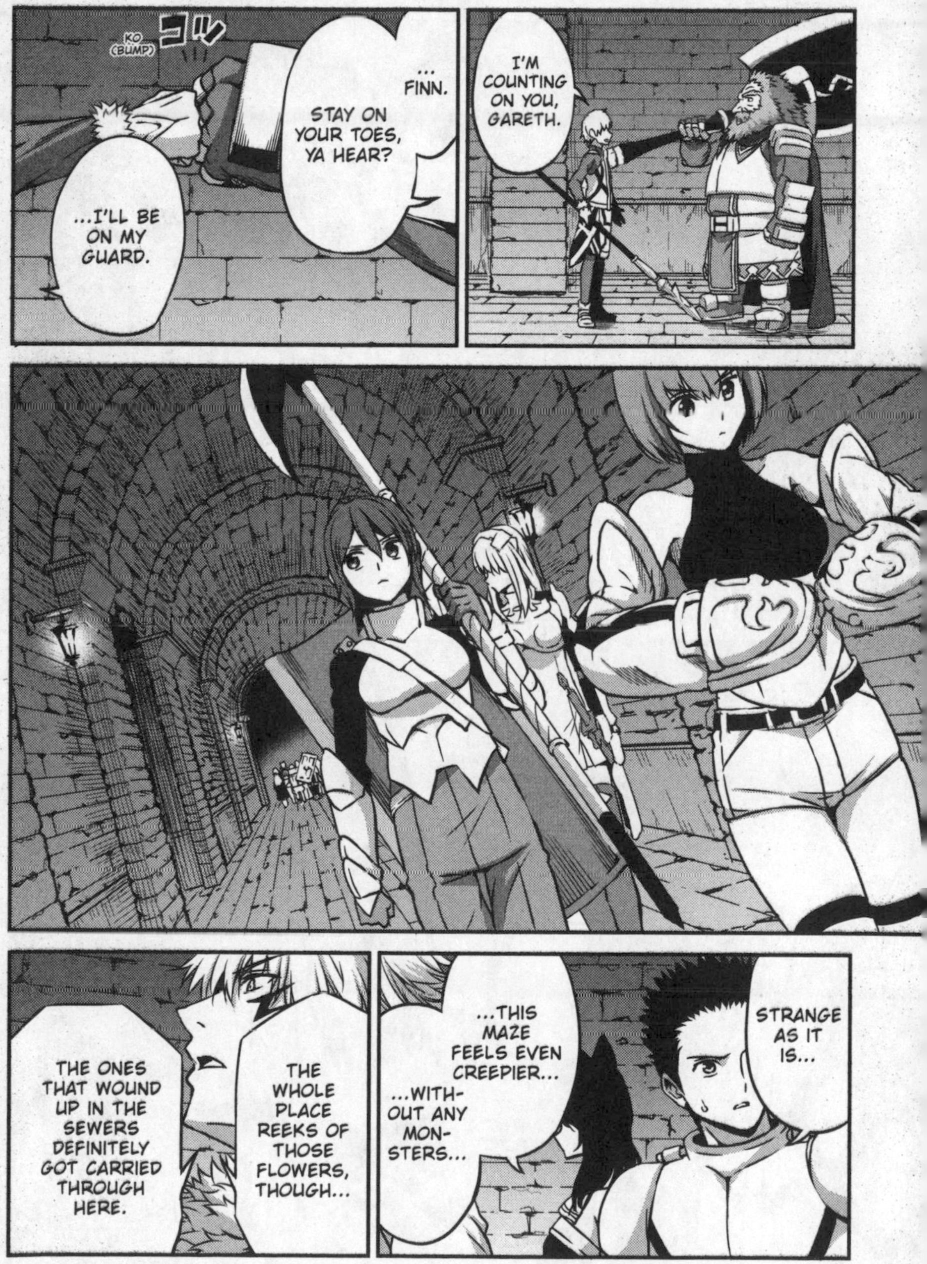
I'M COUNTING ON YOU, GARETH.
...FINN.
STAY ON YOUR TOES, YA HEAR?
KO (BUMP)
...I'LL BE ON MY GUARD.
STRANGE AS IT IS...
...THIS MAZE FEELS EVEN CREEPIER...
...WITH-OUT ANY MON-STERS...
THE WHOLE PLACE REEKS OF THOSE FLOWERS, THOUGH...
THE ONES THAT WOUND UP IN THE SEWERS DEFINITELY GOT CARRIED THROUGH HERE.

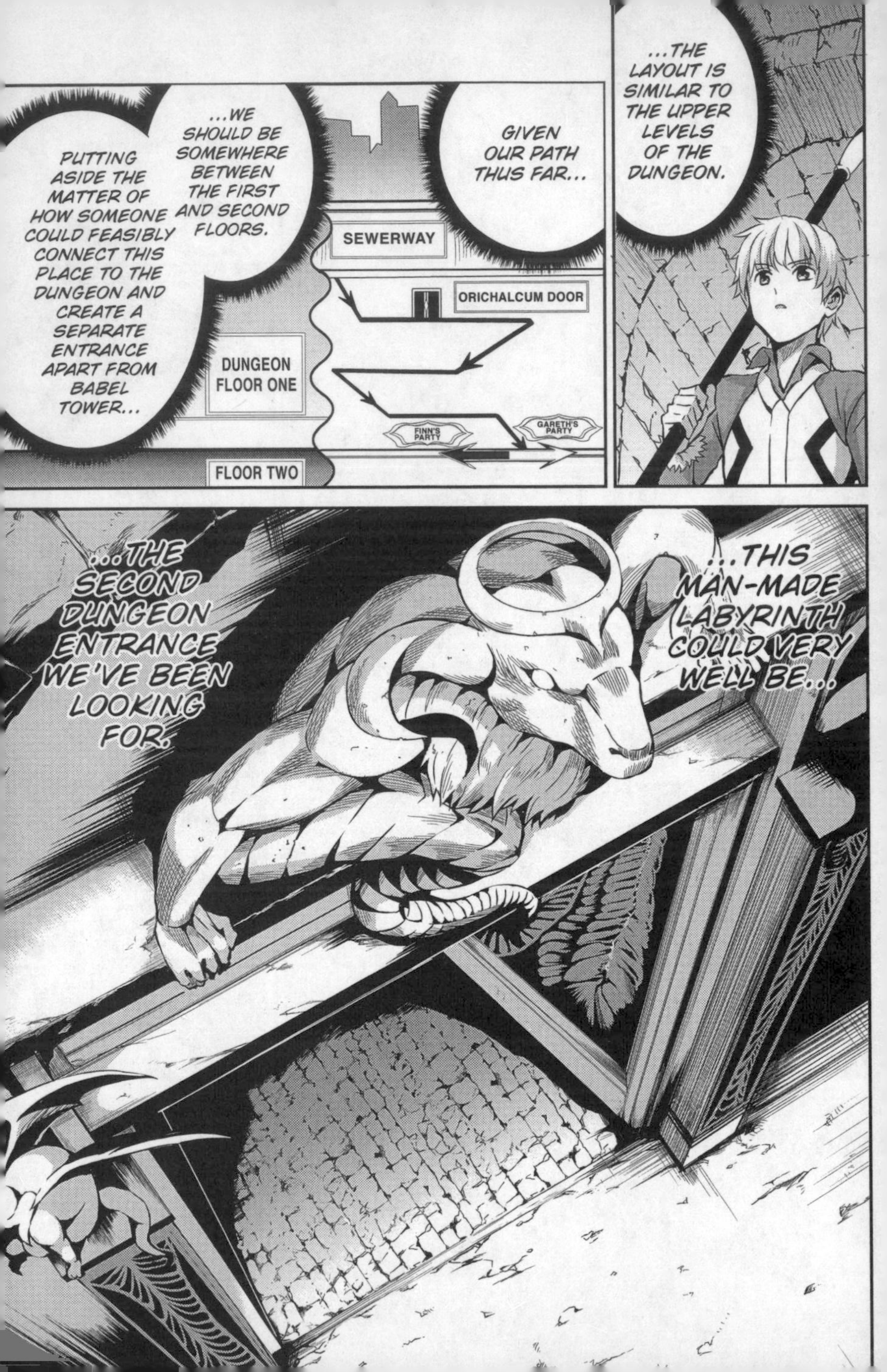
...THE LAYOUT IS SIMILAR TO THE UPPER LEVELS OF THE DUNGEON.
GIVEN OUR PATH THUS FAR...
...WE SHOULD BE SOMEWHERE BETWEEN THE FIRST AND SECOND FLOORS.
PUTTING ASIDE THE MATTER OF HOW SOMEONE COULD FEASIBLY CONNECT THIS PLACE TO THE DUNGEON AND CREATE A SEPARATE ENTRANCE APART FROM BABEL TOWER...
SEWERWAY
ORICHALCUM DOOR
DUNGEON FLOOR ONE
GARETH'S PARTY
FINN'S PARTY
FLOOR TWO
...THIS MAN-MADE LABYRINTH COULD VERY WELL BE...
...THE SECOND DUNGEON ENTRANCE WE'VE BEEN LOOKING FOR.

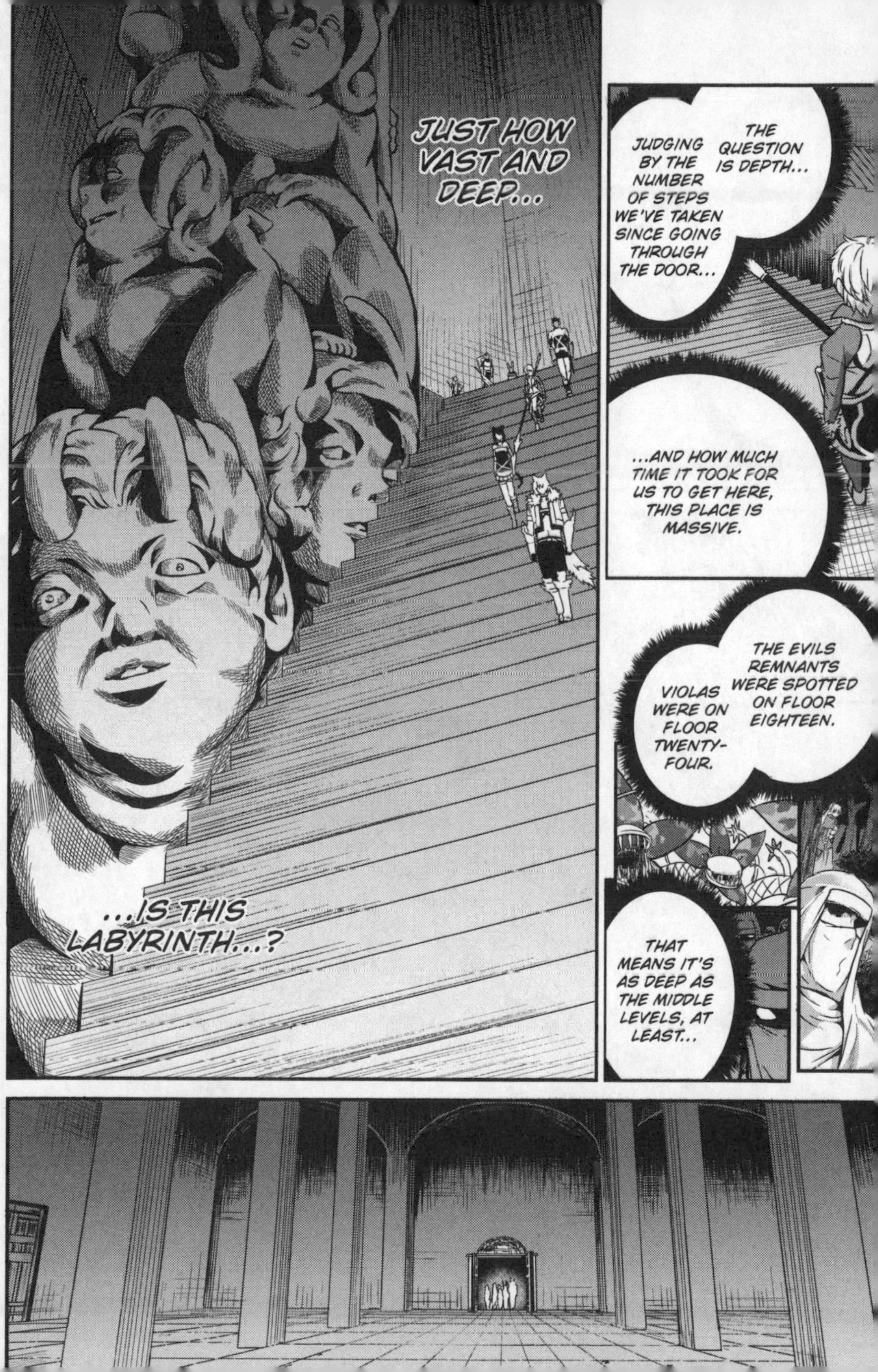
THE QUESTION IS DEPTH...
JUDGING BY THE NUMBER OF STEPS WE'VE TAKEN SINCE GOING THROUGH THE DOOR...
...AND HOW MUCH TIME IT TOOK FOR US TO GET HERE, THIS PLACE IS MASSIVE.
THE EVILS REMNANTS WERE SPOTTED ON FLOOR EIGHTEEN.
VIOLAS WERE ON FLOOR TWENTY-FOUR.
THAT MEANS IT'S AS DEEP AS THE MIDDLE LEVELS, AT LEAST...
JUST HOW VAST AND DEEP...
...IS THIS LABYRINTH...?

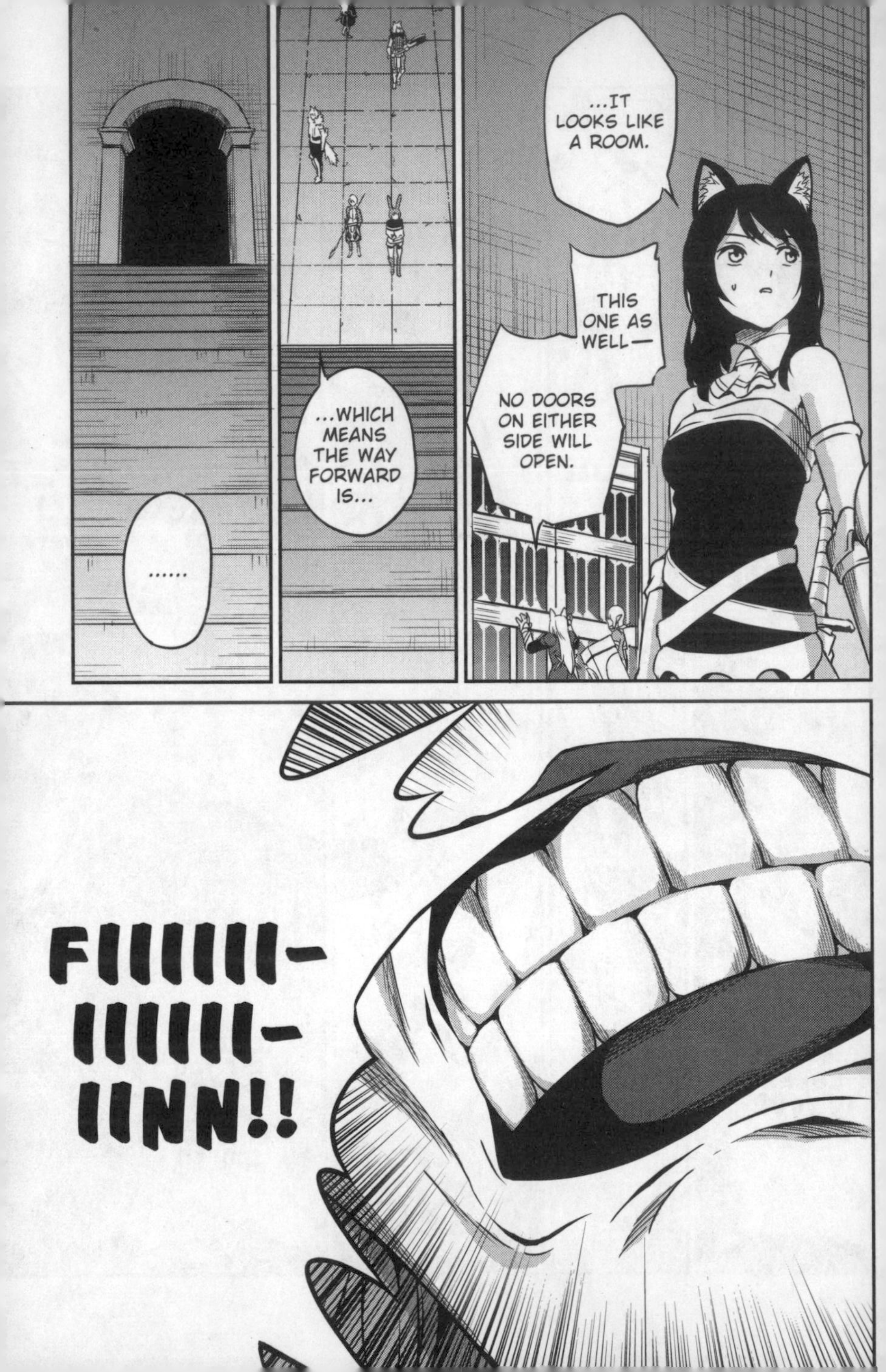
...IT LOOKS LIKE A ROOM.
THIS ONE AS WELL—
NO DOORS ON EITHER SIDE WILL OPEN.
...WHICH MEANS THE WAY FORWARD IS...
......
FIIIIII-IIIIIII-IINN!!

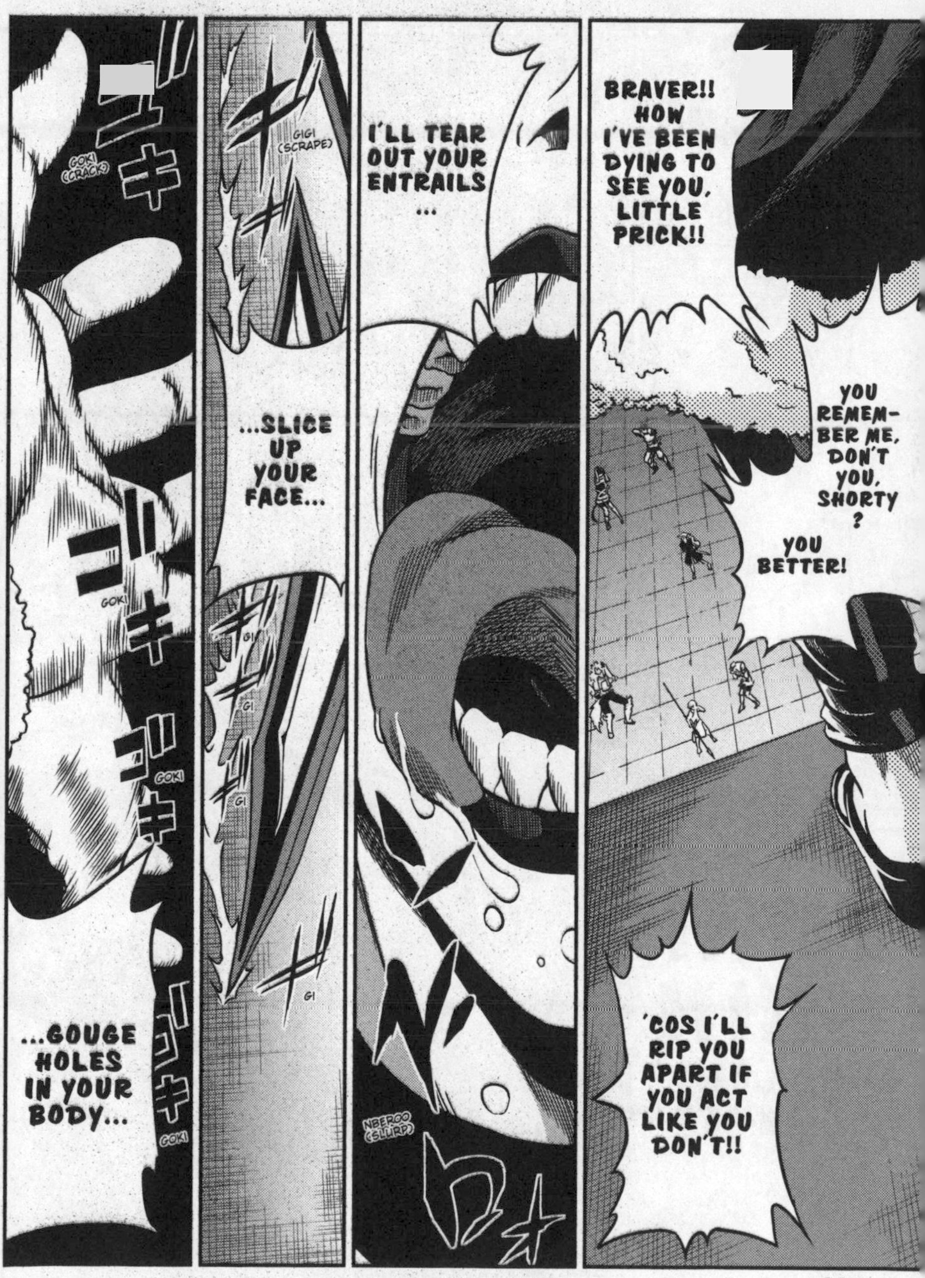
BRAVER!! HOW I'VE BEEN DYING TO SEE YOU, LITTLE PRICK!!
YOU REMEMBER ME, DON'T YOU, SHORTY?
YOU BETTER!
'COS I'LL RIP YOU APART IF YOU ACT LIKE YOU DON'T!!
I'LL TEAR OUT YOUR ENTRAILS...
NBEROO (SLURP)
GIGI (SCRAPE)
...SLICE UP YOUR FACE...
GI
GI
GI
GI
GOKI (CRACK)
GOKI
GOKI
...GOUGE HOLES IN YOUR BODY...
GOKI

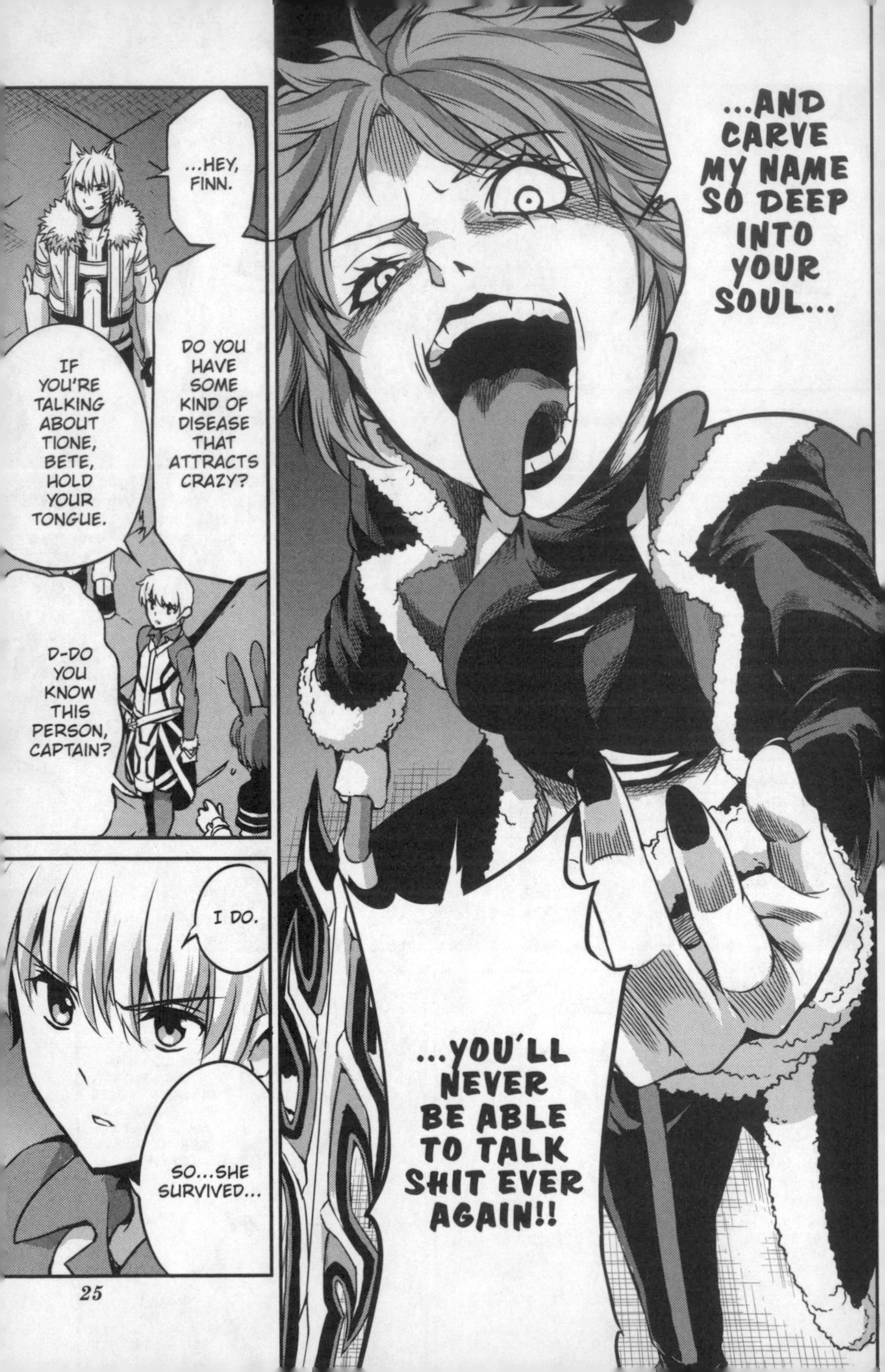
...AND CARVE MY NAME SO DEEP INTO YOUR SOUL...
...YOU'LL NEVER BE ABLE TO TALK SHIT EVER AGAIN!!
...HEY, FINN.
DO YOU HAVE SOME KIND OF DISEASE THAT ATTRACTS CRAZY?
IF YOU'RE TALKING ABOUT TIONE, BETE, HOLD YOUR TONGUE.
D-DO YOU KNOW THIS PERSON, CAPTAIN?
I DO.
SO...SHE SURVIVED...

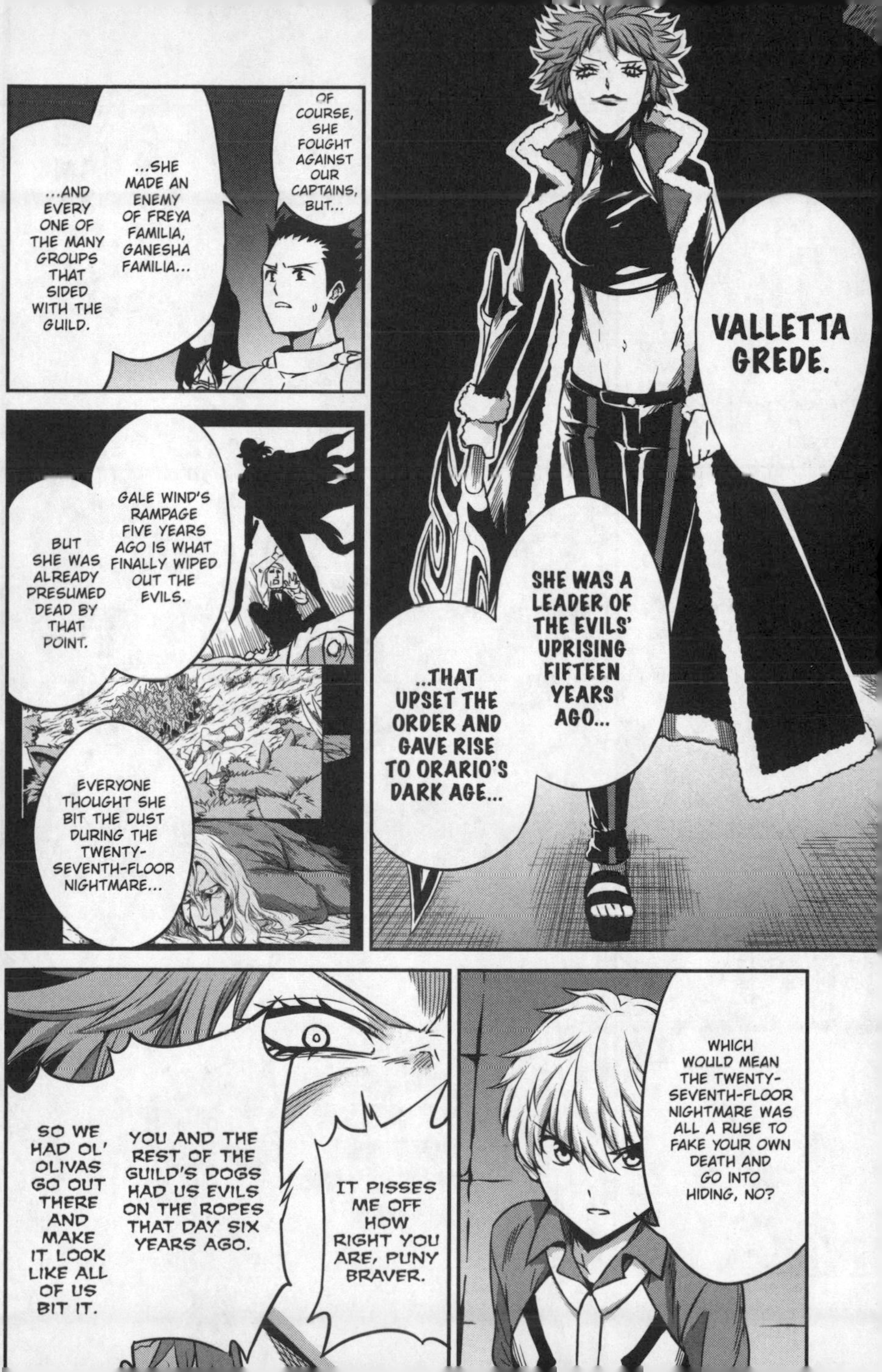
VALLETTA GREDE.
SHE WAS A LEADER OF THE EVILS' UPRISING FIFTEEN YEARS AGO...
...THAT UPSET THE ORDER AND GAVE RISE TO ORARIO'S DARK AGE...
OF COURSE, SHE FOUGHT AGAINST OUR CAPTAINS, BUT...
...SHE MADE AN ENEMY OF FREYA FAMILIA, GANESHA FAMILIA...
...AND EVERY ONE OF THE MANY GROUPS THAT SIDED WITH THE GUILD.
GALE WIND'S RAMPAGE FIVE YEARS AGO IS WHAT FINALLY WIPED OUT THE EVILS.
BUT SHE WAS ALREADY PRESUMED DEAD BY THAT POINT.
EVERYONE THOUGHT SHE BIT THE DUST DURING THE TWENTY-SEVENTH-FLOOR NIGHTMARE...
WHICH WOULD MEAN THE TWENTY-SEVENTH-FLOOR NIGHTMARE WAS ALL A RUSE TO FAKE YOUR OWN DEATH AND GO INTO HIDING, NO?
IT PISSES ME OFF HOW RIGHT YOU ARE, PUNY BRAVER.
YOU AND THE REST OF THE GUILD'S DOGS HAD US EVILS ON THE ROPES THAT DAY SIX YEARS AGO.
SO WE HAD OL' OLIVAS GO OUT THERE AND MAKE IT LOOK LIKE ALL OF US BIT IT.

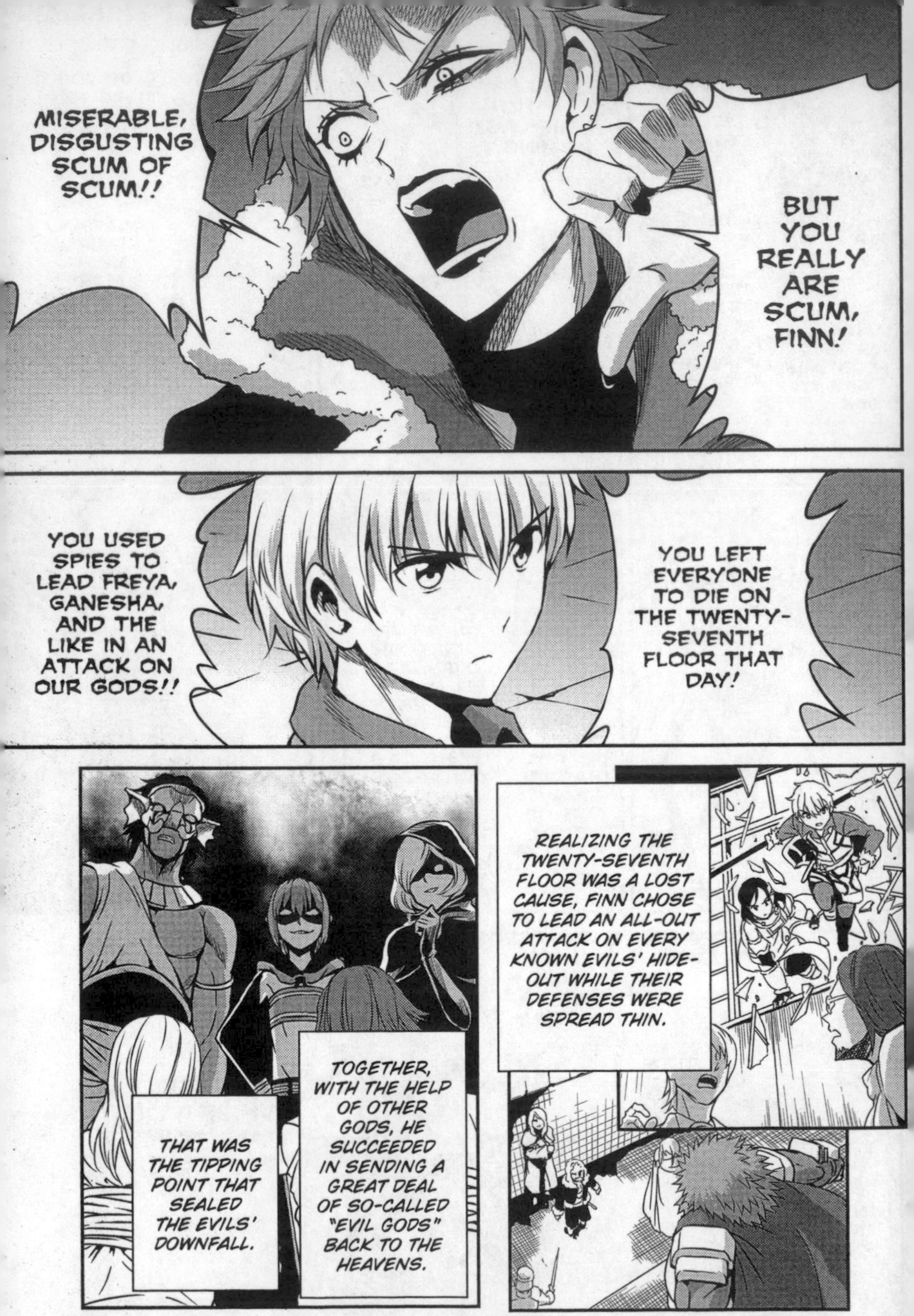
BUT YOU REALLY ARE SCUM, FINN!
MISERABLE, DISGUSTING SCUM OF SCUM!!
YOU LEFT EVERYONE TO DIE ON THE TWENTY-SEVENTH FLOOR THAT DAY!
YOU USED SPIES TO LEAD FREYA, GANESHA, AND THE LIKE IN AN ATTACK ON OUR GODS!!
REALIZING THE TWENTY-SEVENTH FLOOR WAS A LOST CAUSE, FINN CHOSE TO LEAD AN ALL-OUT ATTACK ON EVERY KNOWN EVILS' HIDE-OUT WHILE THEIR DEFENSES WERE SPREAD THIN.
TOGETHER, WITH THE HELP OF OTHER GODS, HE SUCCEEDED IN SENDING A GREAT DEAL OF SO-CALLED "EVIL GODS" BACK TO THE HEAVENS.
THAT WAS THE TIPPING POINT THAT SEALED THE EVILS' DOWNFALL.

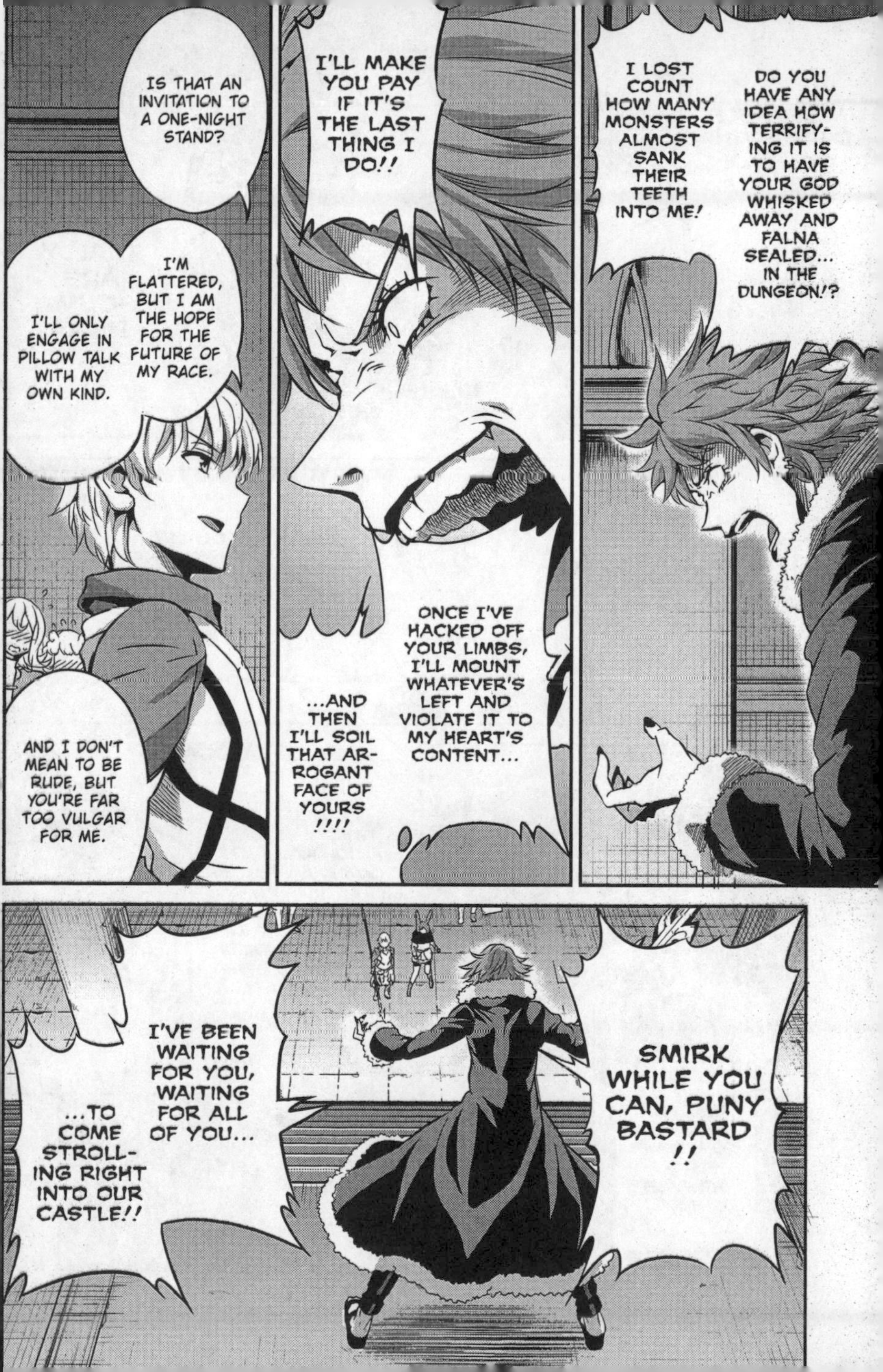
DO YOU HAVE ANY IDEA HOW TERRIFYING IT IS TO HAVE YOUR GOD WHISKED AWAY AND FALNA SEALED... IN THE DUNGEON!?
I LOST COUNT HOW MANY MONSTERS ALMOST SANK THEIR TEETH INTO ME!
I'LL MAKE YOU PAY IF IT'S THE LAST THING I DO!!
ONCE I'VE HACKED OFF YOUR LIMBS, I'LL MOUNT WHATEVER'S LEFT AND VIOLATE IT TO MY HEART'S CONTENT...
...AND THEN I'LL SOIL THAT ARROGANT FACE OF YOURS!!!!
IS THAT AN INVITATION TO A ONE-NIGHT STAND?
I'M FLATTERED, BUT I AM THE HOPE FOR THE FUTURE OF MY RACE.
I'LL ONLY ENGAGE IN PILLOW TALK WITH MY OWN KIND.
AND I DON'T MEAN TO BE RUDE, BUT YOU'RE FAR TOO VULGAR FOR ME.
SMIRK WHILE YOU CAN, PUNY BASTARD!!
I'VE BEEN WAITING FOR YOU, WAITING FOR ALL OF YOU...
...TO COME STROLLING RIGHT INTO OUR CASTLE!!

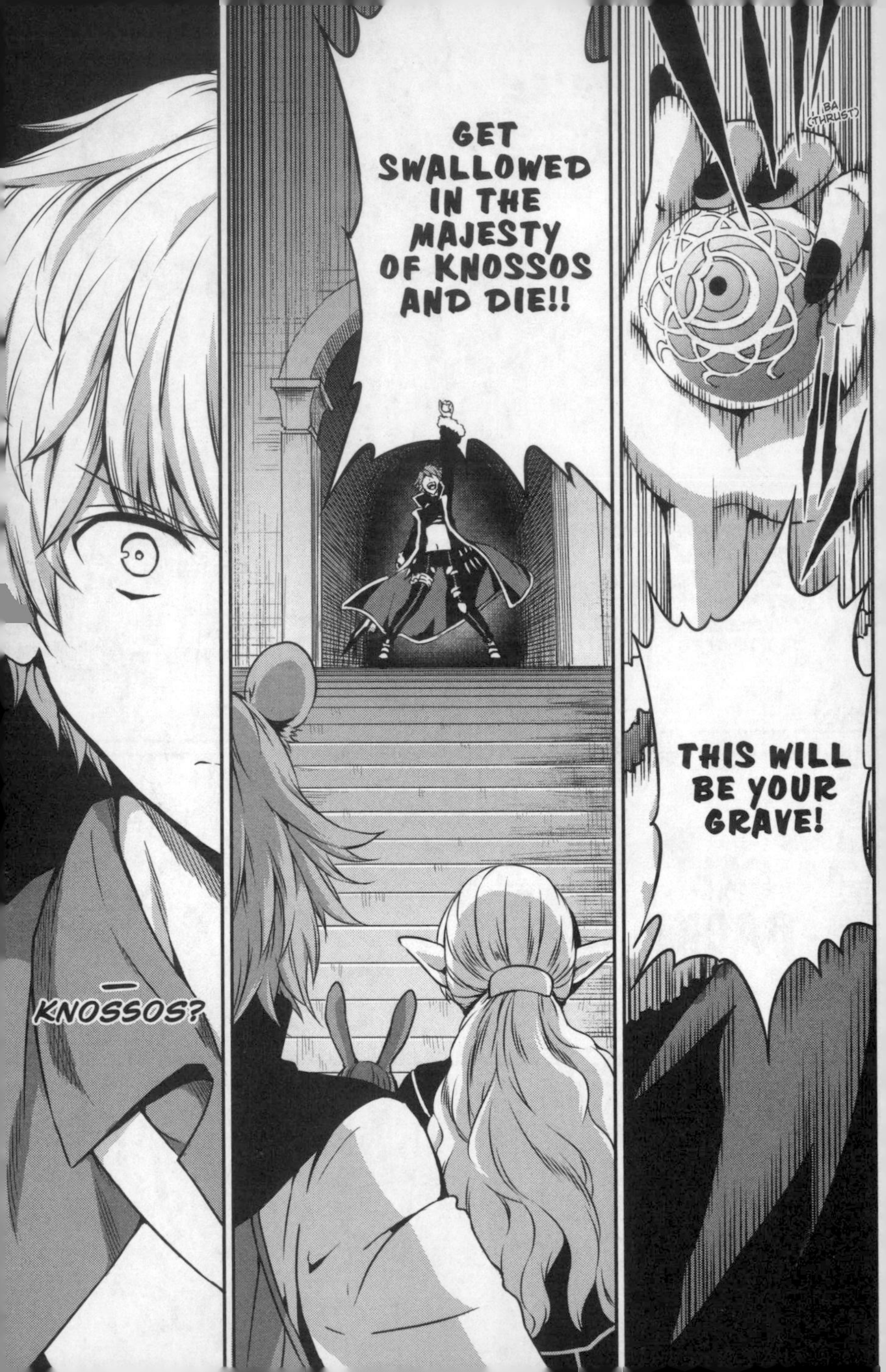
BA (THRUST)
THIS WILL BE YOUR GRAVE!
GET SWALLOWED IN THE MAJESTY OF KNOSSOS AND DIE!!
—KNOSSOS?

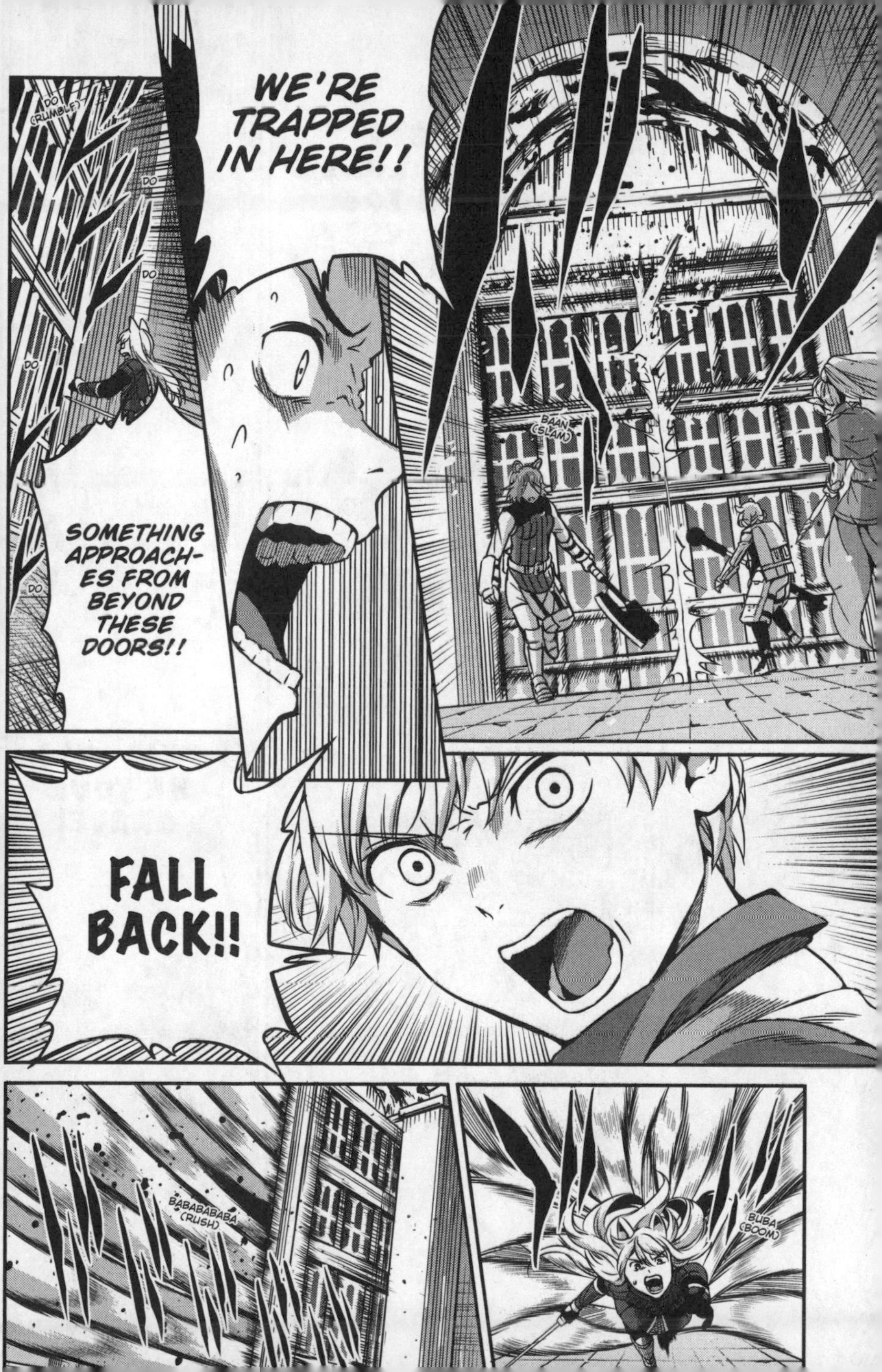
BAAN (SLAM)
WE'RE TRAPPED IN HERE!!
DO (RUMBLE)
DO
DO
DO
DO
SOMETHING APPROACHES FROM BEYOND THESE DOORS!!
FALL BACK!!
BUBA (BOOM)
BABABABABA (RUSH)

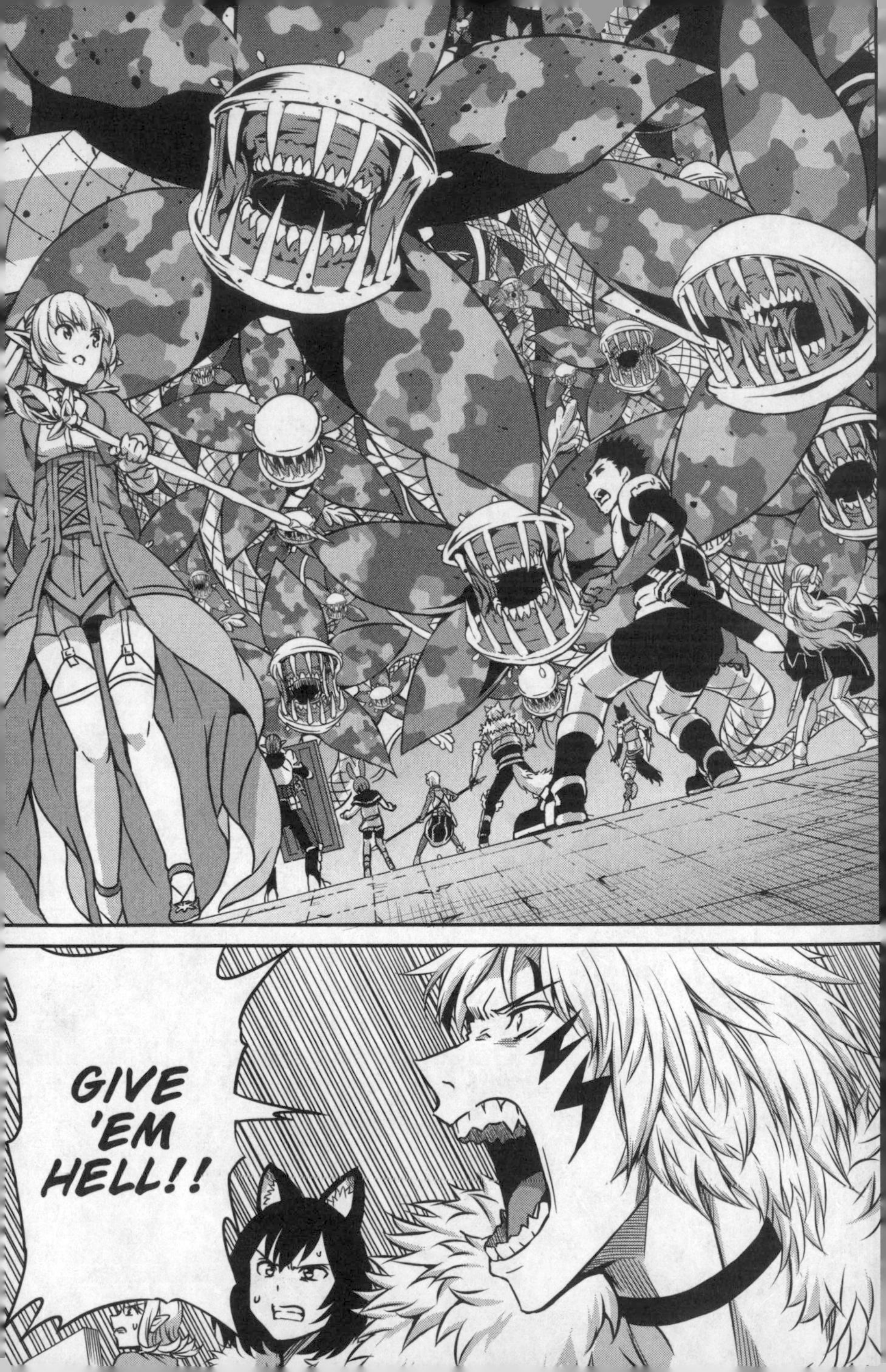
GIVE 'EM HELL!!

Is it WRONG to TRY to PICK-UP GIRLS IN A DUNGEON? ON THE SIDE

Sword Oratoria

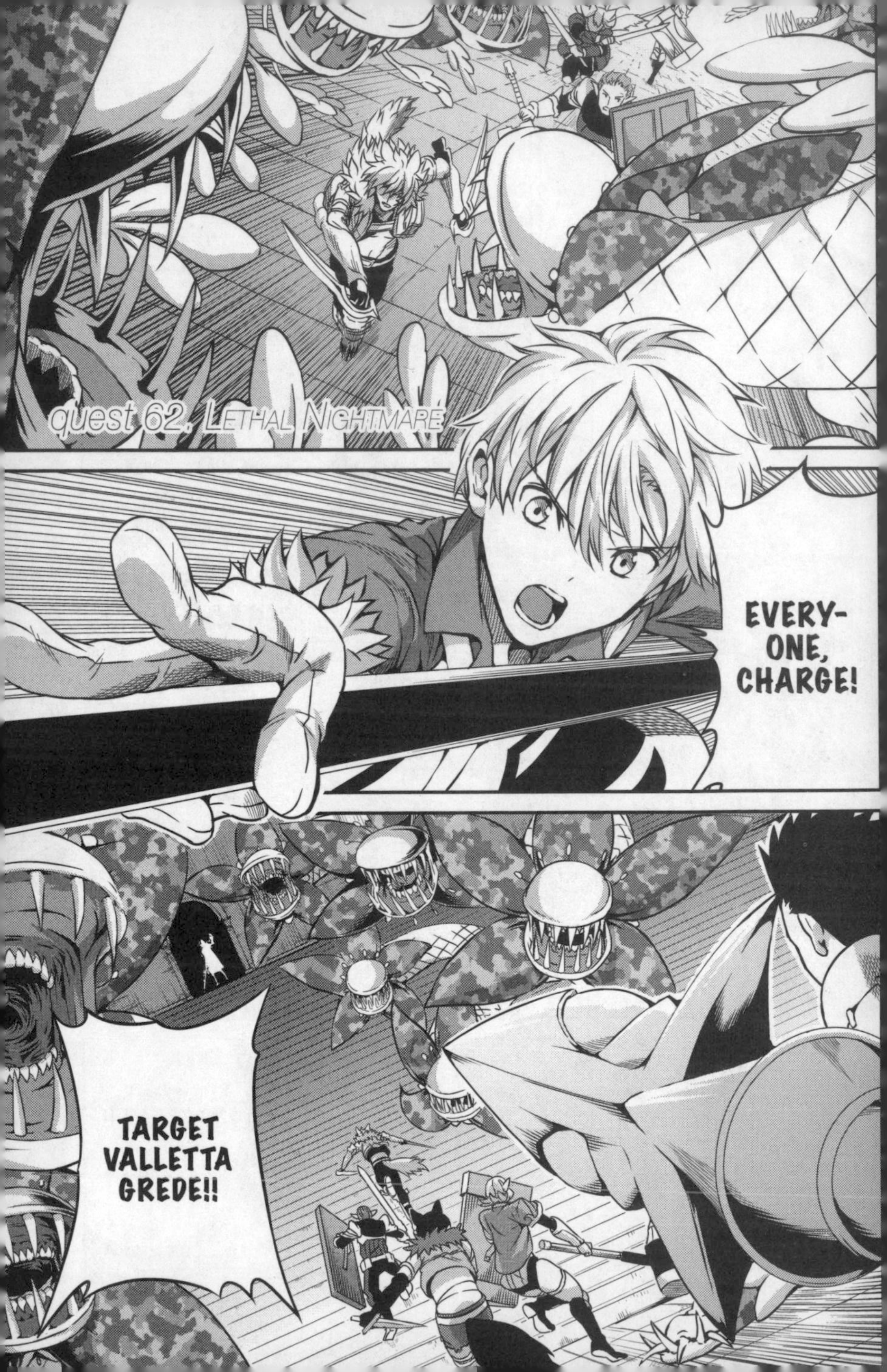
quest 62. Lethal Nightmare
EVERY-ONE, CHARGE!
TARGET VALLETTA GREDE!!

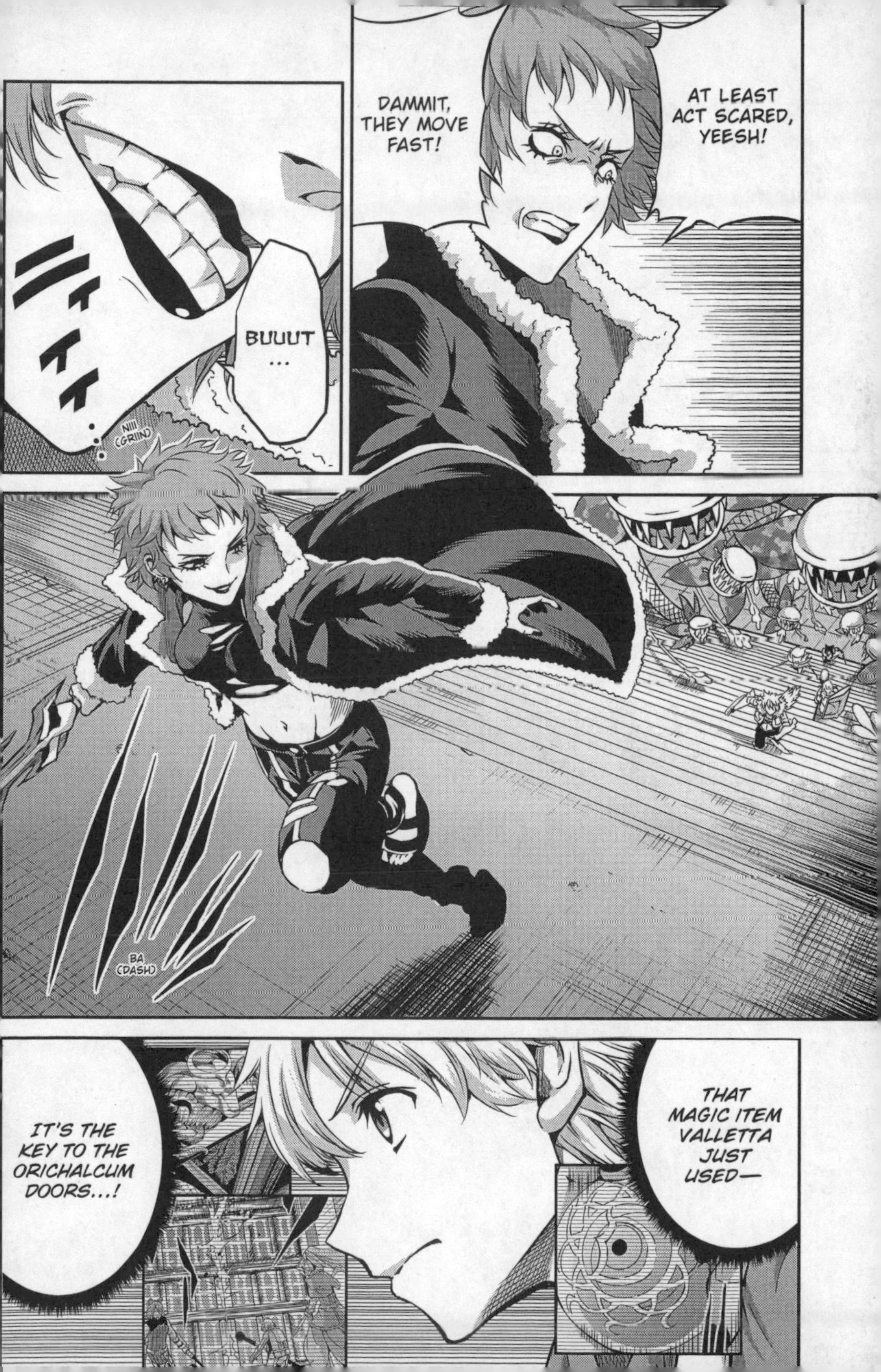
AT LEAST ACT SCARED, YEESH!
DAMMIT, THEY MOVE FAST!
BUUUT ...
NIII (GRIIN)
BA (DASH)
THAT MAGIC ITEM VALLETTA JUST USED—
IT'S THE KEY TO THE ORICHALCUM DOORS...!

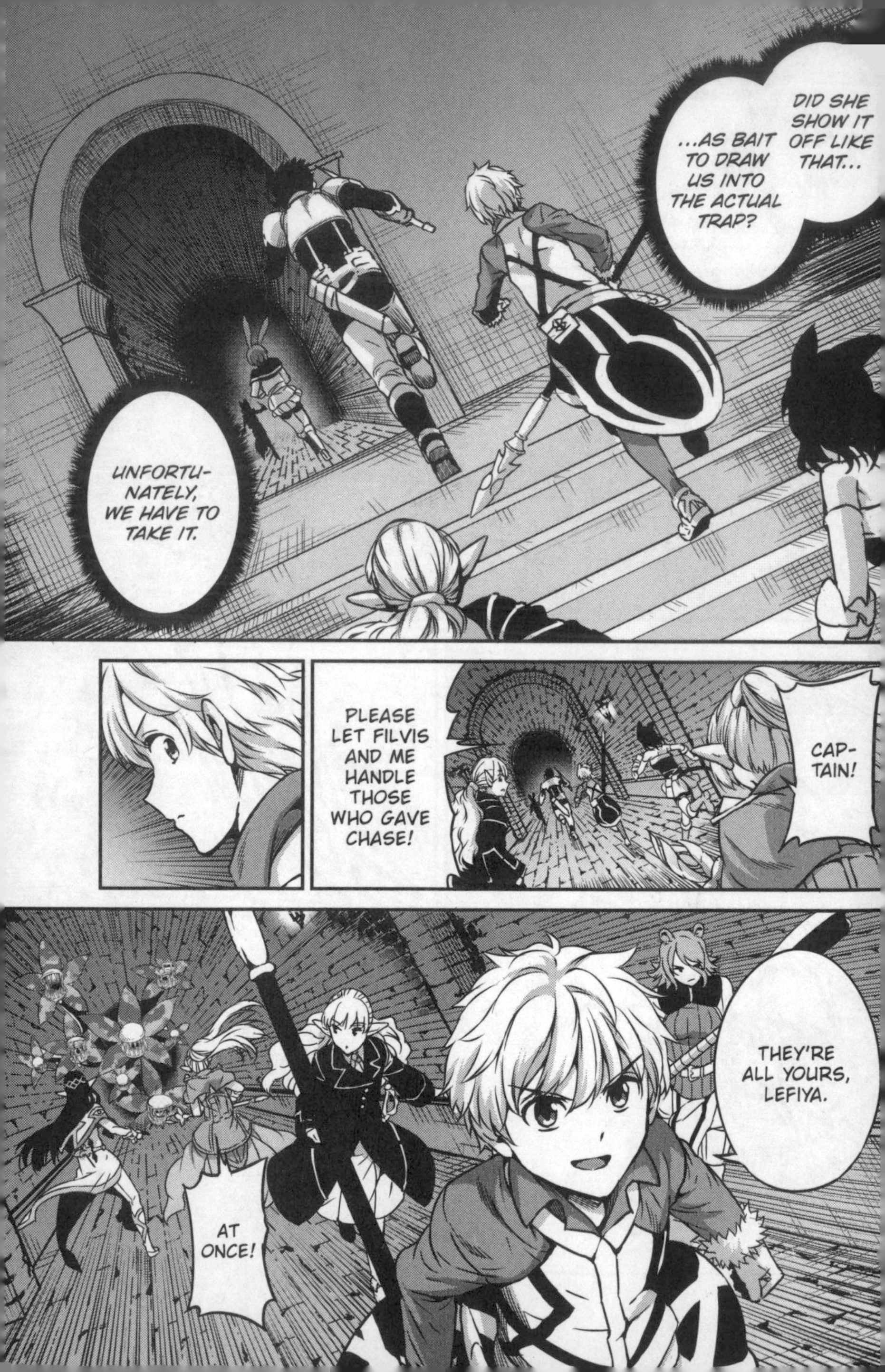
DID SHE SHOW IT OFF LIKE THAT...
...AS BAIT TO DRAW US INTO THE ACTUAL TRAP?
UNFORTU-NATELY, WE HAVE TO TAKE IT.
CAP-TAIN!
PLEASE LET FILVIS AND ME HANDLE THOSE WHO GAVE CHASE!
THEY'RE ALL YOURS, LEFIYA.
AT ONCE!

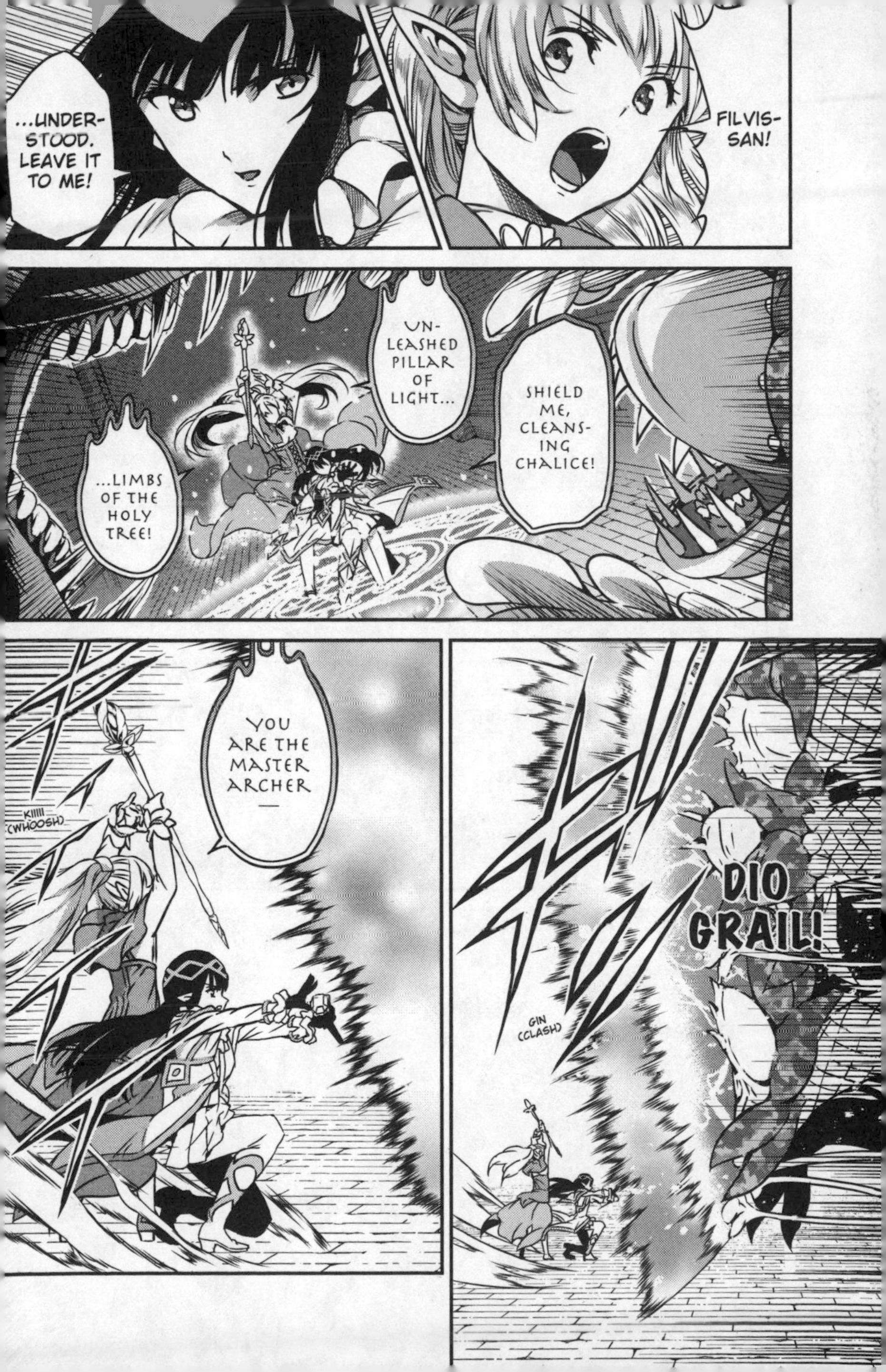
FILVIS-SAN!
...UNDER-STOOD. LEAVE IT TO ME!
SHIELD ME, CLEANS-ING CHALICE!
UN-LEASHED PILLAR OF LIGHT...
...LIMBS OF THE HOLY TREE!
DIO GRAIL!
GIN (CLASH)
KIIIII (WHOOSH)
YOU ARE THE MASTER ARCHER —

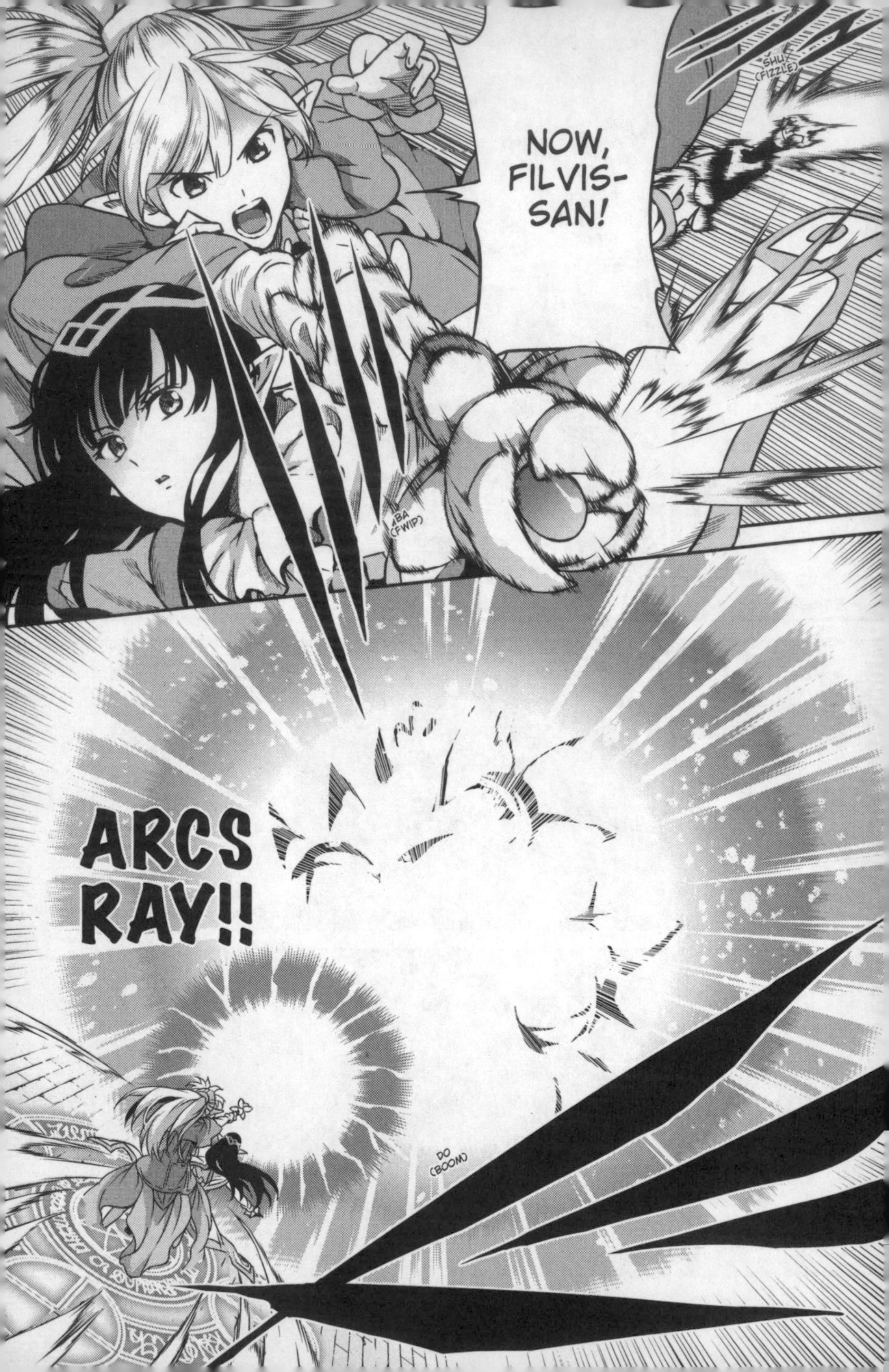
SHU (FIZZLE)
NOW, FILVIS-SAN!
BA (FWIP)
ARCS RAY!!
DO (BOOM)

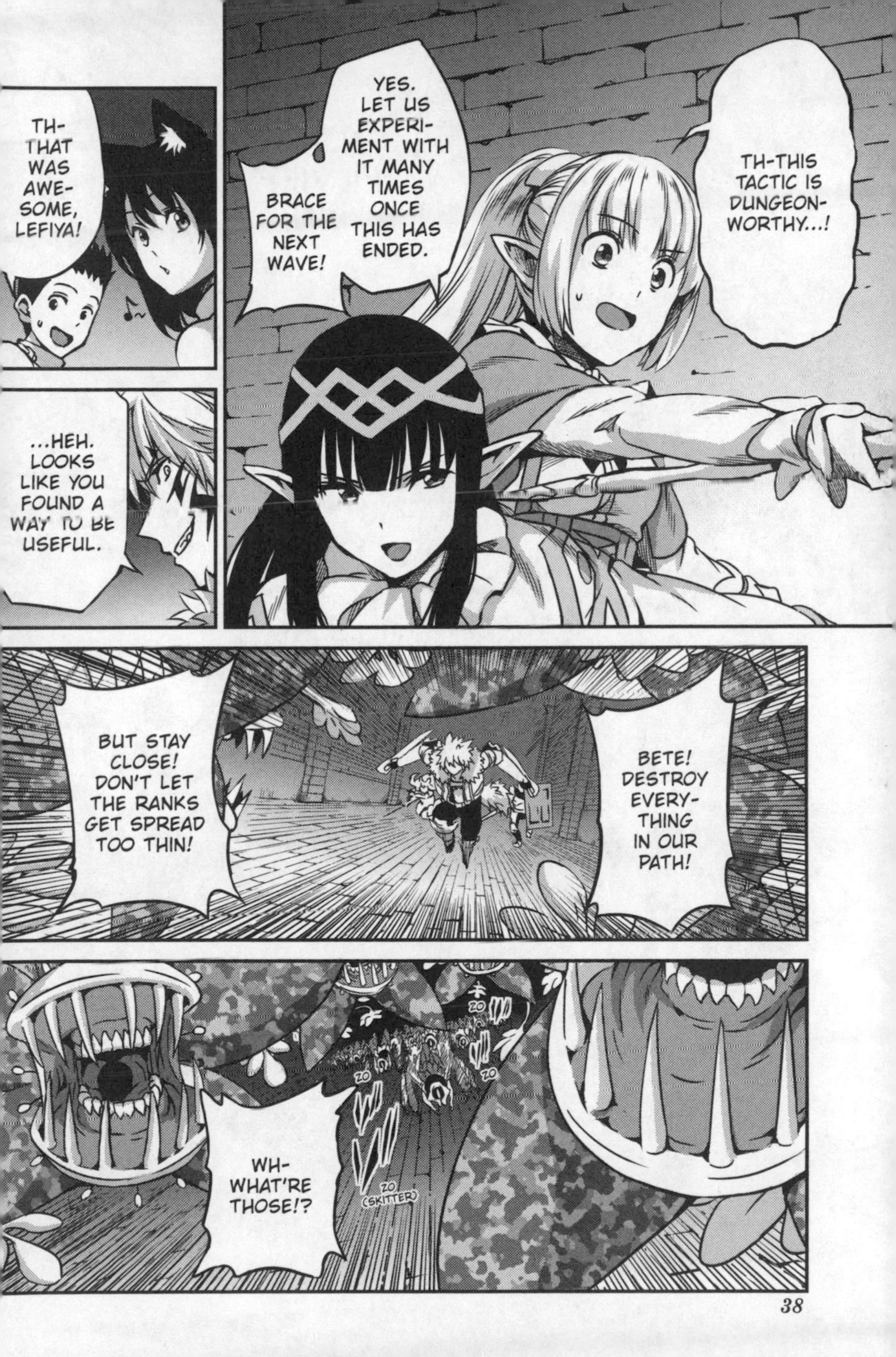
TH-THIS TACTIC IS DUNGEON-WORTHY...!
YES. LET US EXPERIMENT WITH IT MANY TIMES ONCE THIS HAS ENDED.
BRACE FOR THE NEXT WAVE!
TH-THAT WAS AWESOME, LEFIYA!
...HEH. LOOKS LIKE YOU FOUND A WAY TO BE USEFUL.
BETE! DESTROY EVERYTHING IN OUR PATH!
BUT STAY CLOSE! DON'T LET THE RANKS GET SPREAD TOO THIN!
ZO
ZO
ZO
WH-WHAT'RE THOSE!?
ZO (SKITTER)

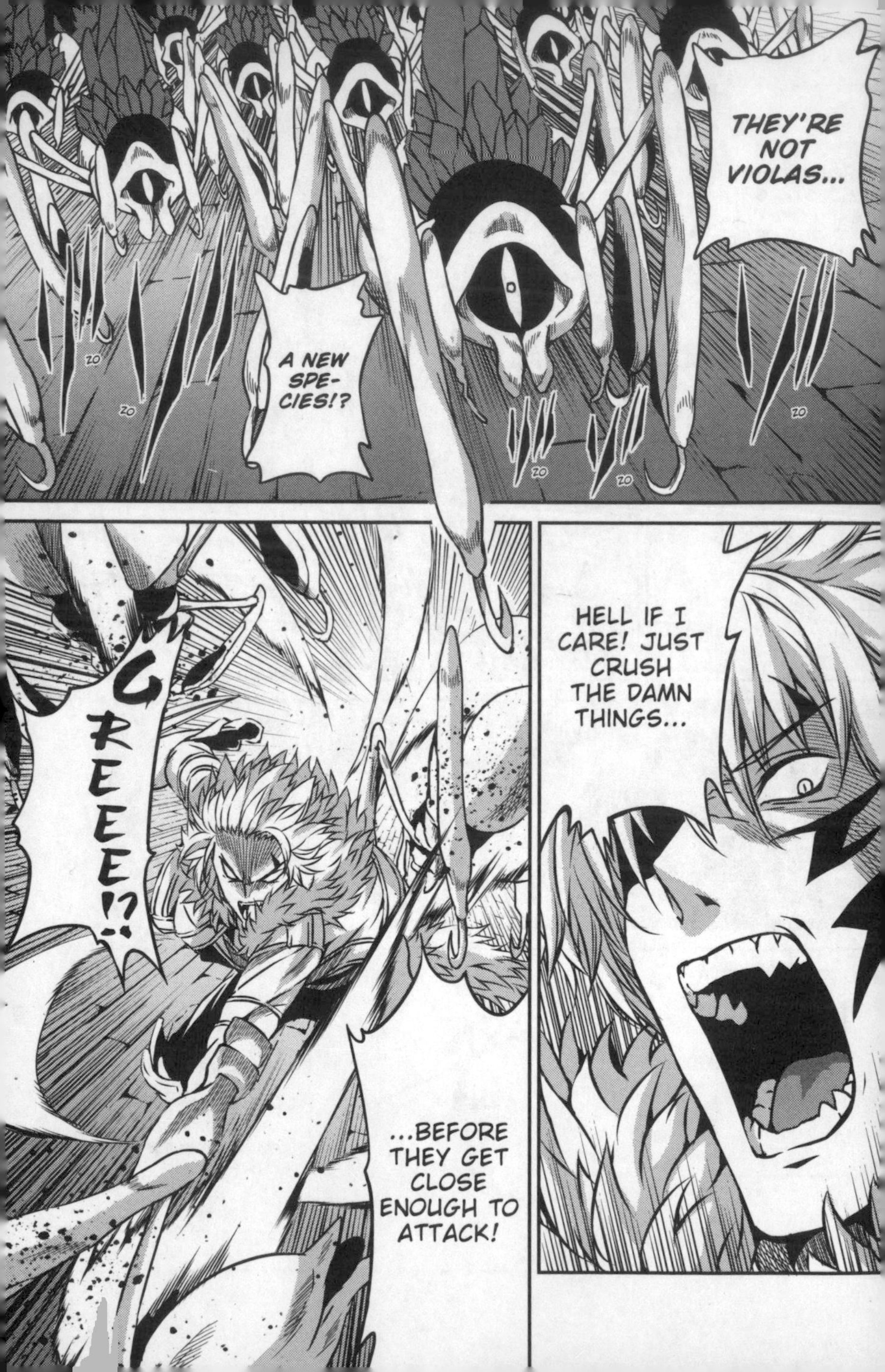
THEY'RE NOT VIOLAS...
A NEW SPE-CIES!?
ZO
ZO
ZO
ZO
ZO
HELL IF I CARE! JUST CRUSH THE DAMN THINGS...
GREEEE!!?
...BEFORE THEY GET CLOSE ENOUGH TO ATTACK!

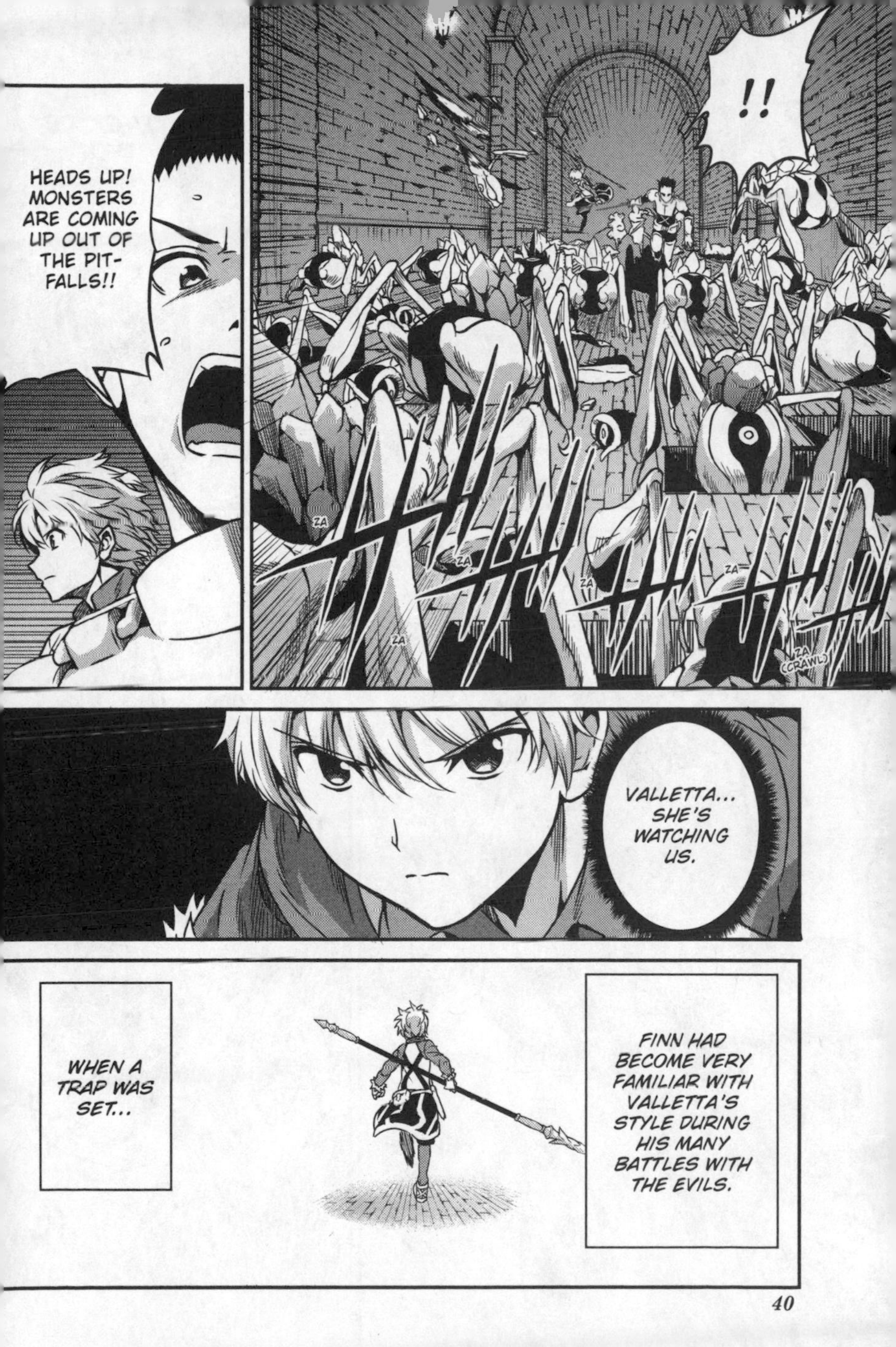
!!
ZA
ZA
ZA
ZA
ZA
ZA (CRAWL)
HEADS UP! MONSTERS ARE COMING UP OUT OF THE PIT-FALLS!!
VALLETTA... SHE'S WATCHING US.
FINN HAD BECOME VERY FAMILIAR WITH VALLETTA'S STYLE DURING HIS MANY BATTLES WITH THE EVILS.
WHEN A TRAP WAS SET...

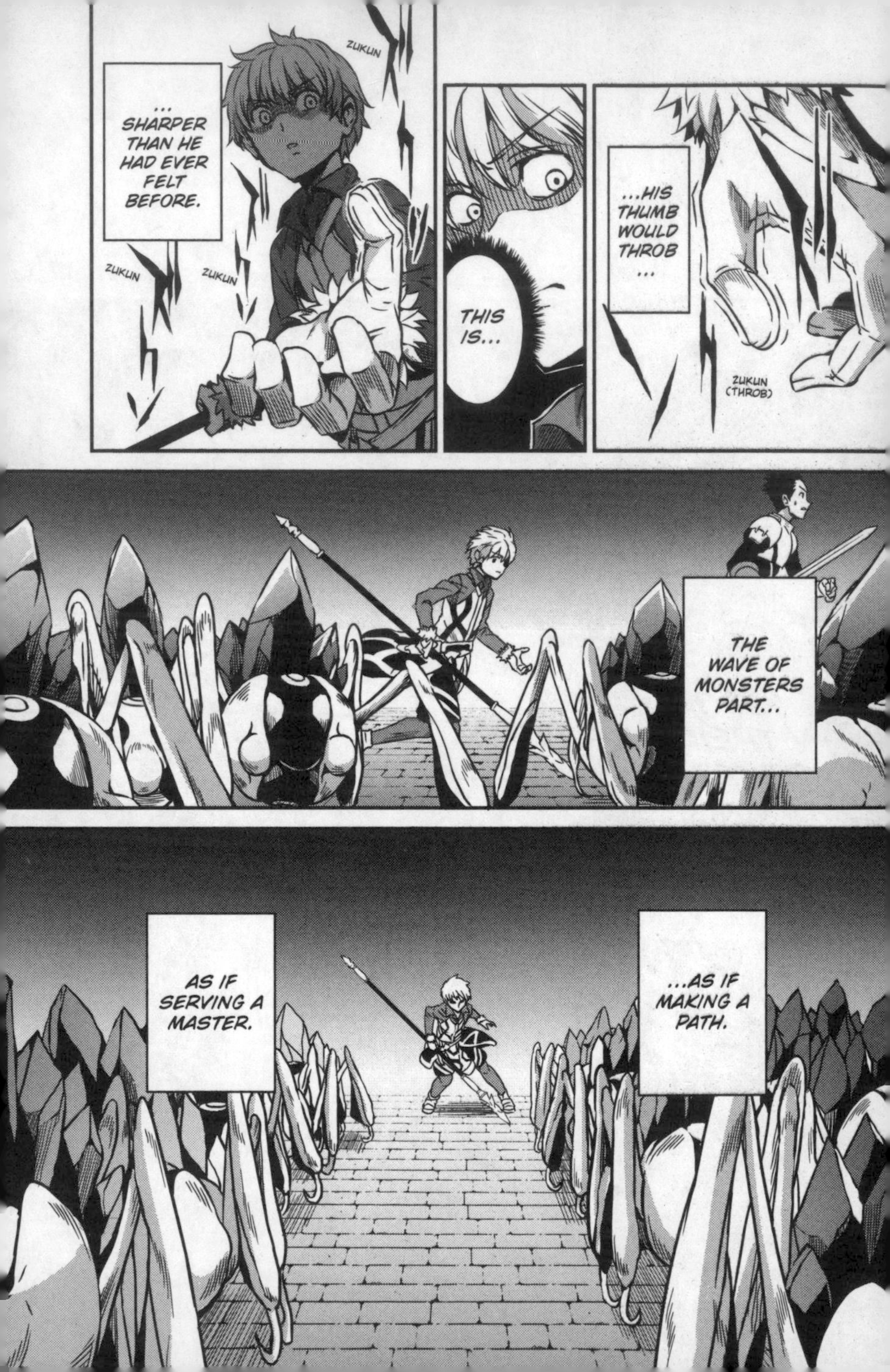
...HIS THUMB WOULD THROB ...
ZUKUN (THROB)
THIS IS...
ZUKUN
... SHARPER THAN HE HAD EVER FELT BEFORE.
ZUKUN
ZUKUN
THE WAVE OF MONSTERS PART...
...AS IF MAKING A PATH.
AS IF SERVING A MASTER.

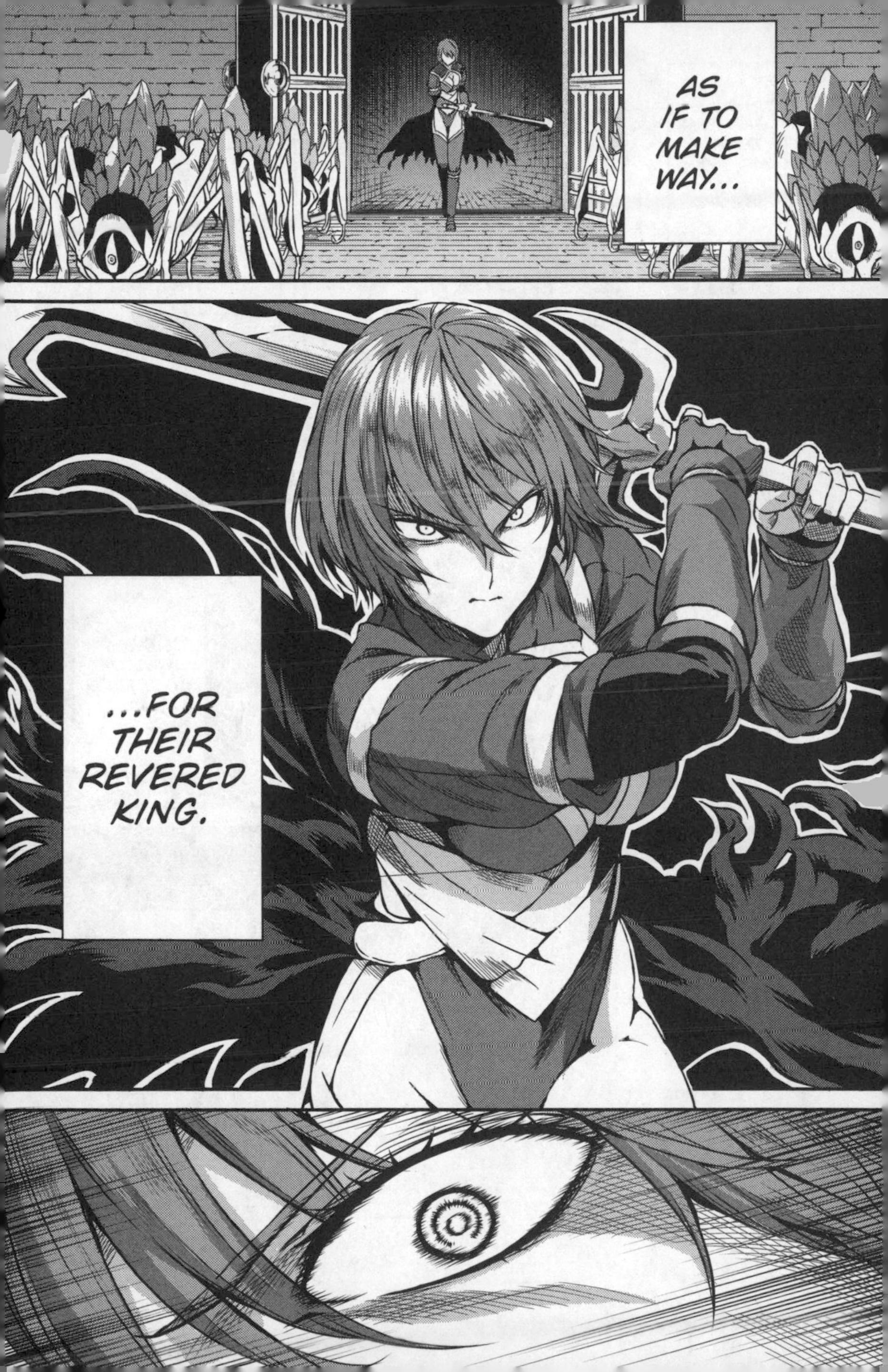
AS IF TO MAKE WAY...
...FOR THEIR REVERED KING.

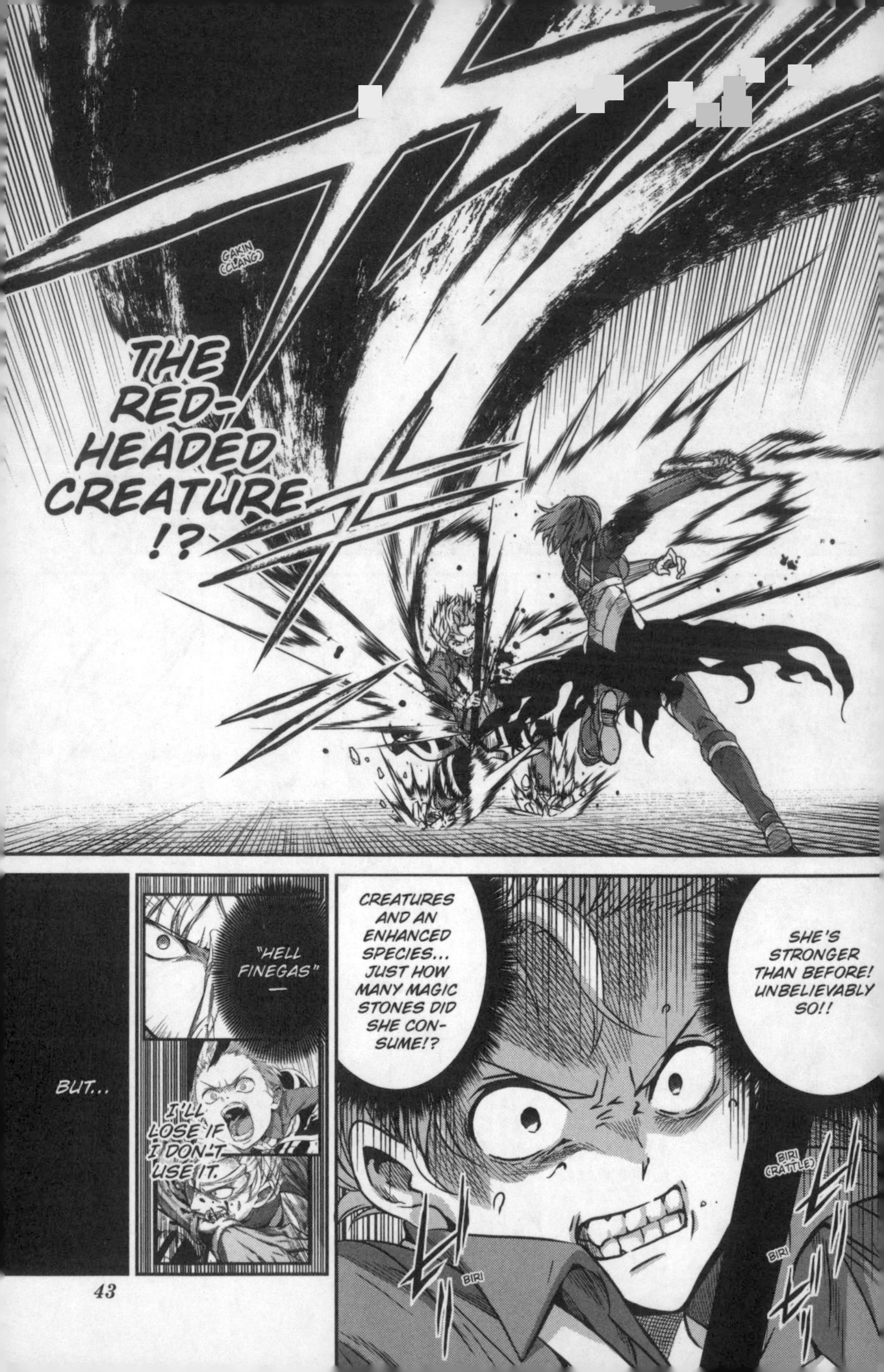
GAKIN (CLANG)
THE RED-HEADED CREATURE!?
SHE'S STRONGER THAN BEFORE! UNBELIEVABLY SO!!
CREATURES AND AN ENHANCED SPECIES... JUST HOW MANY MAGIC STONES DID SHE CONSUME!?
BIRI (RATTLE)
BIRI
BIRI
"HELL FINEGAS" —
I'LL LOSE IF I DON'T USE IT.
BUT...

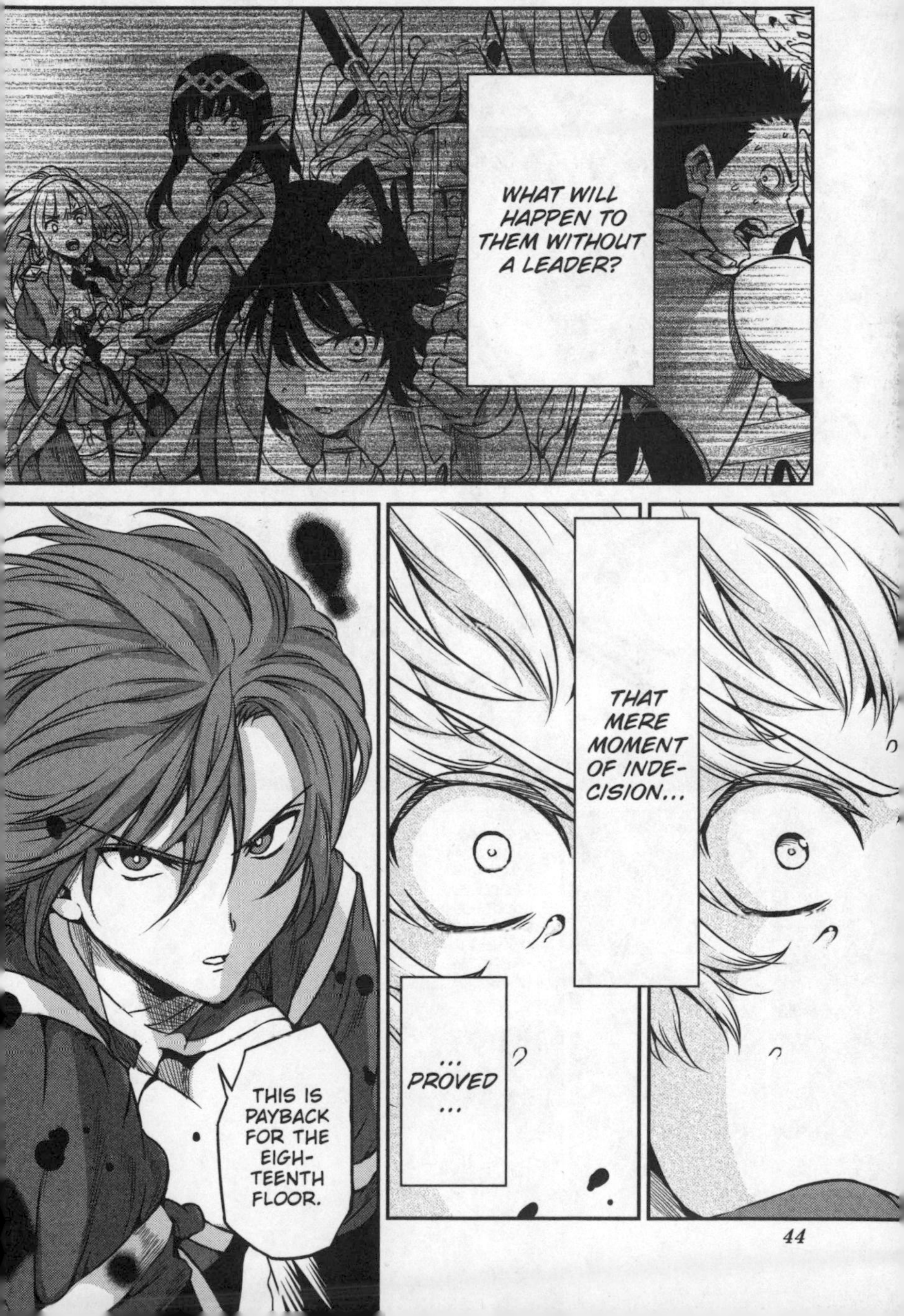
WHAT WILL HAPPEN TO THEM WITHOUT A LEADER?
THAT MERE MOMENT OF INDE-CISION...
...PROVED...
THIS IS PAYBACK FOR THE EIGH-TEENTH FLOOR.

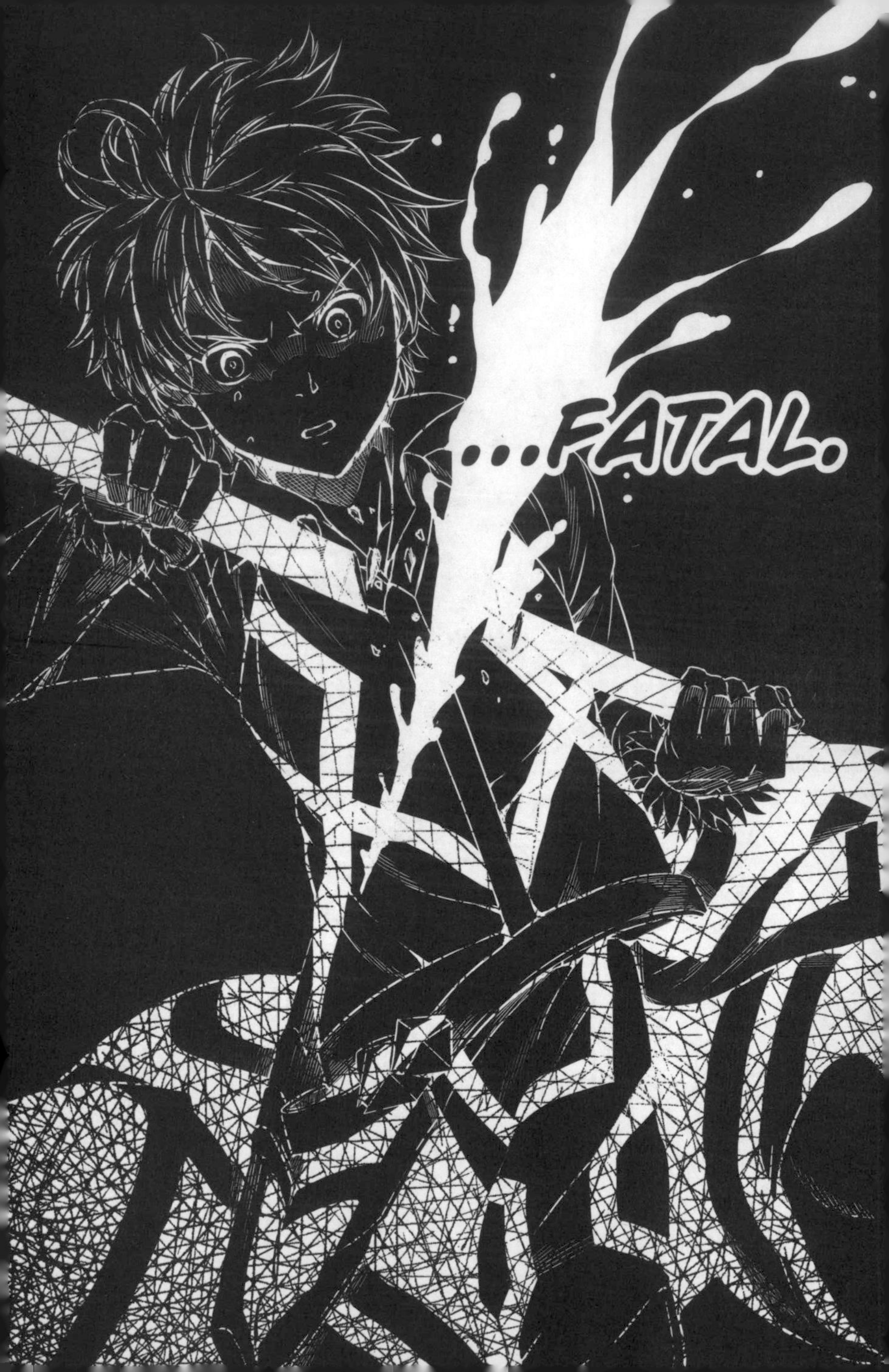
...FATAL.

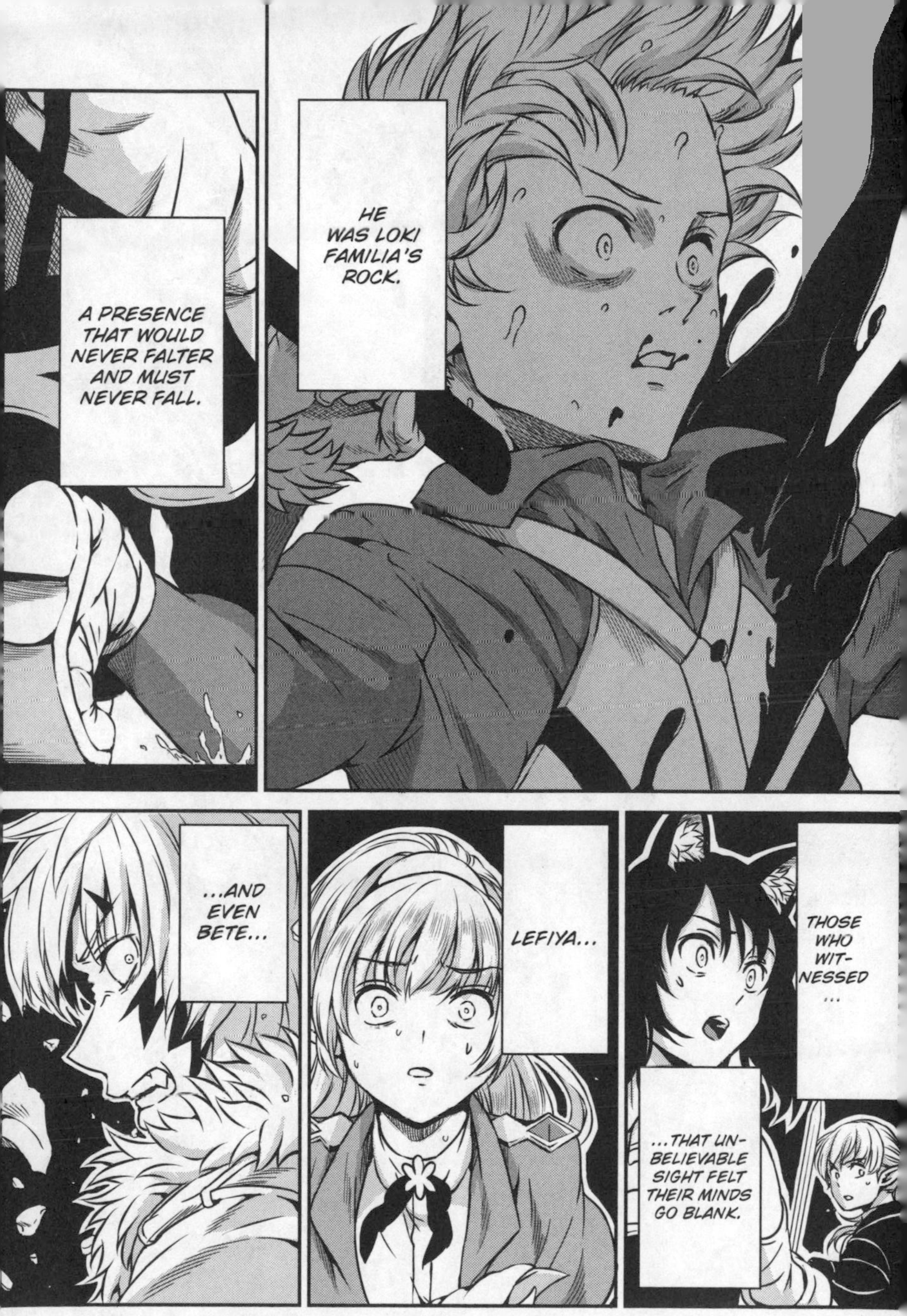
HE WAS LOKI FAMILIA'S ROCK.
A PRESENCE THAT WOULD NEVER FALTER AND MUST NEVER FALL.
THOSE WHO WIT-NESSED ...
...THAT UN-BELIEVABLE SIGHT FELT THEIR MINDS GO BLANK.
LEFIYA...
...AND EVEN BETE...

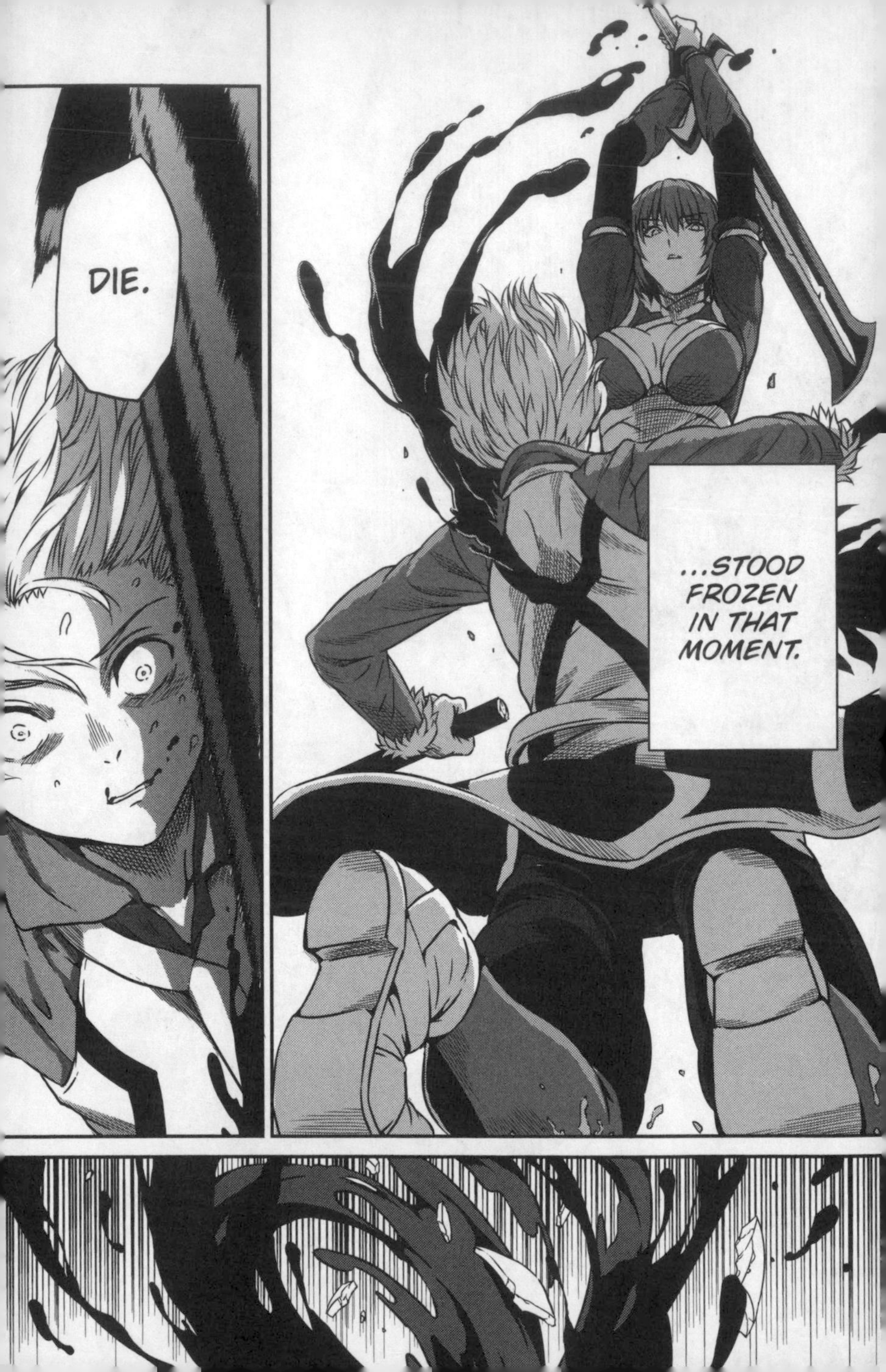
...STOOD FROZEN IN THAT MOMENT.
DIE.

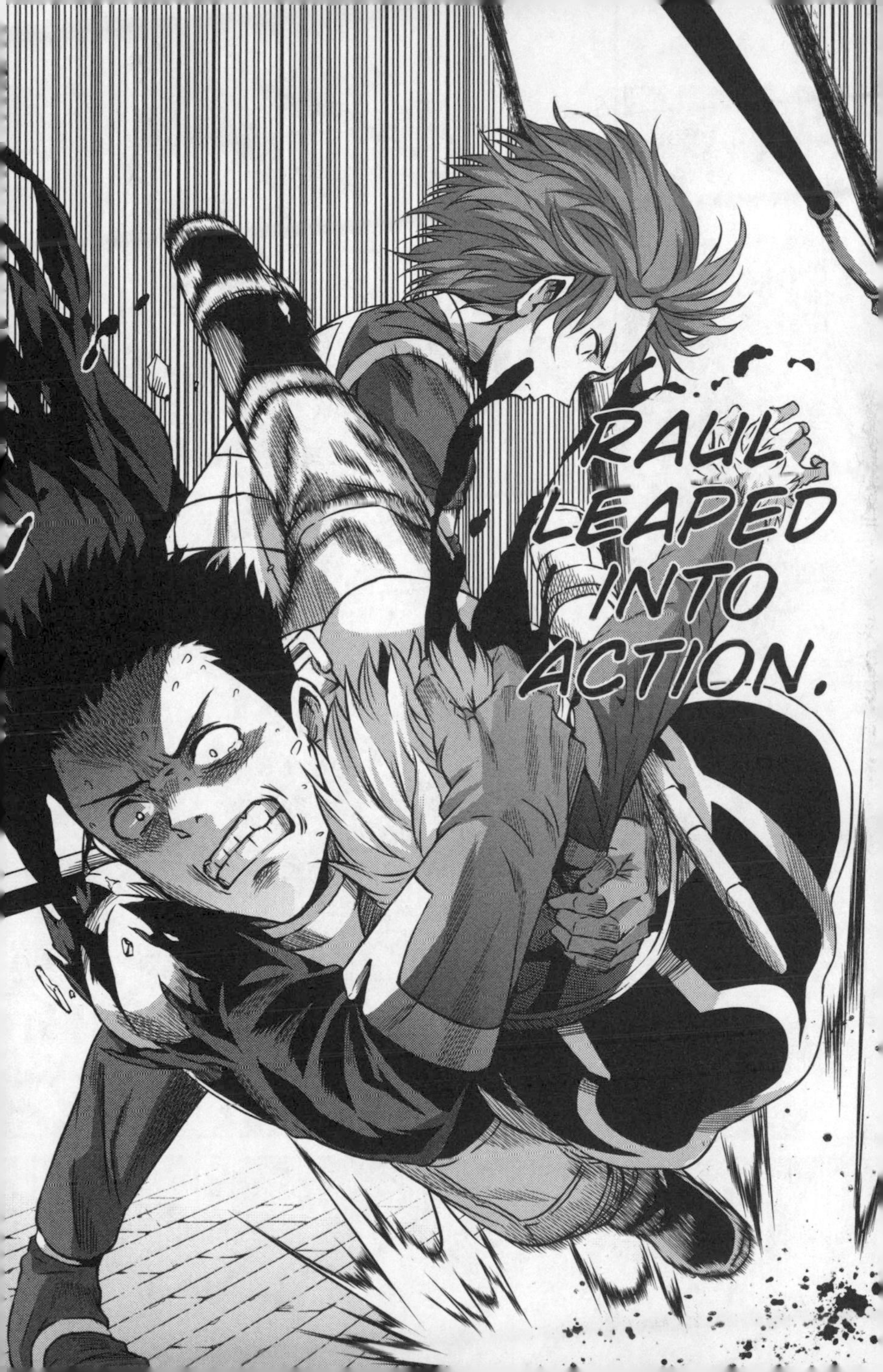
RAUL LEAPED INTO ACTION.

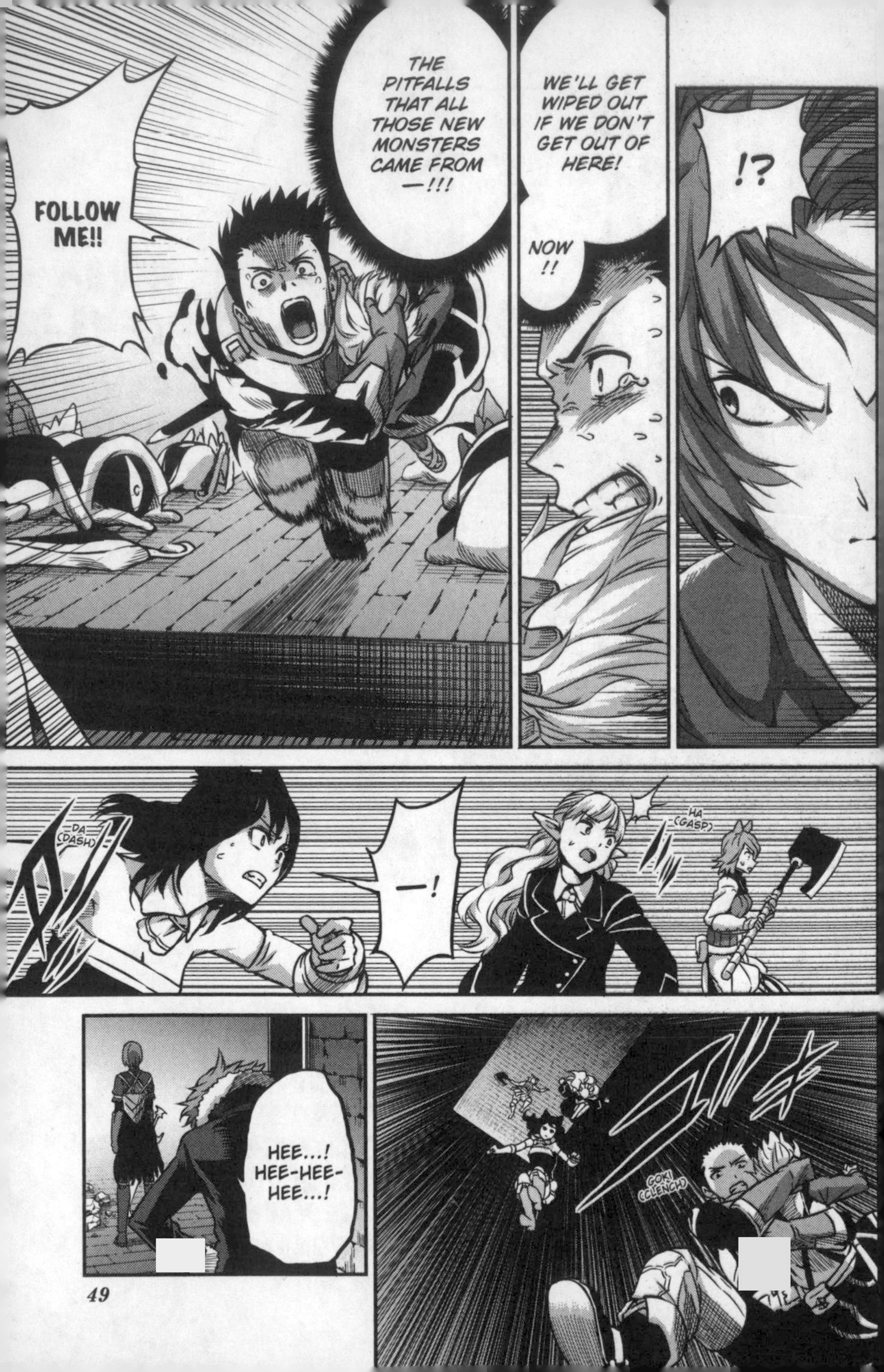
!?
WE'LL GET WIPED OUT IF WE DON'T GET OUT OF HERE!
NOW !!
THE PITFALLS THAT ALL THOSE NEW MONSTERS CAME FROM —!!!
FOLLOW ME!!
HA (GASP)
—!
DA (DASH)
GOKI (CLENCH)
HEE...! HEE-HEE-HEE...!

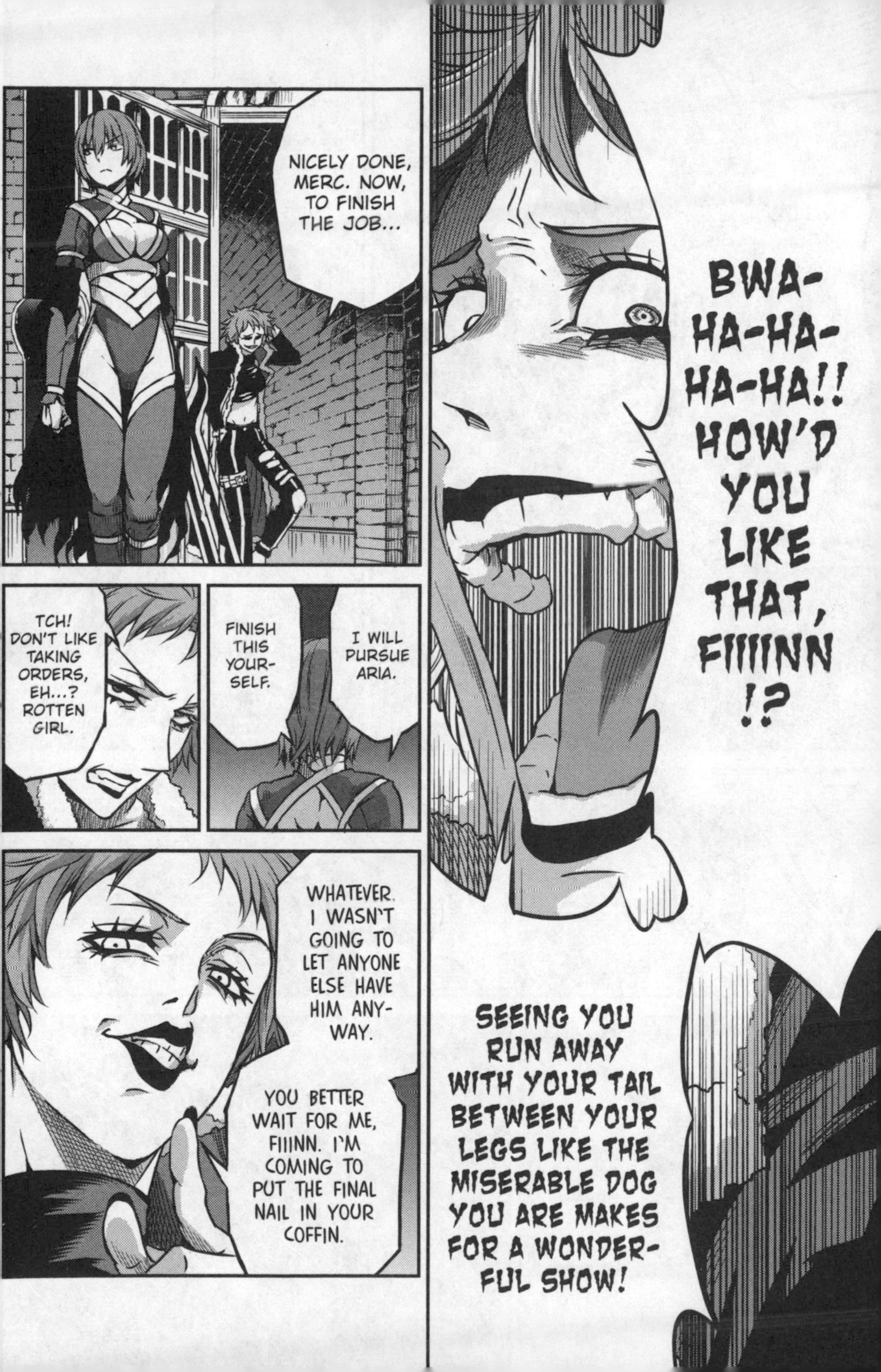
BWA-HA-HA-HA-HA!! HOW'D YOU LIKE THAT, FIIIINN!?
SEEING YOU RUN AWAY WITH YOUR TAIL BETWEEN YOUR LEGS LIKE THE MISERABLE DOG YOU ARE MAKES FOR A WONDERFUL SHOW!
NICELY DONE, MERC. NOW, TO FINISH THE JOB...
I WILL PURSUE ARIA.
FINISH THIS YOURSELF.
TCH! DON'T LIKE TAKING ORDERS, EH...? ROTTEN GIRL.
WHATEVER. I WASN'T GOING TO LET ANYONE ELSE HAVE HIM ANYWAY.
YOU BETTER WAIT FOR ME, FIIINN. I'M COMING TO PUT THE FINAL NAIL IN YOUR COFFIN.

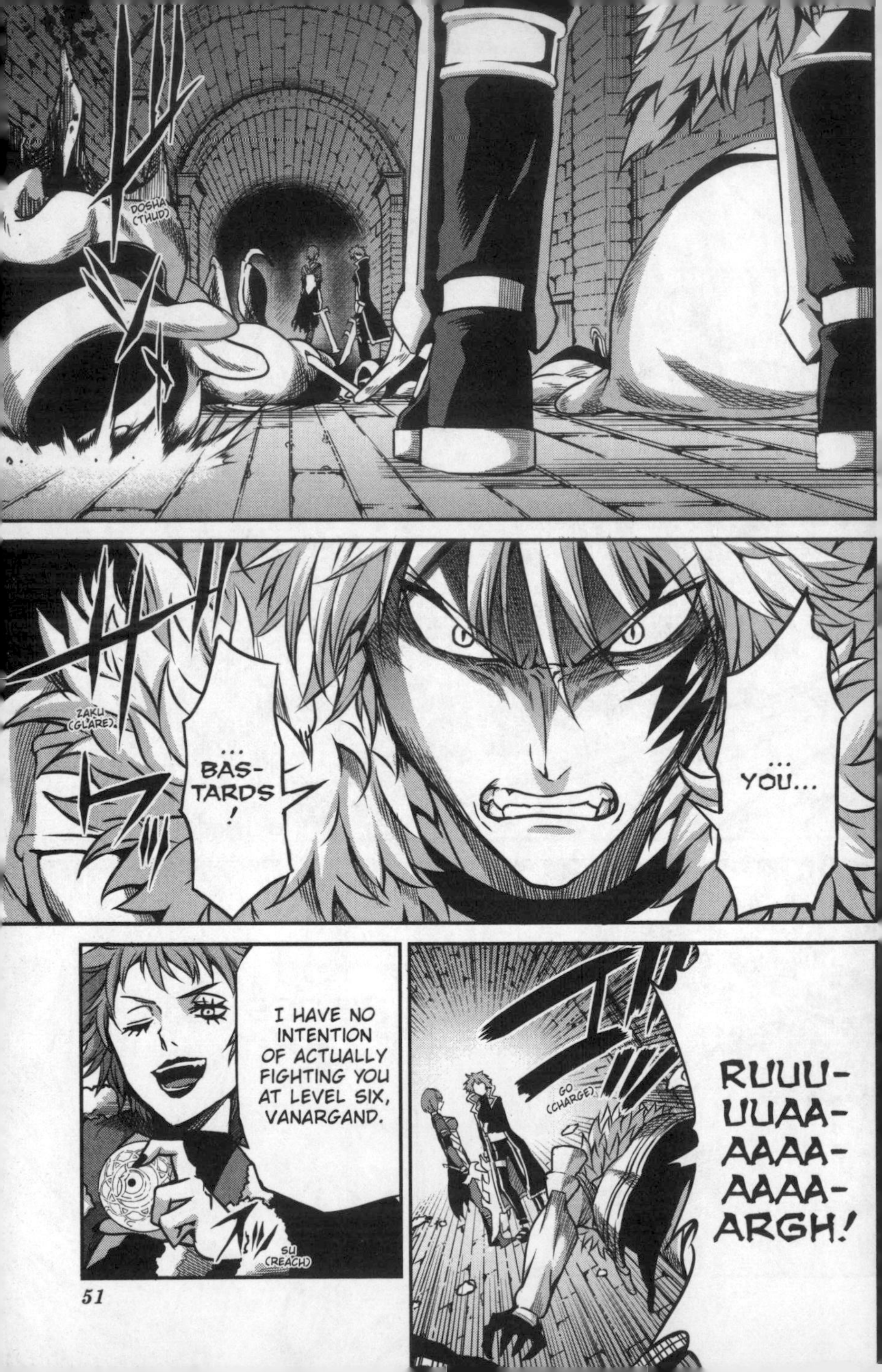
DOSHA (THUD)
... YOU...
... BAS-TARDS!
ZAKU (GLARE)
RUUU-UUAA-AAAA-AAAA-ARGH!
GO (CHARGE)
I HAVE NO INTENTION OF ACTUALLY FIGHTING YOU AT LEVEL SIX, VANARGAND.
SU (REACH)

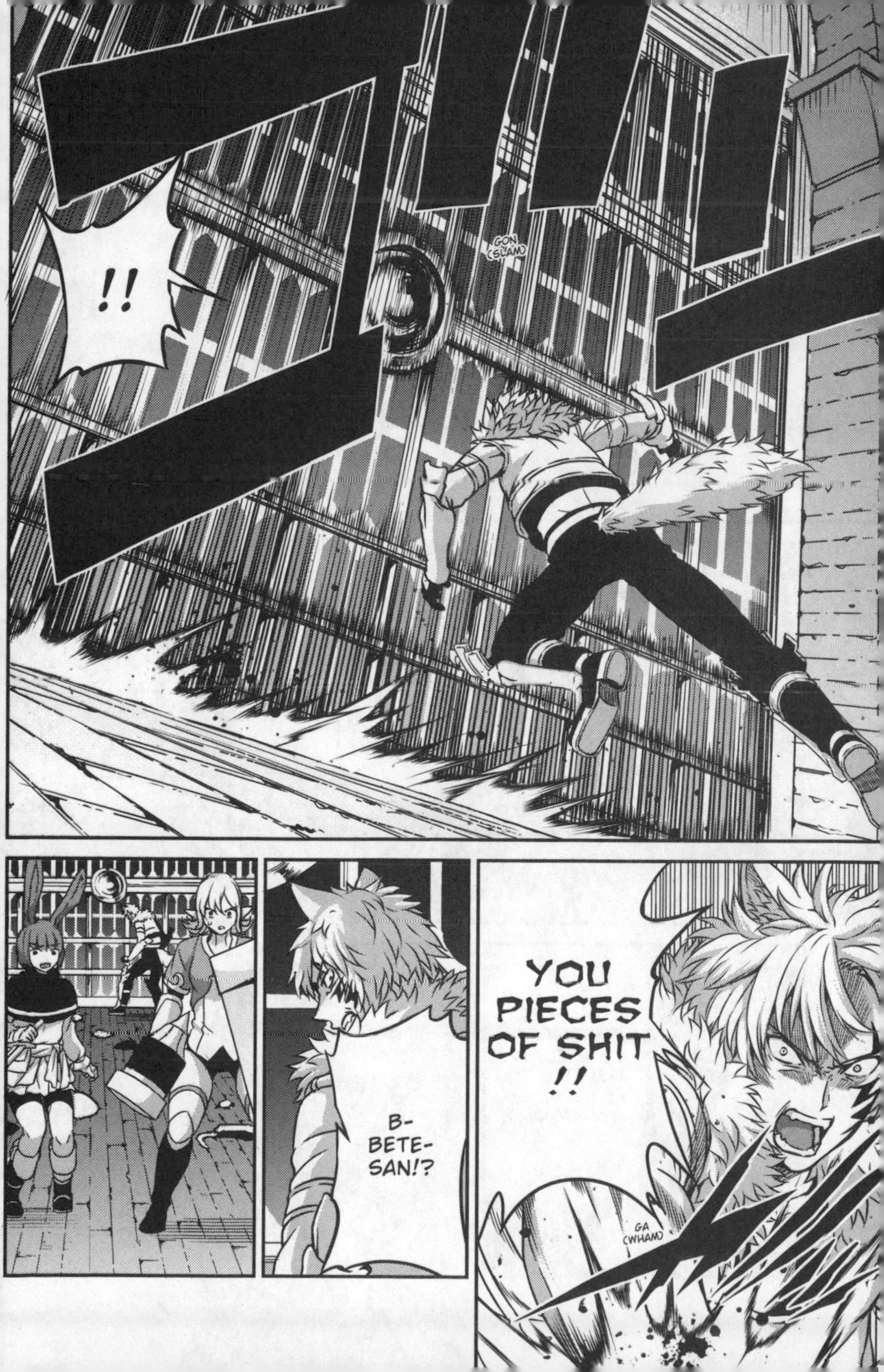
!!
GON (SLAM)
YOU PIECES OF SHIT !!
GA (WHAM)
B- BETE-SAN!?

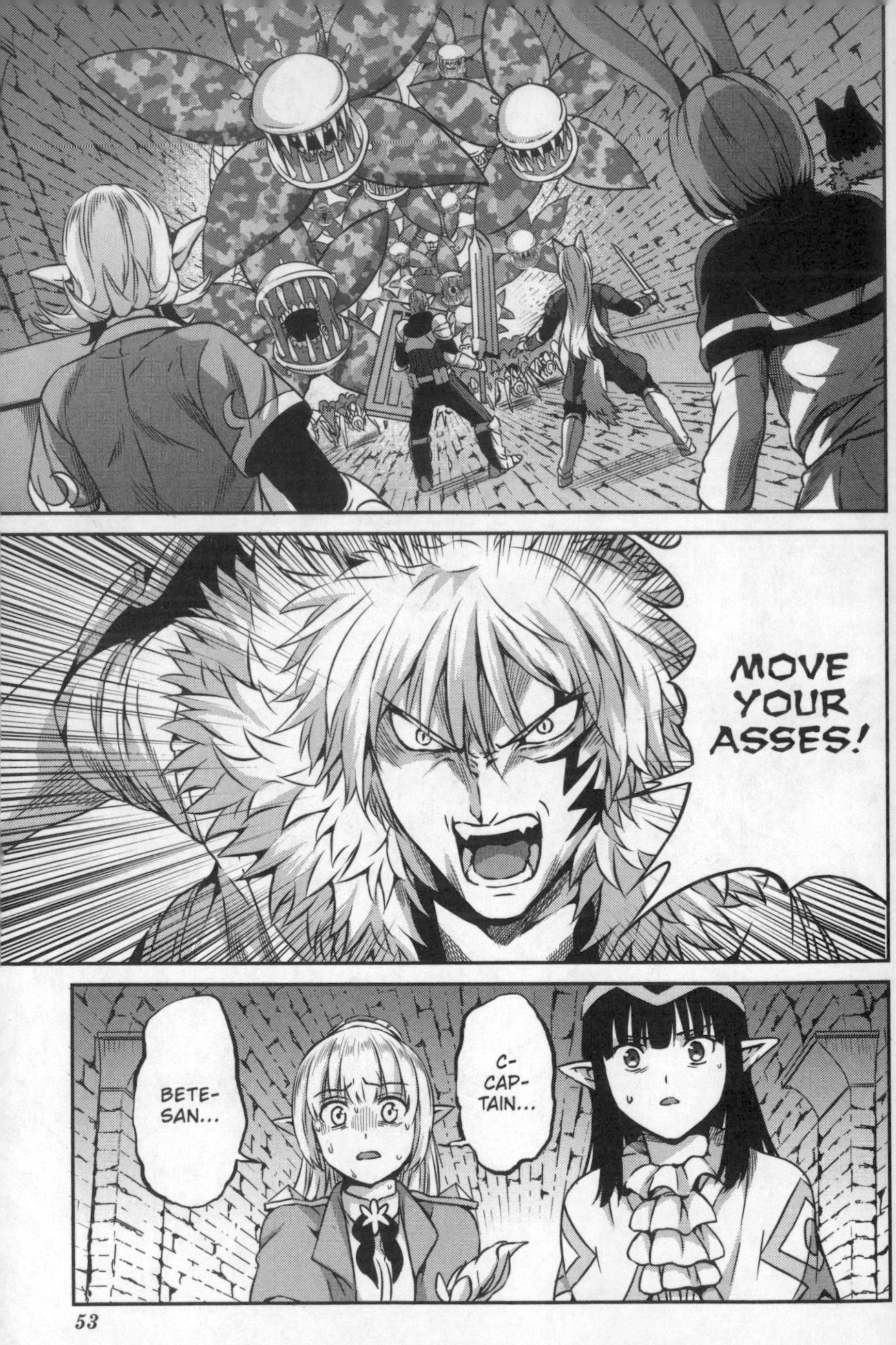
MOVE YOUR ASSES!
C-CAP-TAIN...
BETE-SAN...

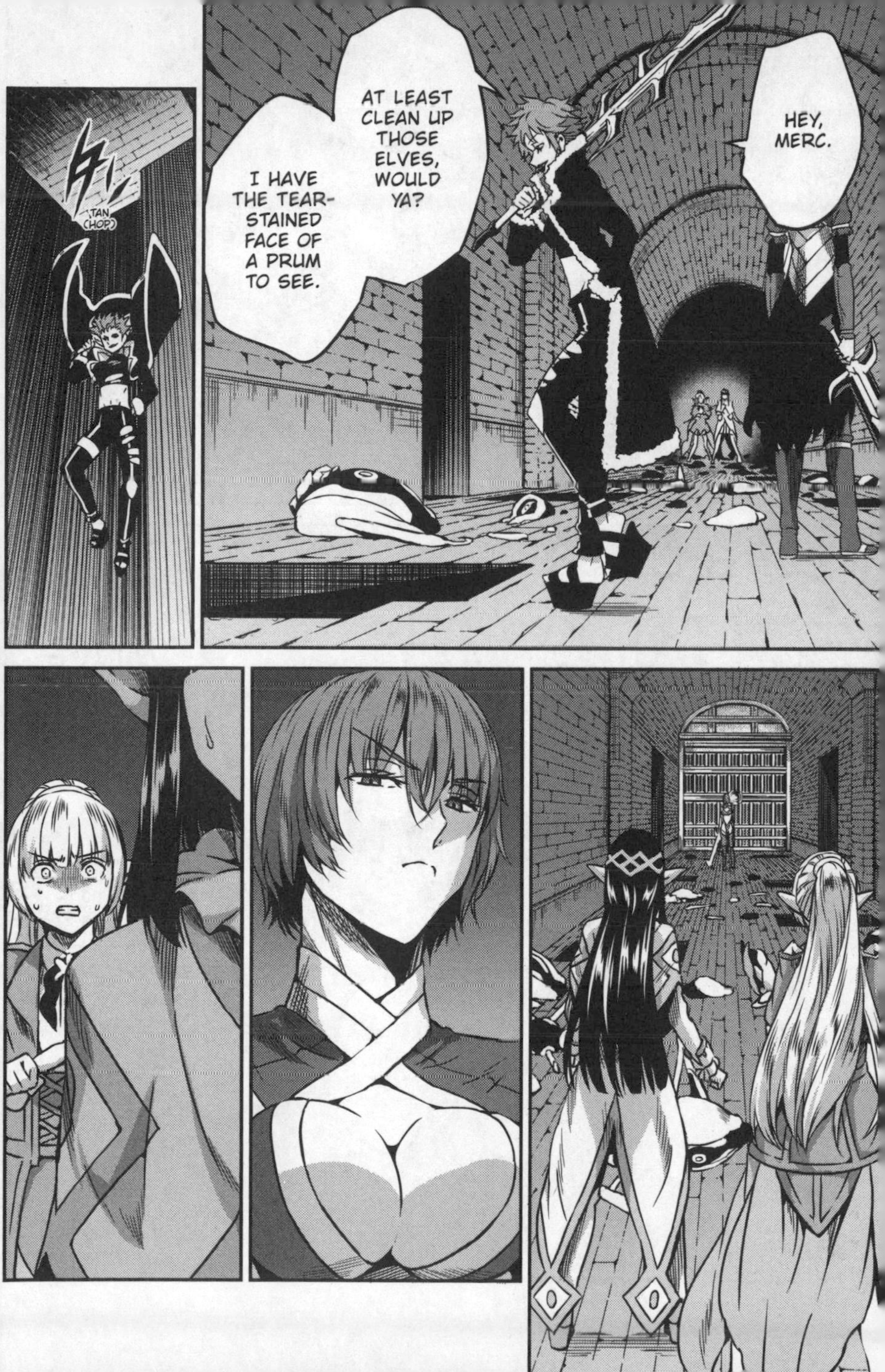
HEY, MERC.
AT LEAST CLEAN UP THOSE ELVES, WOULD YA?
I HAVE THE TEAR-STAINED FACE OF A PRUM TO SEE.
TAN (CHOP)

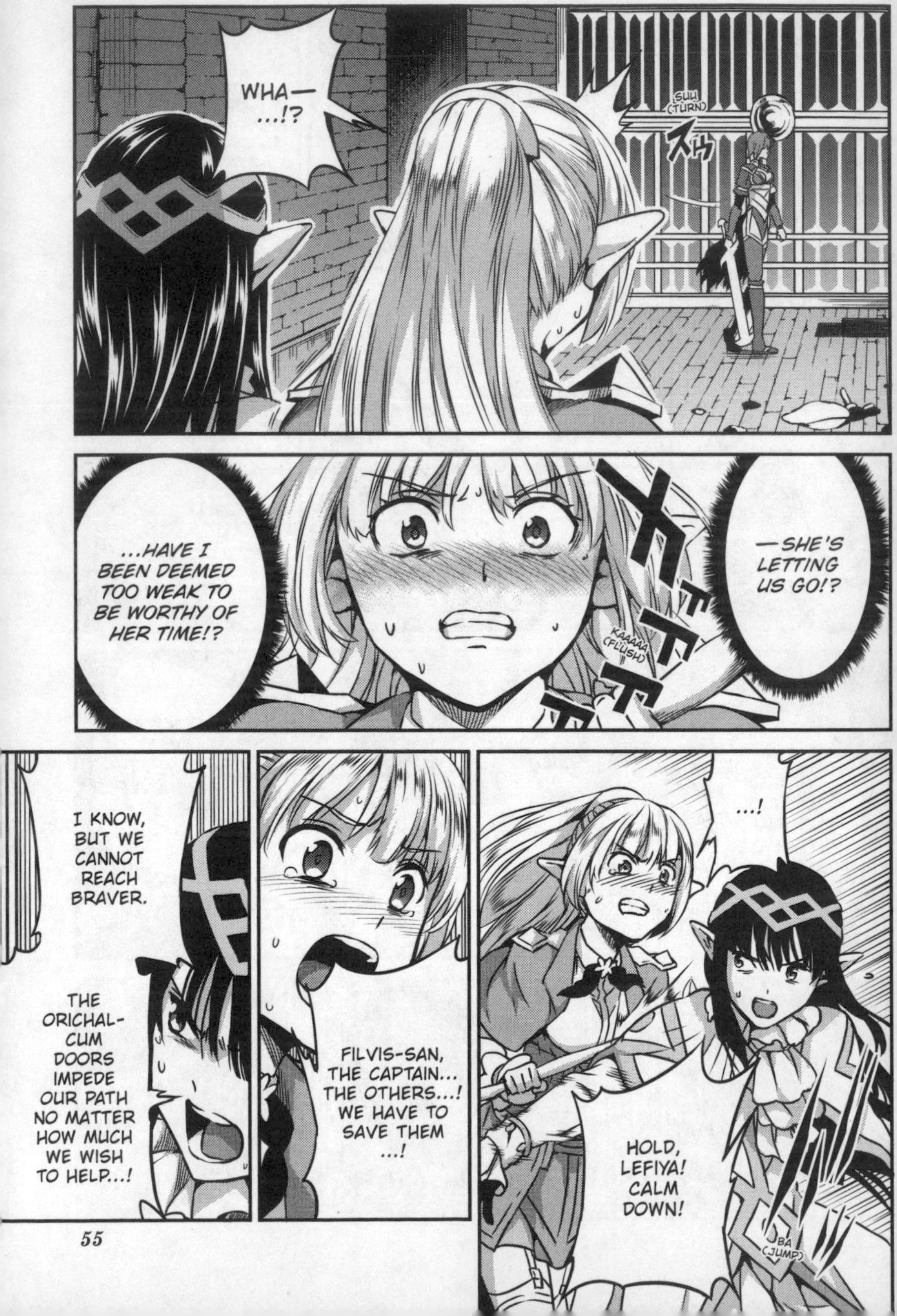
SUU (TURN)
WHA— ...!?
—SHE'S LETTING US GO!?
KAAAAA (FLUSH)
...HAVE I BEEN DEEMED TOO WEAK TO BE WORTHY OF HER TIME!?
...!
HOLD, LEFIYA! CALM DOWN!
BA (JUMP)
FILVIS-SAN, THE CAPTAIN... THE OTHERS...! WE HAVE TO SAVE THEM ...!
I KNOW, BUT WE CANNOT REACH BRAVER.
THE ORICHAL-CUM DOORS IMPEDE OUR PATH NO MATTER HOW MUCH WE WISH TO HELP...!

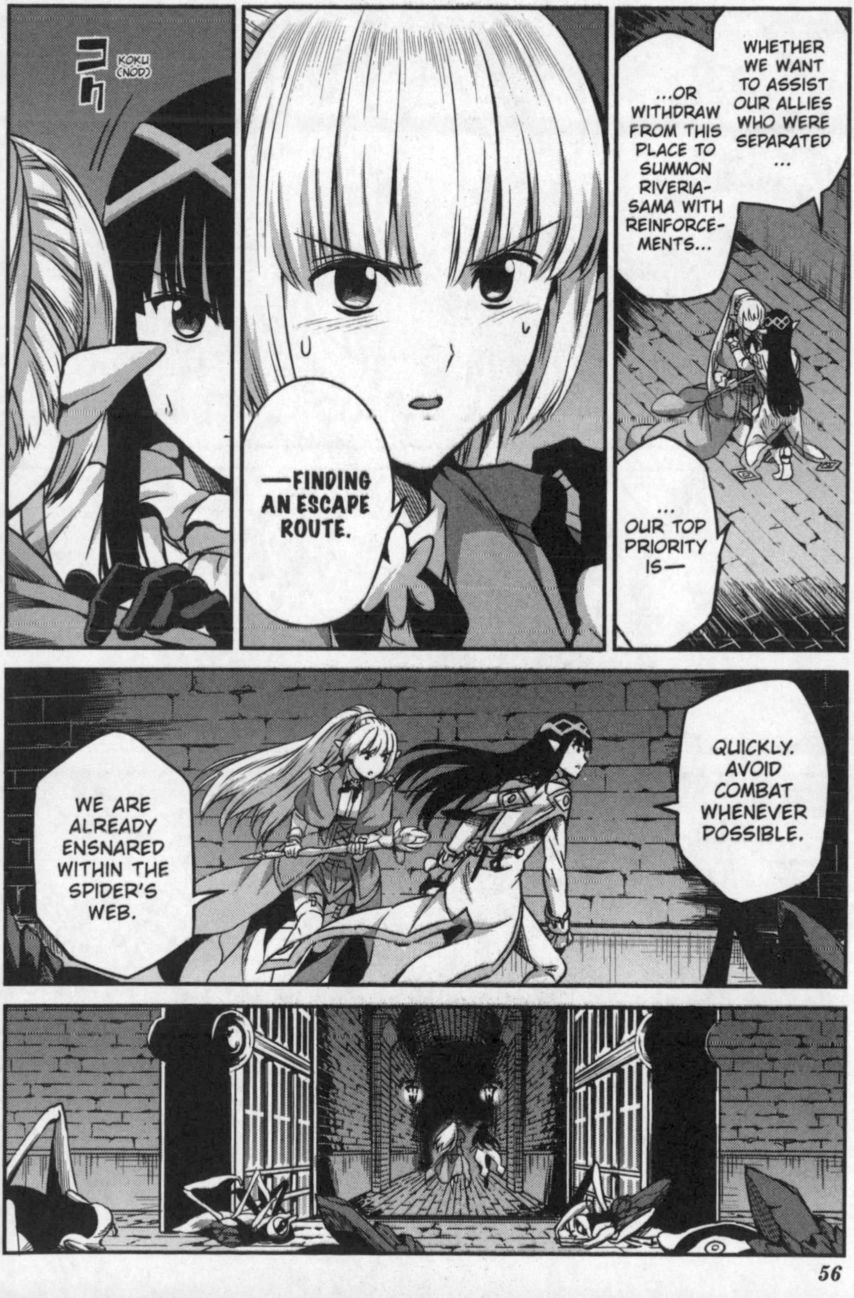
WHETHER WE WANT TO ASSIST OUR ALLIES WHO WERE SEPARATED ...
...OR WITHDRAW FROM THIS PLACE TO SUMMON RIVERIA-SAMA WITH REINFORCE-MENTS...
... OUR TOP PRIORITY IS—
—FINDING AN ESCAPE ROUTE.
KOKU (NOD)
QUICKLY. AVOID COMBAT WHENEVER POSSIBLE.
WE ARE ALREADY ENSNARED WITHIN THE SPIDER'S WEB.

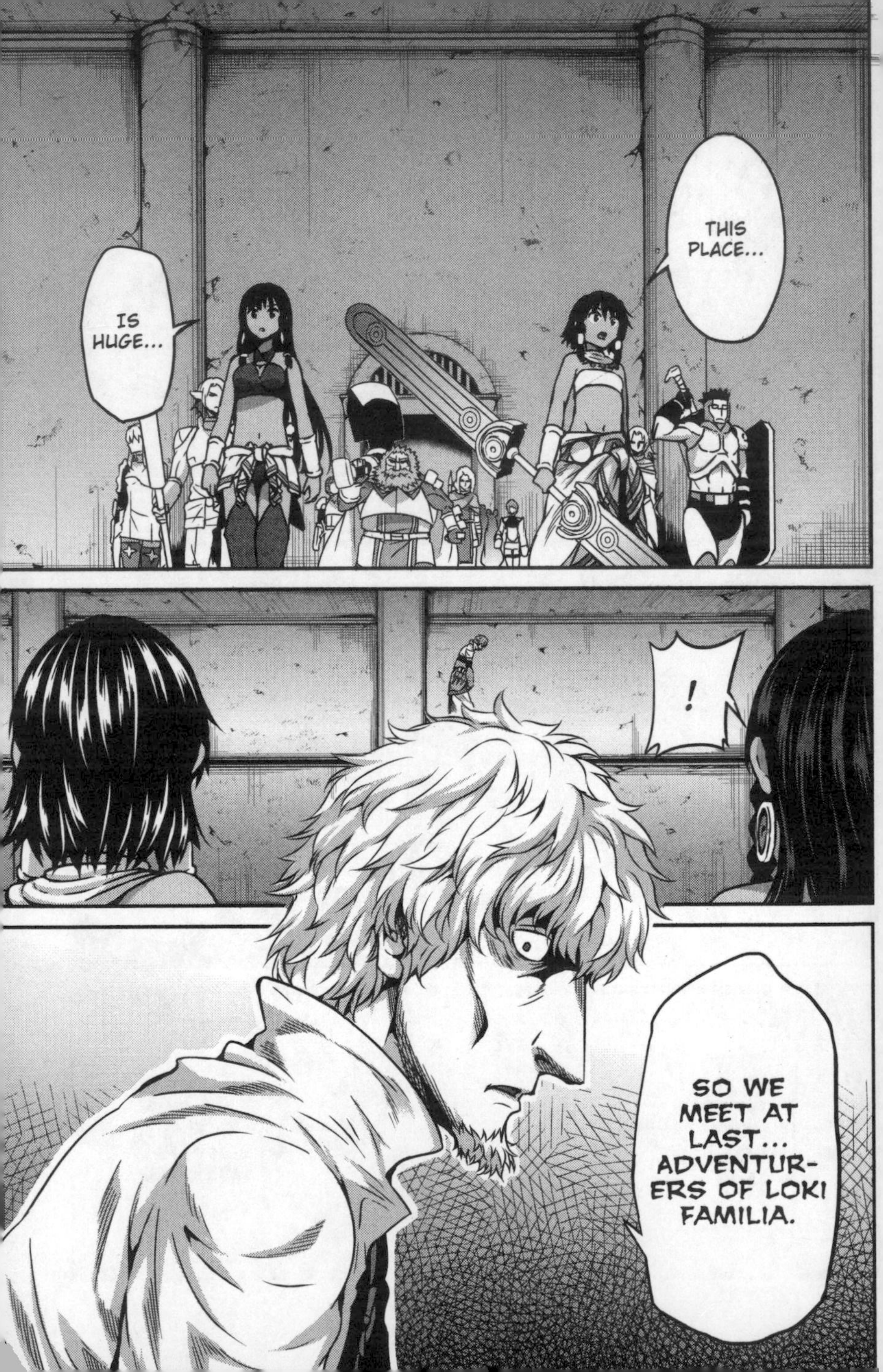
THIS PLACE...
IS HUGE...
!
SO WE MEET AT LAST... ADVENTURERS OF LOKI FAMILIA.

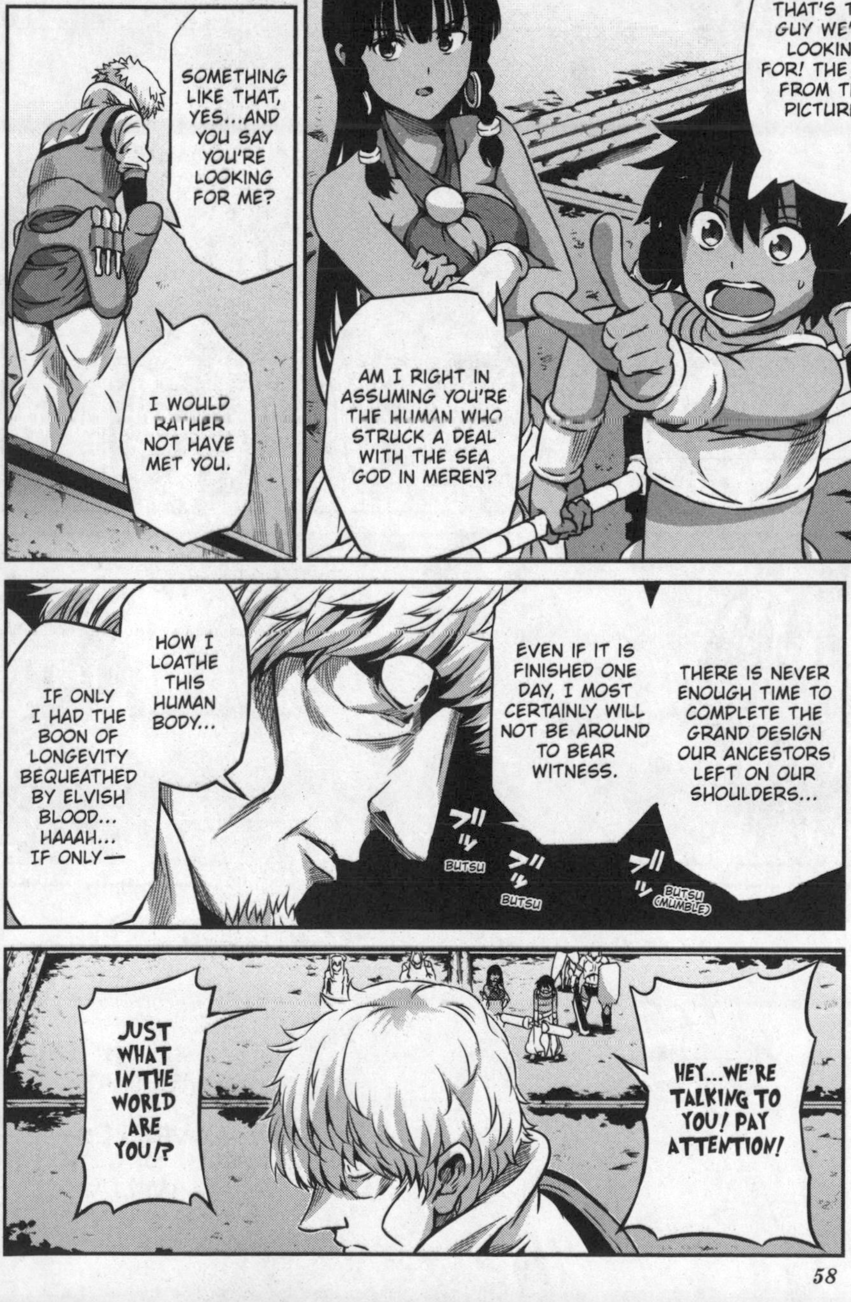
THAT'S THE GUY WE'RE LOOKING FOR! THE ONE FROM THE PICTURE!
AM I RIGHT IN ASSUMING YOU'RE THE HUMAN WHO STRUCK A DEAL WITH THE SEA GOD IN MEREN?
SOMETHING LIKE THAT, YES...AND YOU SAY YOU'RE LOOKING FOR ME?
I WOULD RATHER NOT HAVE MET YOU.
THERE IS NEVER ENOUGH TIME TO COMPLETE THE GRAND DESIGN OUR ANCESTORS LEFT ON OUR SHOULDERS...
EVEN IF IT IS FINISHED ONE DAY, I MOST CERTAINLY WILL NOT BE AROUND TO BEAR WITNESS.
BUTSU (MUMBLE)
BUTSU
BUTSU
HOW I LOATHE THIS HUMAN BODY...
IF ONLY I HAD THE BOON OF LONGEVITY BEQUEATHED BY ELVISH BLOOD... HAAAH... IF ONLY—
HEY...WE'RE TALKING TO YOU! PAY ATTENTION!
JUST WHAT IN THE WORLD ARE YOU!?

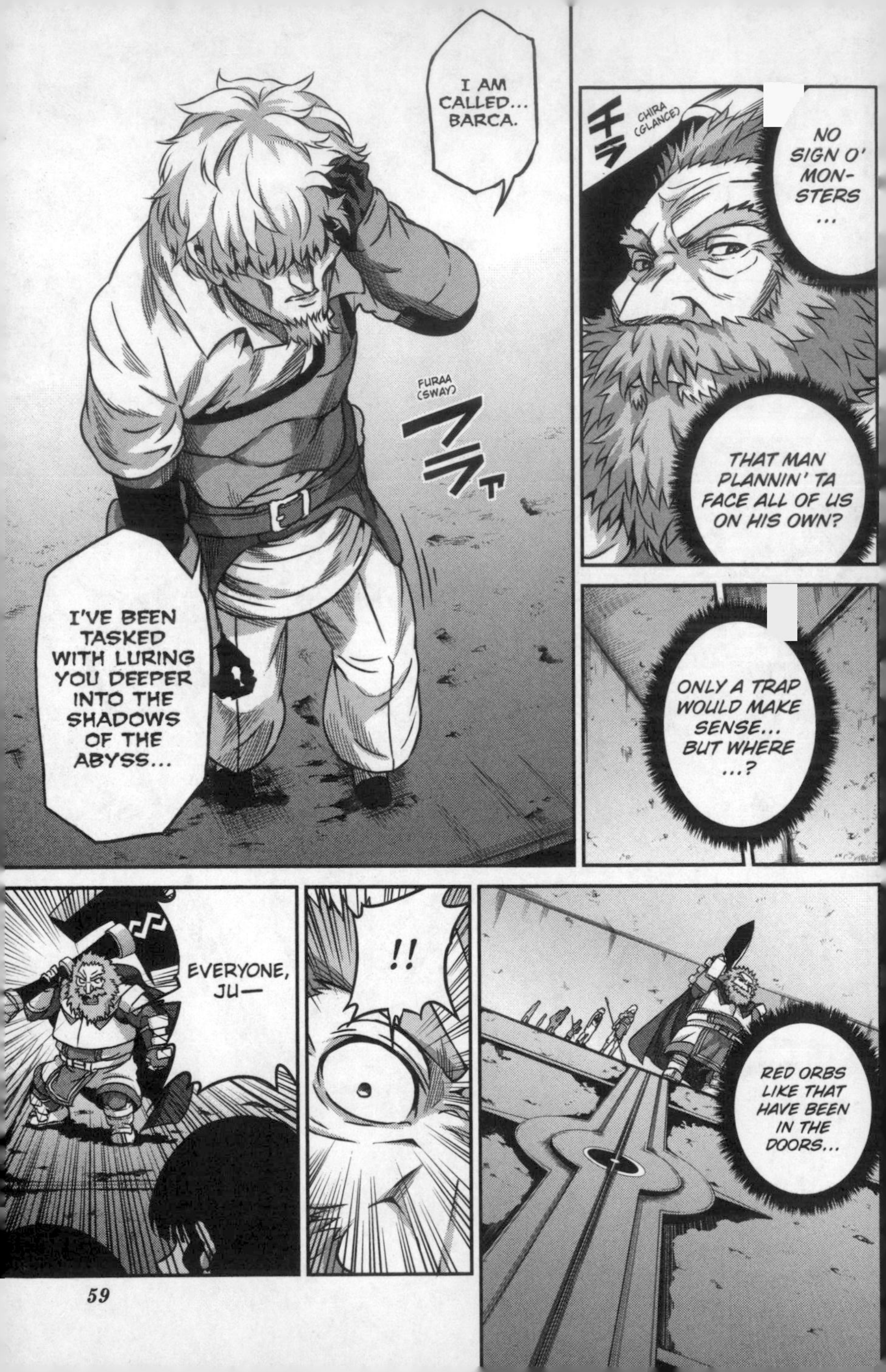
CHIRA (GLANCE)
NO SIGN O' MON-STERS ...
THAT MAN PLANNIN' TA FACE ALL OF US ON HIS OWN?
ONLY A TRAP WOULD MAKE SENSE... BUT WHERE ...?
I AM CALLED... BARCA.
FURAA (SWAY)
I'VE BEEN TASKED WITH LURING YOU DEEPER INTO THE SHADOWS OF THE ABYSS...
RED ORBS LIKE THAT HAVE BEEN IN THE DOORS...
!!
EVERYONE, JU—

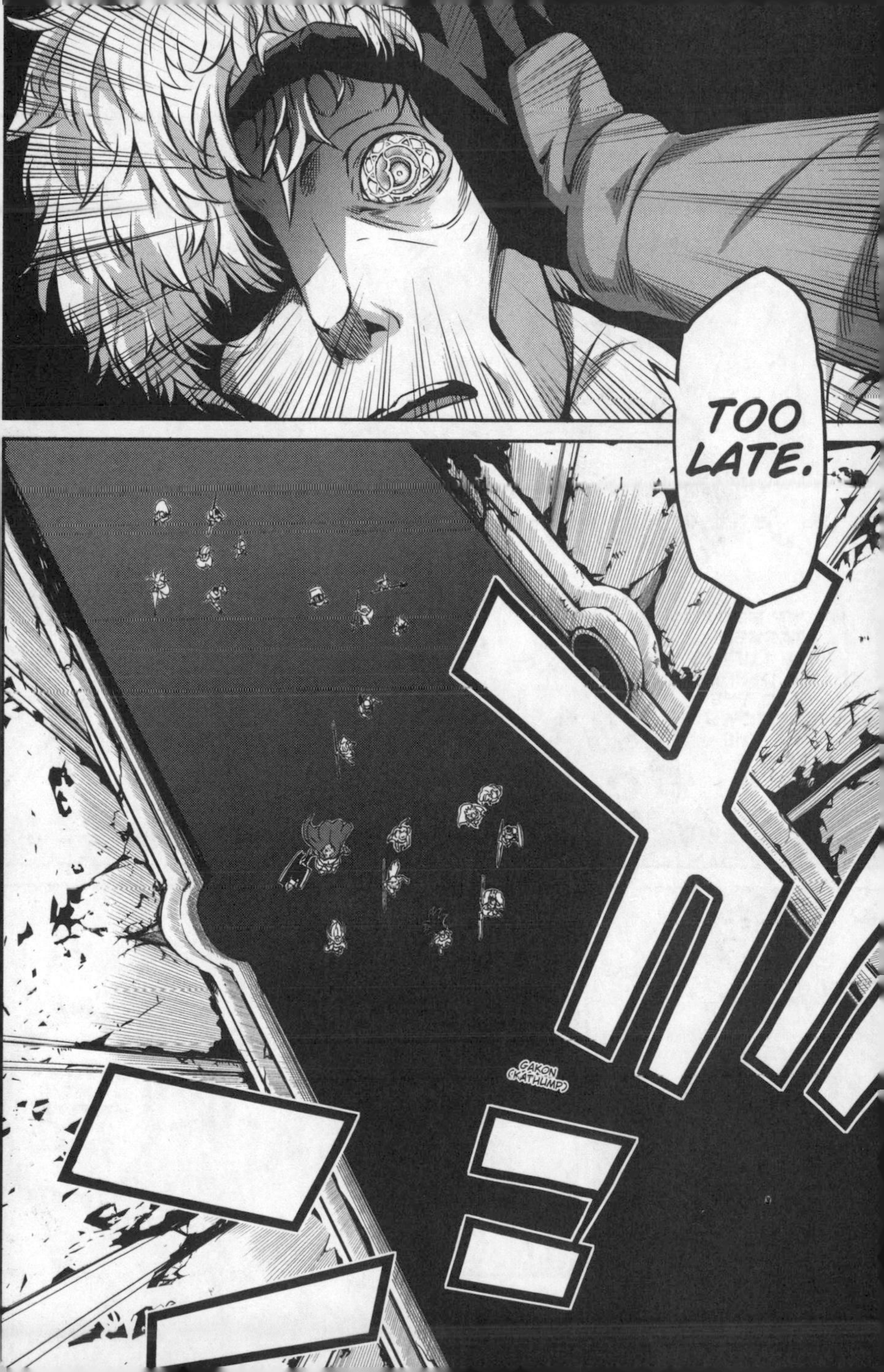
TOO LATE.
GAKON (KATHUMP)

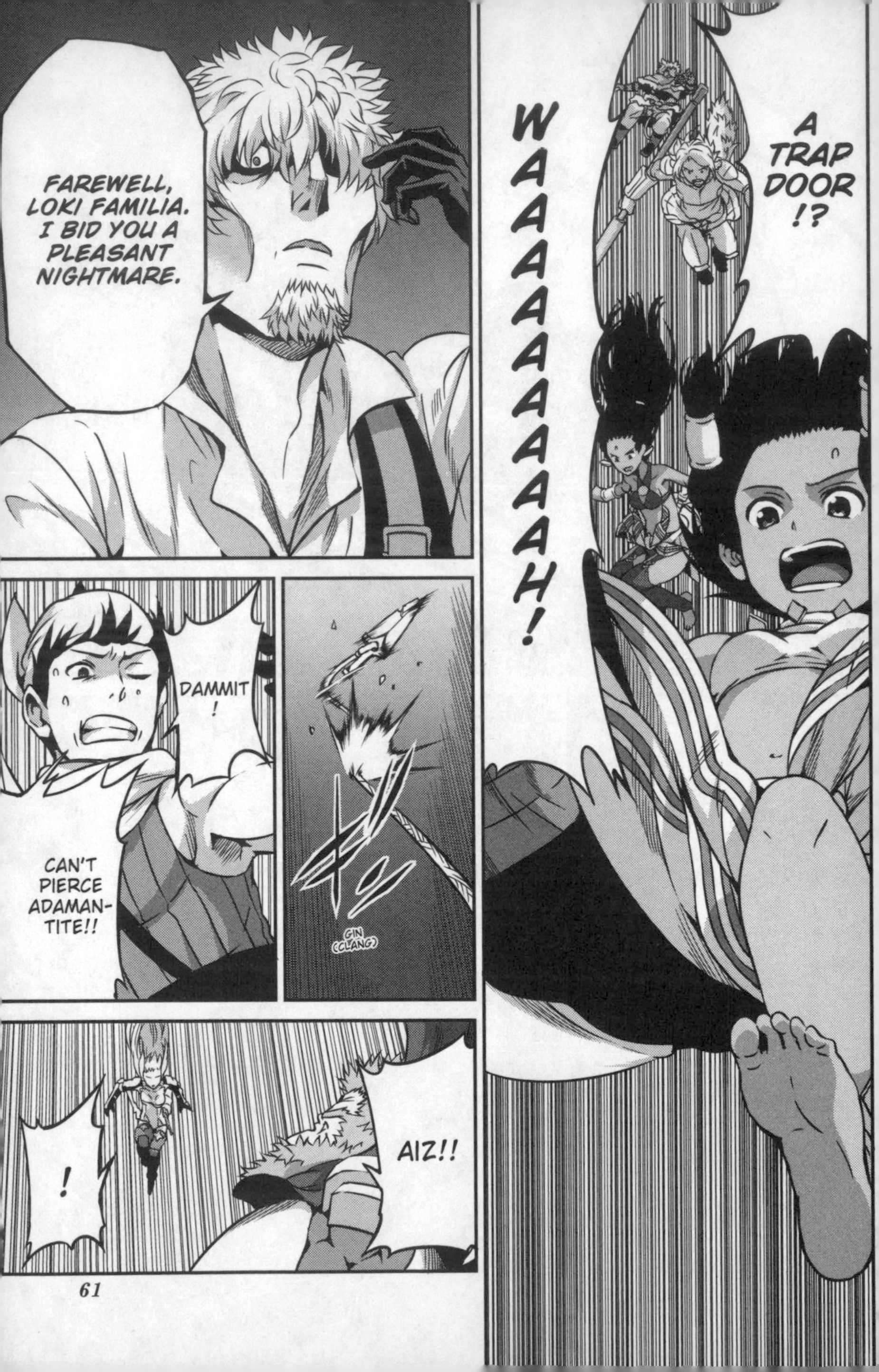
A TRAP DOOR!?
WAAAAAAAAAAAH!
FAREWELL, LOKI FAMILIA. I BID YOU A PLEASANT NIGHTMARE.
GIN (CLANG)
DAMMIT!
CAN'T PIERCE ADAMANTITE!!
AIZ!!
!

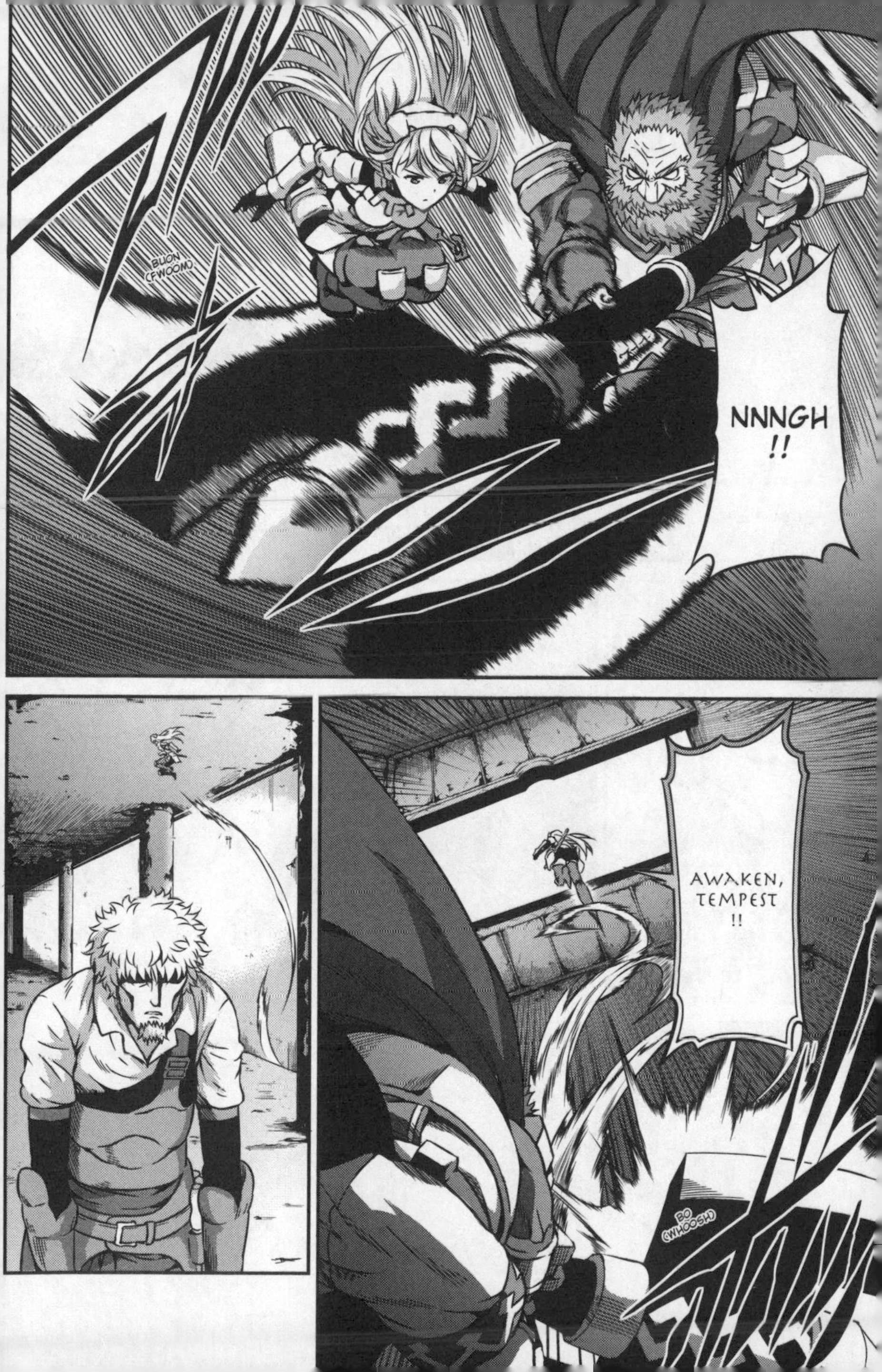
NNNGH !!
BUON (FWOOM)
AWAKEN, TEMPEST !!
BO (WHOOSH)

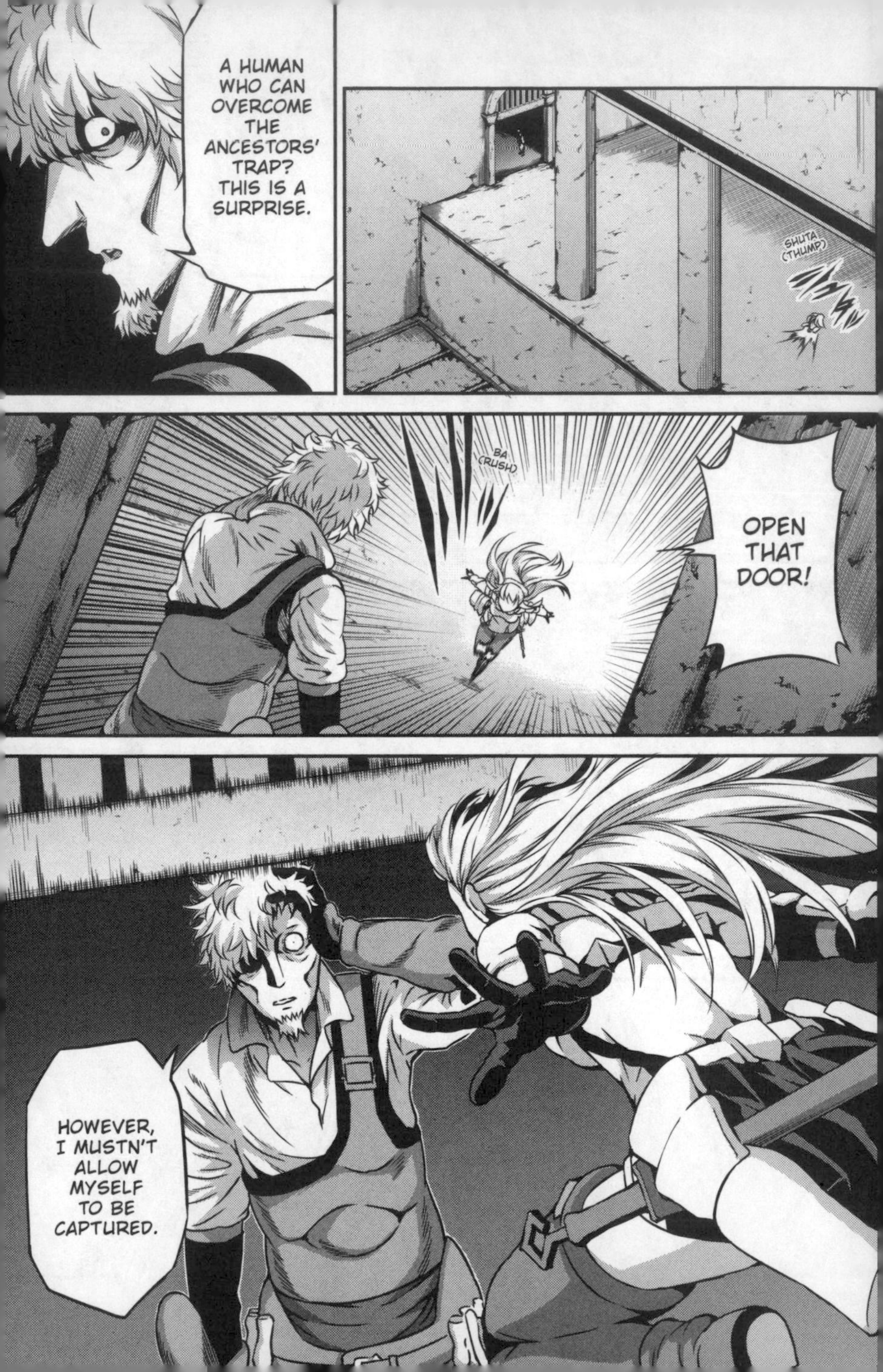
SHUTA (THUMP)
A HUMAN WHO CAN OVERCOME THE ANCESTORS' TRAP? THIS IS A SURPRISE.
OPEN THAT DOOR!
BA (RUSH)
HOWEVER, I MUSTN'T ALLOW MYSELF TO BE CAPTURED.

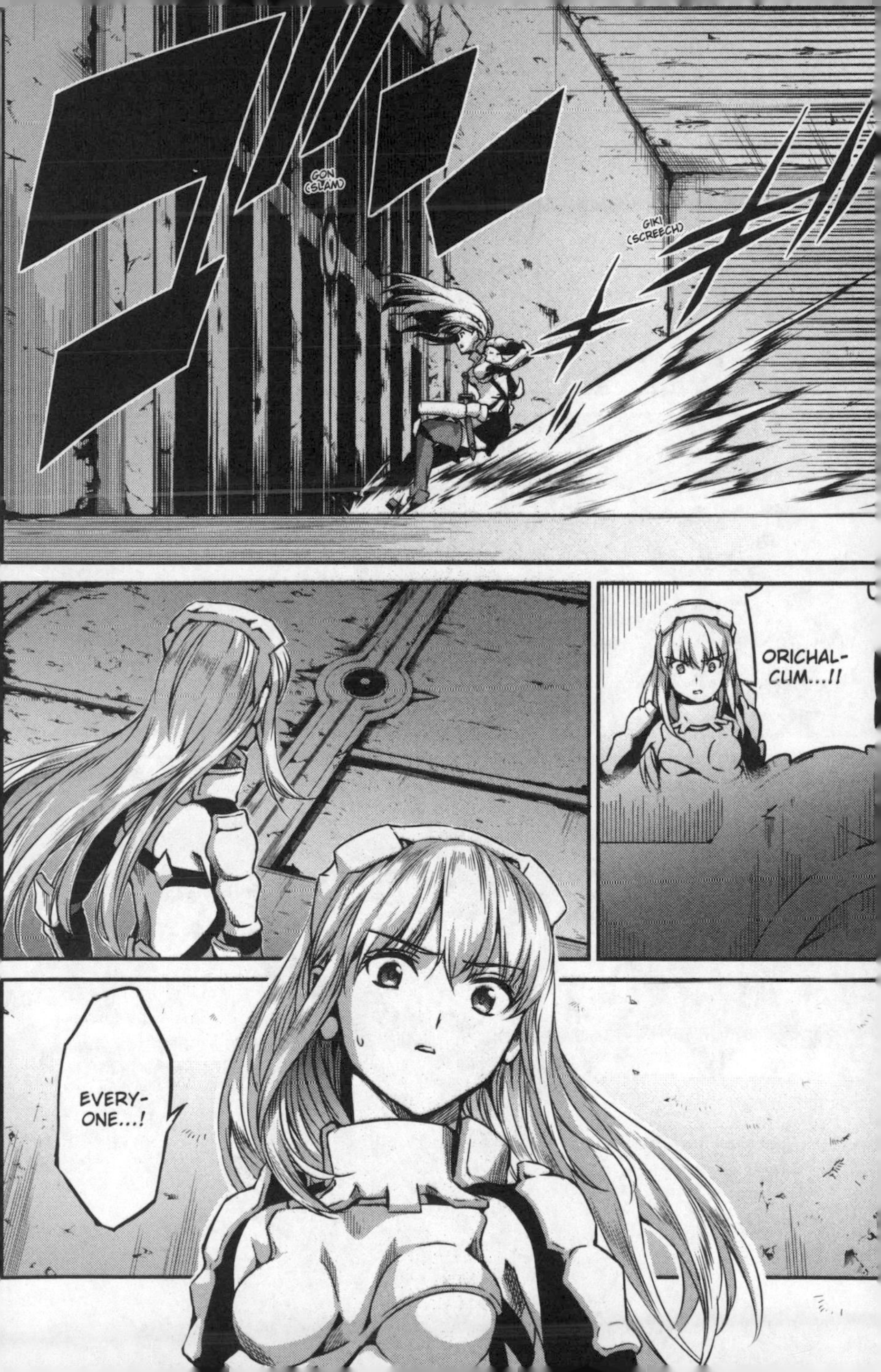
GIKI (SCREECH)
GON (SLAM)
ORICHAL-CUM...!!
EVERY-ONE...!

Is it WRONG to Try to PICK UP GIRLS IN A DUNGEON? ON THE SIDE

Sword Oratoria

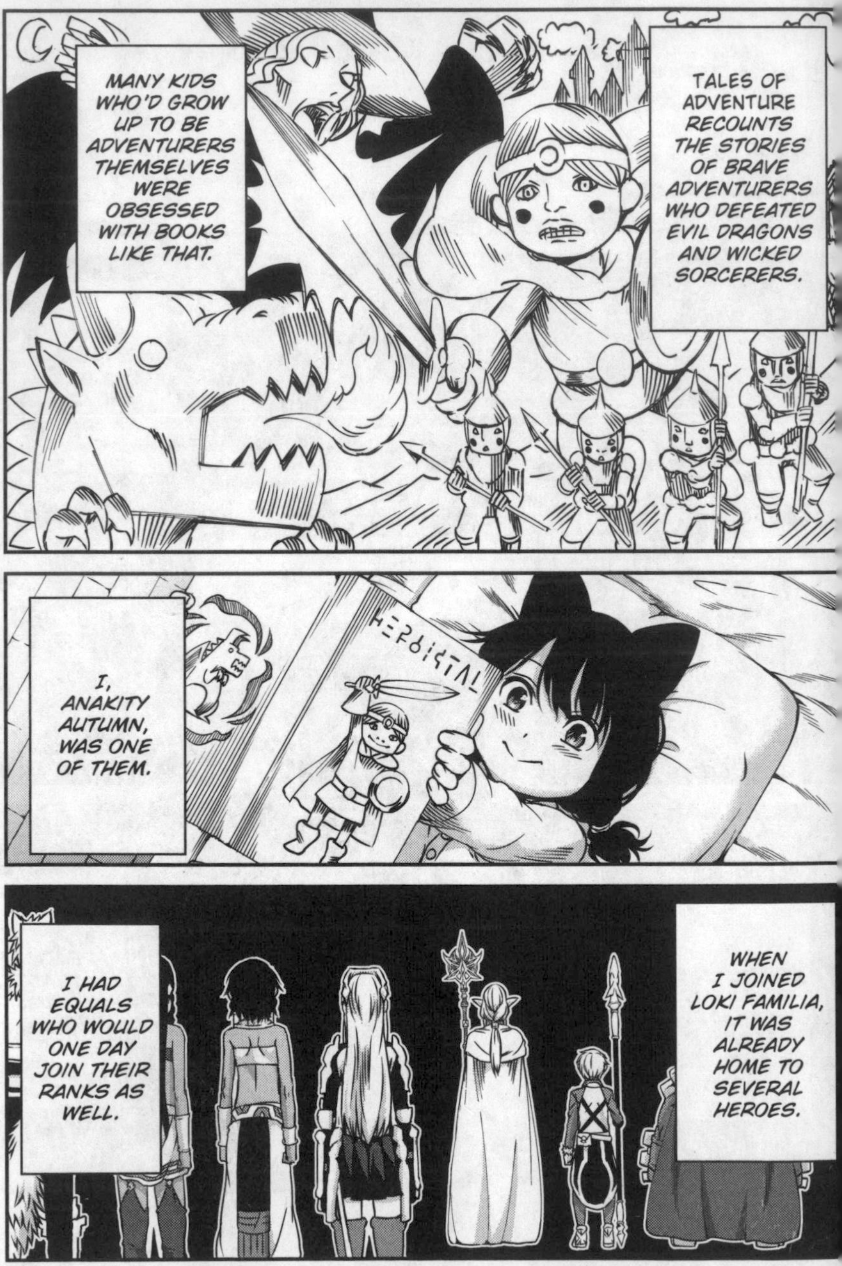
TALES OF ADVENTURE RECOUNTS THE STORIES OF BRAVE ADVENTURERS WHO DEFEATED EVIL DRAGONS AND WICKED SORCERERS.
MANY KIDS WHO'D GROW UP TO BE ADVENTURERS THEMSELVES WERE OBSESSED WITH BOOKS LIKE THAT.
I, ANAKITY AUTUMN, WAS ONE OF THEM.
WHEN I JOINED LOKI FAMILIA, IT WAS ALREADY HOME TO SEVERAL HEROES.
I HAD EQUALS WHO WOULD ONE DAY JOIN THEIR RANKS AS WELL.

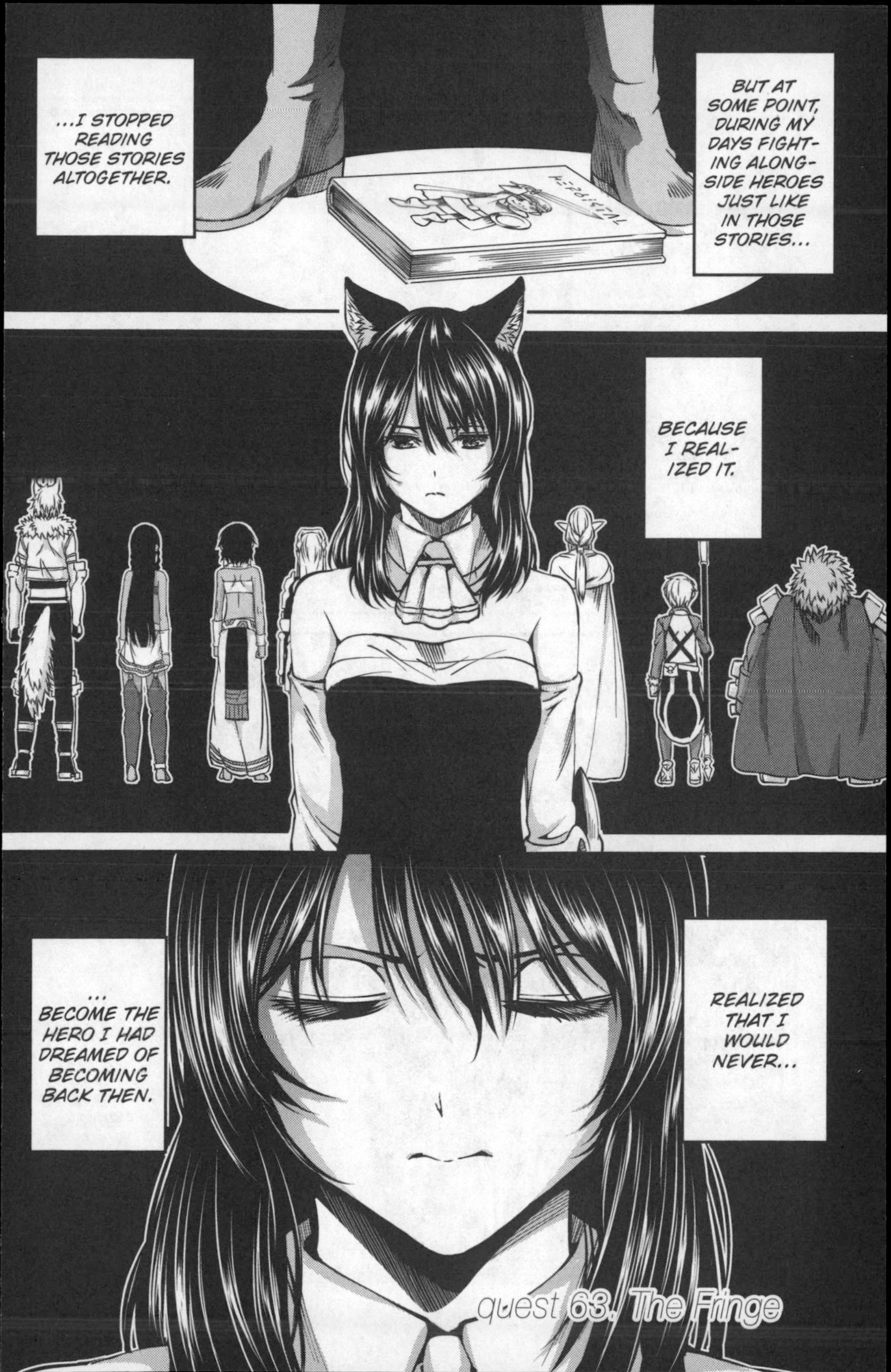
BUT AT SOME POINT, DURING MY DAYS FIGHTING ALONGSIDE HEROES JUST LIKE IN THOSE STORIES...
...I STOPPED READING THOSE STORIES ALTOGETHER.
BECAUSE I REALIZED IT.
REALIZED THAT I WOULD NEVER...
...BECOME THE HERO I HAD DREAMED OF BECOMING BACK THEN.
quest 63. The Fringe

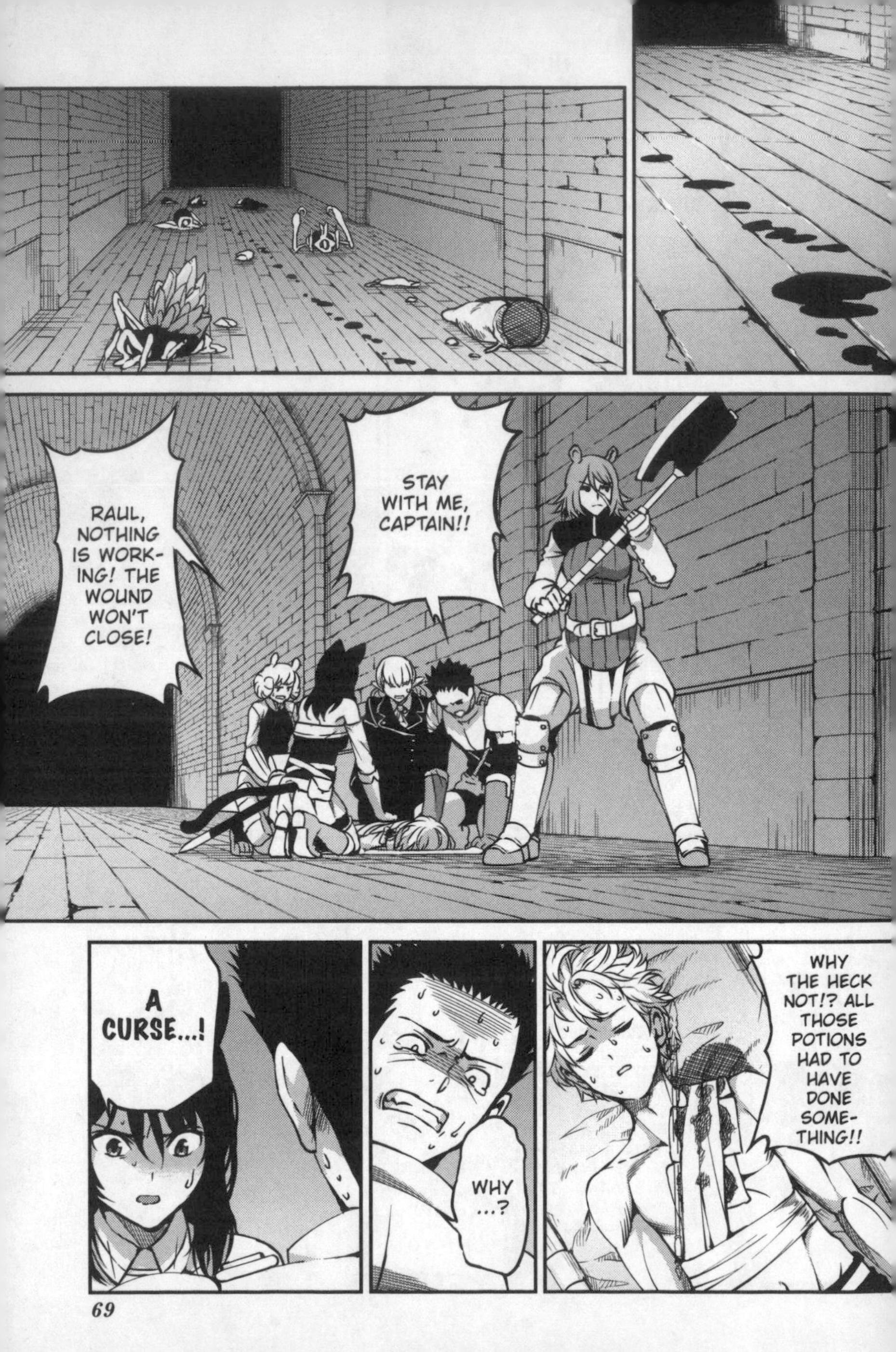
STAY WITH ME, CAPTAIN!!
RAUL, NOTHING IS WORKING! THE WOUND WON'T CLOSE!
WHY THE HECK NOT!? ALL THOSE POTIONS HAD TO HAVE DONE SOMETHING!!
WHY ...?
A CURSE...!

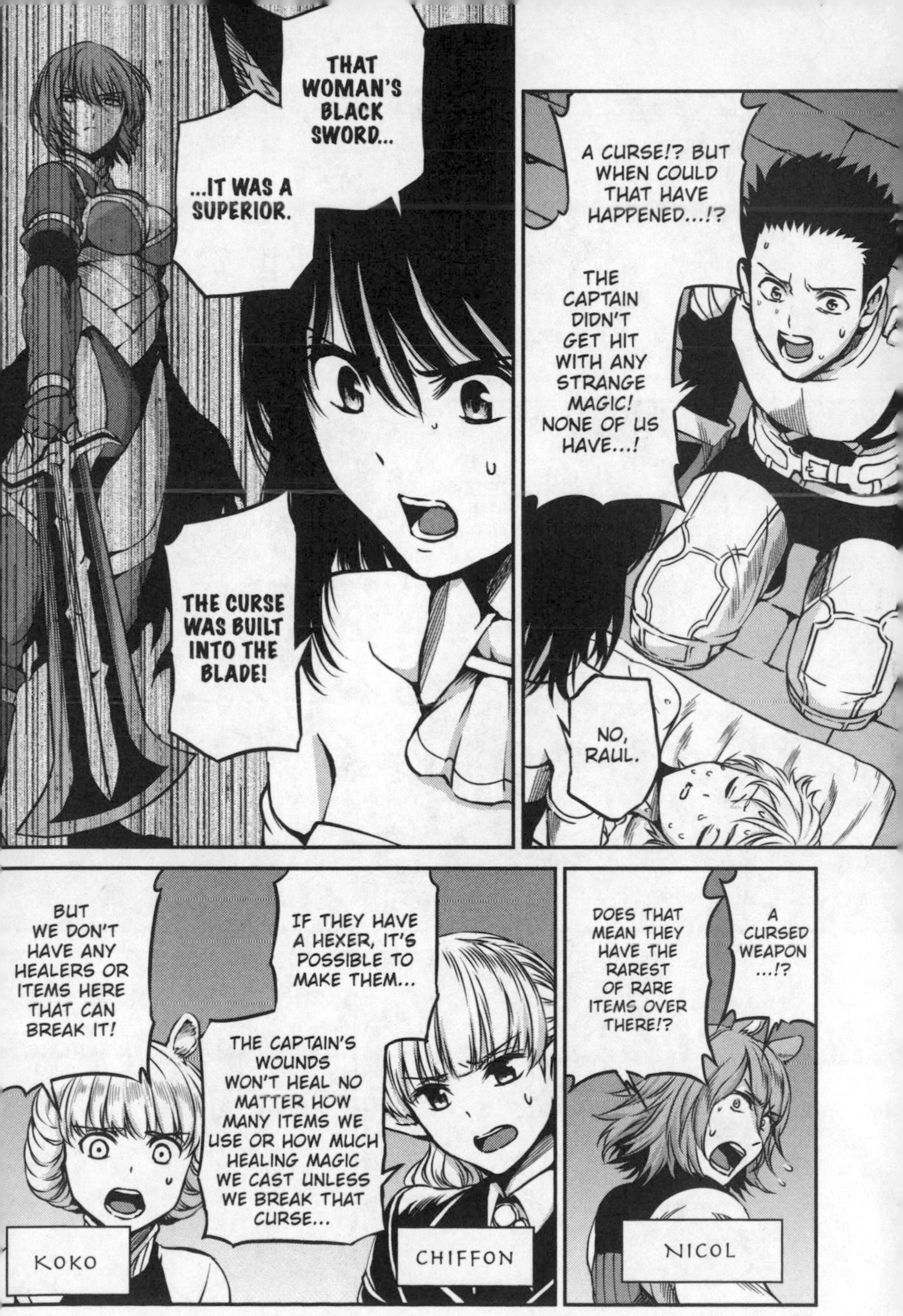
A CURSE!? BUT WHEN COULD THAT HAVE HAPPENED...!?
THE CAPTAIN DIDN'T GET HIT WITH ANY STRANGE MAGIC! NONE OF US HAVE...!
NO, RAUL.
THAT WOMAN'S BLACK SWORD...
...IT WAS A SUPERIOR.
THE CURSE WAS BUILT INTO THE BLADE!
A CURSED WEAPON ...!?
DOES THAT MEAN THEY HAVE THE RAREST OF RARE ITEMS OVER THERE!?
NICOL
IF THEY HAVE A HEXER, IT'S POSSIBLE TO MAKE THEM...
THE CAPTAIN'S WOUNDS WON'T HEAL NO MATTER HOW MANY ITEMS WE USE OR HOW MUCH HEALING MAGIC WE CAST UNLESS WE BREAK THAT CURSE...
CHIFFON
BUT WE DON'T HAVE ANY HEALERS OR ITEMS HERE THAT CAN BREAK IT!
KOKO

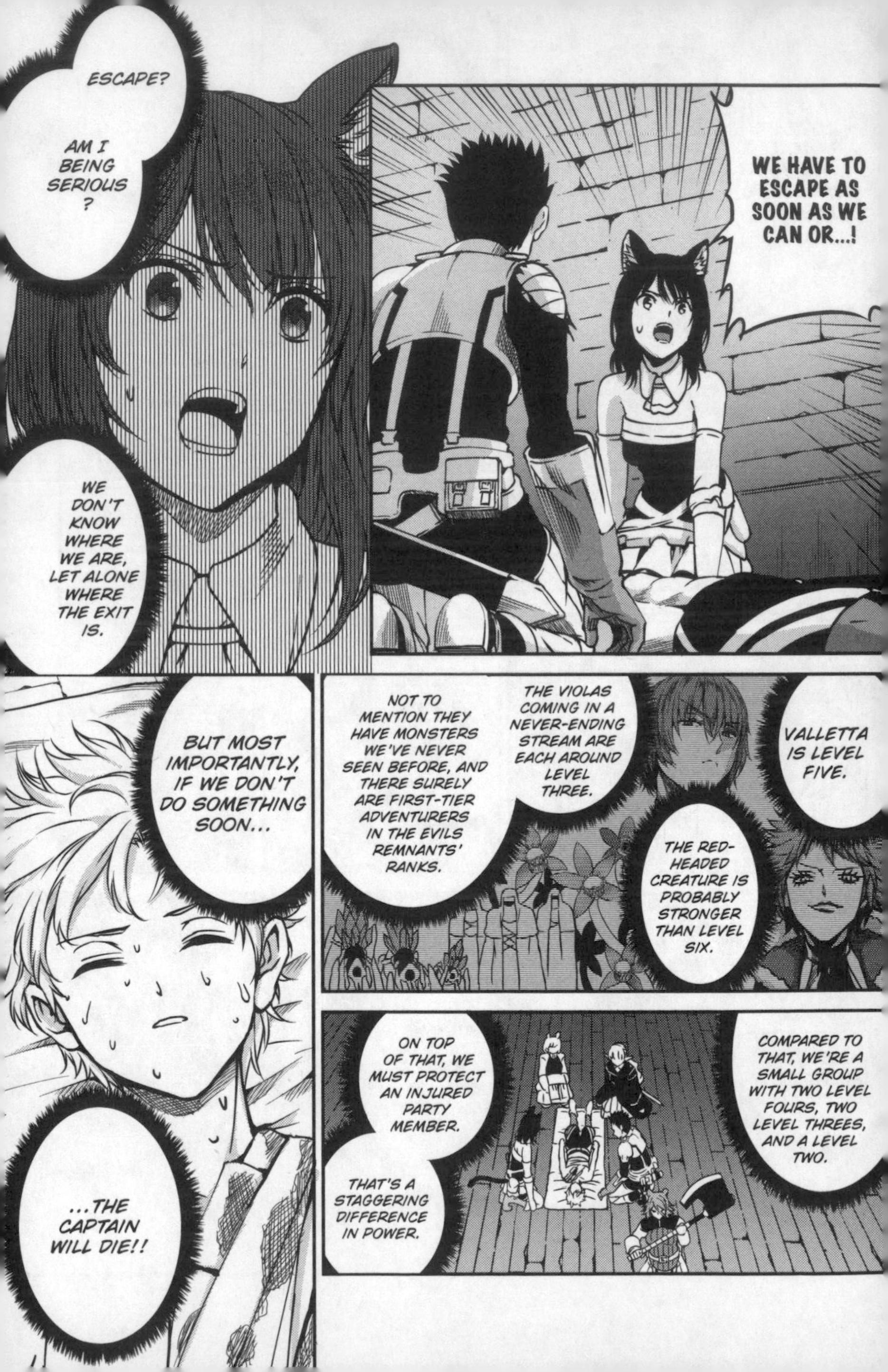

WE HAVE TO ESCAPE AS SOON AS WE CAN OR...!
ESCAPE?
AM I BEING SERIOUS?
WE DON'T KNOW WHERE WE ARE, LET ALONE WHERE THE EXIT IS.
VALLETTA IS LEVEL FIVE.
THE RED-HEADED CREATURE IS PROBABLY STRONGER THAN LEVEL SIX.
THE VIOLAS COMING IN A NEVER-ENDING STREAM ARE EACH AROUND LEVEL THREE.
NOT TO MENTION THEY HAVE MONSTERS WE'VE NEVER SEEN BEFORE, AND THERE SURELY ARE FIRST-TIER ADVENTURERS IN THE EVILS REMNANTS' RANKS.
COMPARED TO THAT, WE'RE A SMALL GROUP WITH TWO LEVEL FOURS, TWO LEVEL THREES, AND A LEVEL TWO.
ON TOP OF THAT, WE MUST PROTECT AN INJURED PARTY MEMBER.
THAT'S A STAGGERING DIFFERENCE IN POWER.
BUT MOST IMPORTANTLY, IF WE DON'T DO SOMETHING SOON...
...THE CAPTAIN WILL DIE!!

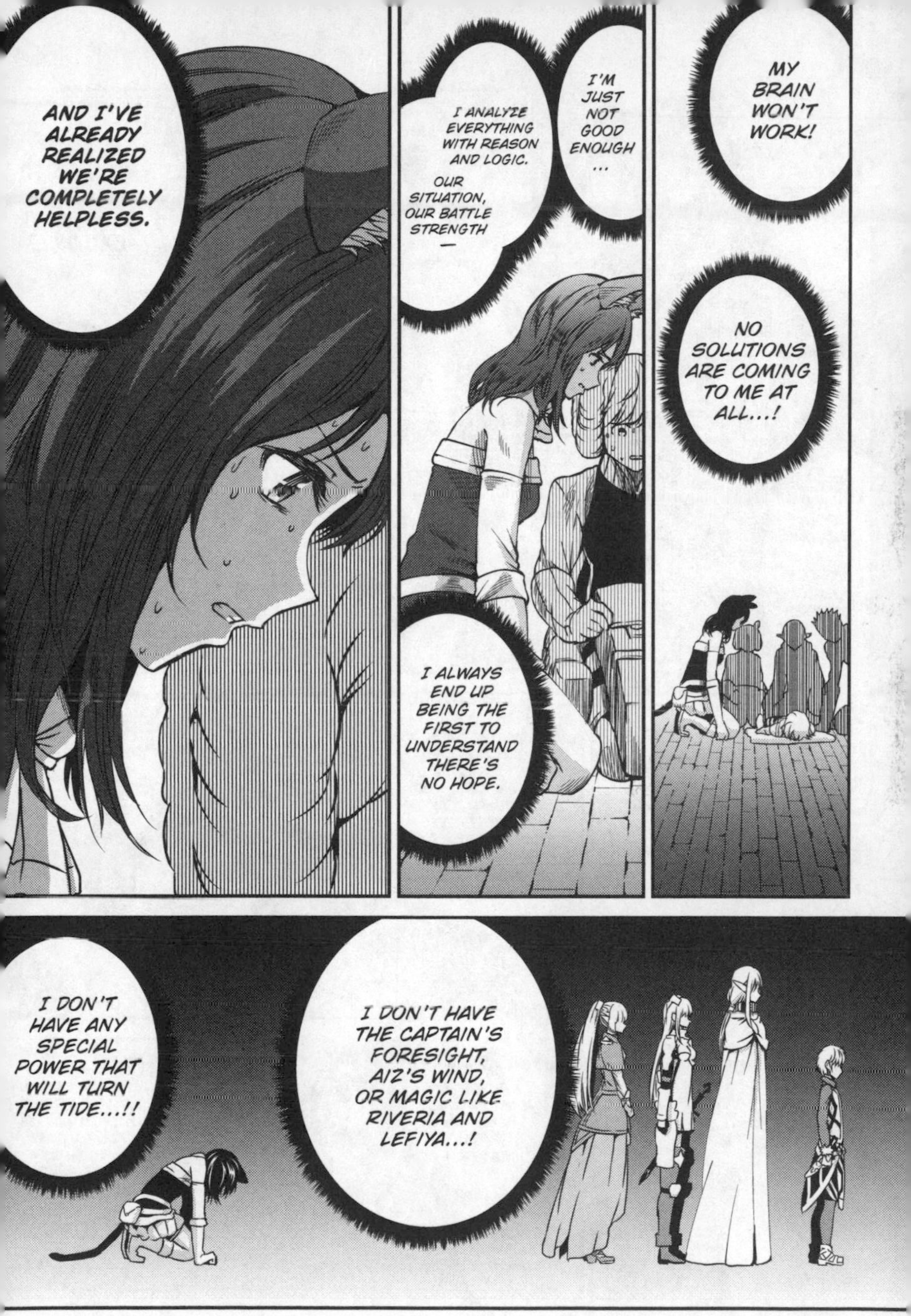
MY BRAIN WON'T WORK!
NO SOLUTIONS ARE COMING TO ME AT ALL...!
I'M JUST NOT GOOD ENOUGH...
I ANALYZE EVERYTHING WITH REASON AND LOGIC.
OUR SITUATION, OUR BATTLE STRENGTH—
I ALWAYS END UP BEING THE FIRST TO UNDERSTAND THERE'S NO HOPE.
AND I'VE ALREADY REALIZED WE'RE COMPLETELY HELPLESS.
I DON'T HAVE THE CAPTAIN'S FORESIGHT, AIZ'S WIND, OR MAGIC LIKE RIVERIA AND LEFIYA...!
I DON'T HAVE ANY SPECIAL POWER THAT WILL TURN THE TIDE...!!

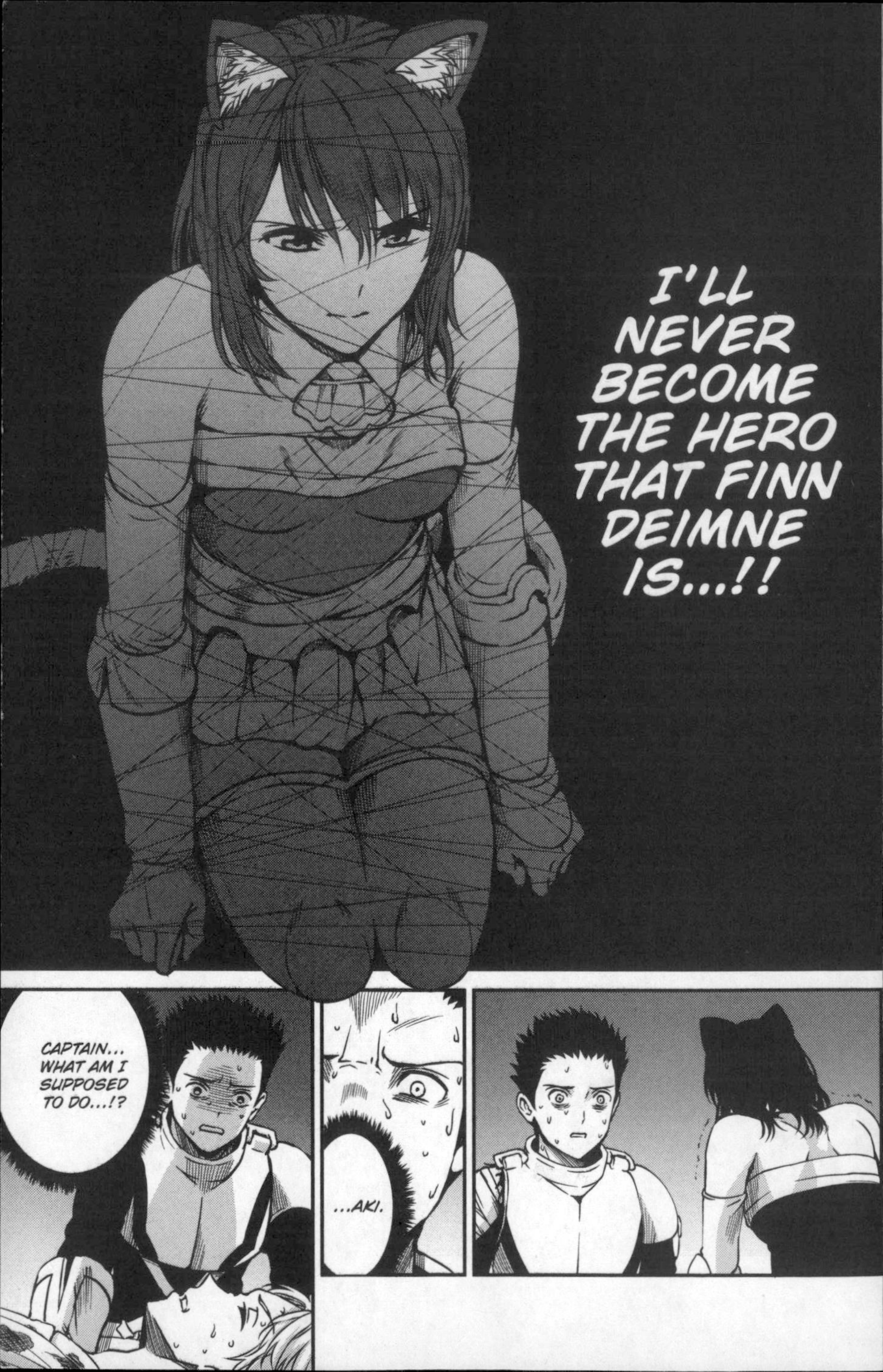
I'LL NEVER BECOME THE HERO THAT FINN DEIMNE IS...!!
...AKI.
CAPTAIN... WHAT AM I SUPPOSED TO DO...!?

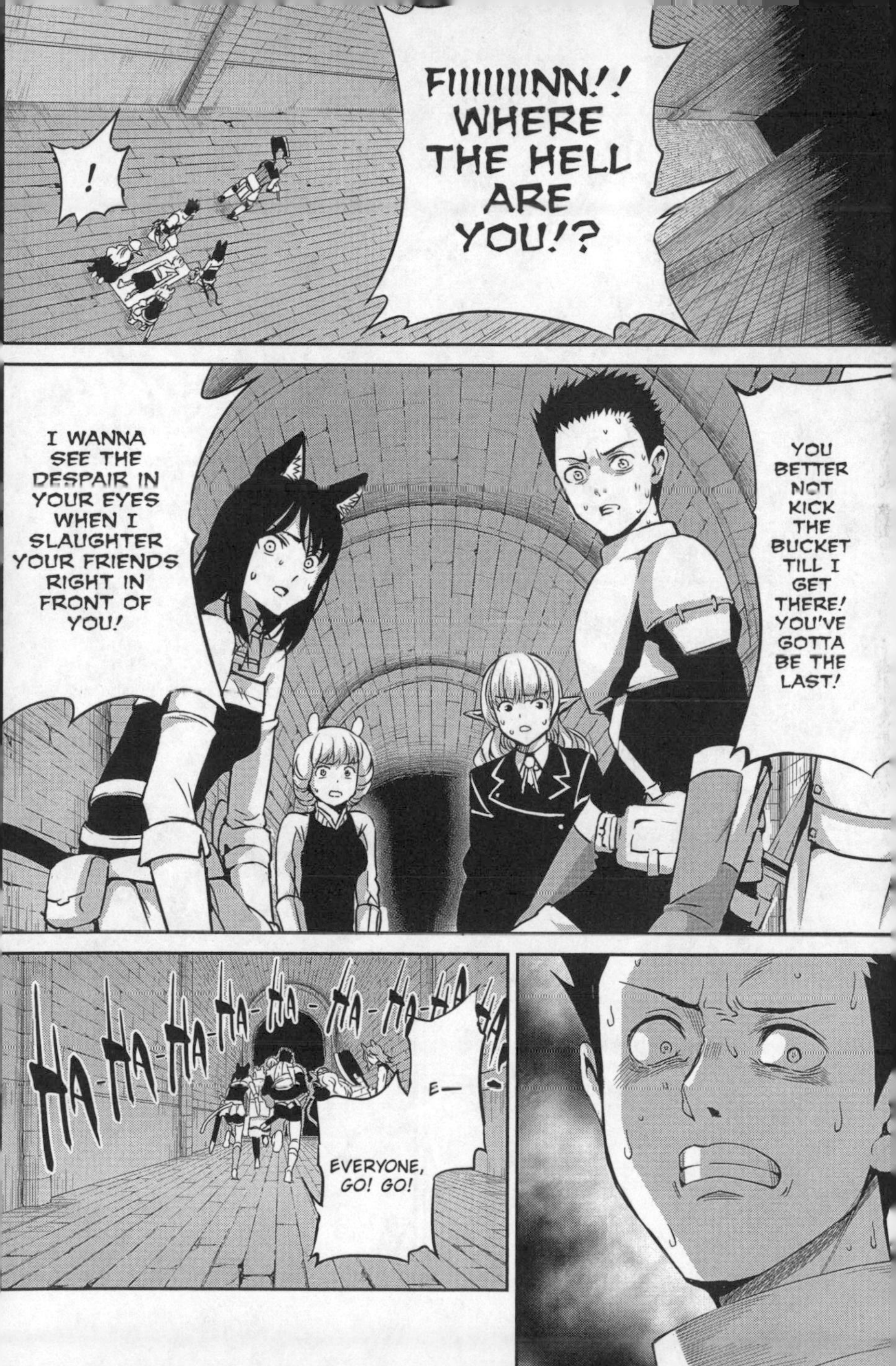
FIIIIIIINN!! WHERE THE HELL ARE YOU!?
!
YOU BETTER NOT KICK THE BUCKET TILL I GET THERE! YOU'VE GOTTA BE THE LAST!
I WANNA SEE THE DESPAIR IN YOUR EYES WHEN I SLAUGHTER YOUR FRIENDS RIGHT IN FRONT OF YOU!
E—
EVERYONE, GO! GO!
HA-HA-HA-HA-HA-HA-HA-HA-HA-HA-HA

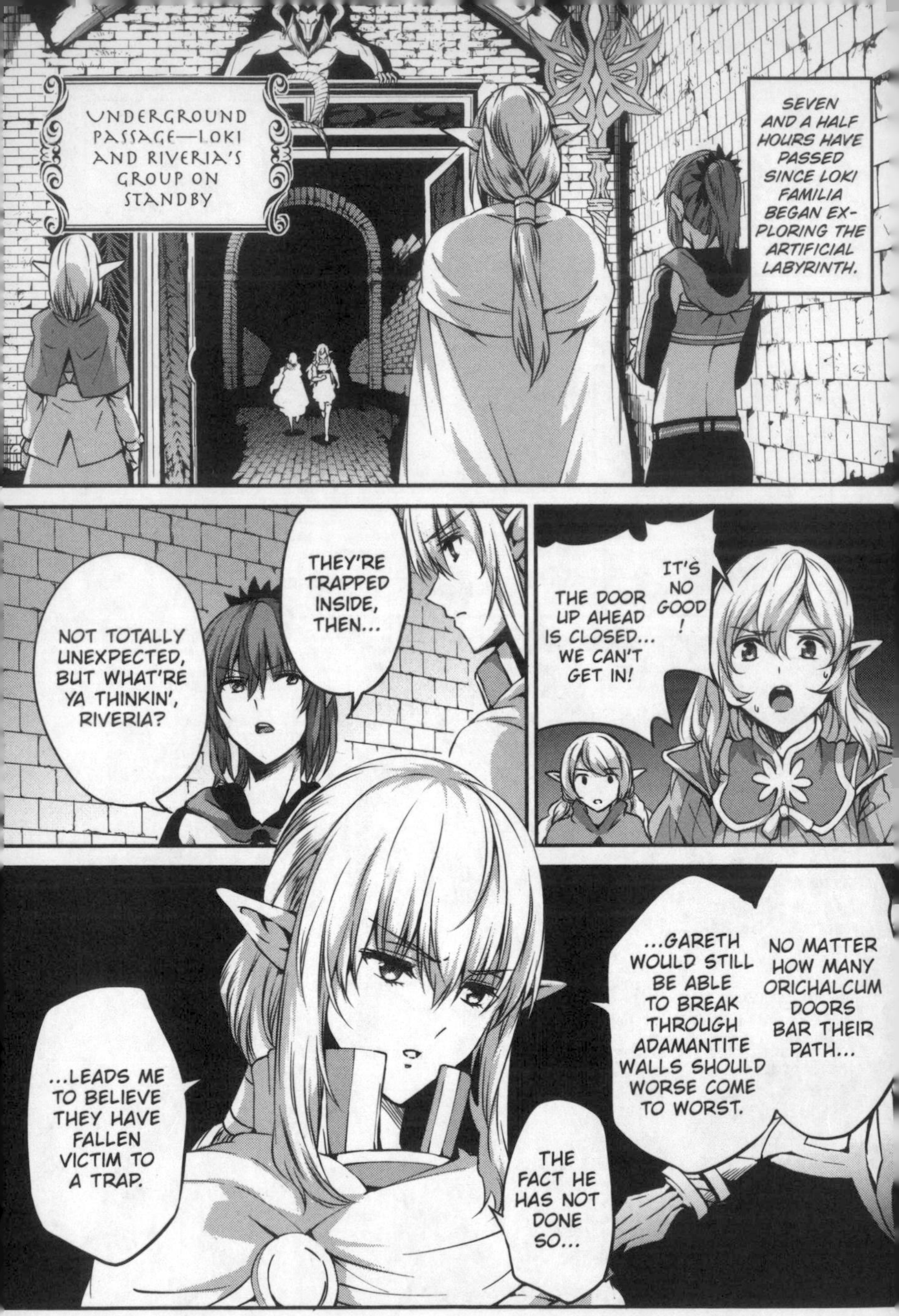
SEVEN AND A HALF HOURS HAVE PASSED SINCE LOKI FAMILIA BEGAN EX-PLORING THE ARTIFICIAL LABYRINTH.
UNDERGROUND PASSAGE—LOKI AND RIVERIA'S GROUP ON STANDBY
IT'S NO GOOD!
THE DOOR UP AHEAD IS CLOSED... WE CAN'T GET IN!
THEY'RE TRAPPED INSIDE, THEN...
NOT TOTALLY UNEXPECTED, BUT WHAT'RE YA THINKIN', RIVERIA?
NO MATTER HOW MANY ORICHALCUM DOORS BAR THEIR PATH...
...GARETH WOULD STILL BE ABLE TO BREAK THROUGH ADAMANTITE WALLS SHOULD WORSE COME TO WORST.
THE FACT HE HAS NOT DONE SO...
...LEADS ME TO BELIEVE THEY HAVE FALLEN VICTIM TO A TRAP.

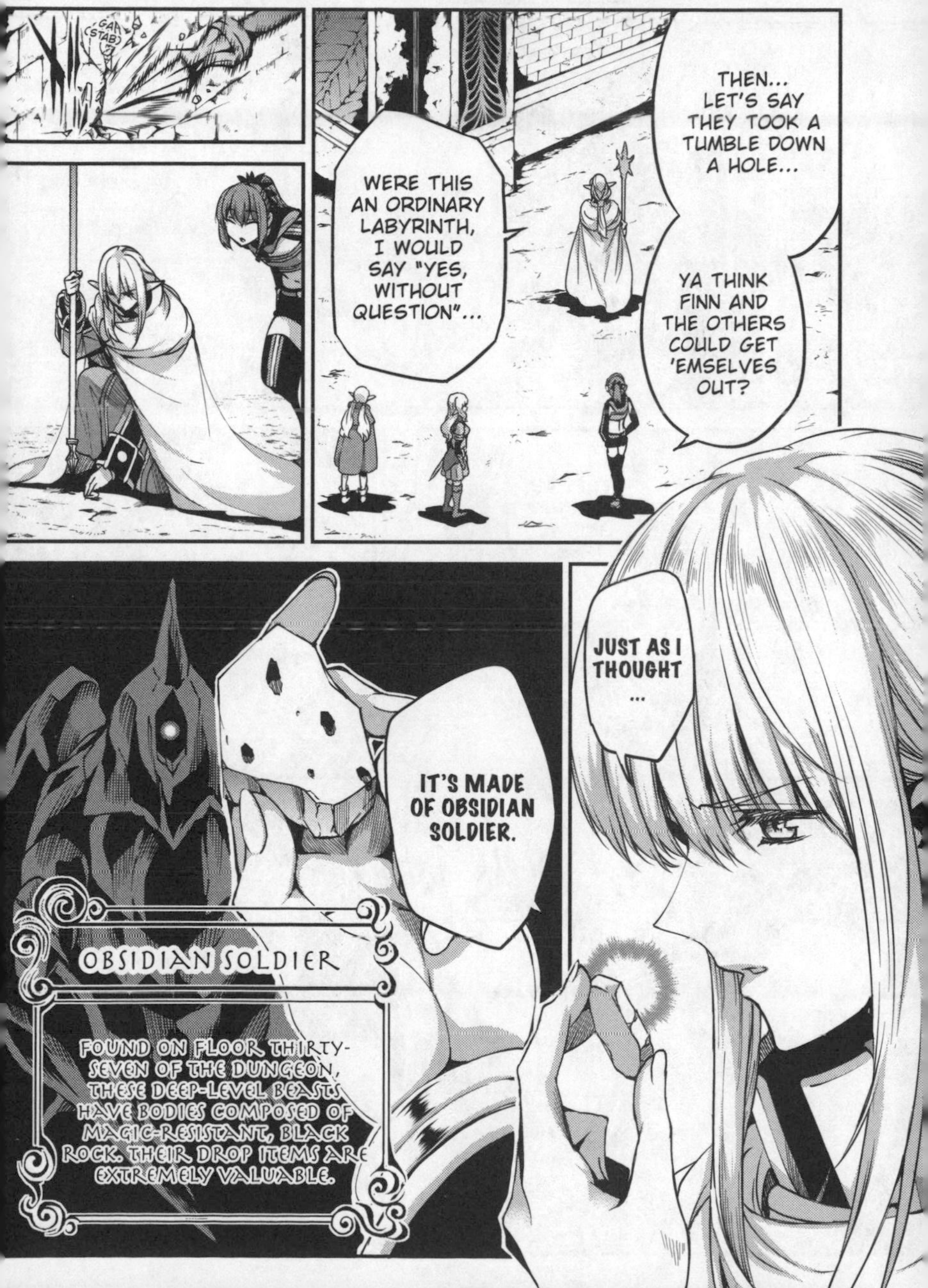
THEN... LET'S SAY THEY TOOK A TUMBLE DOWN A HOLE...
YA THINK FINN AND THE OTHERS COULD GET 'EMSELVES OUT?
WERE THIS AN ORDINARY LABYRINTH, I WOULD SAY "YES, WITHOUT QUESTION"...
GA (STAB)
JUST AS I THOUGHT...
IT'S MADE OF OBSIDIAN SOLDIER.
OBSIDIAN SOLDIER
FOUND ON FLOOR THIRTY-SEVEN OF THE DUNGEON, THESE DEEP-LEVEL BEASTS HAVE BODIES COMPOSED OF MAGIC-RESISTANT, BLACK ROCK. THEIR DROP ITEMS ARE EXTREMELY VALUABLE.

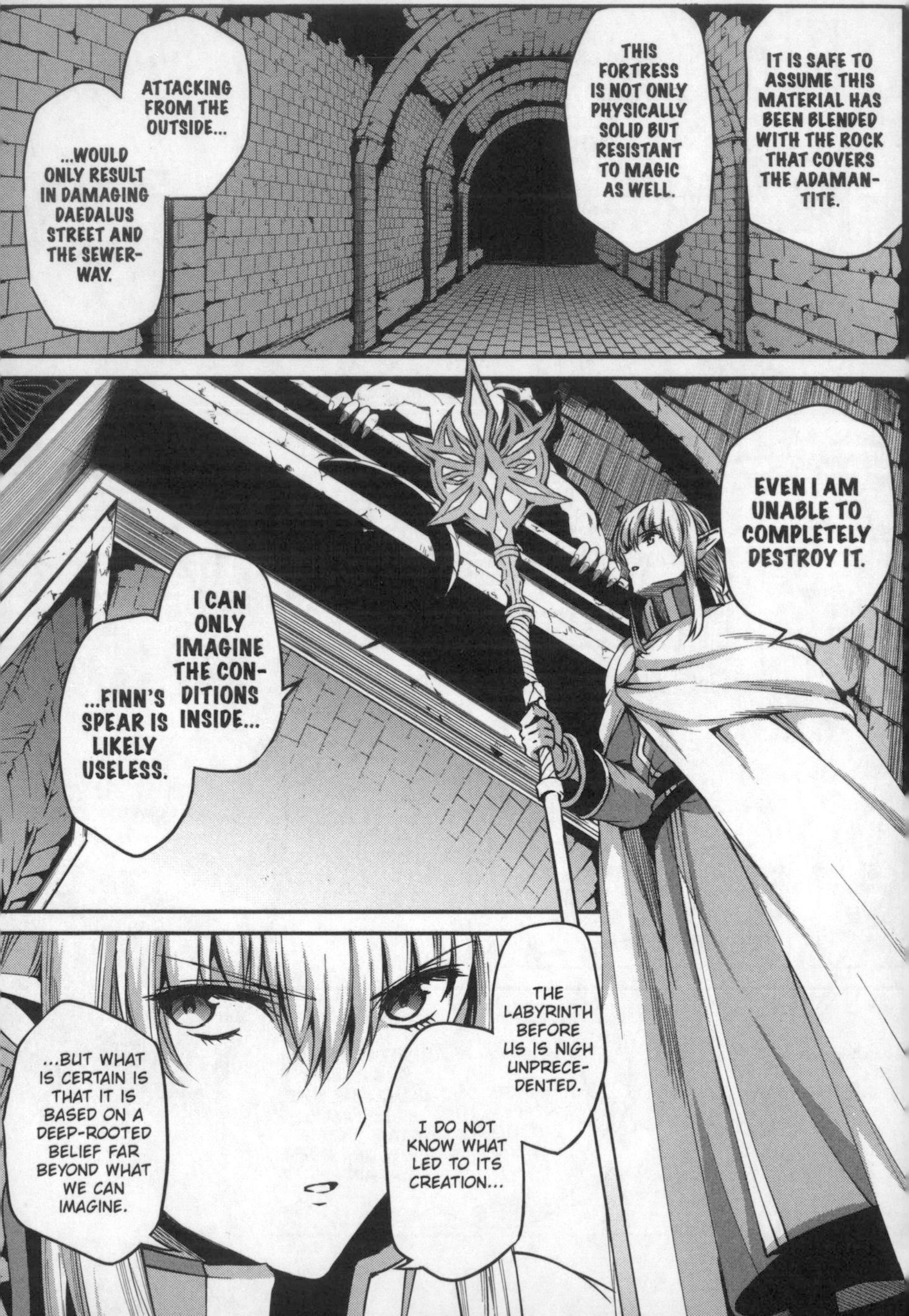
IT IS SAFE TO ASSUME THIS MATERIAL HAS BEEN BLENDED WITH THE ROCK THAT COVERS THE ADAMANTITE.
THIS FORTRESS IS NOT ONLY PHYSICALLY SOLID BUT RESISTANT TO MAGIC AS WELL.
ATTACKING FROM THE OUTSIDE...
...WOULD ONLY RESULT IN DAMAGING DAEDALUS STREET AND THE SEWERWAY.
EVEN I AM UNABLE TO COMPLETELY DESTROY IT.
I CAN ONLY IMAGINE THE CONDITIONS INSIDE...
...FINN'S SPEAR IS LIKELY USELESS.
THE LABYRINTH BEFORE US IS NIGH UNPRECEDENTED.
I DO NOT KNOW WHAT LED TO ITS CREATION...
...BUT WHAT IS CERTAIN IS THAT IT IS BASED ON A DEEP-ROOTED BELIEF FAR BEYOND WHAT WE CAN IMAGINE.

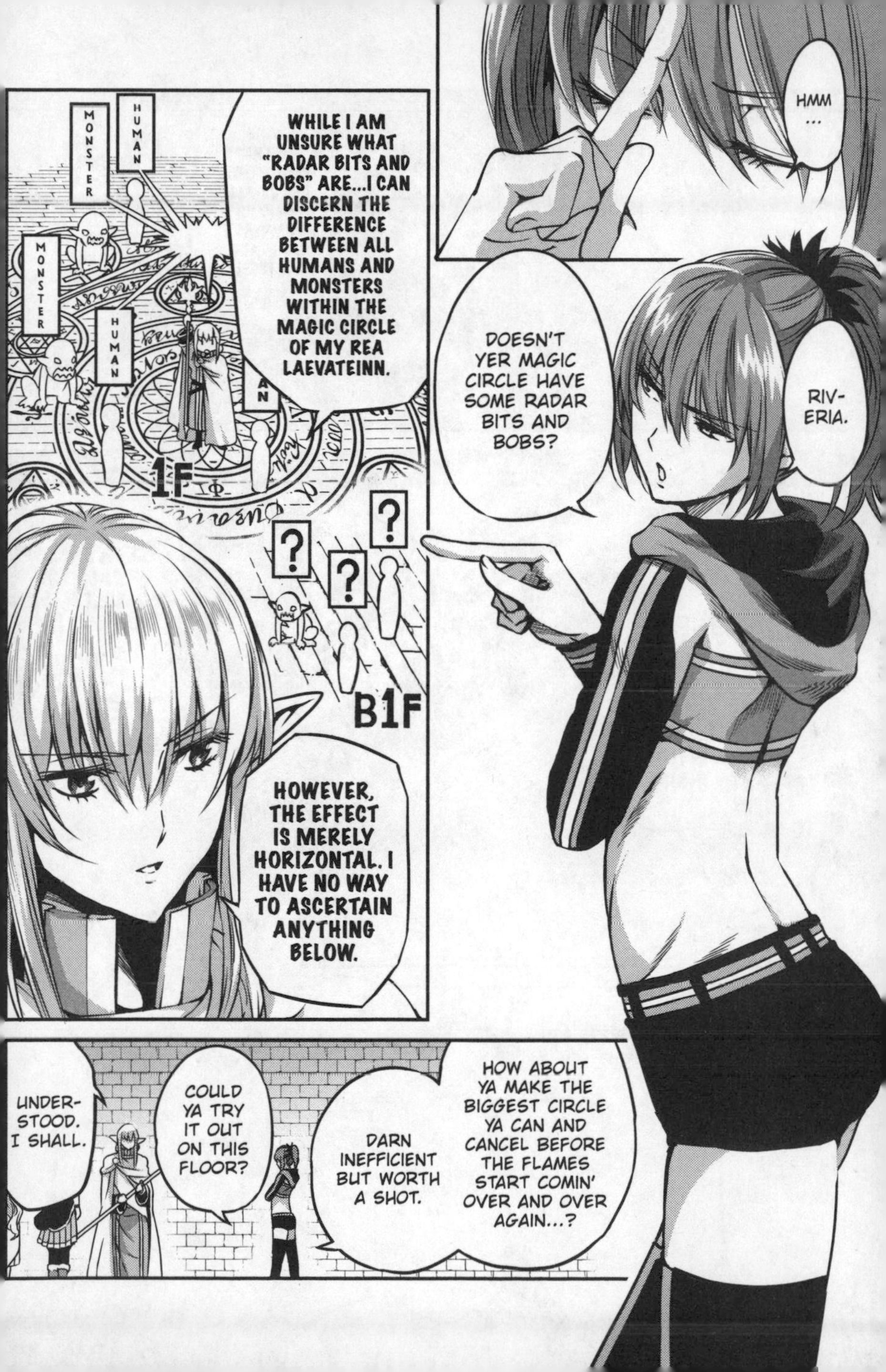
HMM...
RIV-ERIA.
DOESN'T YER MAGIC CIRCLE HAVE SOME RADAR BITS AND BOBS?
WHILE I AM UNSURE WHAT "RADAR BITS AND BOBS" ARE...I CAN DISCERN THE DIFFERENCE BETWEEN ALL HUMANS AND MONSTERS WITHIN THE MAGIC CIRCLE OF MY REA LAEVATEINN.
HUMAN
MONSTER
MONSTER
HUMAN
1F
?
?
?
B1F
HOWEVER, THE EFFECT IS MERELY HORIZONTAL. I HAVE NO WAY TO ASCERTAIN ANYTHING BELOW.
HOW ABOUT YA MAKE THE BIGGEST CIRCLE YA CAN AND CANCEL BEFORE THE FLAMES START COMIN' OVER AND OVER AGAIN...?
DARN INEFFICIENT BUT WORTH A SHOT.
COULD YA TRY IT OUT ON THIS FLOOR?
UNDER-STOOD. I SHALL.

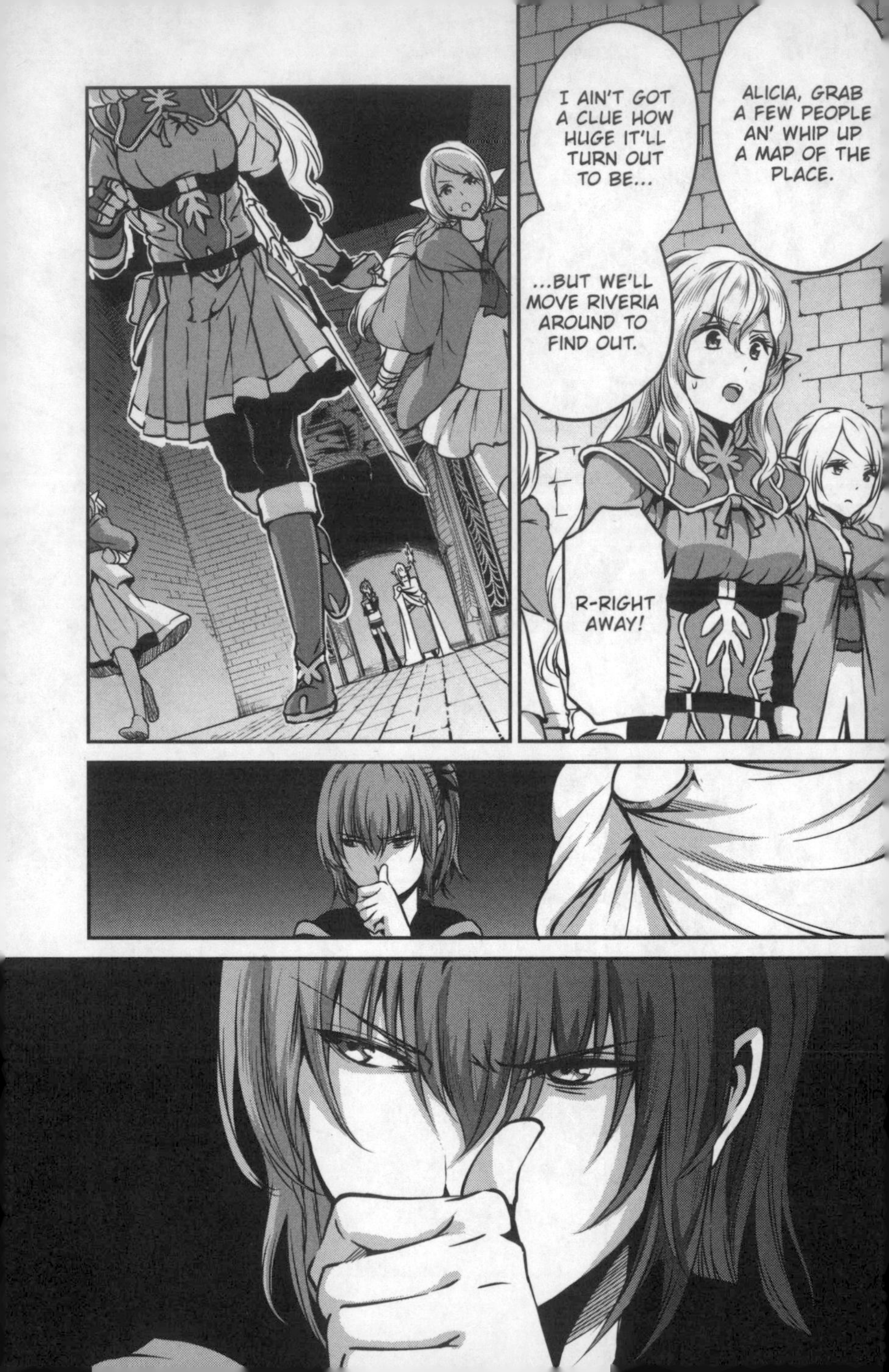
ALICIA, GRAB A FEW PEOPLE AN' WHIP UP A MAP OF THE PLACE.
I AIN'T GOT A CLUE HOW HUGE IT'LL TURN OUT TO BE...
...BUT WE'LL MOVE RIVERIA AROUND TO FIND OUT.
R-RIGHT AWAY!

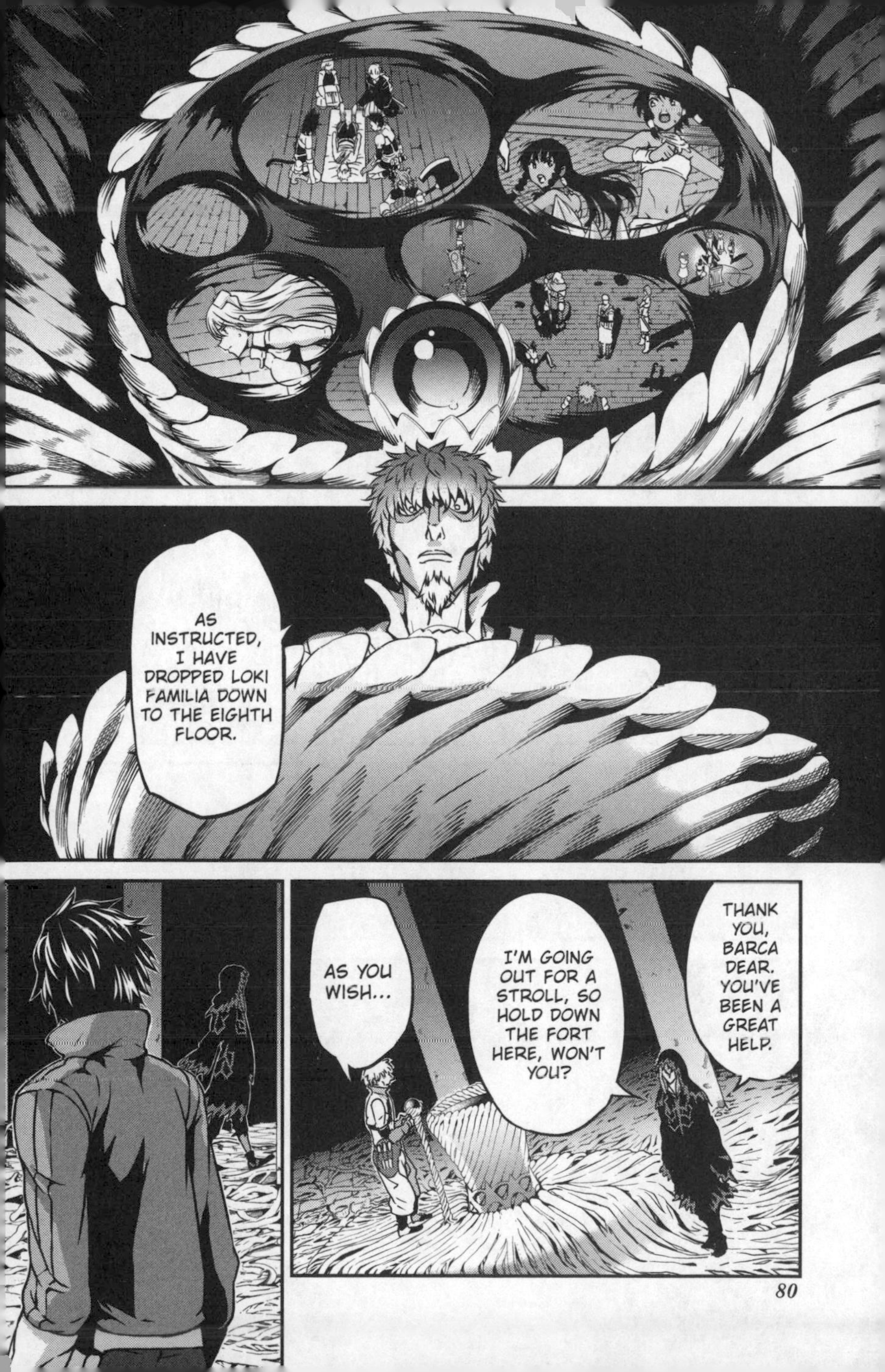
AS INSTRUCTED, I HAVE DROPPED LOKI FAMILIA DOWN TO THE EIGHTH FLOOR.
THANK YOU, BARCA DEAR. YOU'VE BEEN A GREAT HELP.
I'M GOING OUT FOR A STROLL, SO HOLD DOWN THE FORT HERE, WON'T YOU?
AS YOU WISH...

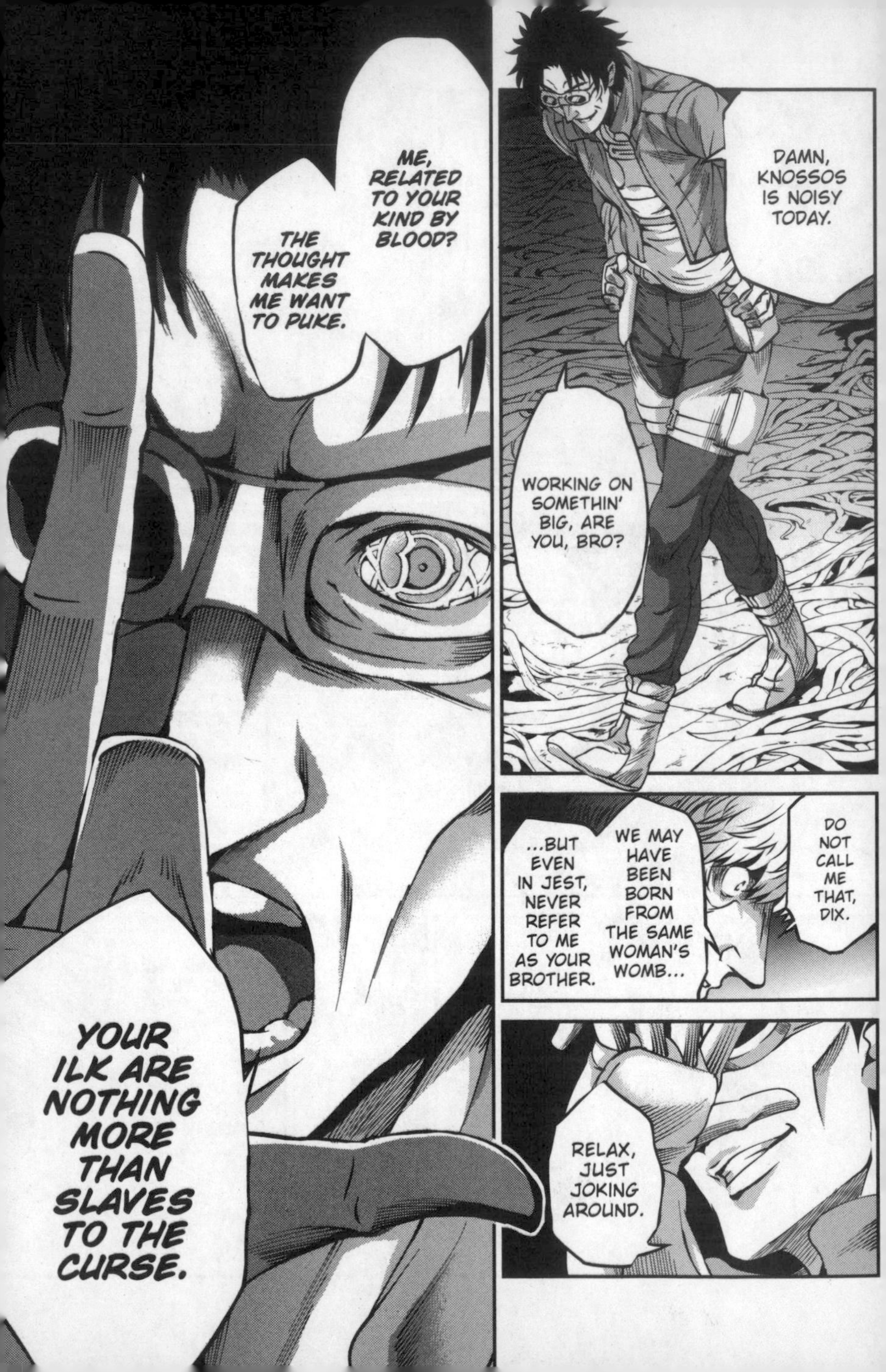
DAMN, KNOSSOS IS NOISY TODAY.
WORKING ON SOMETHIN' BIG, ARE YOU, BRO?
DO NOT CALL ME THAT, DIX.
WE MAY HAVE BEEN BORN FROM THE SAME WOMAN'S WOMB...
...BUT EVEN IN JEST, NEVER REFER TO ME AS YOUR BROTHER.
RELAX, JUST JOKING AROUND.
ME, RELATED TO YOUR KIND BY BLOOD?
THE THOUGHT MAKES ME WANT TO PUKE.
YOUR ILK ARE NOTHING MORE THAN SLAVES TO THE CURSE.

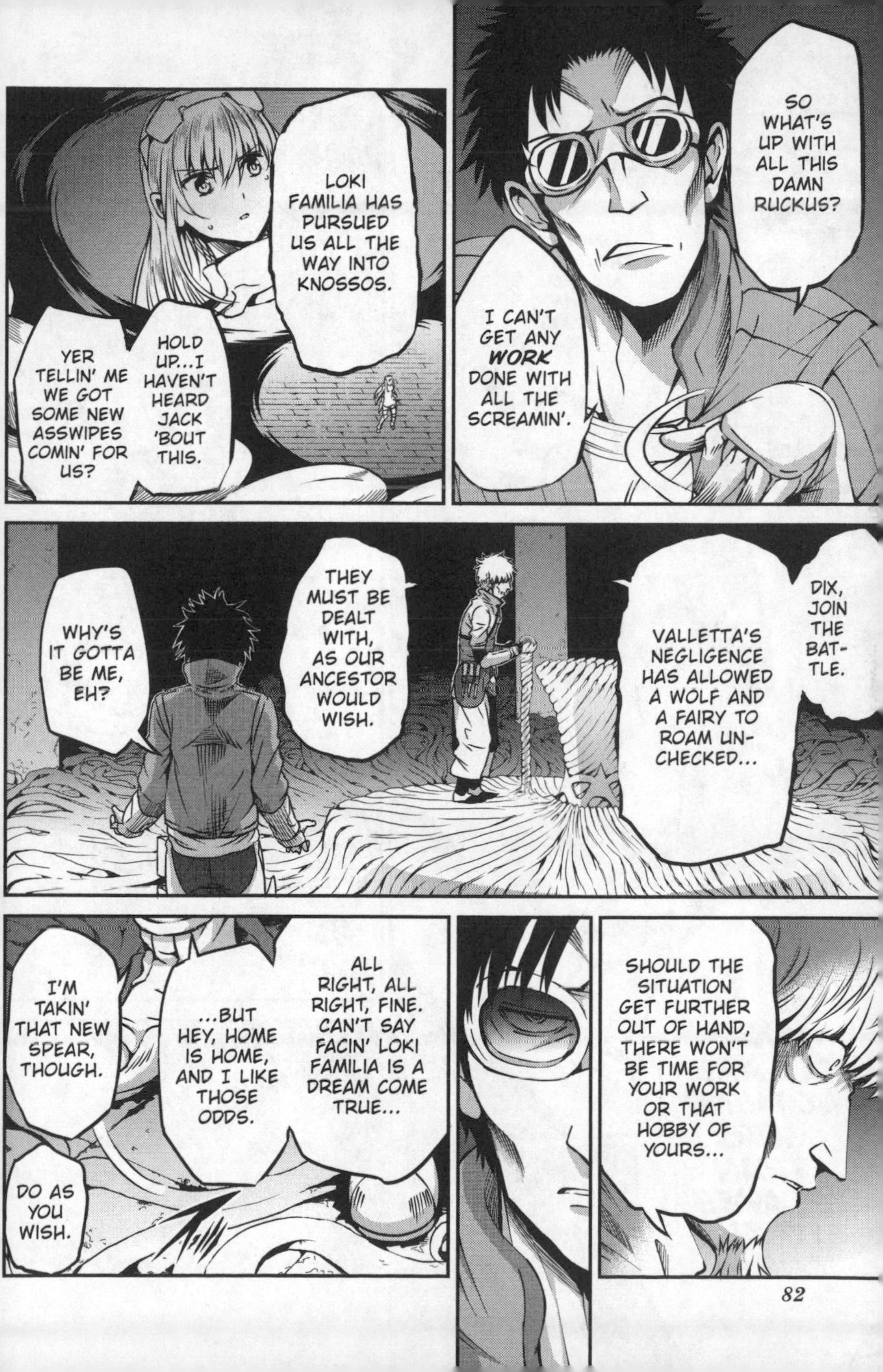
SO WHAT'S UP WITH ALL THIS DAMN RUCKUS?
I CAN'T GET ANY **WORK** DONE WITH ALL THE SCREAMIN'.
LOKI FAMILIA HAS PURSUED US ALL THE WAY INTO KNOSSOS.
HOLD UP...I HAVEN'T HEARD JACK 'BOUT THIS.
YER TELLIN' ME WE GOT SOME NEW ASSWIPES COMIN' FOR US?
DIX, JOIN THE BAT-TLE.
VALLETTA'S NEGLIGENCE HAS ALLOWED A WOLF AND A FAIRY TO ROAM UN-CHECKED...
THEY MUST BE DEALT WITH, AS OUR ANCESTOR WOULD WISH.
WHY'S IT GOTTA BE ME, EH?
SHOULD THE SITUATION GET FURTHER OUT OF HAND, THERE WON'T BE TIME FOR YOUR WORK OR THAT HOBBY OF YOURS...
ALL RIGHT, ALL RIGHT, FINE. CAN'T SAY FACIN' LOKI FAMILIA IS A DREAM COME TRUE...
...BUT HEY, HOME IS HOME, AND I LIKE THOSE ODDS.
I'M TAKIN' THAT NEW SPEAR, THOUGH.
DO AS YOU WISH.

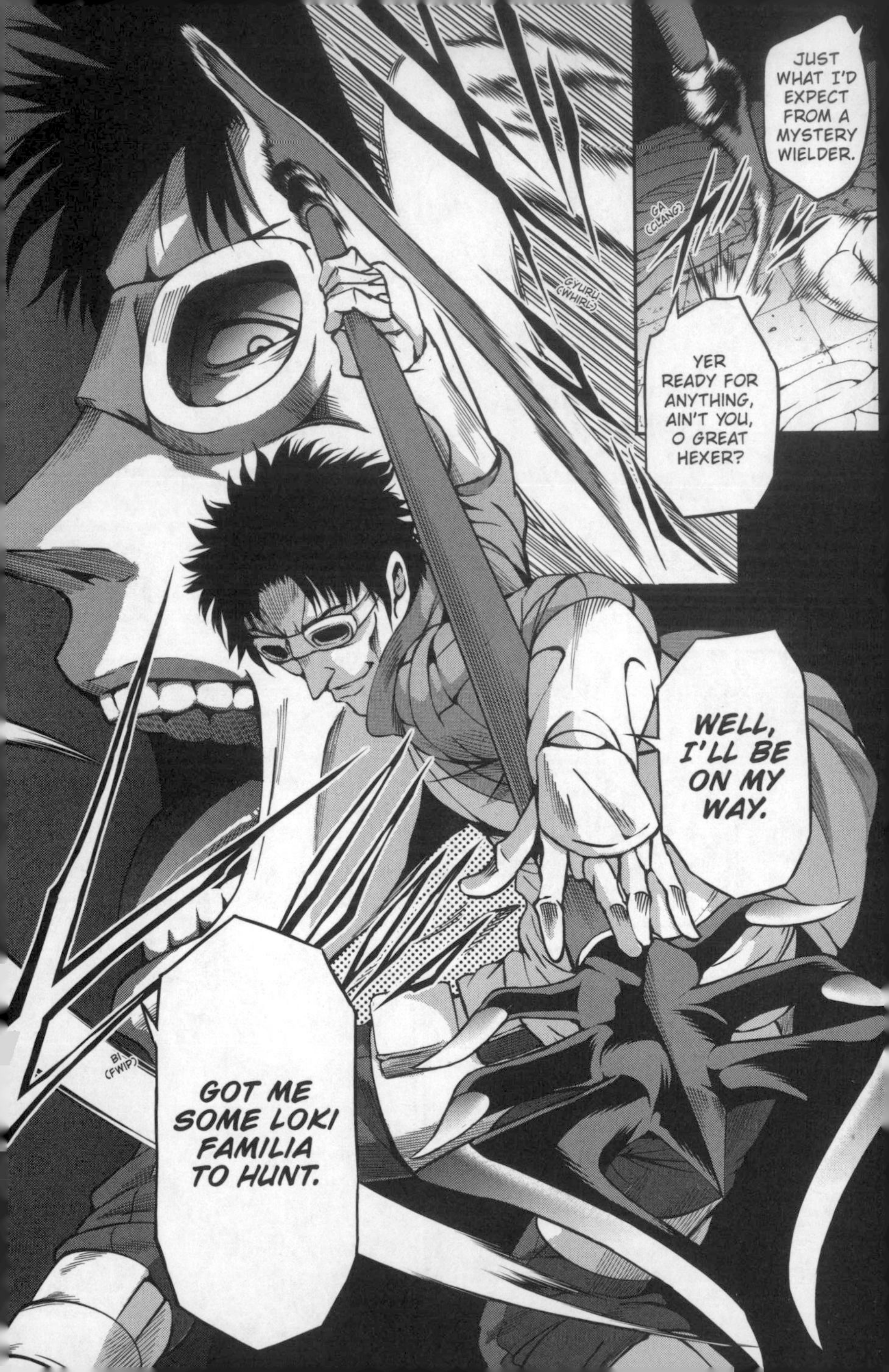
JUST WHAT I'D EXPECT FROM A MYSTERY WIELDER.
GA (CLANG)
YER READY FOR ANYTHING, AIN'T YOU, O GREAT HEXER?
GYURU (WHIRL)
WELL, I'LL BE ON MY WAY.
BI (FWIP)
GOT ME SOME LOKI FAMILIA TO HUNT.

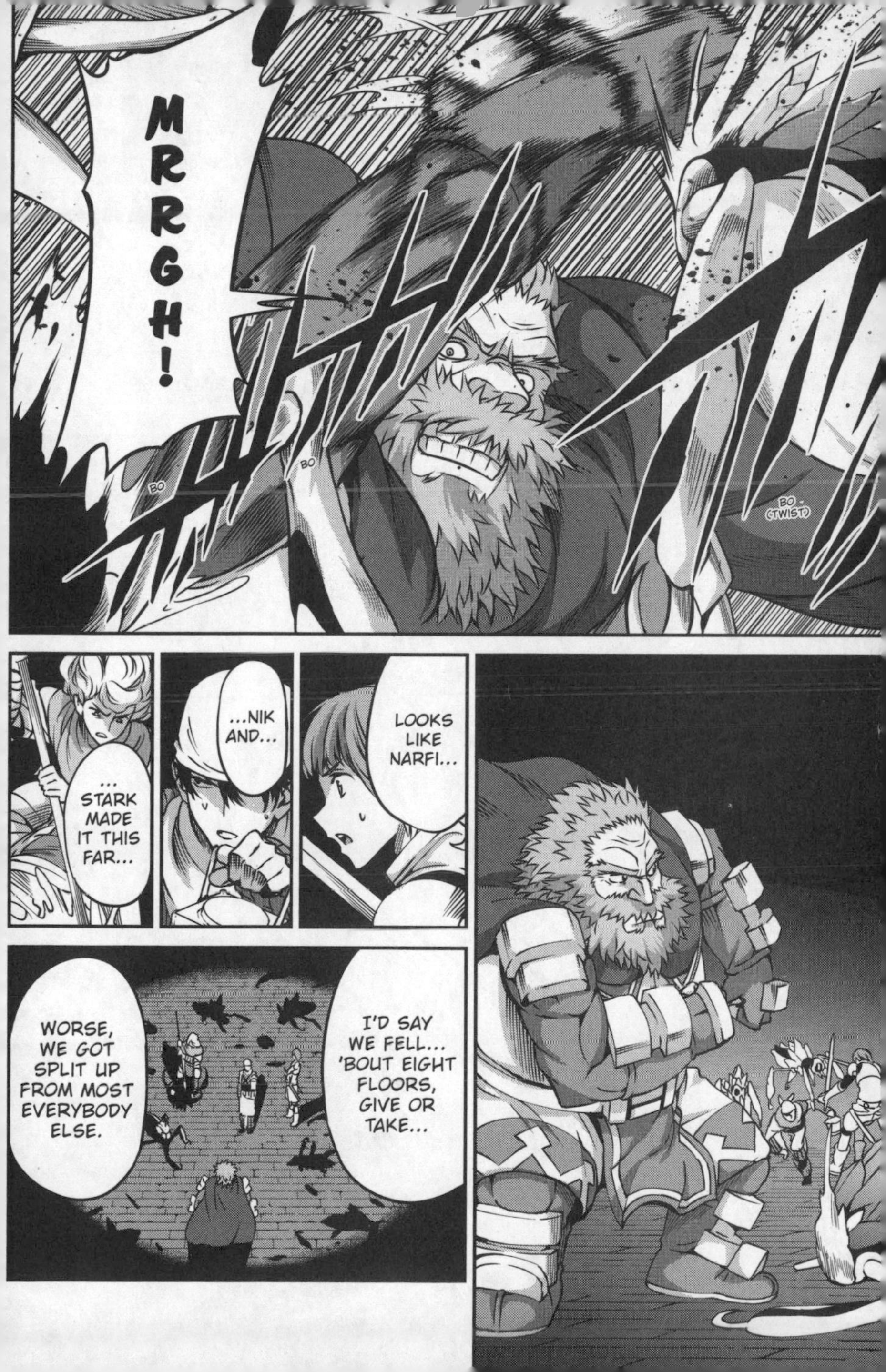
MRRGH!
BO (TWIST)
BO
BO
LOOKS LIKE NARFI...
...NIK AND...
...STARK MADE IT THIS FAR...
I'D SAY WE FELL... 'BOUT EIGHT FLOORS, GIVE OR TAKE...
WORSE, WE GOT SPLIT UP FROM MOST EVERYBODY ELSE.

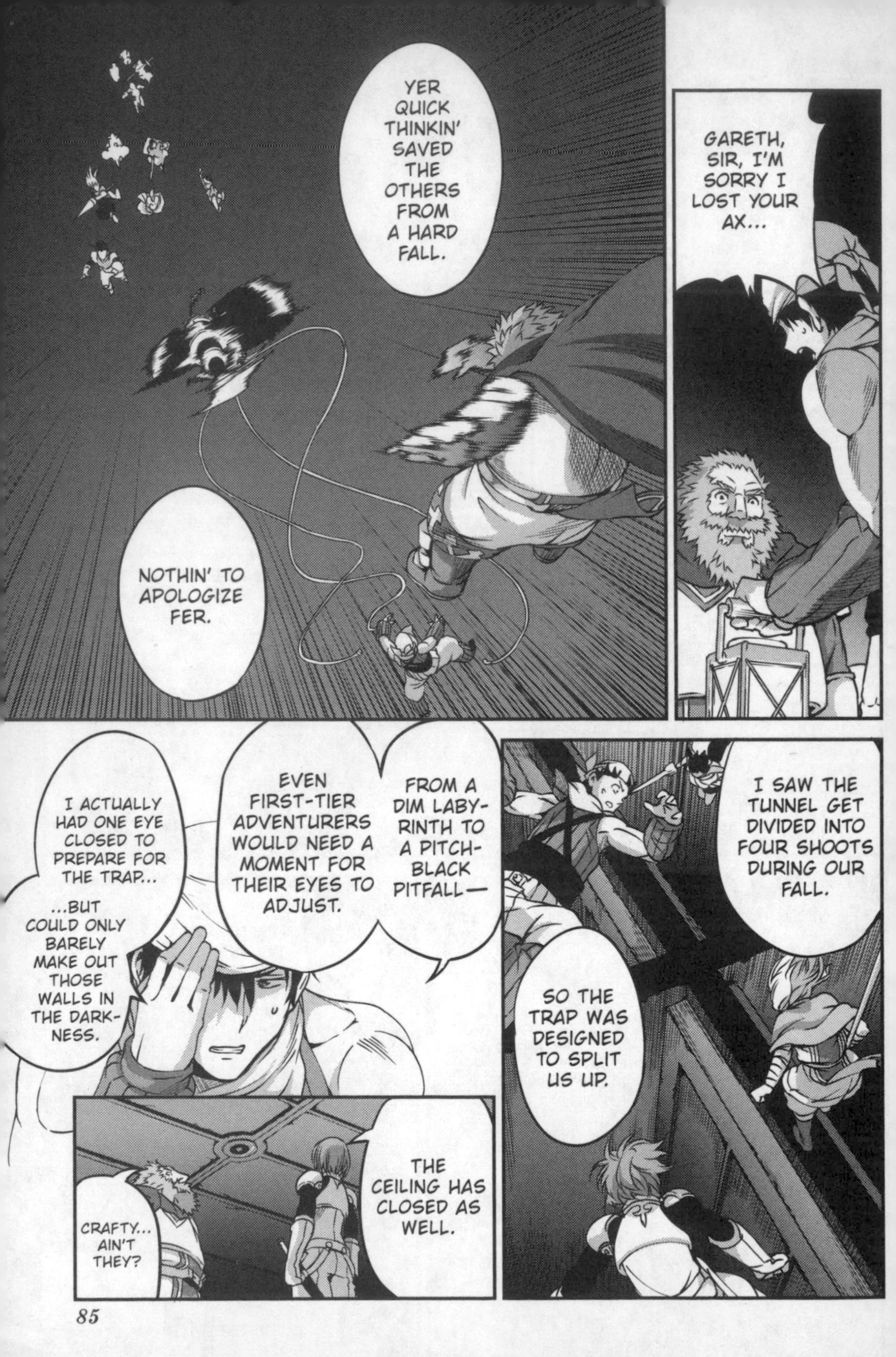
GARETH, SIR, I'M SORRY I LOST YOUR AX...
YER QUICK THINKIN' SAVED THE OTHERS FROM A HARD FALL.
NOTHIN' TO APOLOGIZE FER.
I SAW THE TUNNEL GET DIVIDED INTO FOUR SHOOTS DURING OUR FALL.
SO THE TRAP WAS DESIGNED TO SPLIT US UP.
FROM A DIM LABY-RINTH TO A PITCH-BLACK PITFALL—
EVEN FIRST-TIER ADVENTURERS WOULD NEED A MOMENT FOR THEIR EYES TO ADJUST.
I ACTUALLY HAD ONE EYE CLOSED TO PREPARE FOR THE TRAP...
...BUT COULD ONLY BARELY MAKE OUT THOSE WALLS IN THE DARK-NESS.
THE CEILING HAS CLOSED AS WELL.
CRAFTY... AIN'T THEY?

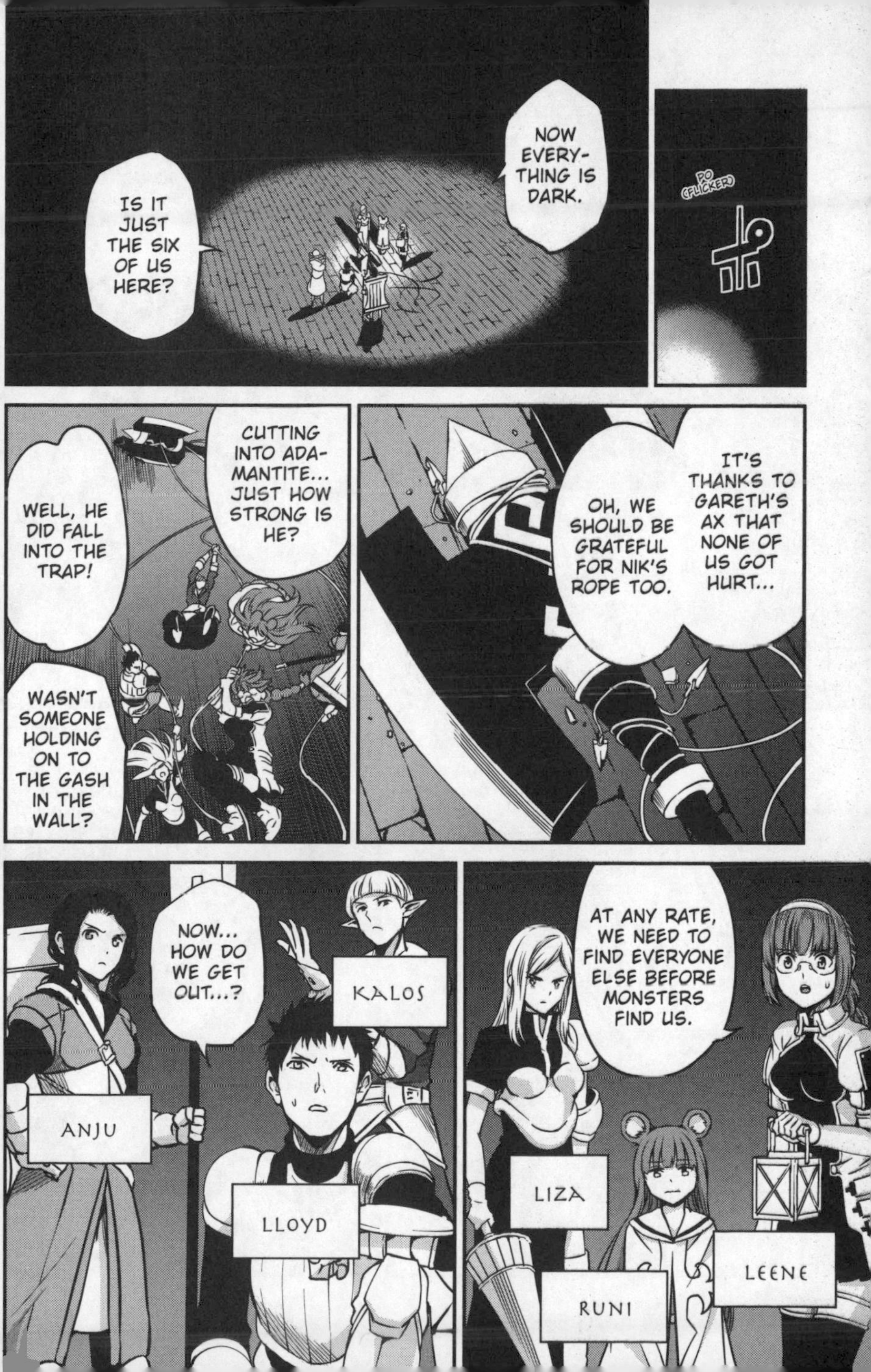
PO (FLICKER)
NOW EVERY-THING IS DARK.
IS IT JUST THE SIX OF US HERE?
IT'S THANKS TO GARETH'S AX THAT NONE OF US GOT HURT...
OH, WE SHOULD BE GRATEFUL FOR NIK'S ROPE TOO.
CUTTING INTO ADA-MANTITE... JUST HOW STRONG IS HE?
WELL, HE DID FALL INTO THE TRAP!
WASN'T SOMEONE HOLDING ON TO THE GASH IN THE WALL?
AT ANY RATE, WE NEED TO FIND EVERYONE ELSE BEFORE MONSTERS FIND US.
LIZA
LEENE
RUNI
NOW... HOW DO WE GET OUT...?
KALOS
ANJU
LLOYD

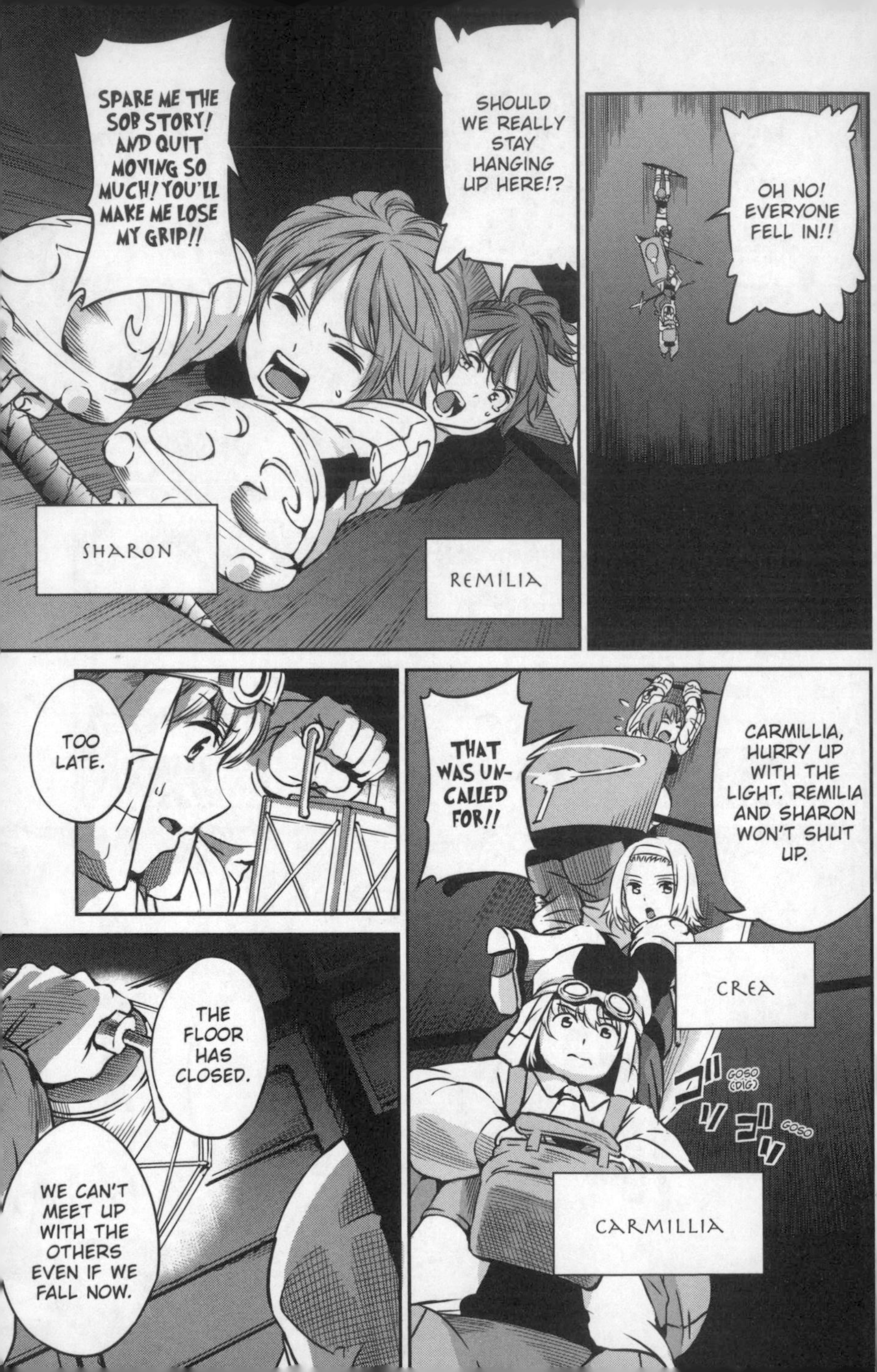
OH NO! EVERYONE FELL IN!!
SHOULD WE REALLY STAY HANGING UP HERE!?
SPARE ME THE SOB STORY! AND QUIT MOVING SO MUCH! YOU'LL MAKE ME LOSE MY GRIP!!
REMILIA
SHARON
CARMILLIA, HURRY UP WITH THE LIGHT. REMILIA AND SHARON WON'T SHUT UP.
THAT WAS UN-CALLED FOR!!
CREA
GOSO (DIG)
GOSO
CARMILLIA
TOO LATE.
THE FLOOR HAS CLOSED.
WE CAN'T MEET UP WITH THE OTHERS EVEN IF WE FALL NOW.

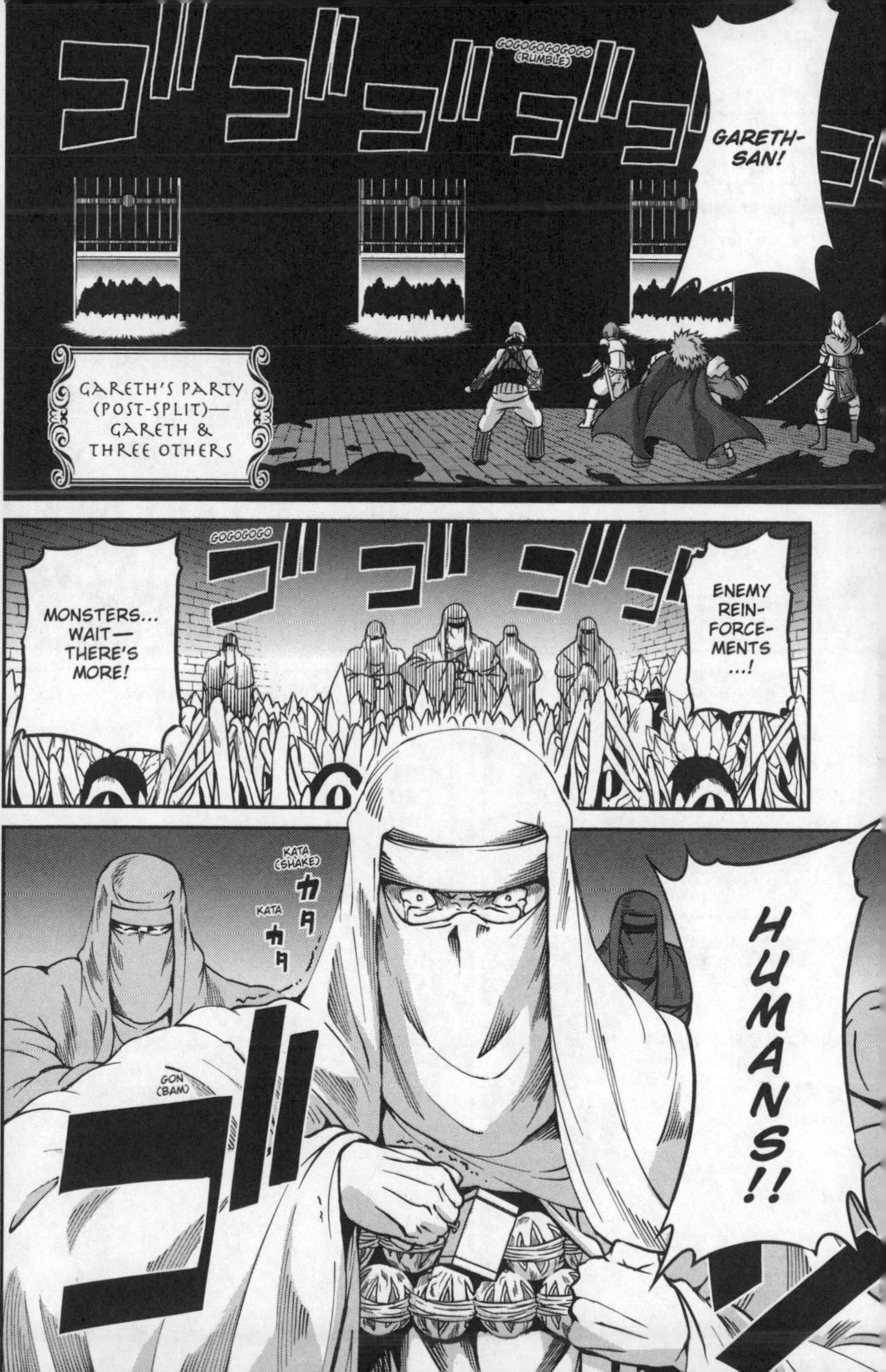
GARETH-SAN!
GOGOGOGOGOGO (RUMBLE)
GARETH'S PARTY (POST-SPLIT)— GARETH & THREE OTHERS
ENEMY REIN-FORCE-MENTS ...!
GOGOGOGO
MONSTERS... WAIT— THERE'S MORE!
HUMANS!!
KATA (SHAKE)
KATA
GON (BAM)

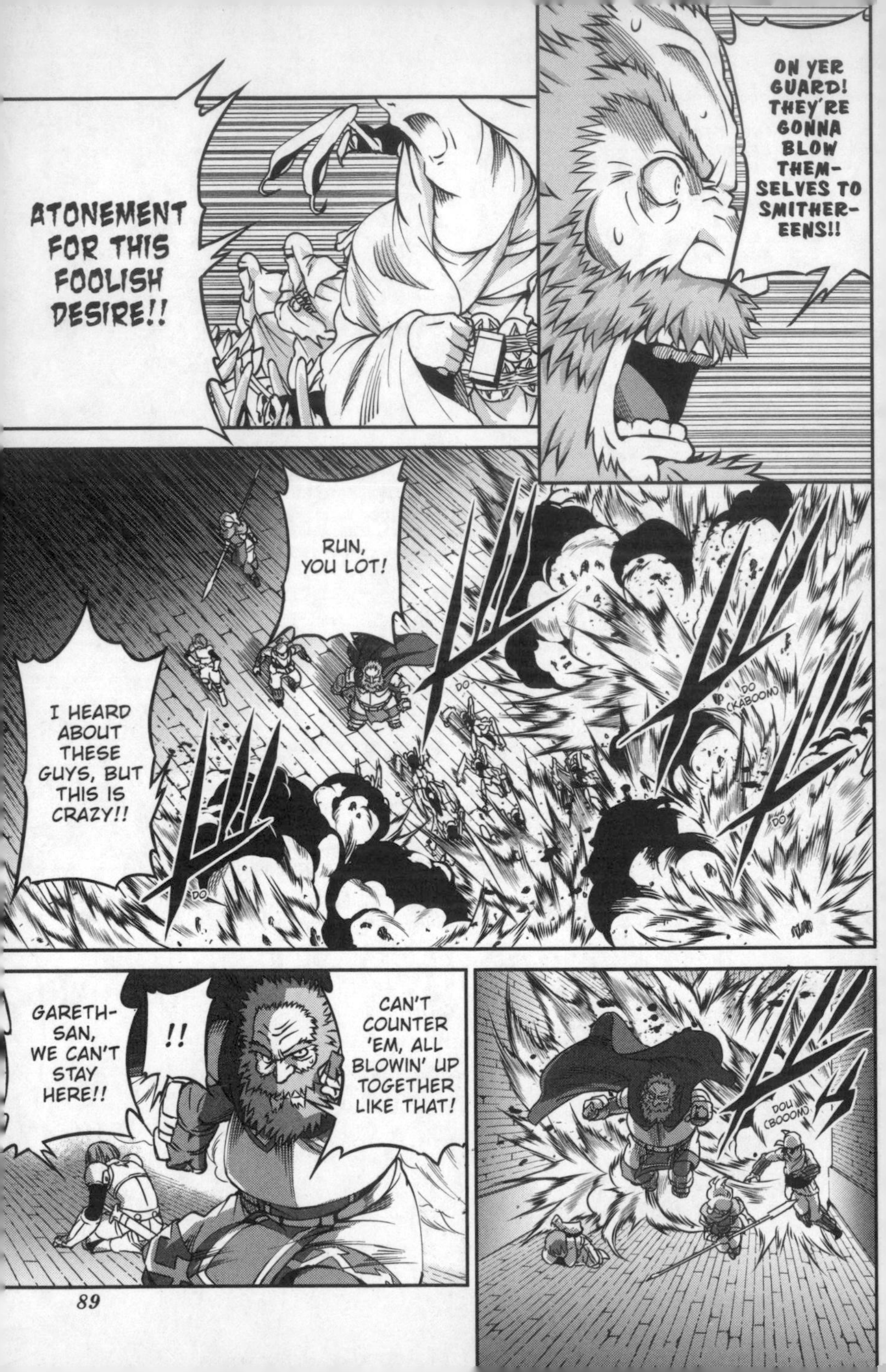

ON YER GUARD! THEY'RE GONNA BLOW THEM-SELVES TO SMITHER-EENS!!
ATONEMENT FOR THIS FOOLISH DESIRE!!
DO (KABOOM)
DO
DO
RUN, YOU LOT!
I HEARD ABOUT THESE GUYS, BUT THIS IS CRAZY!!
DO
DOU (BOOOM)
CAN'T COUNTER 'EM, ALL BLOWIN' UP TOGETHER LIKE THAT!
!!
GARETH-SAN, WE CAN'T STAY HERE!!

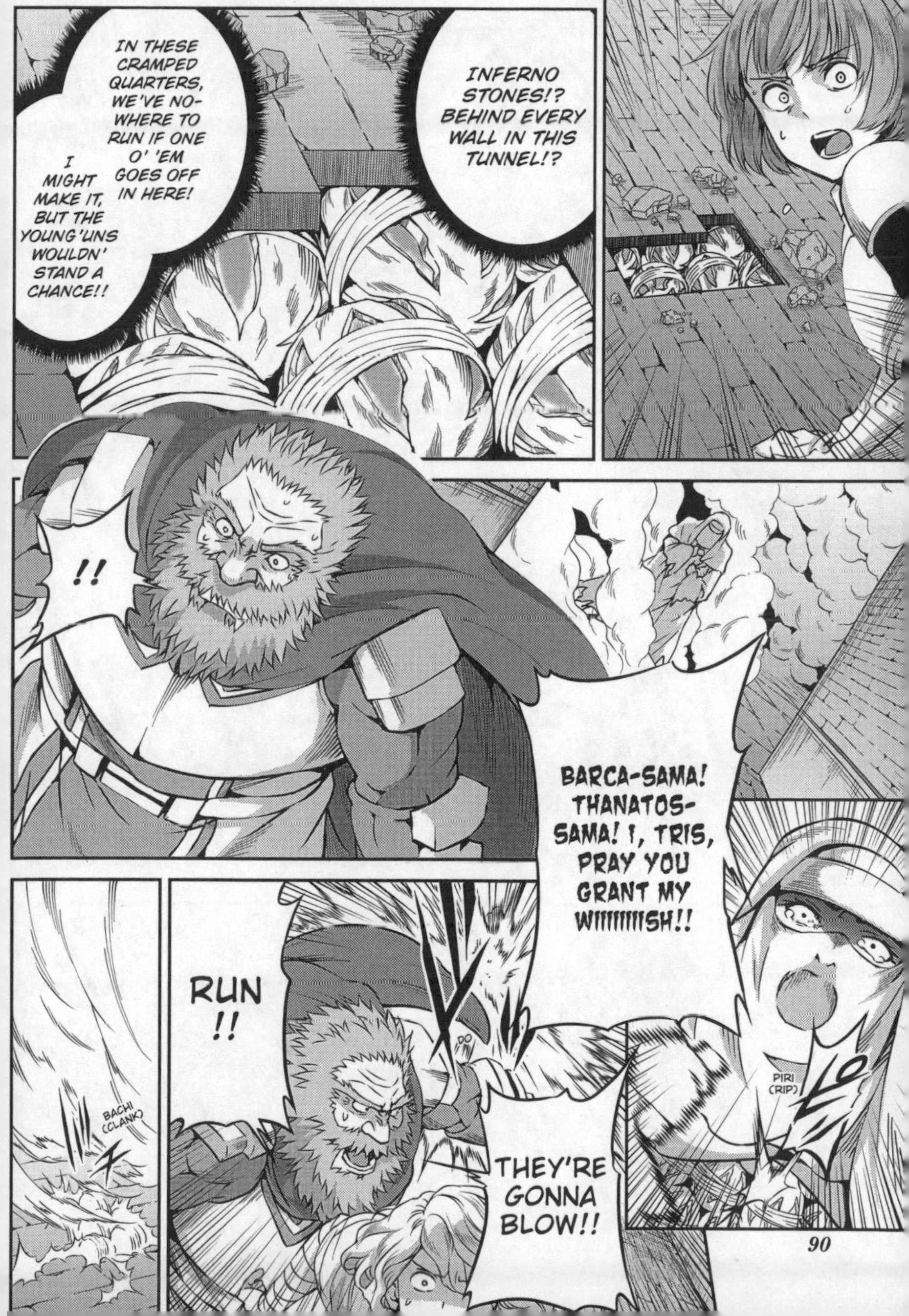
INFERNO STONES!? BEHIND EVERY WALL IN THIS TUNNEL!?
IN THESE CRAMPED QUARTERS, WE'VE NO-WHERE TO RUN IF ONE O' 'EM GOES OFF IN HERE!
I MIGHT MAKE IT, BUT THE YOUNG'UNS WOULDN' STAND A CHANCE!!
!!
BARCA-SAMA! THANATOS-SAMA! I, TRIS, PRAY YOU GRANT MY WIIIIIIIISH!!
PIRI (RIP)
DO
RUN!!
THEY'RE GONNA BLOW!!
BACHI (CLANK)

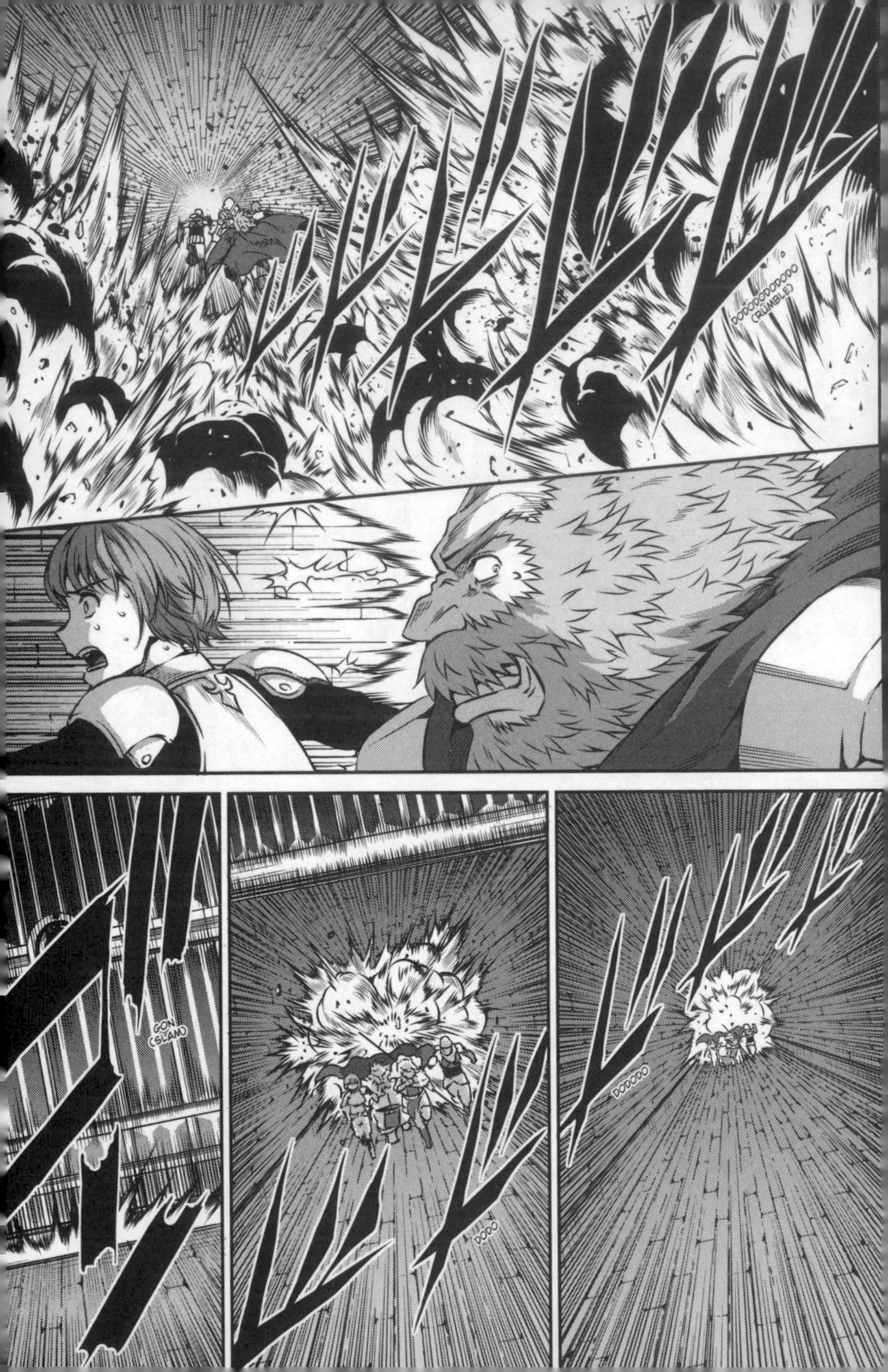
DODODODODODO
(RUMBLE)
DODODO
DODO
GON
(SLAM)

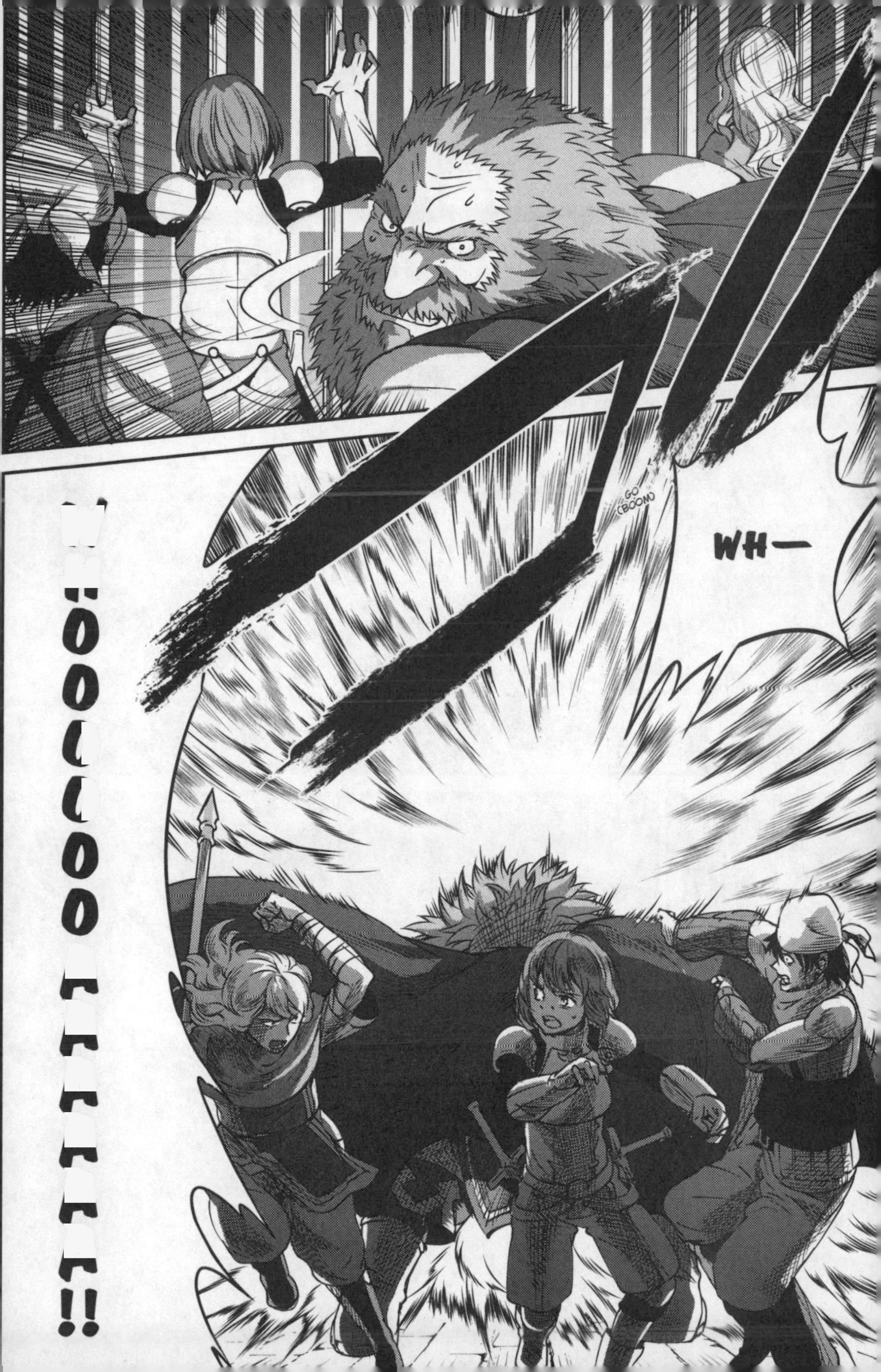
WH—
GO
(BOON)

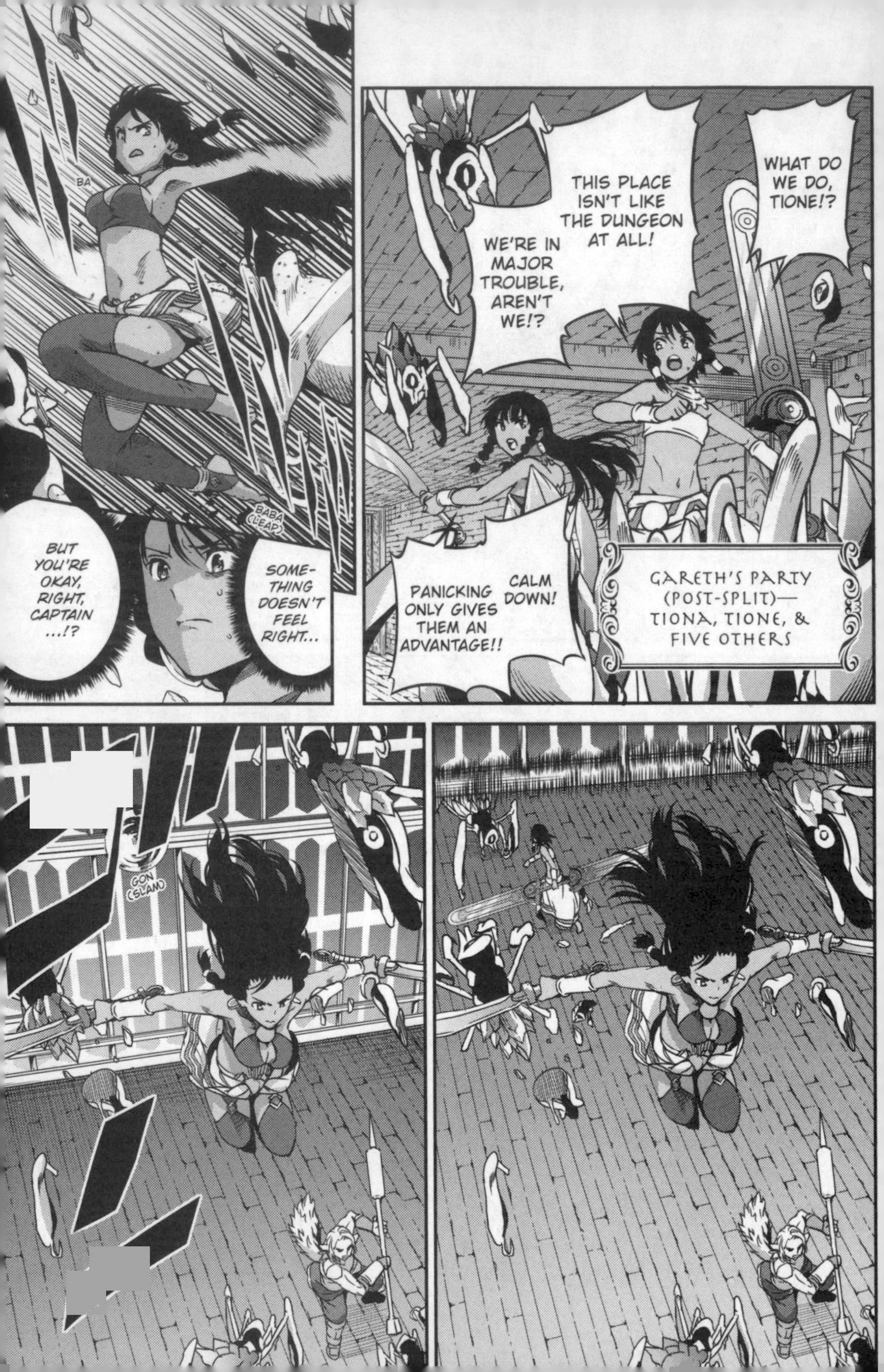
WHAT DO WE DO, TIONE!?
THIS PLACE ISN'T LIKE THE DUNGEON AT ALL!
WE'RE IN MAJOR TROUBLE, AREN'T WE!?
GARETH'S PARTY (POST-SPLIT)—TIONA, TIONE, & FIVE OTHERS
CALM DOWN!
PANICKING ONLY GIVES THEM AN ADVANTAGE!!
BA
BABA (LEAP)
SOME-THING DOESN'T FEEL RIGHT...
BUT YOU'RE OKAY, RIGHT, CAPTAIN ...!?
GON (SLAM)

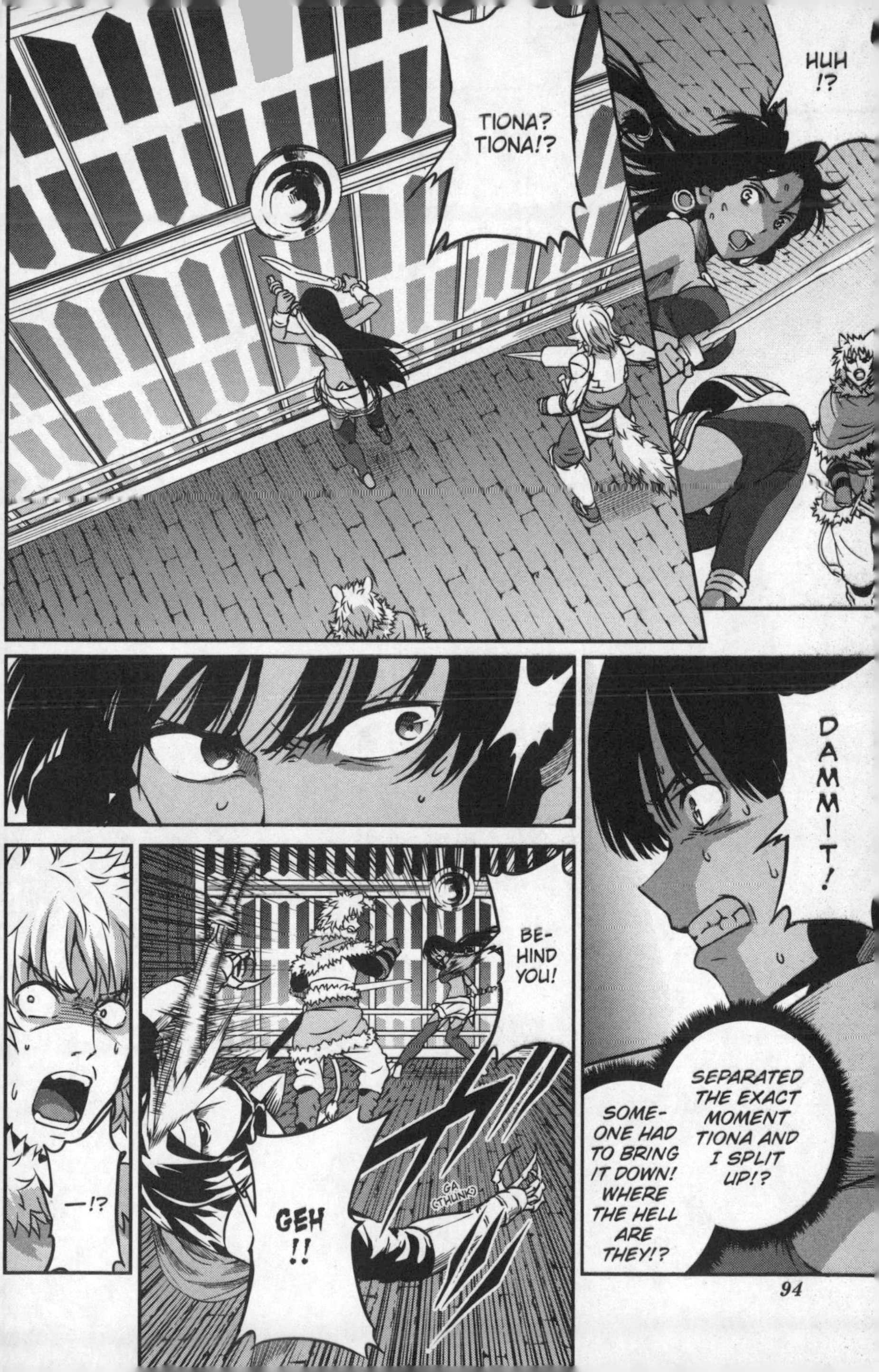
HUH!?
TIONA? TIONA!?
DAMMIT!
SOME-ONE HAD TO BRING IT DOWN! WHERE THE HELL ARE THEY!?
SEPARATED THE EXACT MOMENT TIONA AND I SPLIT UP!?
BE-HIND YOU!
GA (THUNK)
GEH!!
—!?

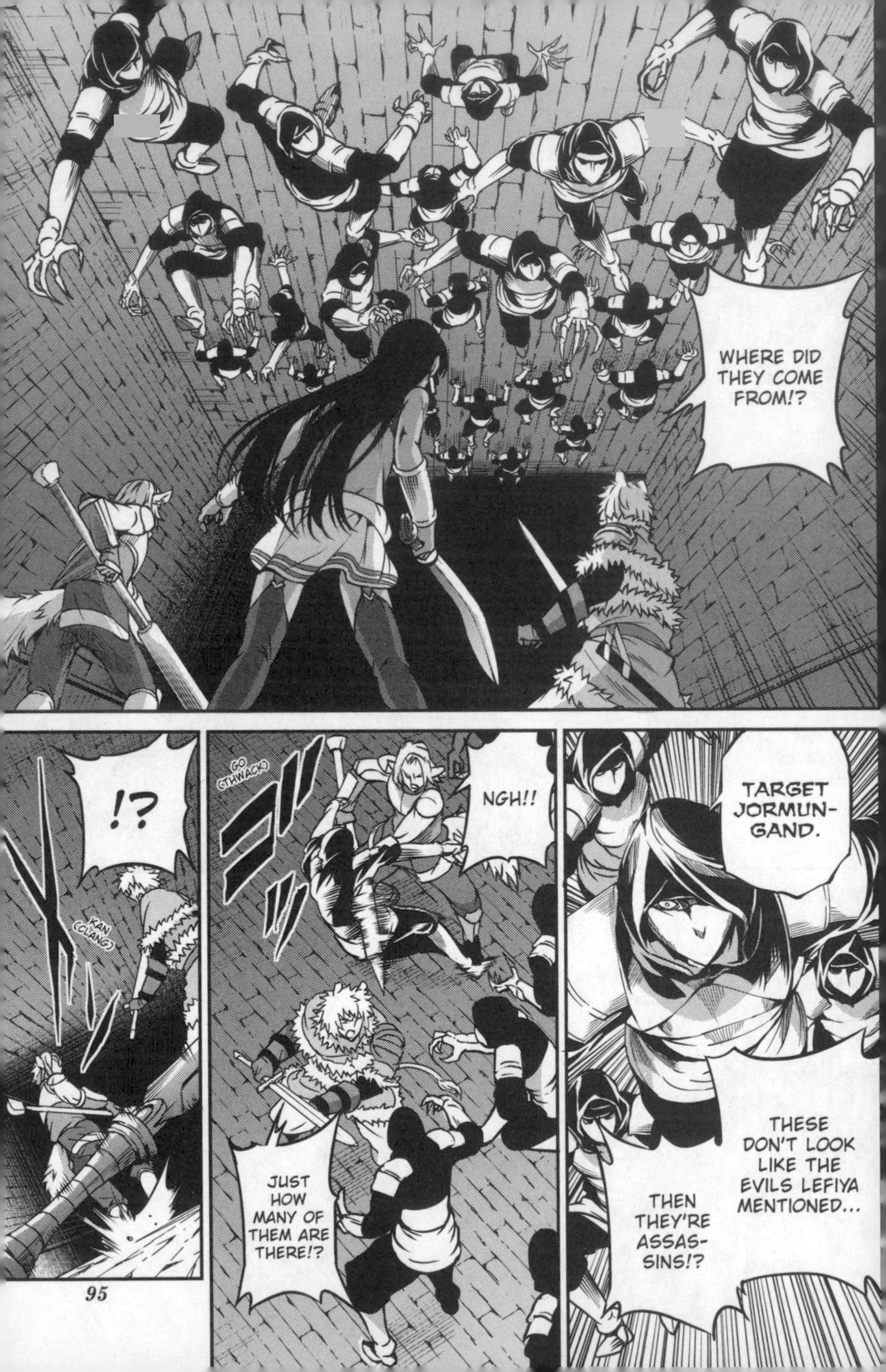
WHERE DID THEY COME FROM!?
TARGET JORMUN-GAND.
THESE DON'T LOOK LIKE THE EVILS LEFIYA MENTIONED...
THEN THEY'RE ASSAS-SINS!?
GO (THWACK)
NGH!!
JUST HOW MANY OF THEM ARE THERE!?
!?
KAN (CLANG)

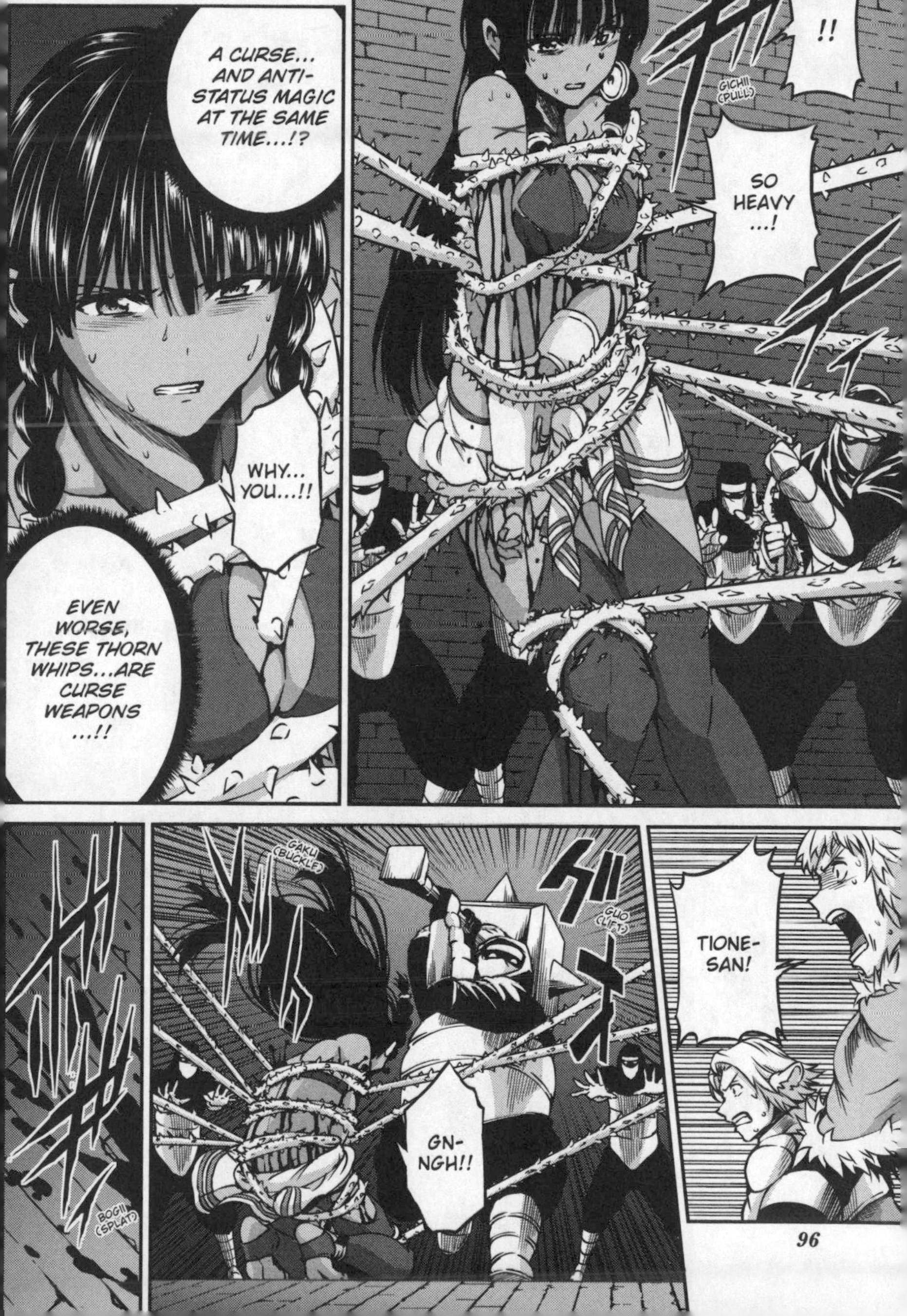
!!
GICHII (PULL)
SO HEAVY ...!
A CURSE... AND ANTI-STATUS MAGIC AT THE SAME TIME...!?
WHY... YOU...!!
EVEN WORSE, THESE THORN WHIPS...ARE CURSE WEAPONS ...!!
TIONE-SAN!
GAKU (BUCKLE)
GUO (LIFT)
GN-NGH!!
BOGII (SPLAT)

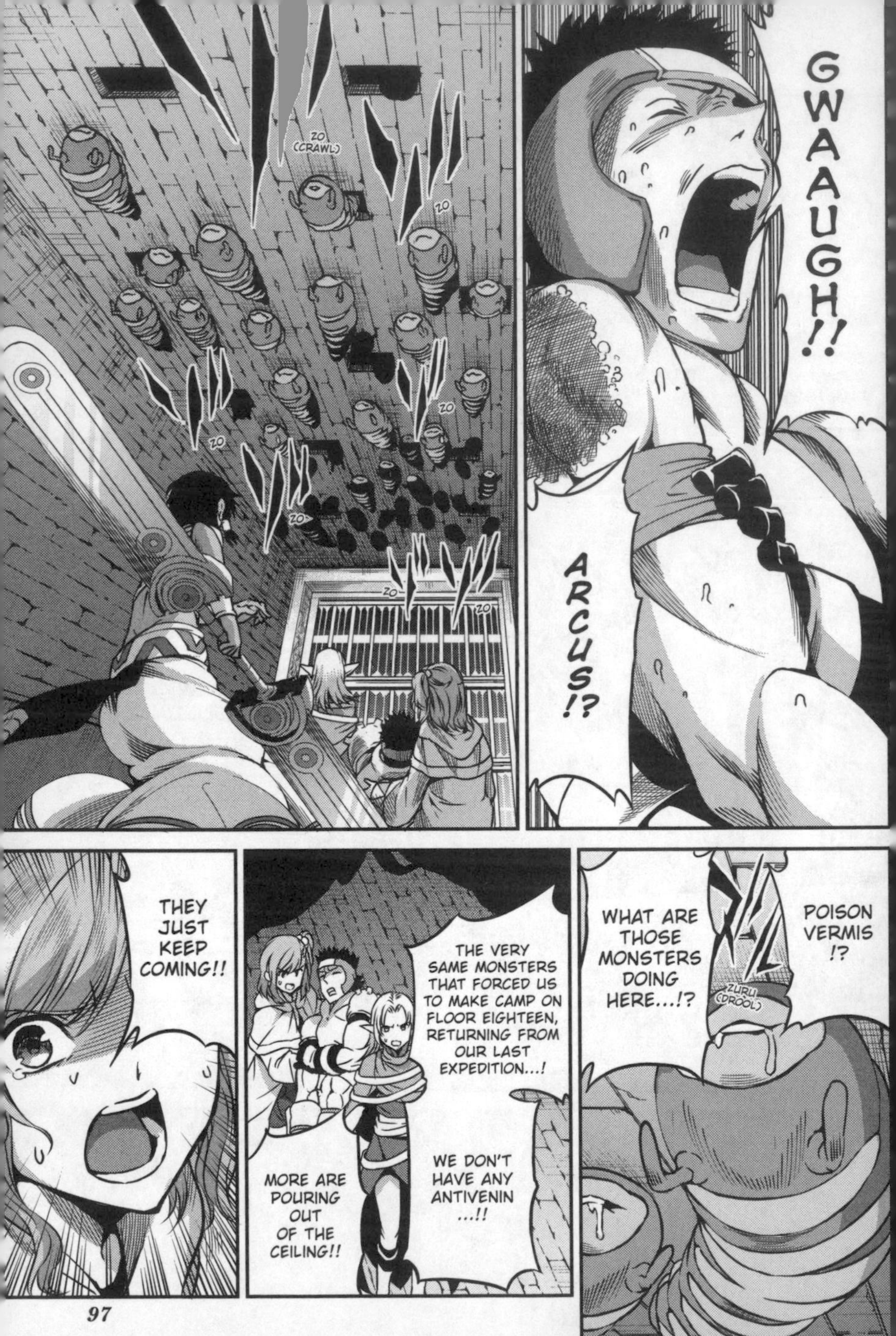
GWAAUGH!!
ARCUS!?
ZO (CRAWL)
ZO
ZO
ZO
ZO
ZO
ZO
POISON VERMIS!?
WHAT ARE THOSE MONSTERS DOING HERE...!?
ZURU (DROOL)
THE VERY SAME MONSTERS THAT FORCED US TO MAKE CAMP ON FLOOR EIGHTEEN, RETURNING FROM OUR LAST EXPEDITION...!
WE DON'T HAVE ANY ANTIVENIN...!!
MORE ARE POURING OUT OF THE CEILING!!
THEY JUST KEEP COMING!!

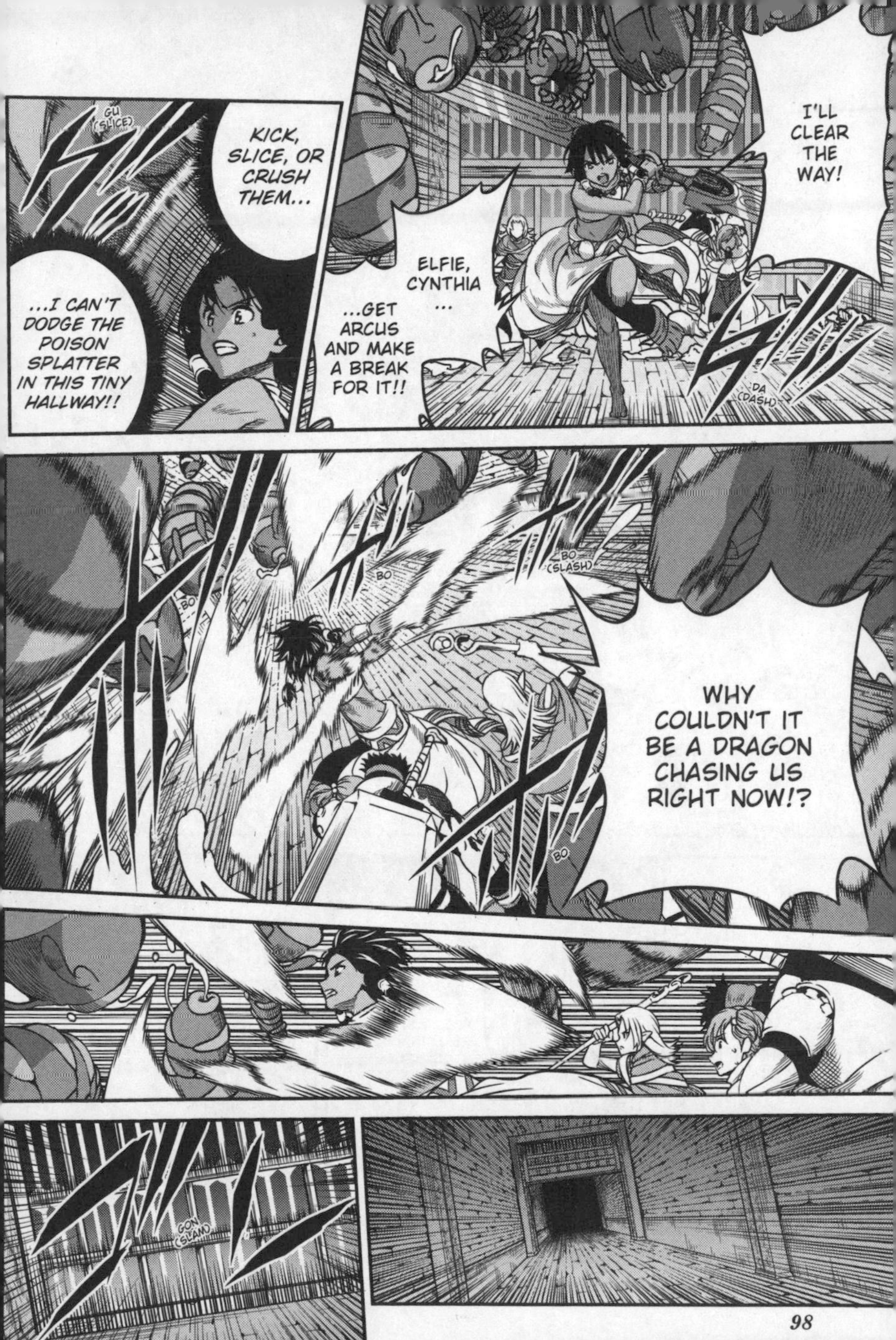
I'LL CLEAR THE WAY!
ELFIE, CYNTHIA ...
...GET ARCUS AND MAKE A BREAK FOR IT!!
DA (DASH)
GU (SLICE)
KICK, SLICE, OR CRUSH THEM...
...I CAN'T DODGE THE POISON SPLATTER IN THIS TINY HALLWAY!!
BO (SLASH)
BO
BO
BO
WHY COULDN'T IT BE A DRAGON CHASING US RIGHT NOW!?
GON (SLAM)

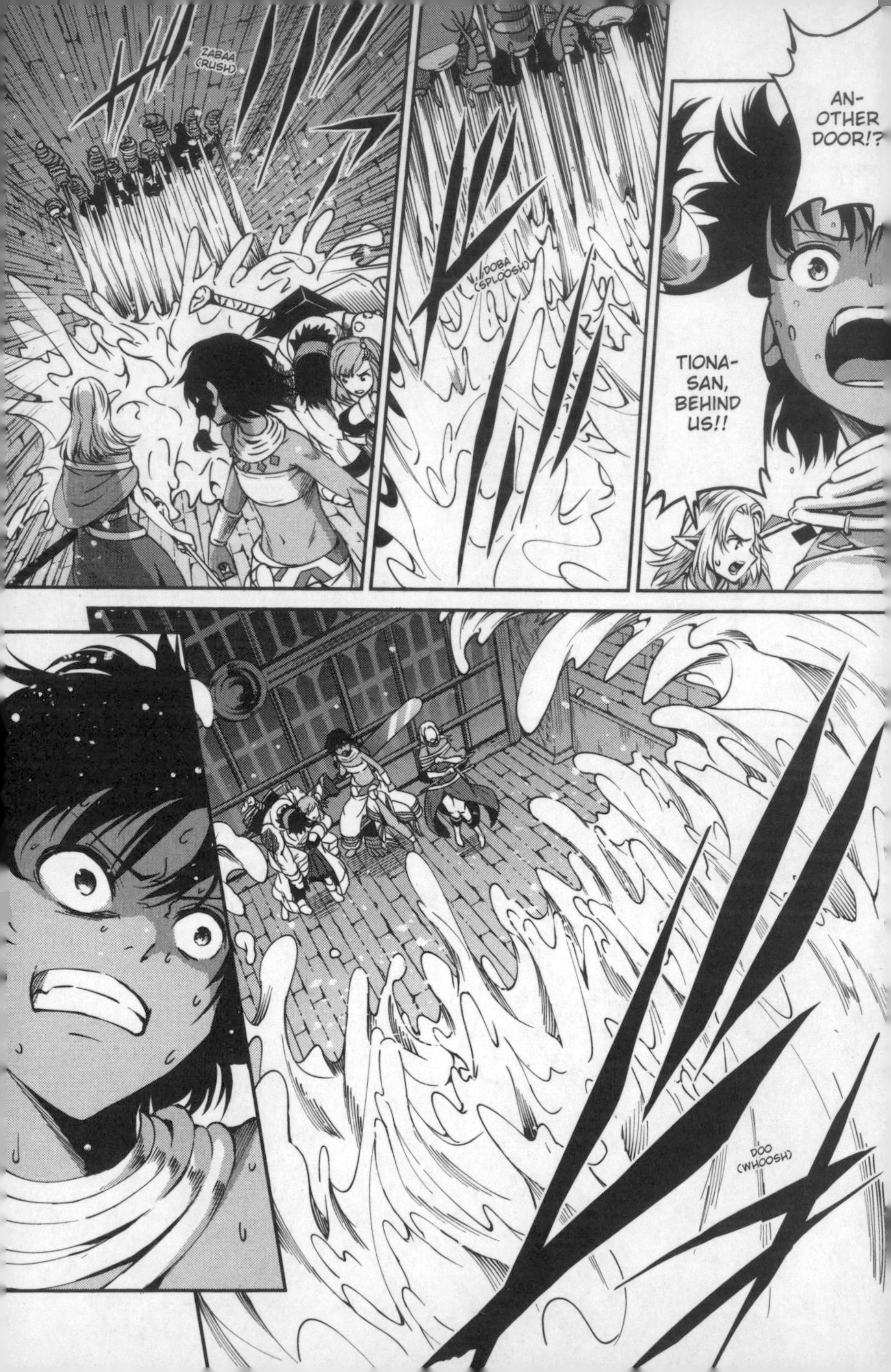
AN-OTHER DOOR!?
TIONA-SAN, BEHIND US!!
DOBA (SPLOOSH)
ZABAA (RUSH)
DOO (WHOOSH)

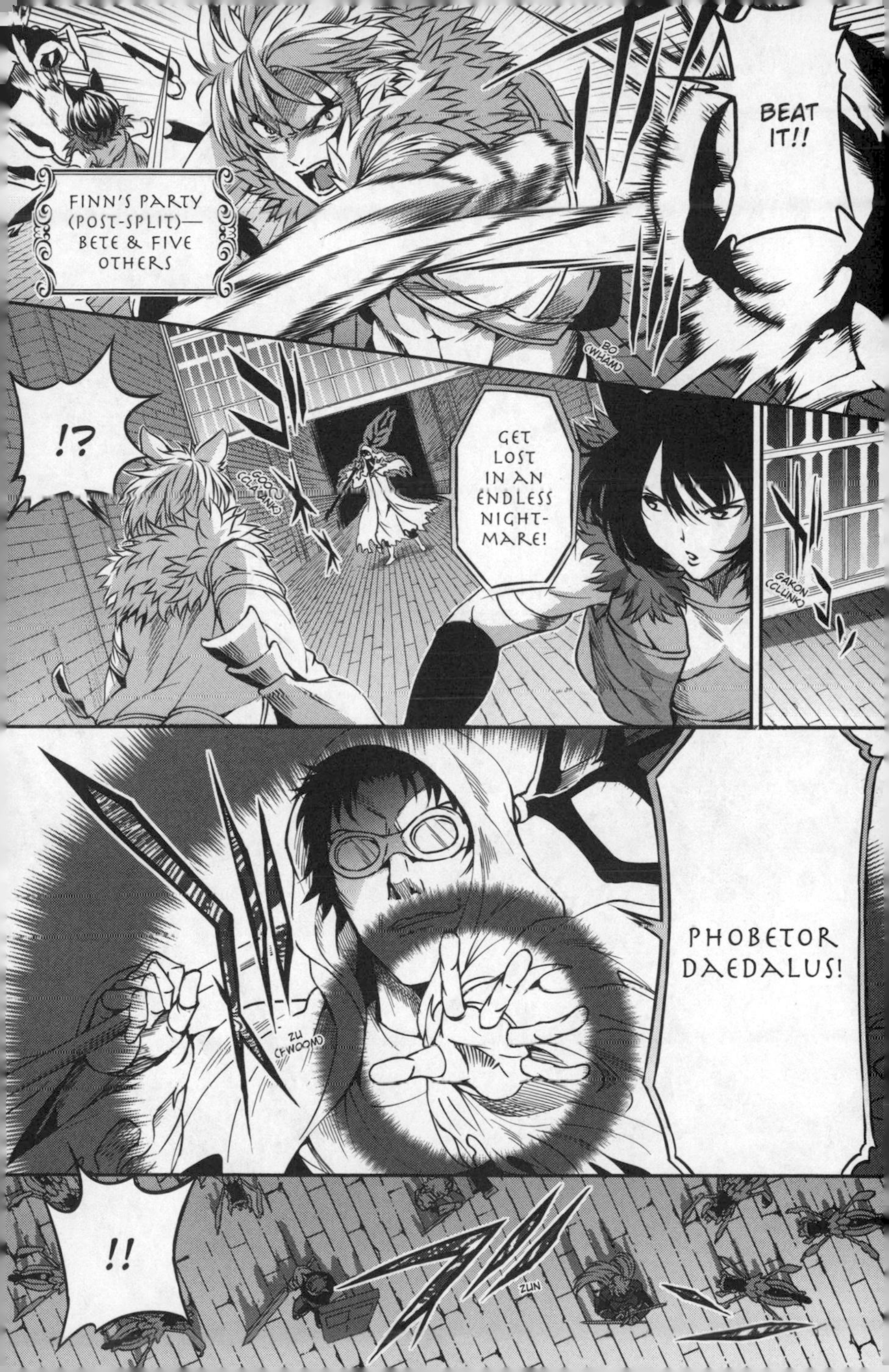
BEAT IT!!
FINN'S PARTY (POST-SPLIT)— BETE & FIVE OTHERS
BO (WHAM)
GET LOST IN AN ENDLESS NIGHTMARE!
GAKON (CLUNK)
GOO (CLANK)
!?
PHOBETOR DAEDALUS!
ZU (FWOOM)
ZUN
!!

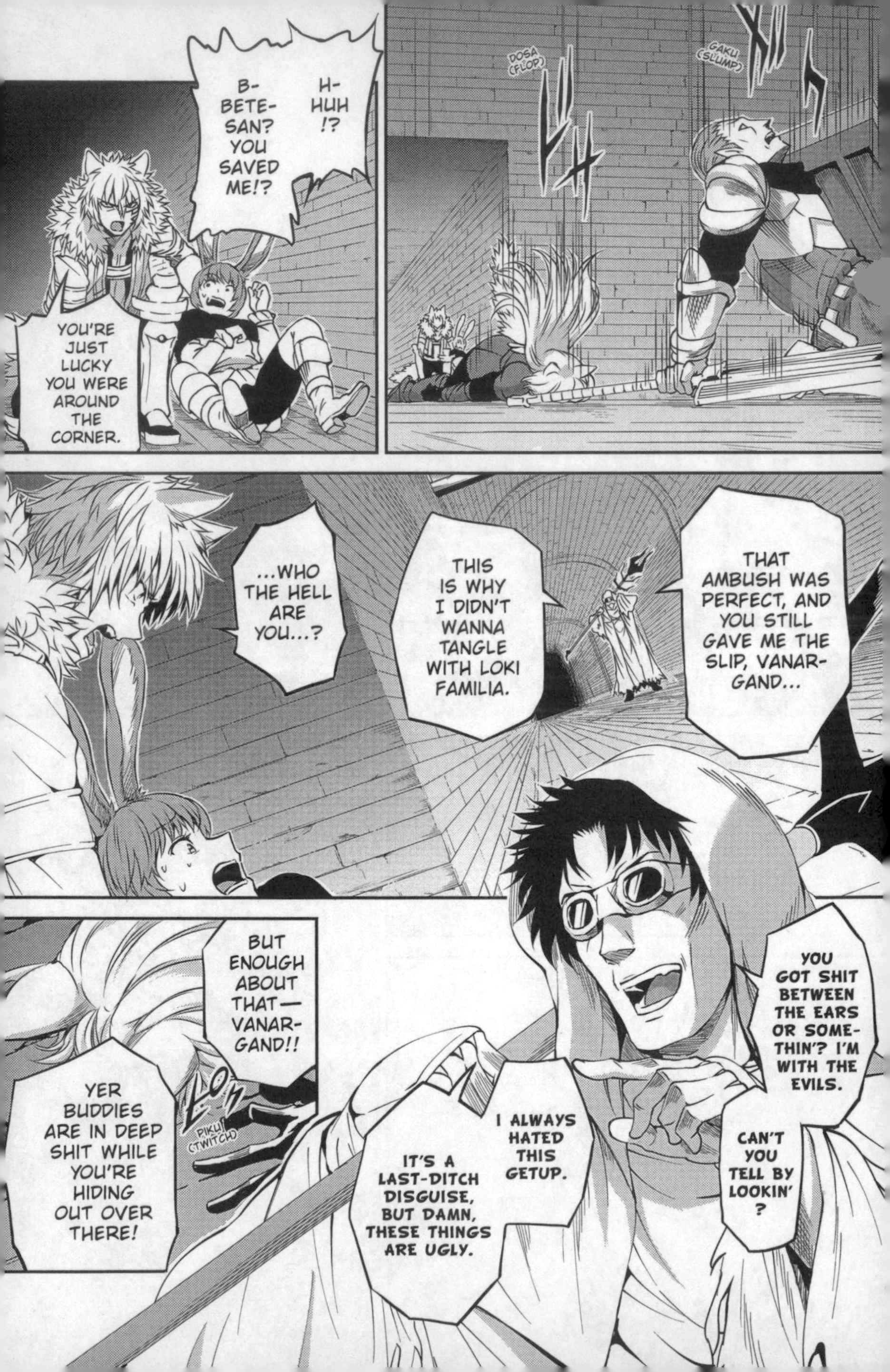
GAKU (SLUMP)
DOSA (FLOP)
H-HUH!?
B-BETE-SAN? YOU SAVED ME!?
YOU'RE JUST LUCKY YOU WERE AROUND THE CORNER.
THAT AMBUSH WAS PERFECT, AND YOU STILL GAVE ME THE SLIP, VANARGAND...
THIS IS WHY I DIDN'T WANNA TANGLE WITH LOKI FAMILIA.
...WHO THE HELL ARE YOU...?
YOU GOT SHIT BETWEEN THE EARS OR SOMETHIN'? I'M WITH THE EVILS.
CAN'T YOU TELL BY LOOKIN'?
I ALWAYS HATED THIS GETUP.
IT'S A LAST-DITCH DISGUISE, BUT DAMN, THESE THINGS ARE UGLY.
BUT ENOUGH ABOUT THAT—VANARGAND!!
PIKU (TWITCH)
YER BUDDIES ARE IN DEEP SHIT WHILE YOU'RE HIDING OUT OVER THERE!

OOOOROOO
CROAD

...!?

G-GUYS
!?

GA
CWHAMD

GASH!
CSLASH!

A CON-
FUSION
CURSE...!

102

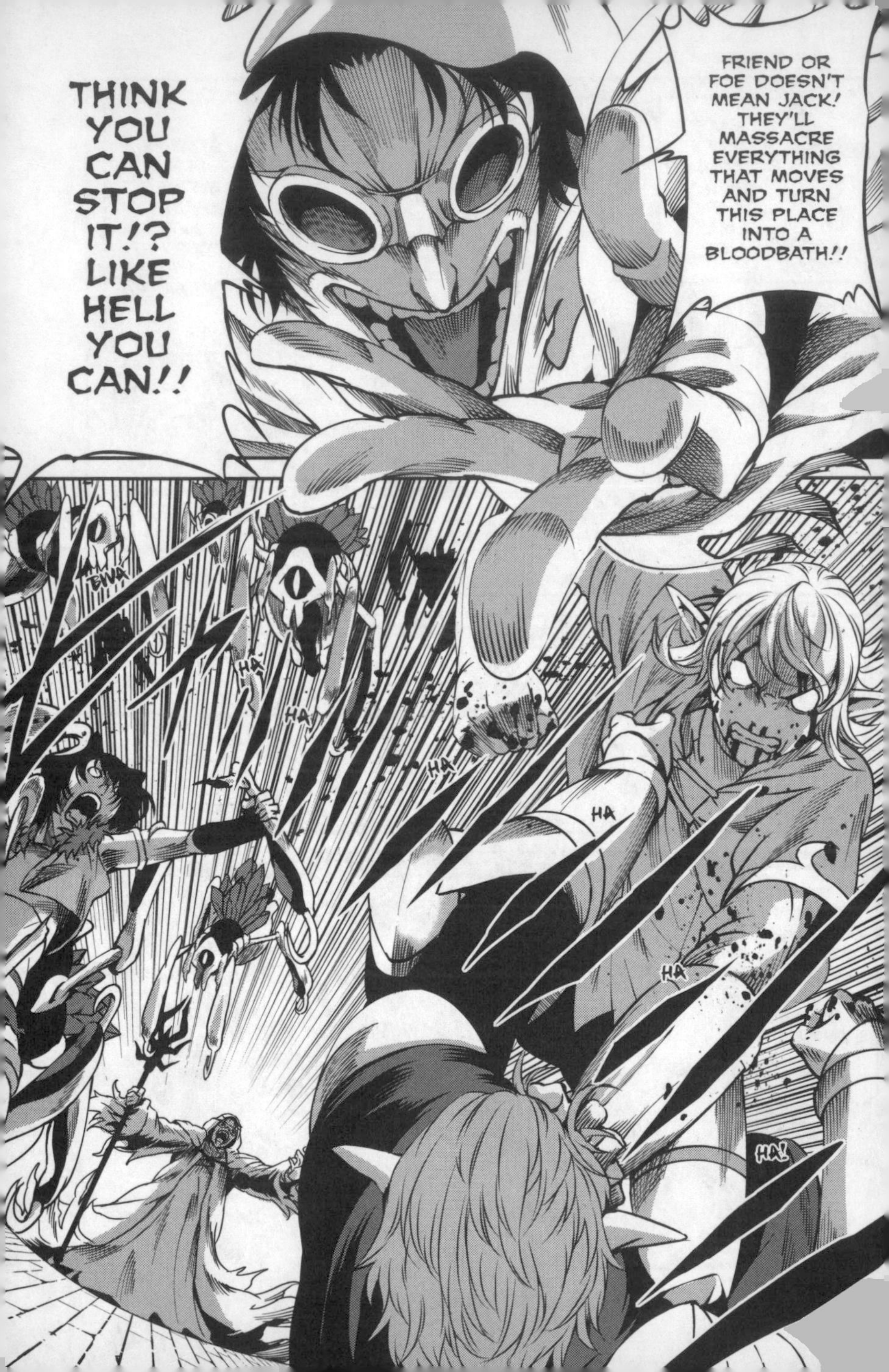
FRIEND OR FOE DOESN'T MEAN JACK! THEY'LL MASSACRE EVERYTHING THAT MOVES AND TURN THIS PLACE INTO A BLOODBATH!!
THINK YOU CAN STOP IT!? LIKE HELL YOU CAN!!
HA
HA
HA!
BWA
HA
HA
HA

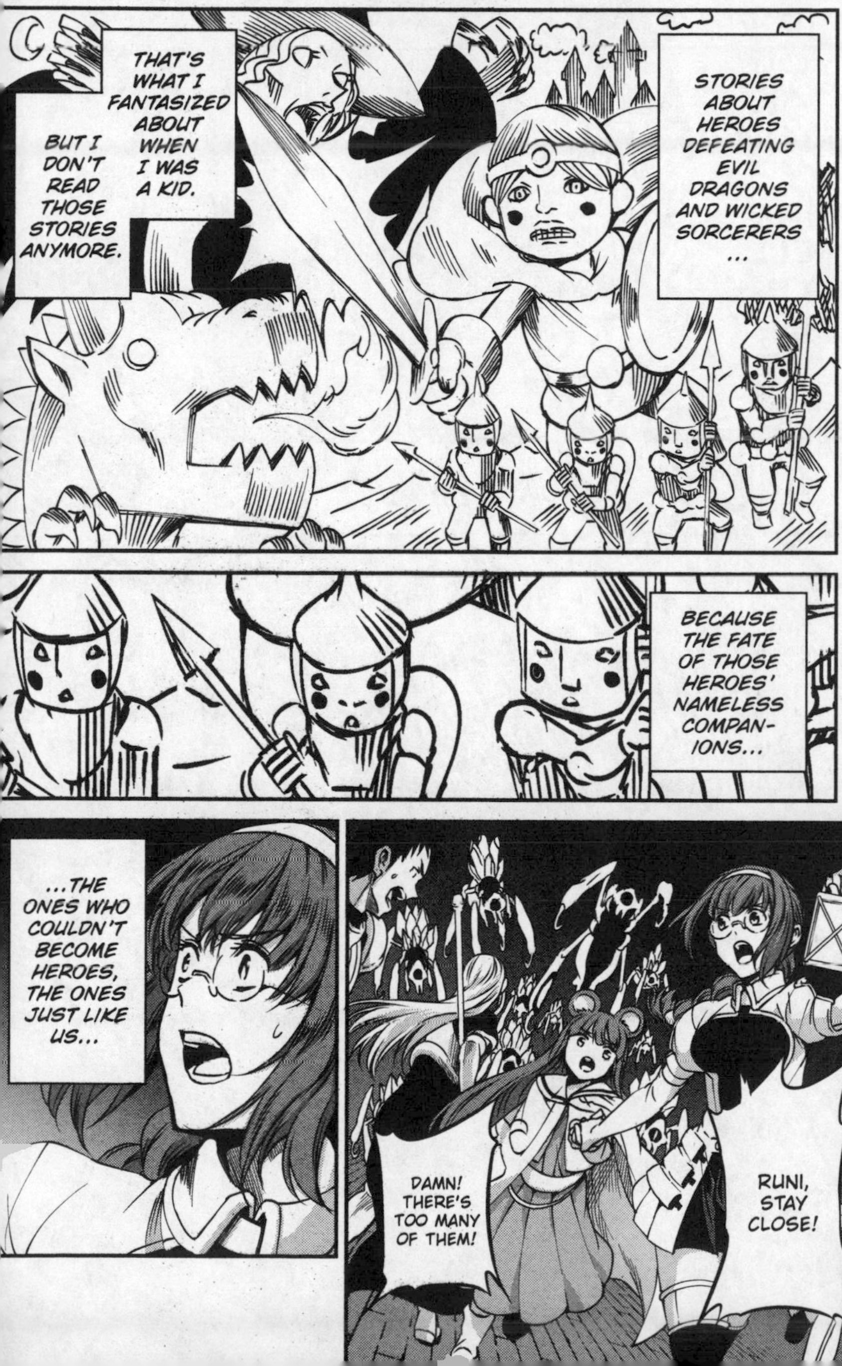
STORIES ABOUT HEROES DEFEATING EVIL DRAGONS AND WICKED SORCERERS...
THAT'S WHAT I FANTASIZED ABOUT WHEN I WAS A KID.
BUT I DON'T READ THOSE STORIES ANYMORE.
BECAUSE THE FATE OF THOSE HEROES' NAMELESS COMPAN-IONS...
RUNI, STAY CLOSE!
DAMN! THERE'S TOO MANY OF THEM!
...THE ONES WHO COULDN'T BECOME HEROES, THE ONES JUST LIKE US...

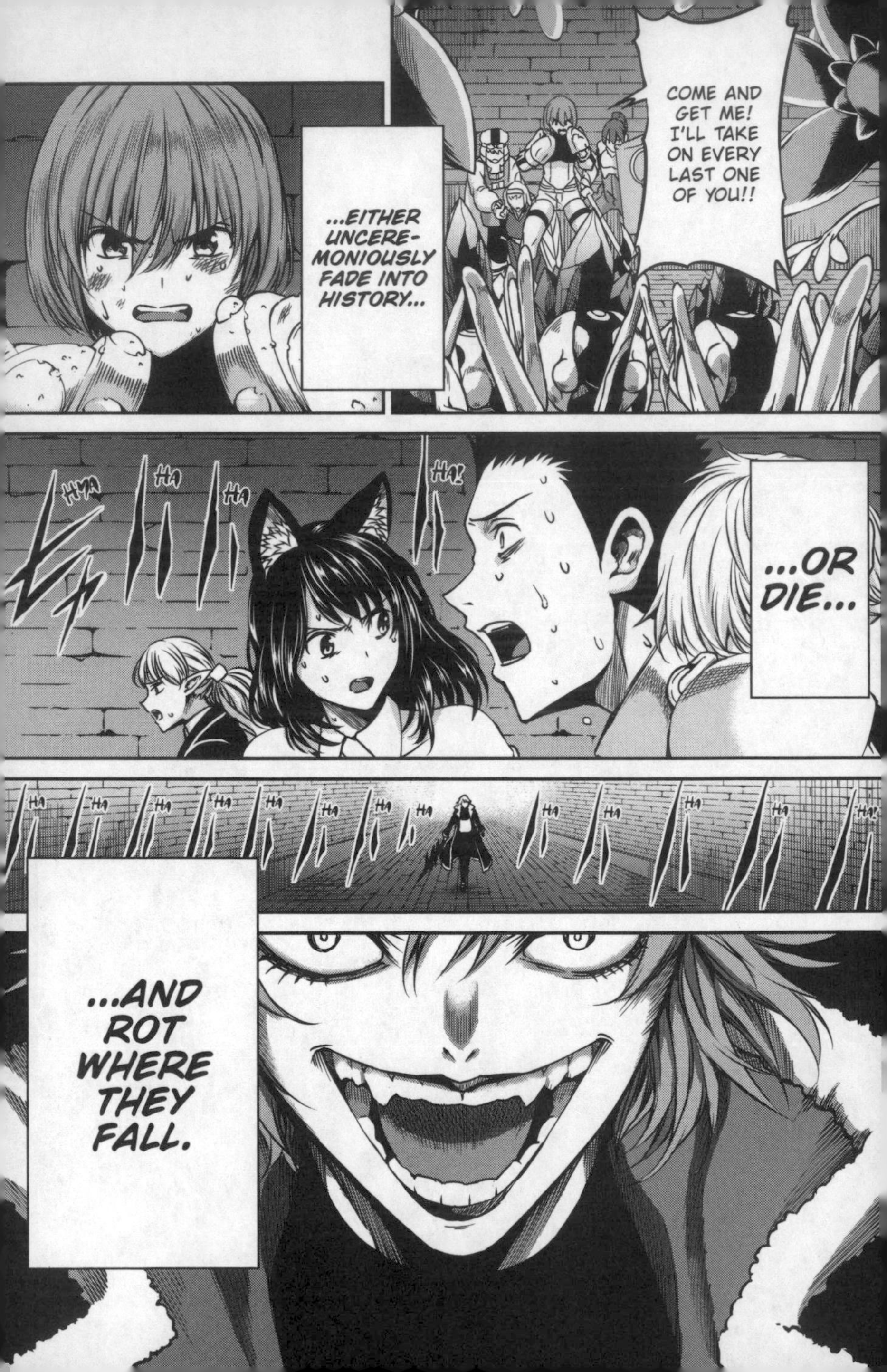
COME AND GET ME! I'LL TAKE ON EVERY LAST ONE OF YOU!!
...EITHER UNCERE-MONIOUSLY FADE INTO HISTORY...
...OR DIE...
HA!
HA
HA
HYA
HA!
HA
HA
HA
HA
HA
HA
HA
HA
HA
HA
HA
...AND ROT WHERE THEY FALL.

Is it WRONG to TRY to PICK UP GIRLS in a DUNGEON? ON THE SIDE

Sword Oratoria

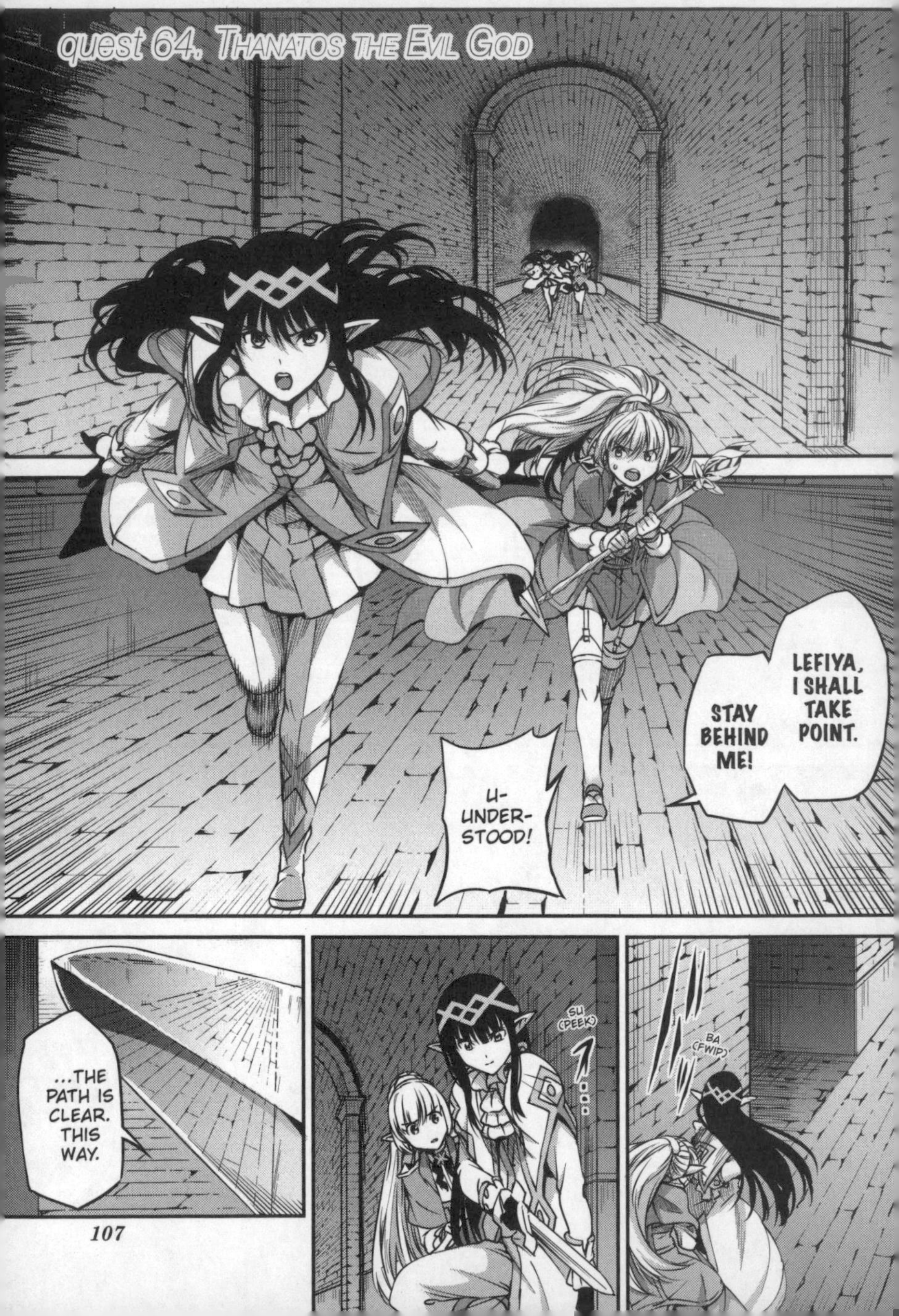
quest 64. Thanatos the Evil God
LEFIYA, I SHALL TAKE POINT.
STAY BEHIND ME!
U-UNDERSTOOD!
BA (FWIP)
SU (PEEK)
...THE PATH IS CLEAR. THIS WAY.

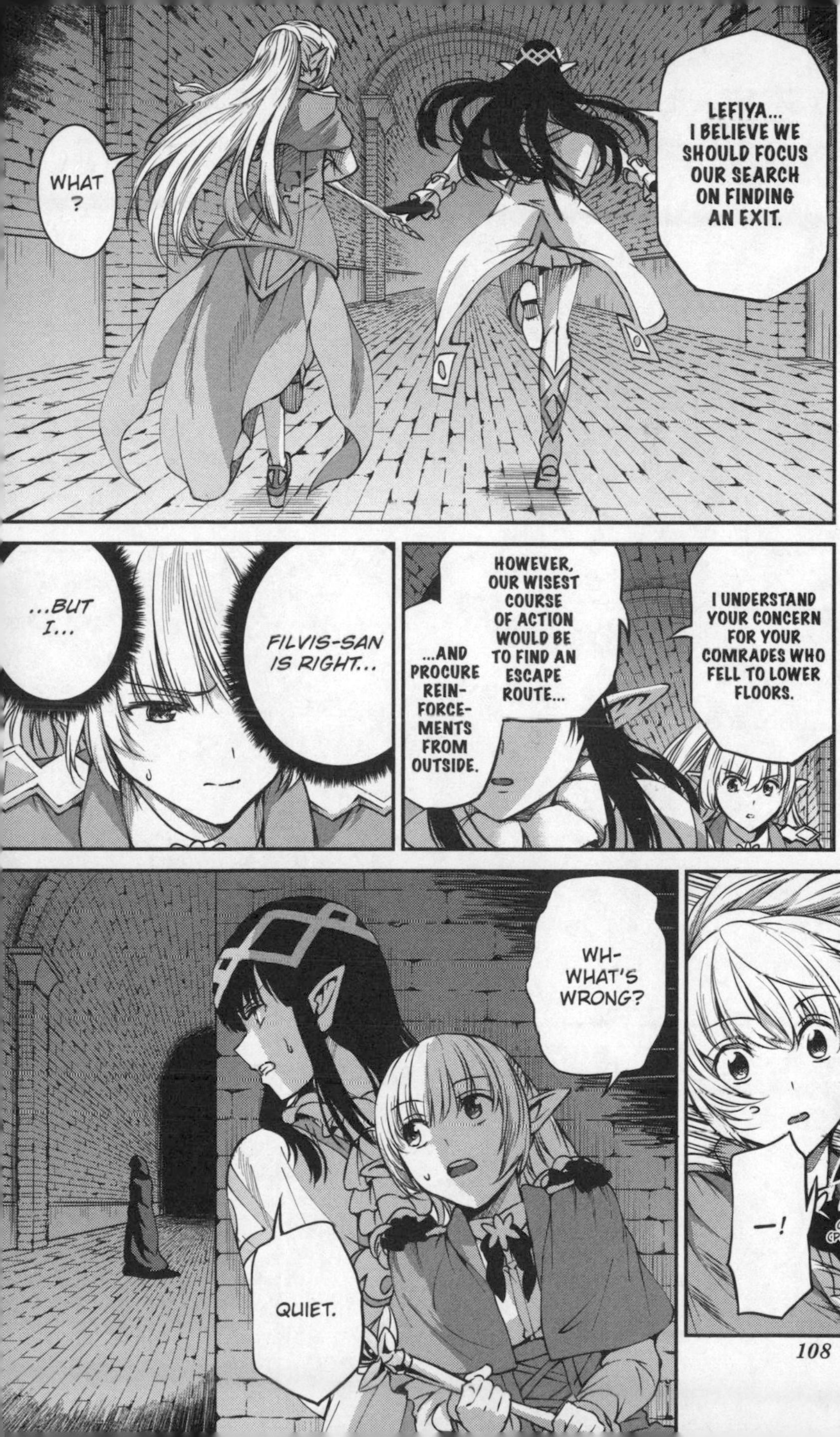
LEFIYA... I BELIEVE WE SHOULD FOCUS OUR SEARCH ON FINDING AN EXIT.
WHAT?
I UNDERSTAND YOUR CONCERN FOR YOUR COMRADES WHO FELL TO LOWER FLOORS.
HOWEVER, OUR WISEST COURSE OF ACTION WOULD BE TO FIND AN ESCAPE ROUTE...
...AND PROCURE REIN-FORCE-MENTS FROM OUTSIDE.
FILVIS-SAN IS RIGHT...
...BUT I...
GUI (PULL)
—!
WH-WHAT'S WRONG?
QUIET.

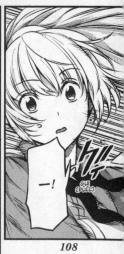

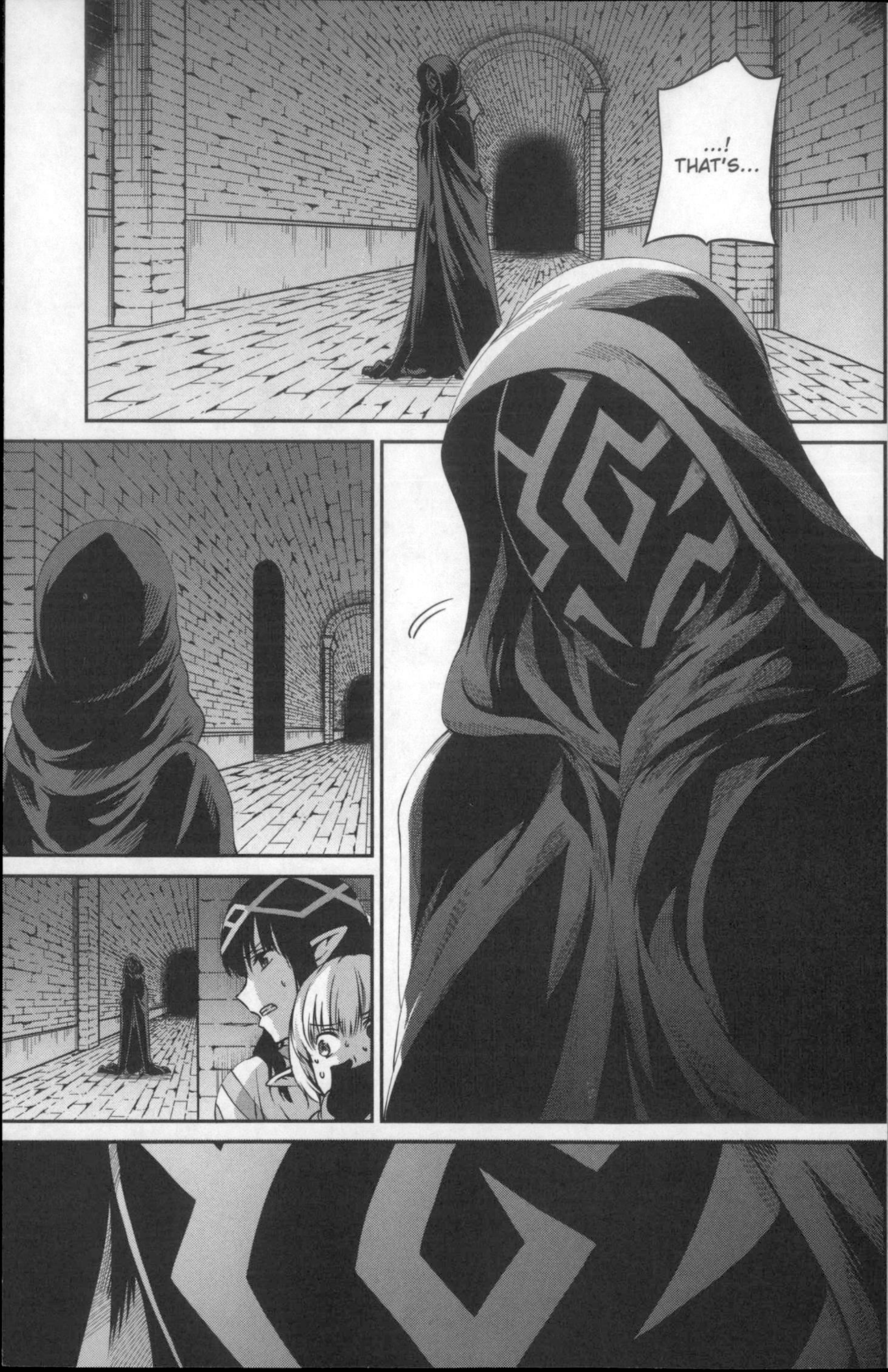
...! THAT'S...

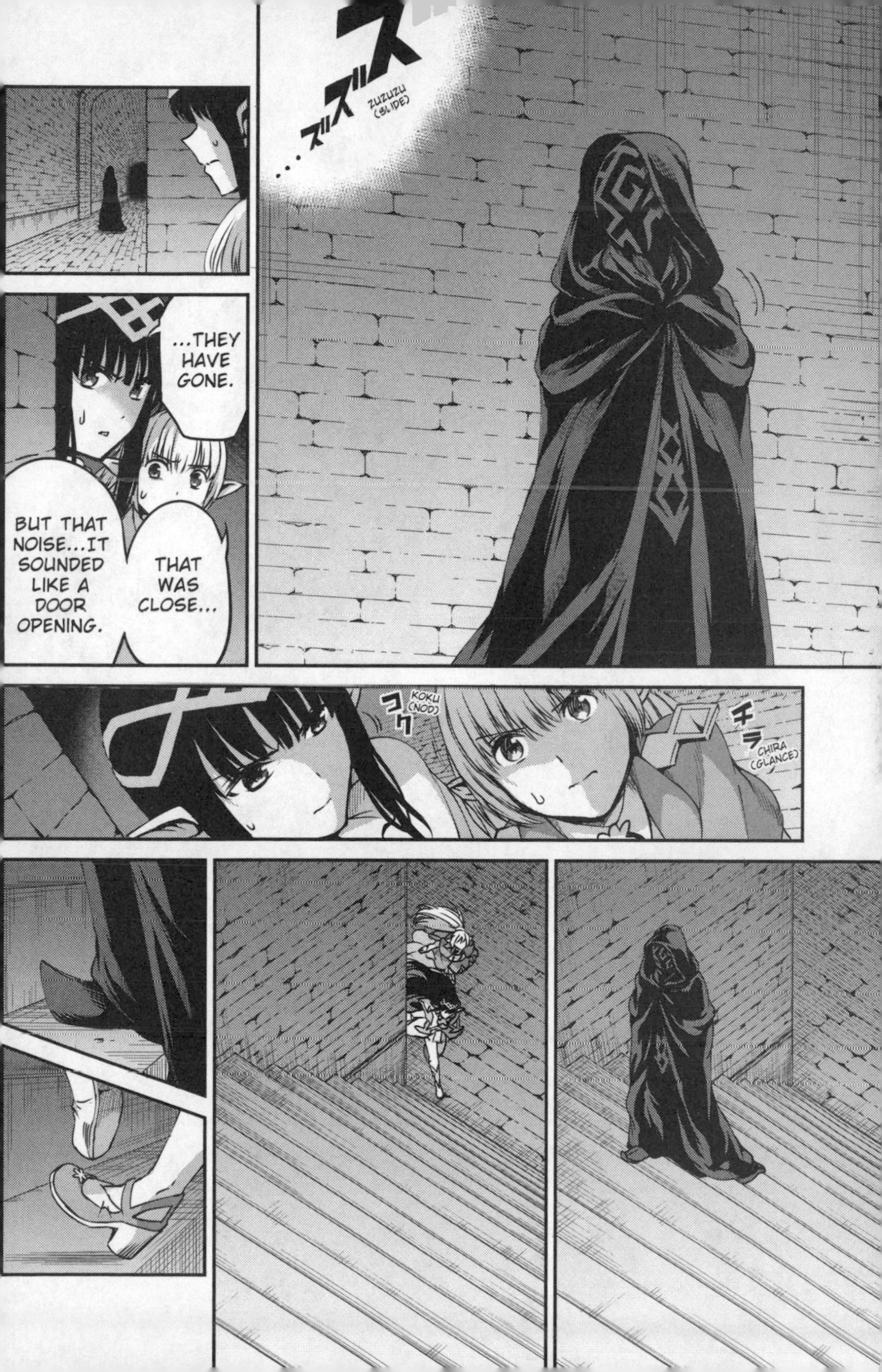
...ズズズ
ZUZUZU (SLIDE)
...THEY HAVE GONE.
THAT WAS CLOSE...
BUT THAT NOISE...IT SOUNDED LIKE A DOOR OPENING.
チラ
CHIRA (GLANCE)
コク
KOKU (NOD)

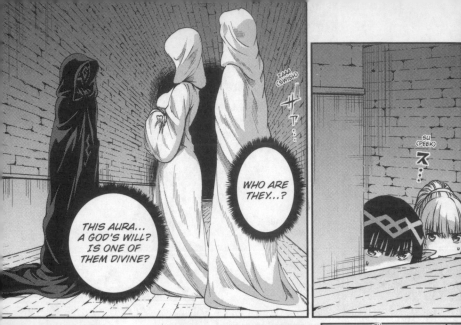

ZAAA
(SWISH)

WHO ARE THEY...?

THIS AURA... A GOD'S WILL? IS ONE OF THEM DIVINE?

SU
(PEEK)

WHERE DO YOU THINK THEY'RE OFF TO?

I DO NOT KNOW. HOW- EVER...

KURL
(WHIRL)

ZAAAA

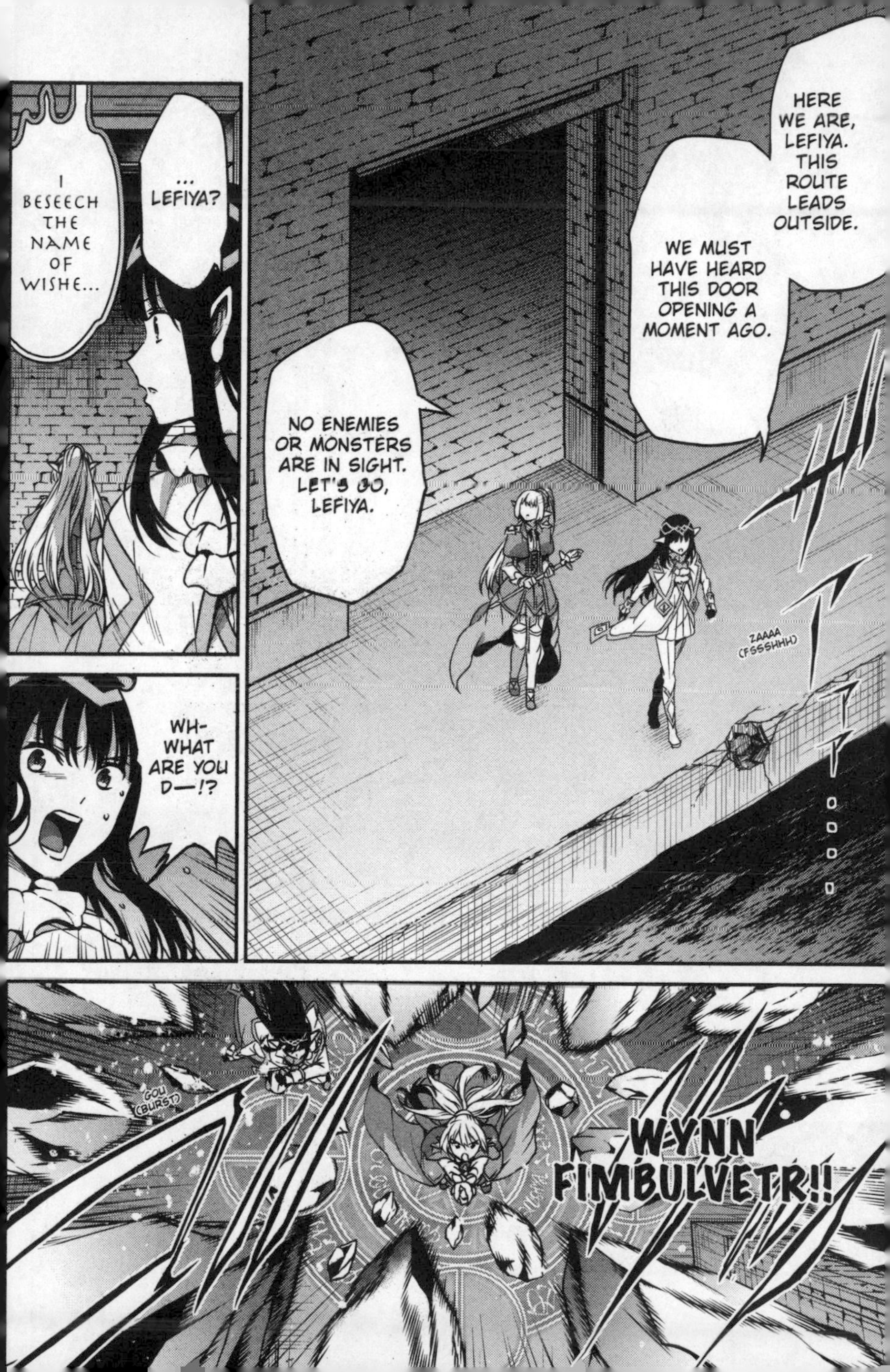
HERE WE ARE, LEFIYA. THIS ROUTE LEADS OUTSIDE.
WE MUST HAVE HEARD THIS DOOR OPENING A MOMENT AGO.
NO ENEMIES OR MONSTERS ARE IN SIGHT. LET'S GO, LEFIYA.
ZAAAA (FSSSHHH)
...LEFIYA?
I BESEECH THE NAME OF WISHE...
WH-WHAT ARE YOU D—!?
GOU (BURST)
WYNN FIMBULVETR!!

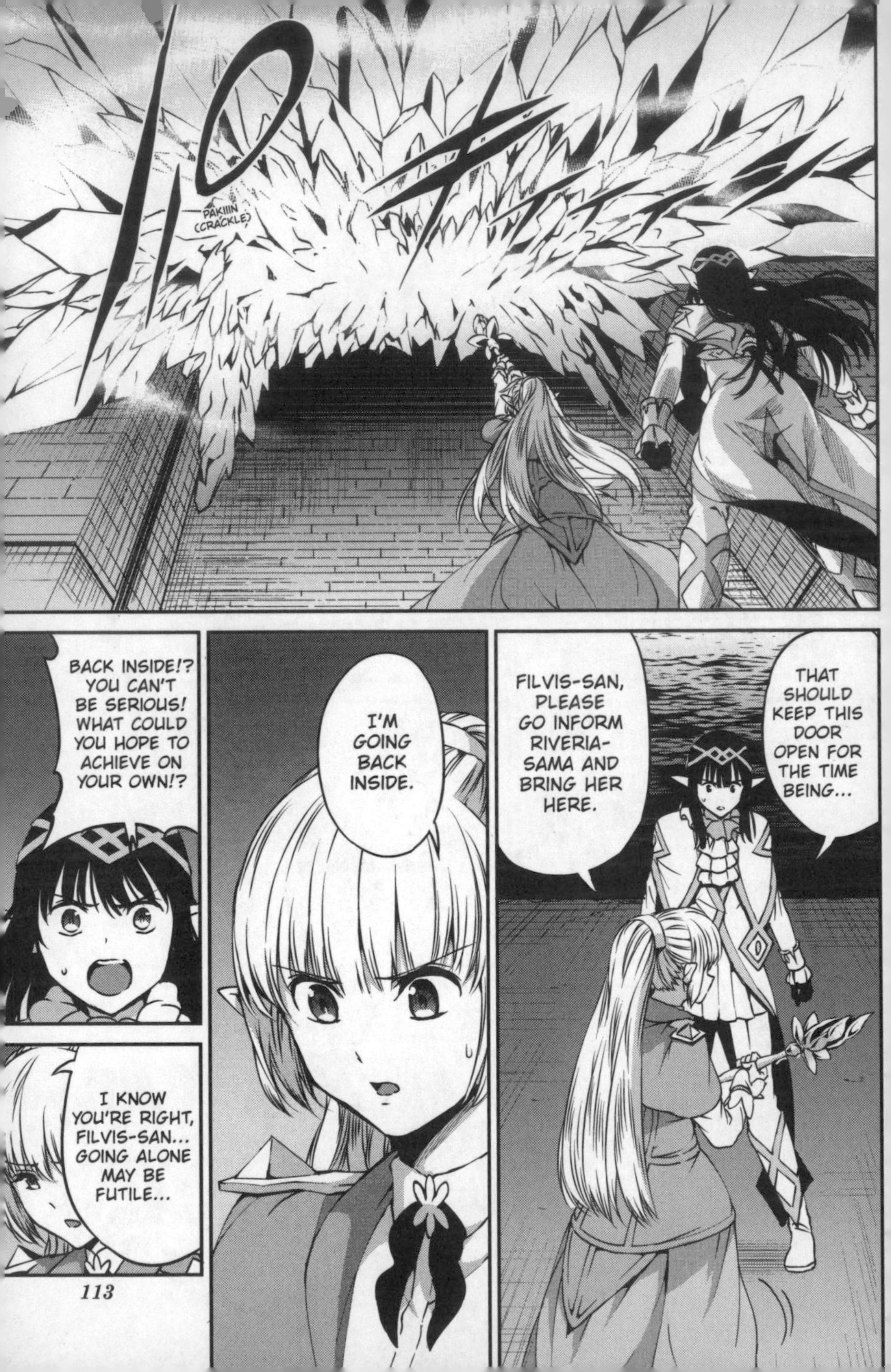
PAKIIIN (CRACKLE)
THAT SHOULD KEEP THIS DOOR OPEN FOR THE TIME BEING...
FILVIS-SAN, PLEASE GO INFORM RIVERIA-SAMA AND BRING HER HERE.
I'M GOING BACK INSIDE.
BACK INSIDE!? YOU CAN'T BE SERIOUS! WHAT COULD YOU HOPE TO ACHIEVE ON YOUR OWN!?
I KNOW YOU'RE RIGHT, FILVIS-SAN... GOING ALONE MAY BE FUTILE...

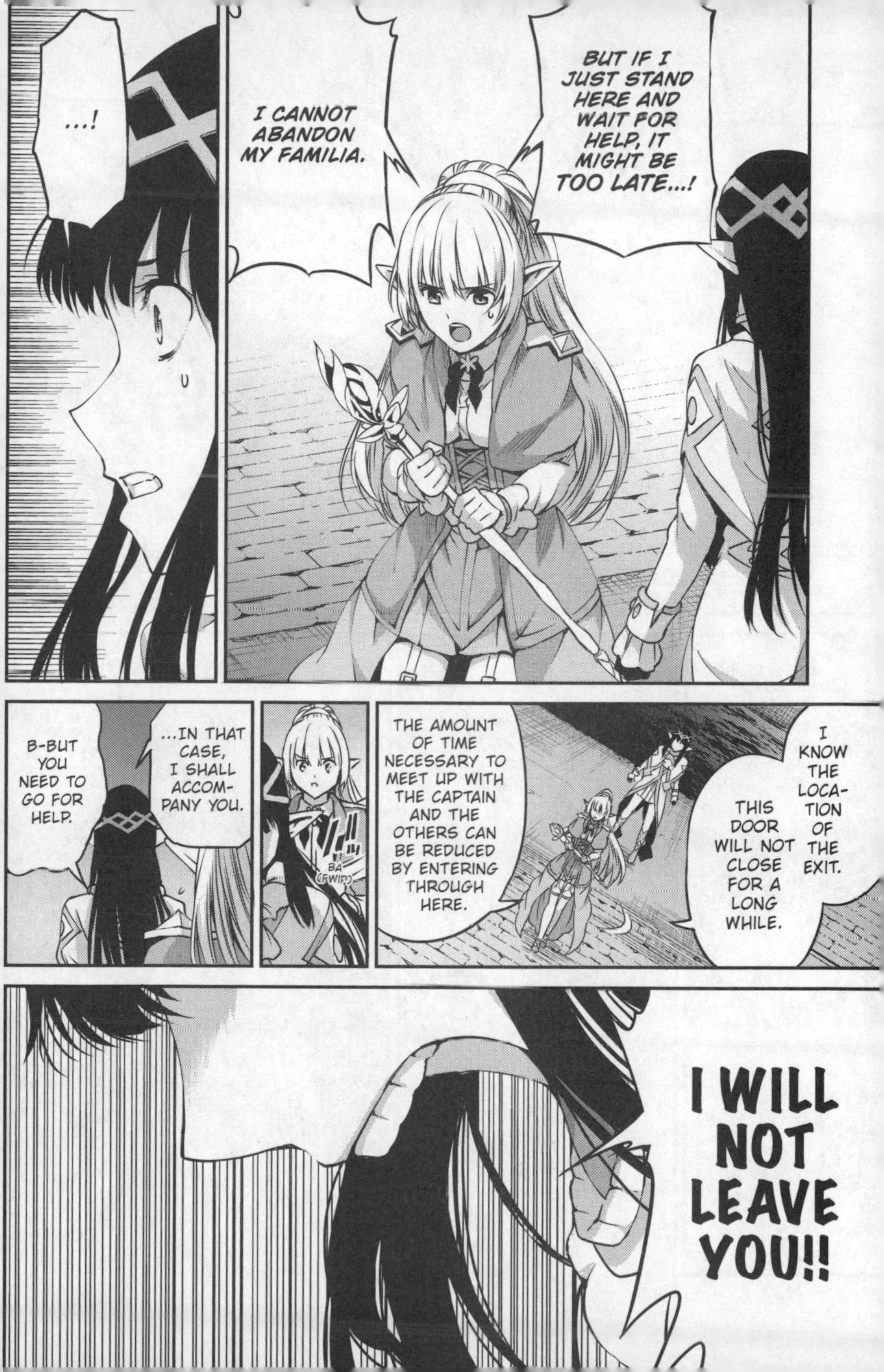

I CANNOT ABANDON MY FAMILIA.
BUT IF I JUST STAND HERE AND WAIT FOR HELP, IT MIGHT BE TOO LATE...!
...!
I KNOW THE LOCATION OF THE EXIT.
THIS DOOR WILL NOT CLOSE FOR A LONG WHILE.
THE AMOUNT OF TIME NECESSARY TO MEET UP WITH THE CAPTAIN AND THE OTHERS CAN BE REDUCED BY ENTERING THROUGH HERE.
BA (FWIP)
...IN THAT CASE, I SHALL ACCOMPANY YOU.
B-BUT YOU NEED TO GO FOR HELP.
I WILL NOT LEAVE YOU!!

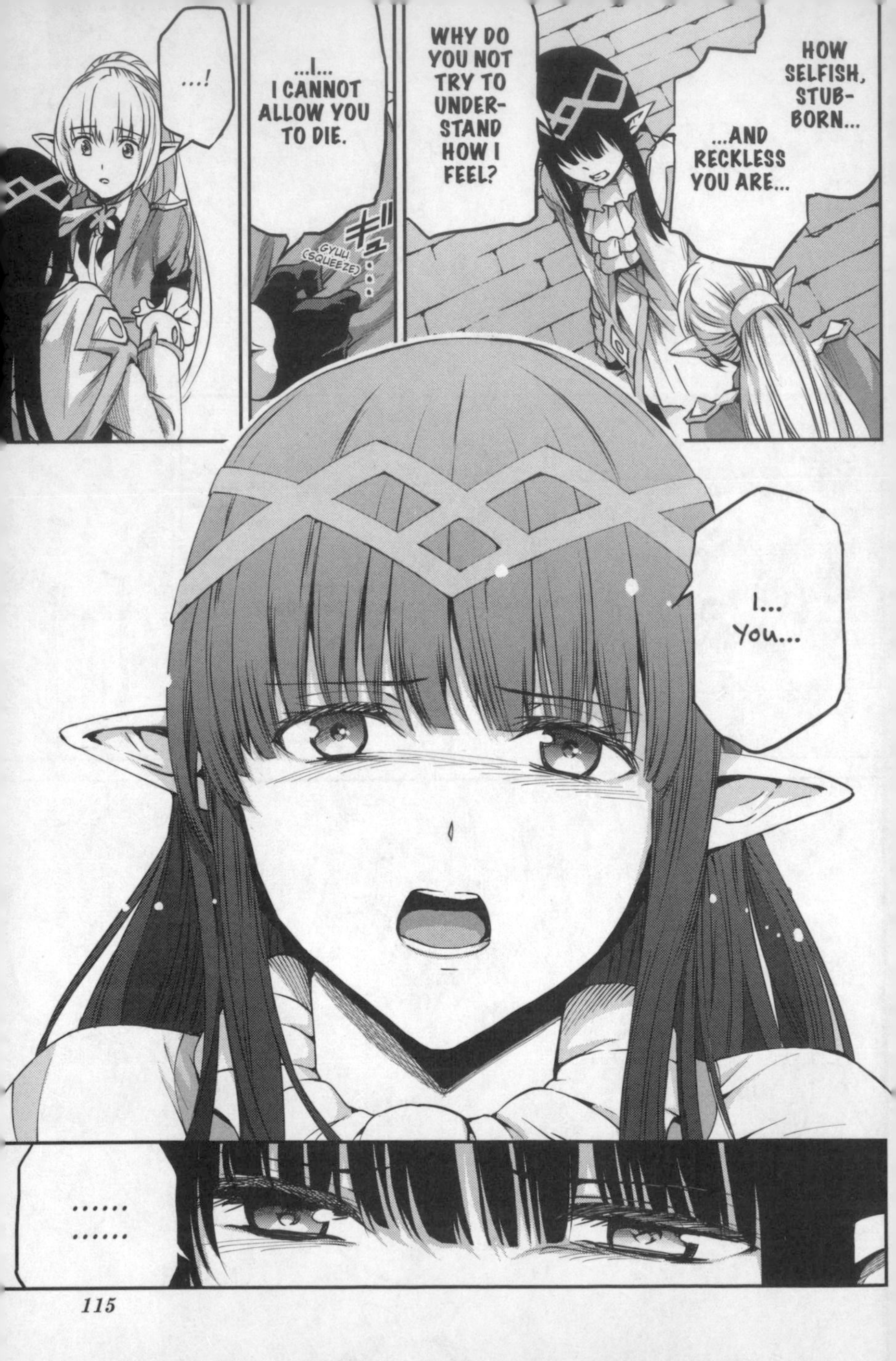
HOW SELFISH, STUB-BORN...
...AND RECKLESS YOU ARE...
WHY DO YOU NOT TRY TO UNDER-STAND HOW I FEEL?
...I... I CANNOT ALLOW YOU TO DIE.
GYUU (SQUEEZE)
...!
I... You...
......
......

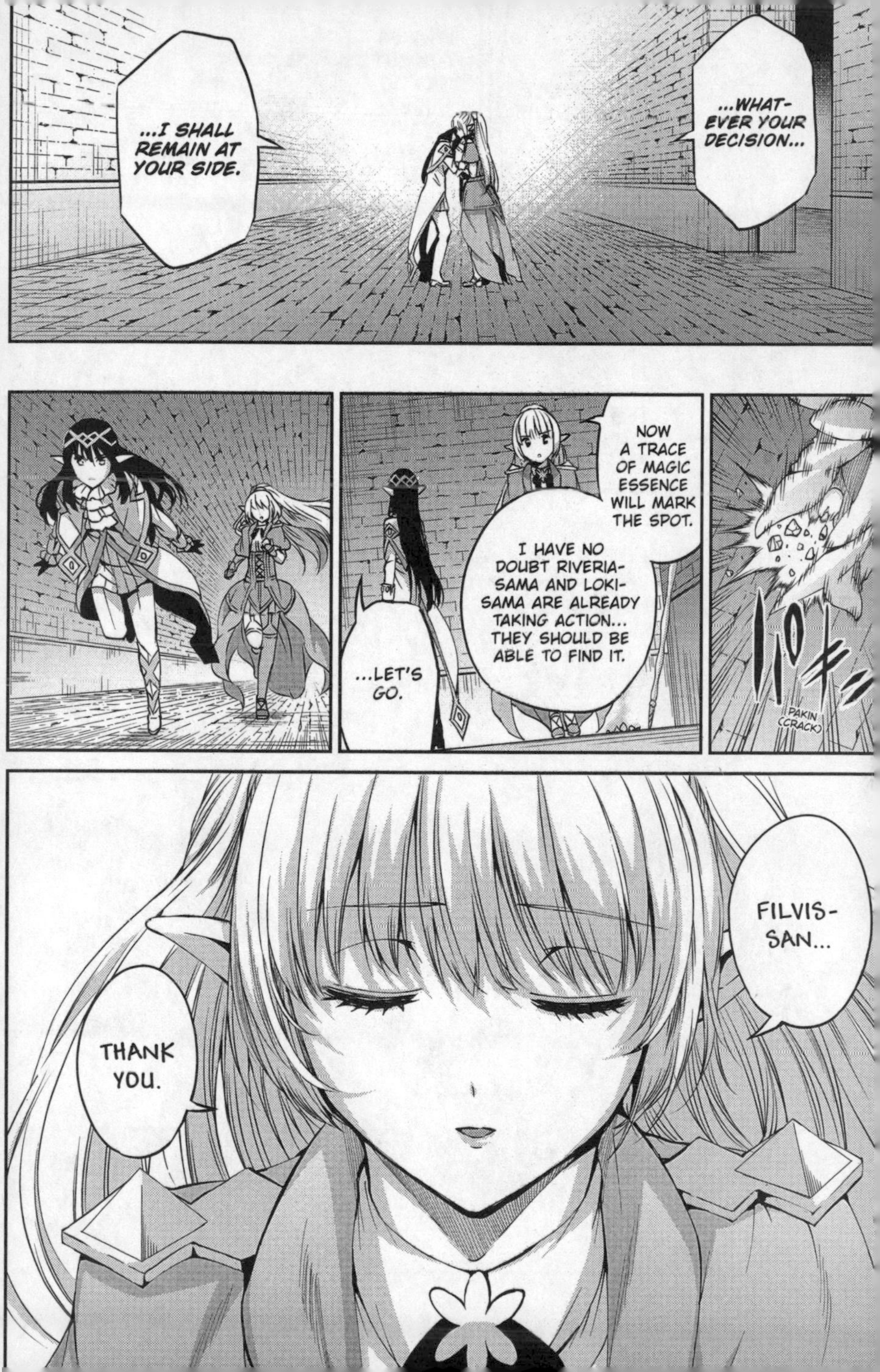
...WHAT-EVER YOUR DECISION...
...I SHALL REMAIN AT YOUR SIDE.
PAKIN (CRACK)
NOW A TRACE OF MAGIC ESSENCE WILL MARK THE SPOT.
I HAVE NO DOUBT RIVERIA-SAMA AND LOKI-SAMA ARE ALREADY TAKING ACTION... THEY SHOULD BE ABLE TO FIND IT.
...LET'S GO.
FILVIS-SAN...
THANK YOU.

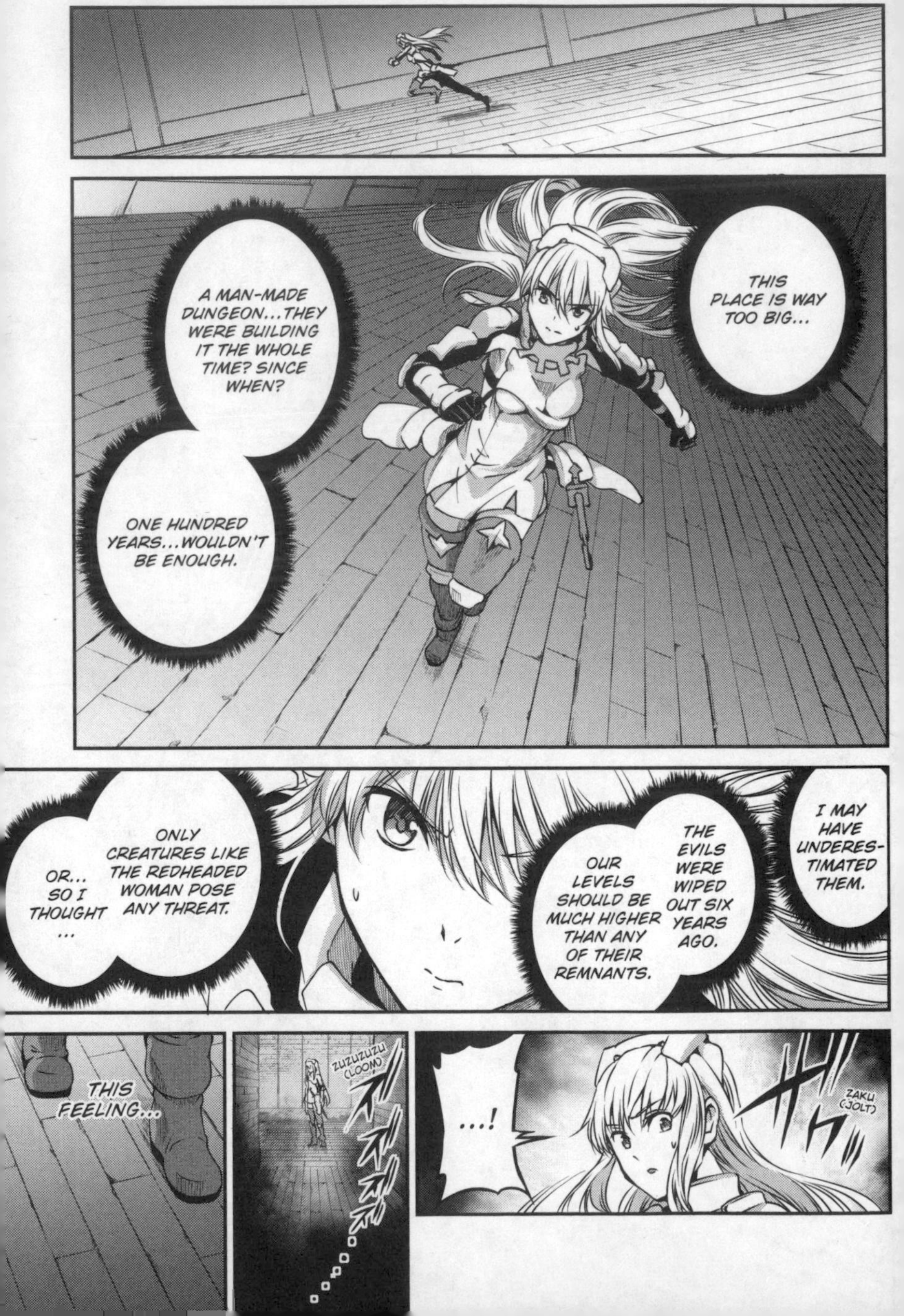
THIS PLACE IS WAY TOO BIG...
A MAN-MADE DUNGEON...THEY WERE BUILDING IT THE WHOLE TIME? SINCE WHEN?
ONE HUNDRED YEARS...WOULDN'T BE ENOUGH.
I MAY HAVE UNDERES-TIMATED THEM.
THE EVILS WERE WIPED OUT SIX YEARS AGO.
OUR LEVELS SHOULD BE MUCH HIGHER THAN ANY OF THEIR REMNANTS.
ONLY CREATURES LIKE THE REDHEADED WOMAN POSE ANY THREAT.
OR... SO I THOUGHT ...
ZAKU (JOLT)
...!
ZUZUZUZU (LOOM)
THIS FEELING...

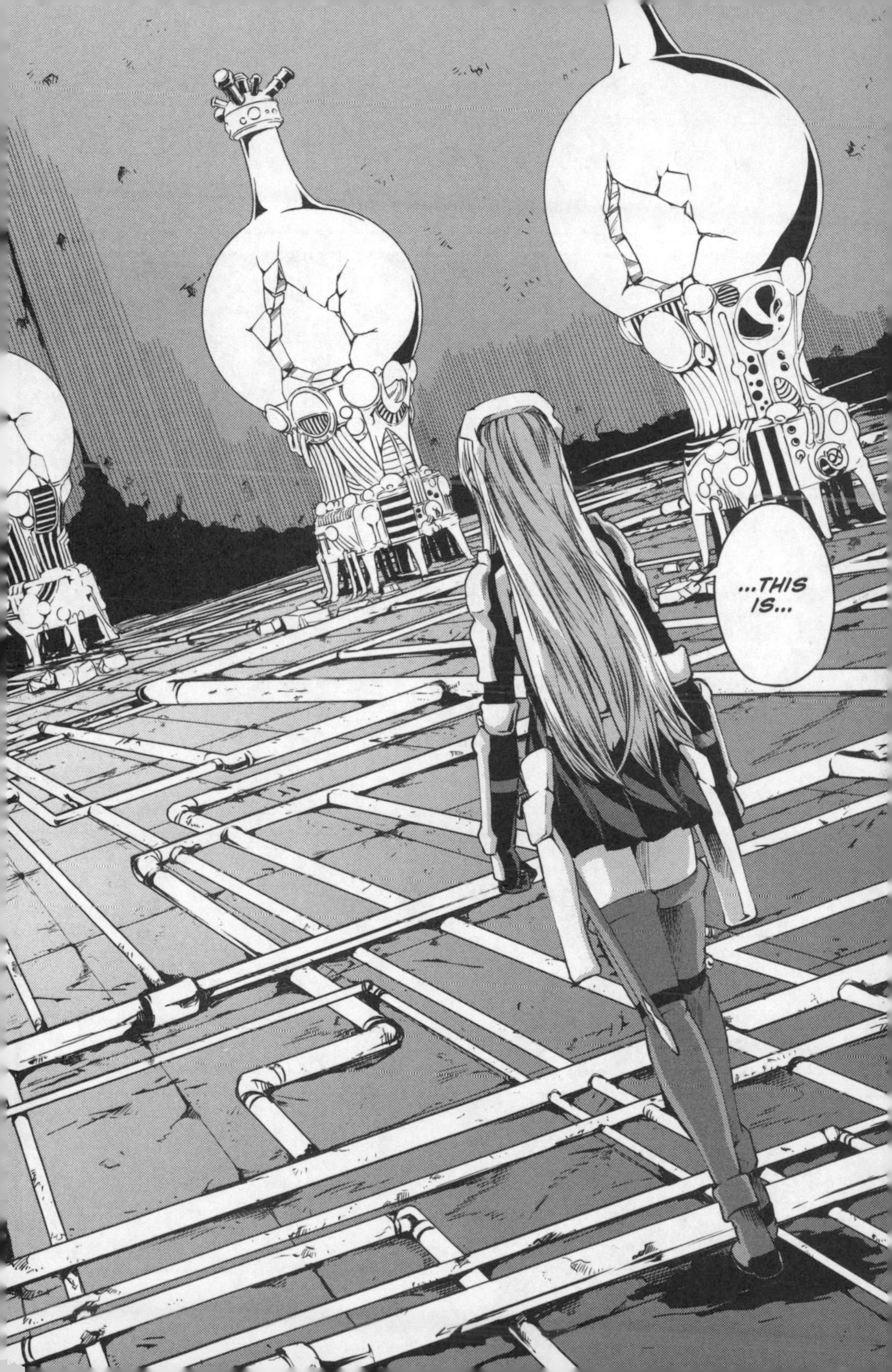
...THIS IS...

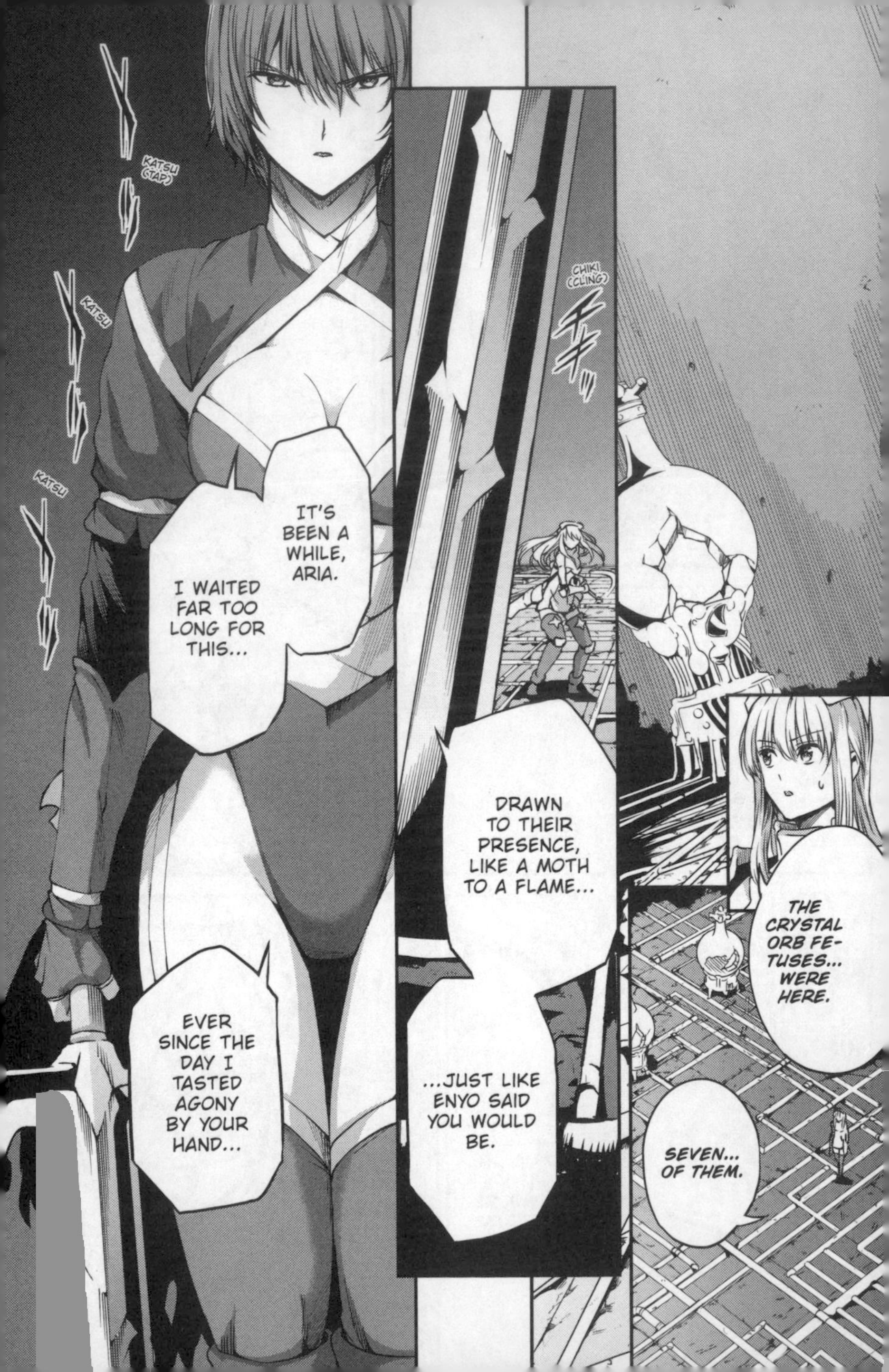
THE CRYSTAL ORB FE-TUSES... WERE HERE.
SEVEN... OF THEM.
CHIKI (CLING)
DRAWN TO THEIR PRESENCE, LIKE A MOTH TO A FLAME...
...JUST LIKE ENYO SAID YOU WOULD BE.
KATSU (TAP)
KATSU
KATSU
IT'S BEEN A WHILE, ARIA.
I WAITED FAR TOO LONG FOR THIS...
EVER SINCE THE DAY I TASTED AGONY BY YOUR HAND...

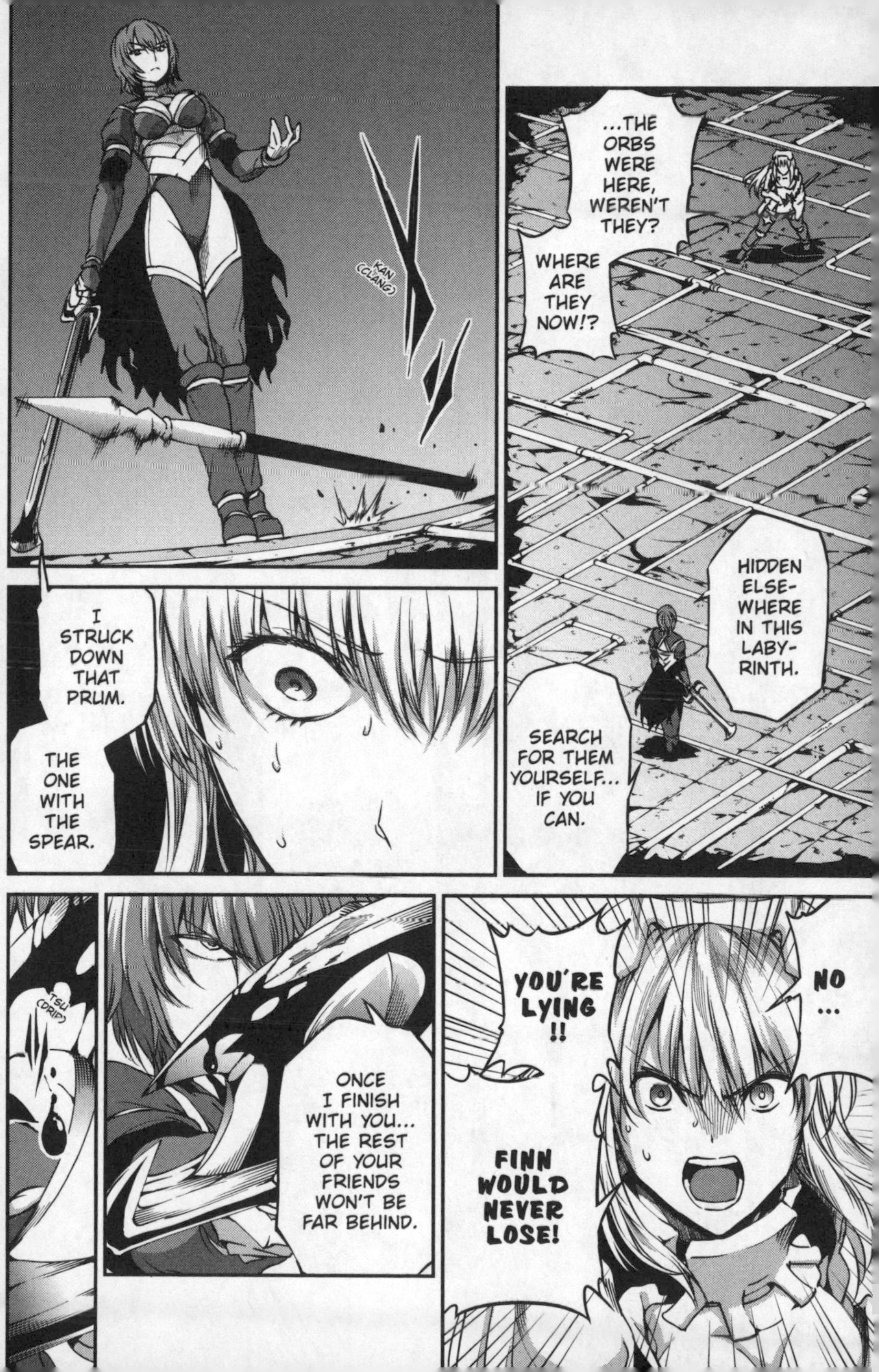
...THE ORBS WERE HERE, WEREN'T THEY?
WHERE ARE THEY NOW!?
HIDDEN ELSEWHERE IN THIS LABYRINTH.
SEARCH FOR THEM YOURSELF... IF YOU CAN.
KAN (CLANG)
I STRUCK DOWN THAT PRUM.
THE ONE WITH THE SPEAR.
NO...
YOU'RE LYING!!
FINN WOULD NEVER LOSE!
ONCE I FINISH WITH YOU... THE REST OF YOUR FRIENDS WON'T BE FAR BEHIND.
TSU (DRIP)

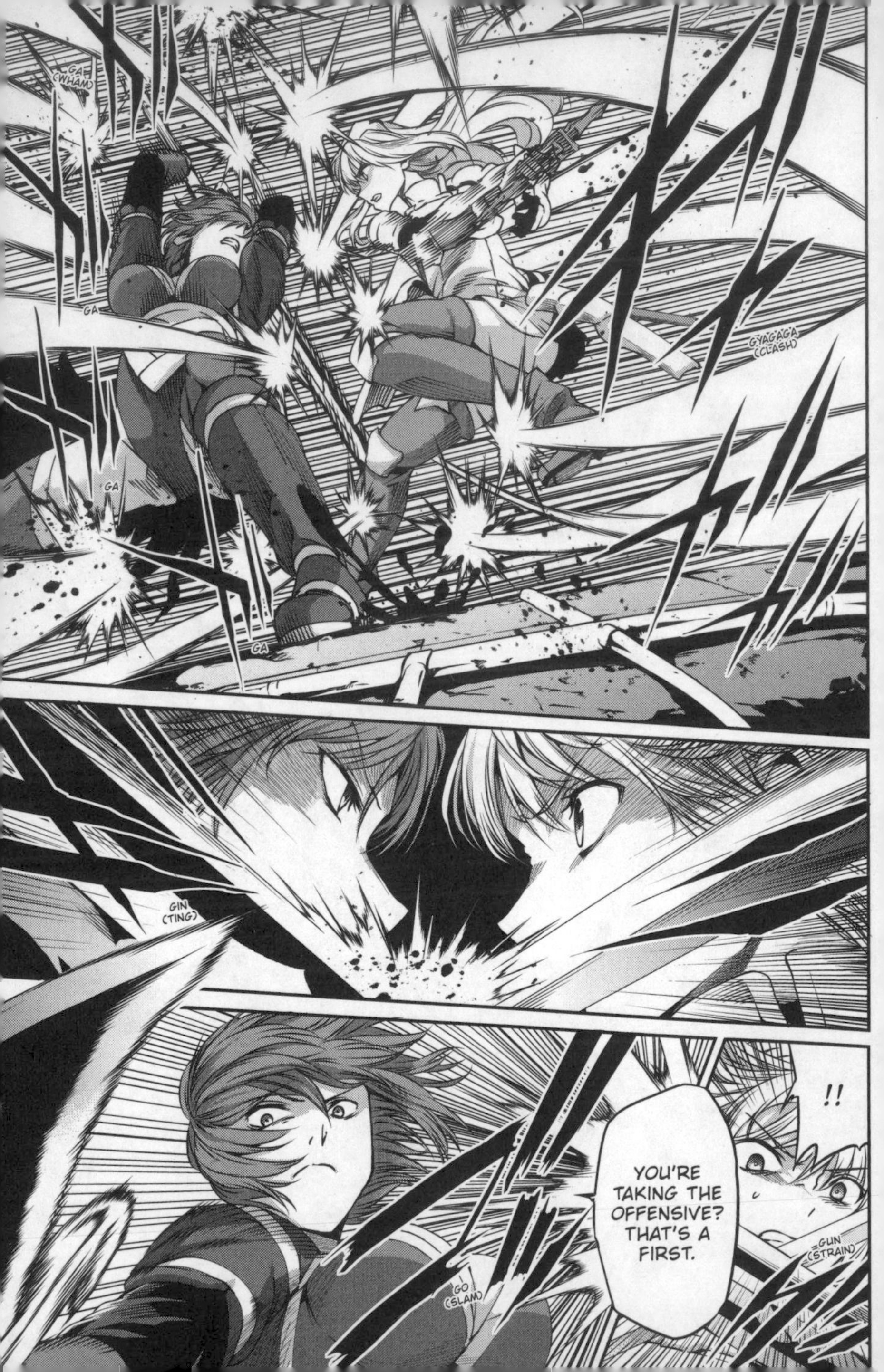
GA (WHAM)
GYAGAGA (CLASH)
GA
GA
GA
GIN (TING)
!!
GUN (STRAIN)
YOU'RE TAKING THE OFFENSIVE? THAT'S A FIRST.
GO (SLAM)

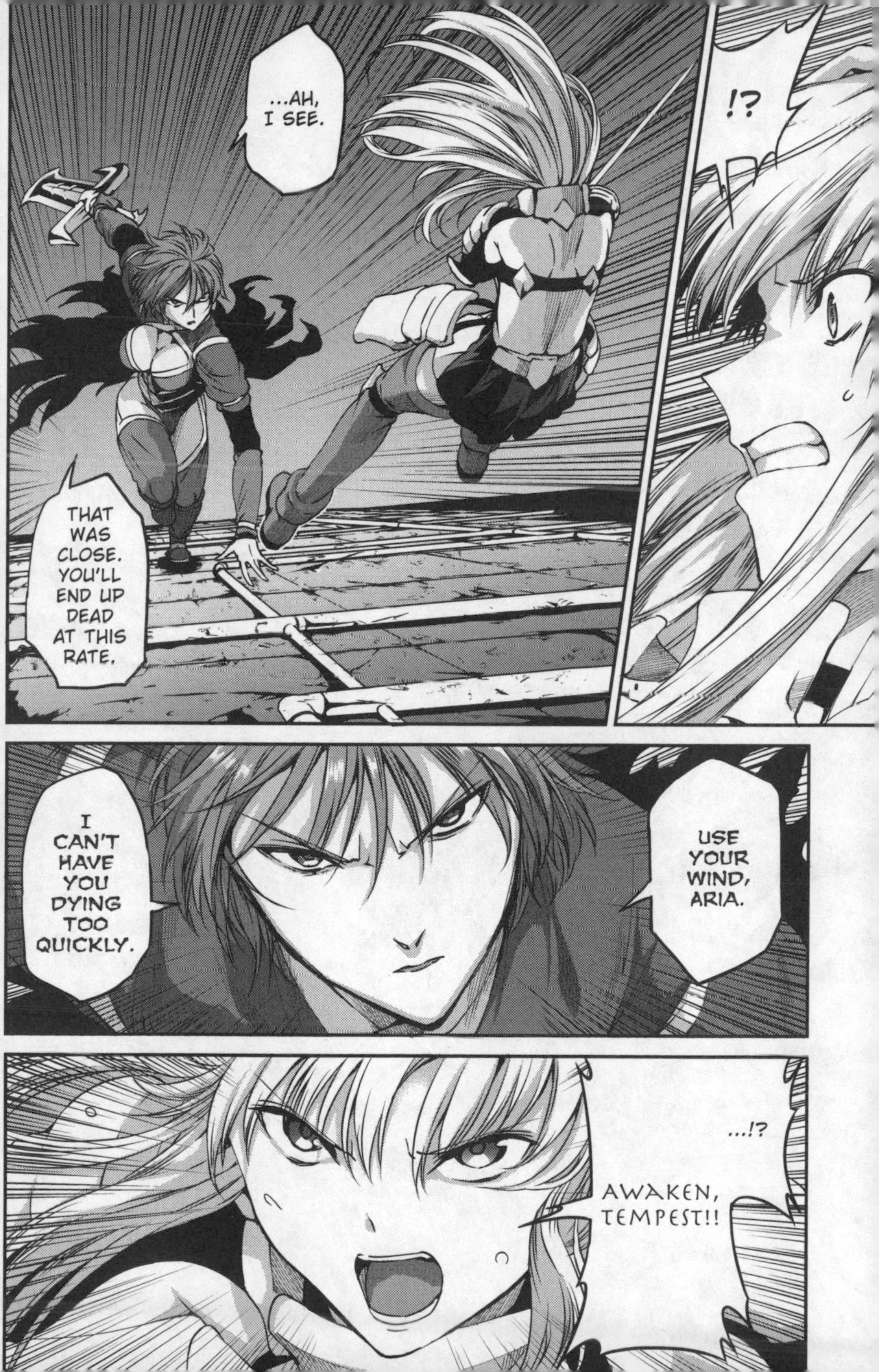
!?
...AH, I SEE.
THAT WAS CLOSE. YOU'LL END UP DEAD AT THIS RATE.
USE YOUR WIND, ARIA.
I CAN'T HAVE YOU DYING TOO QUICKLY.
...!?
AWAKEN, TEMPEST!!

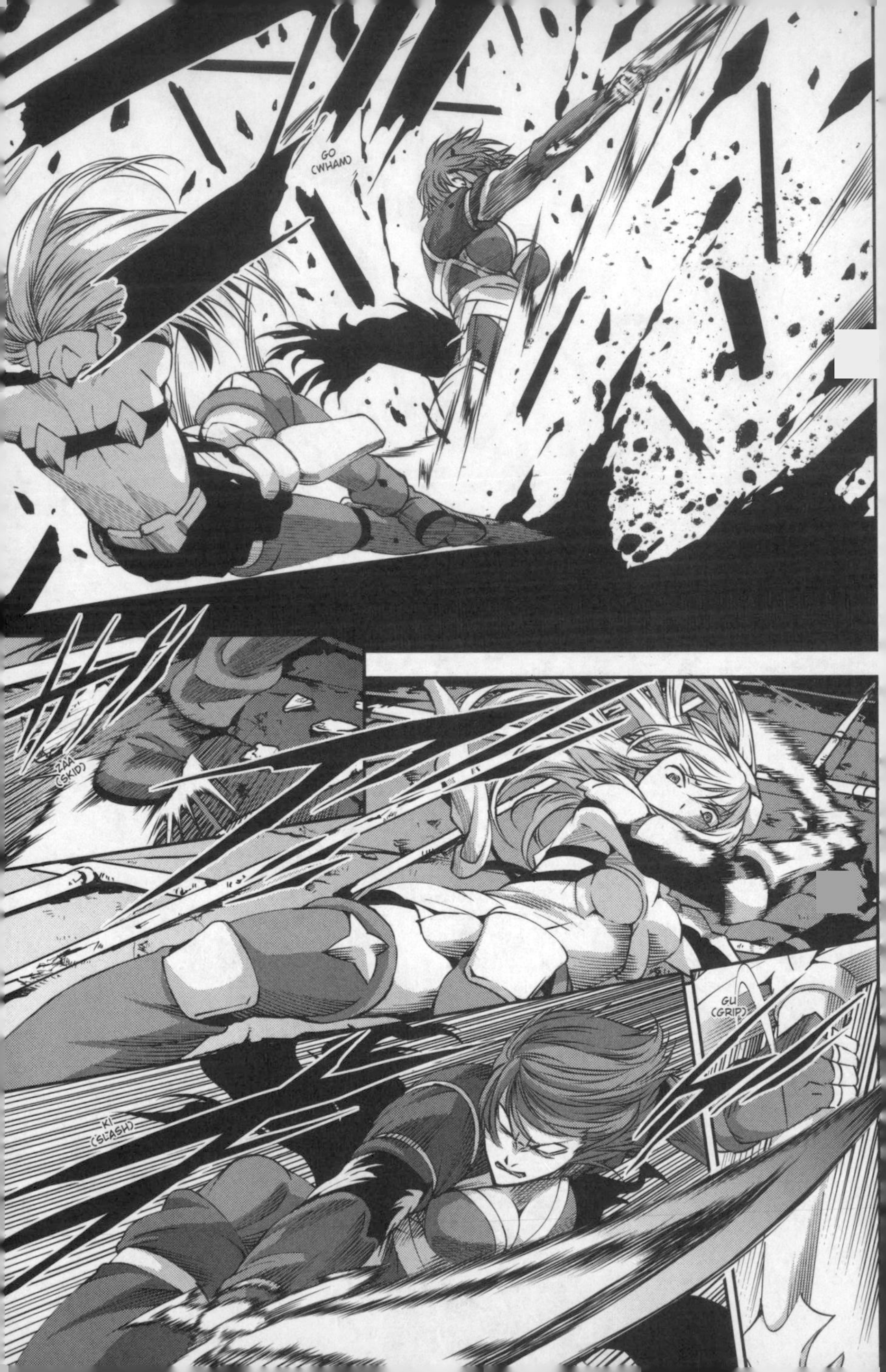
GO
(WHAM)
ZAA
(SKID)
GU
(GRIP)
KI
(SLASH)

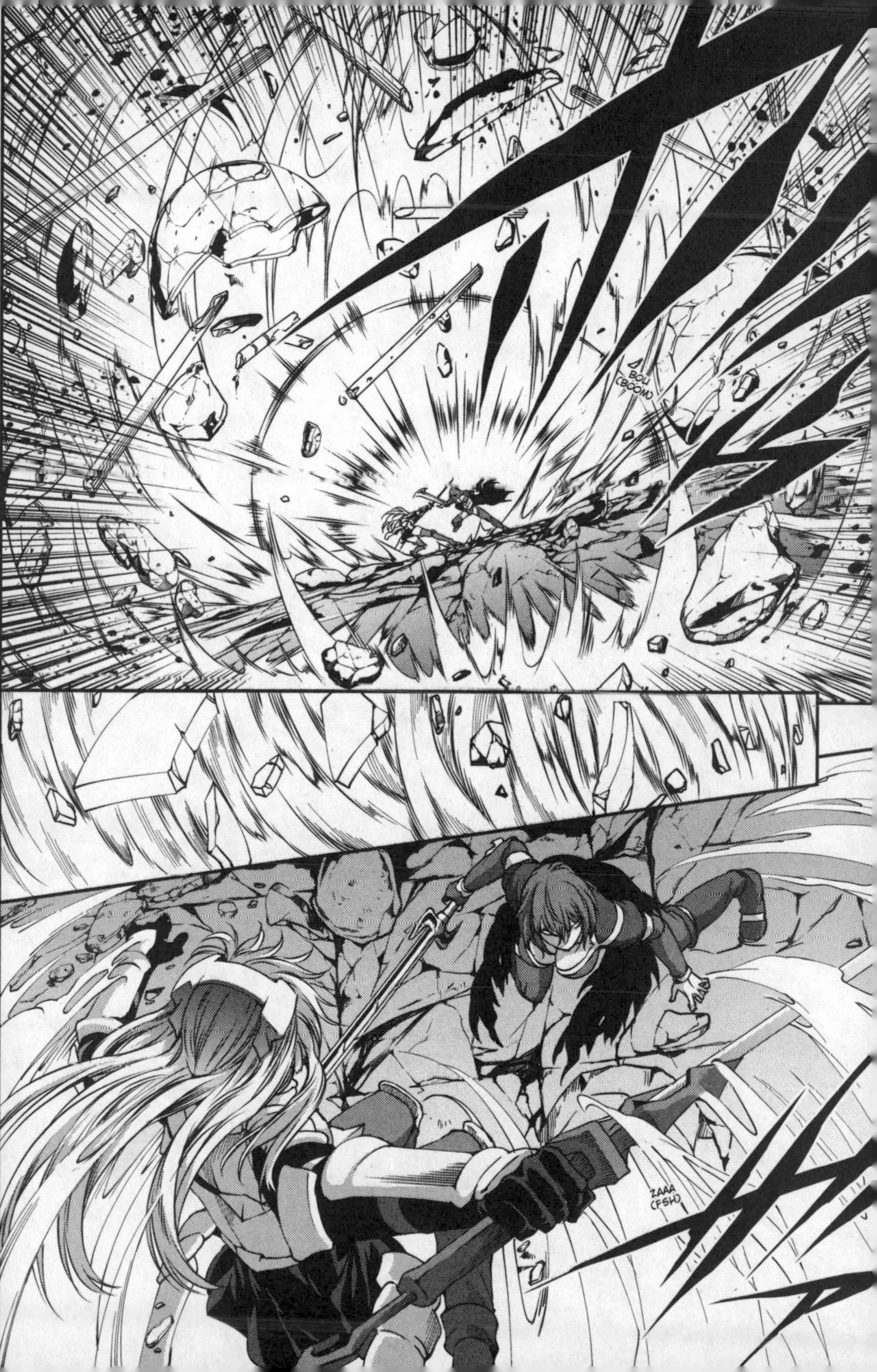
BOU
(BOOM)
ZAAA
(FSH)

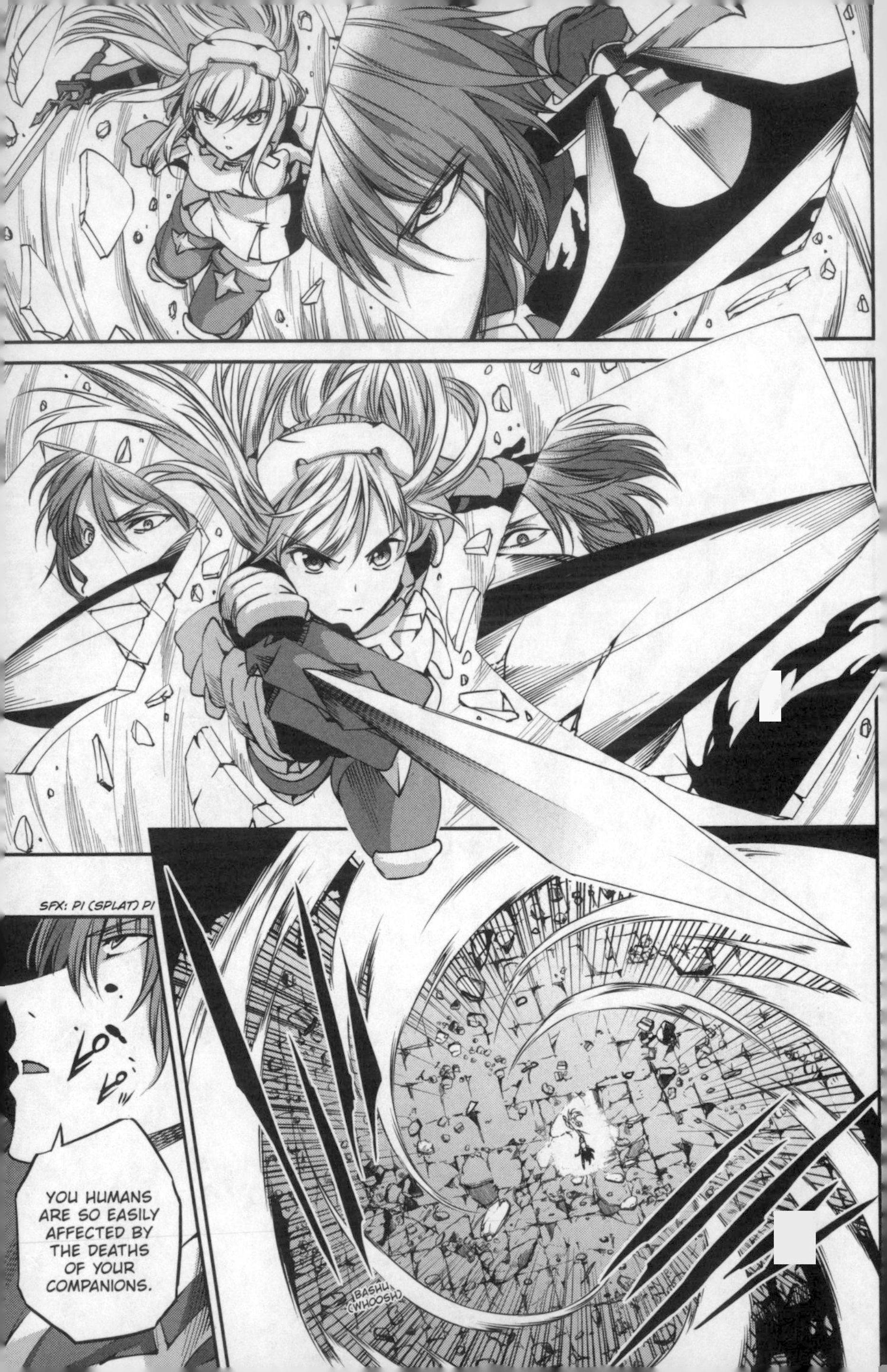
BASHU (WHOOSH)
SFX: PI (SPLAT) PI
YOU HUMANS ARE SO EASILY AFFECTED BY THE DEATHS OF YOUR COMPANIONS.

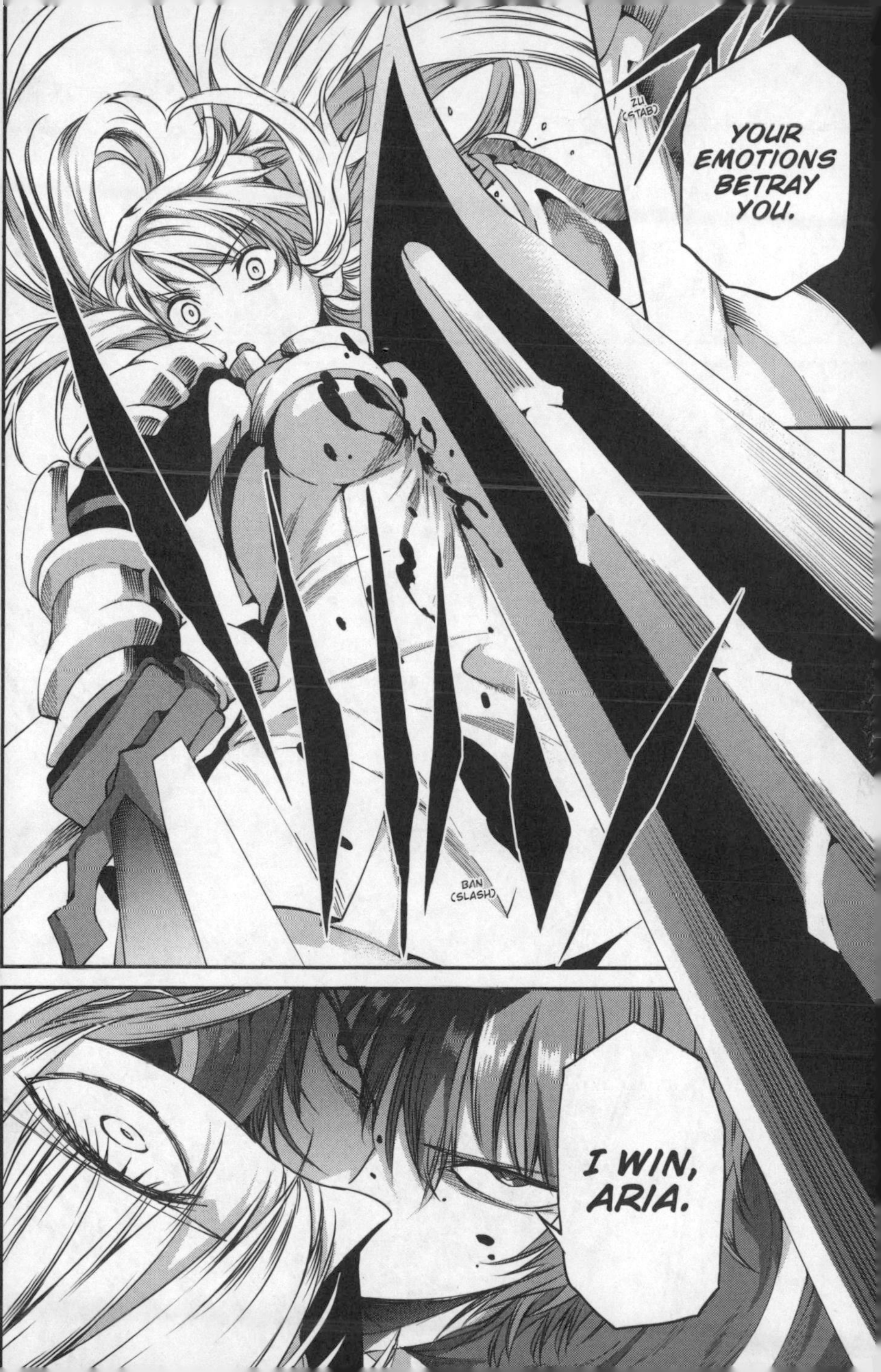
ZU (STAB)
YOUR EMOTIONS BETRAY YOU.
BAN (SLASH)
I WIN, ARIA.

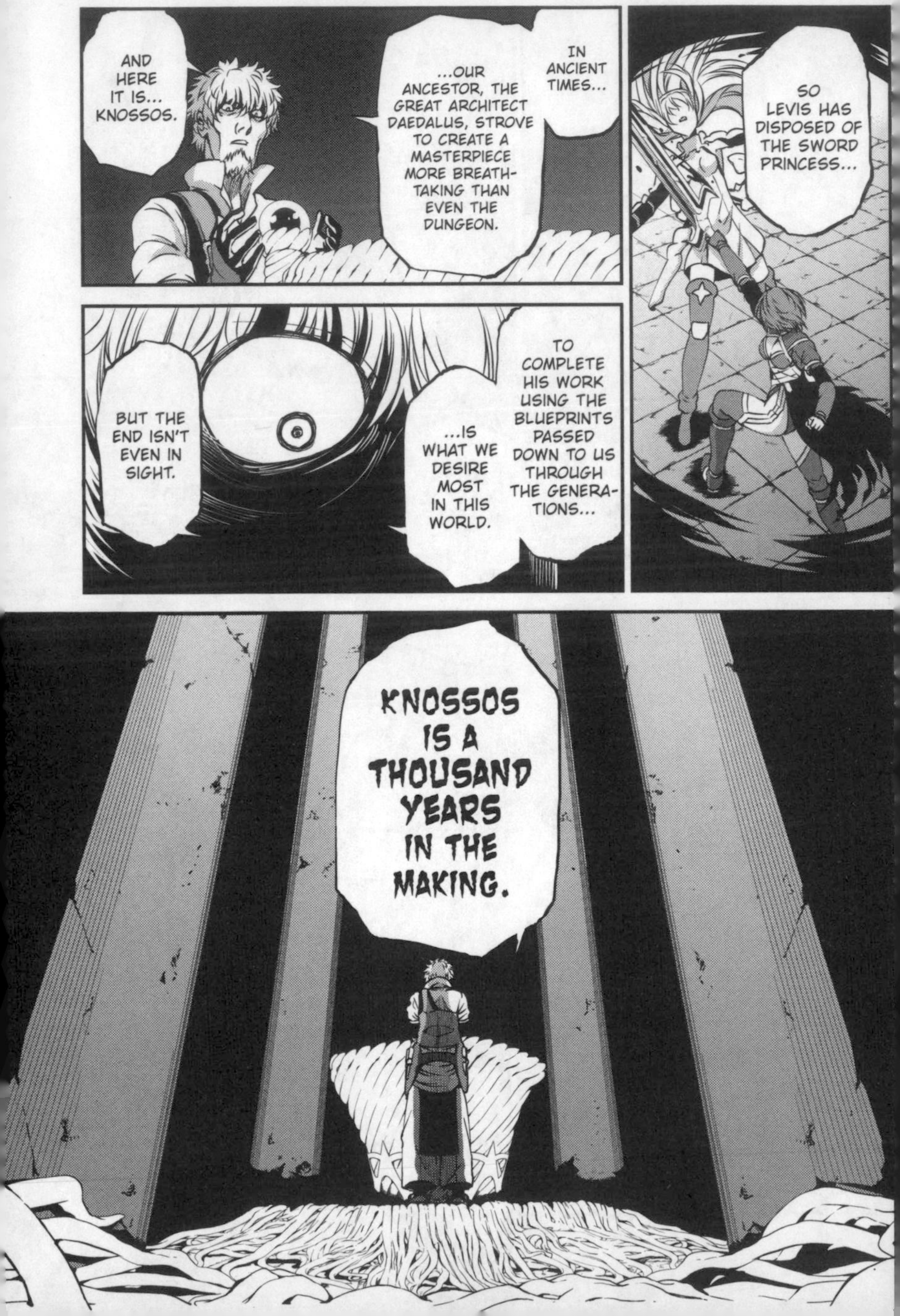
SO LEVIS HAS DISPOSED OF THE SWORD PRINCESS...
IN ANCIENT TIMES...
...OUR ANCESTOR, THE GREAT ARCHITECT DAEDALUS, STROVE TO CREATE A MASTERPIECE MORE BREATH-TAKING THAN EVEN THE DUNGEON.
AND HERE IT IS... KNOSSOS.
TO COMPLETE HIS WORK USING THE BLUEPRINTS PASSED DOWN TO US THROUGH THE GENERA-TIONS...
...IS WHAT WE DESIRE MOST IN THIS WORLD.
BUT THE END ISN'T EVEN IN SIGHT.
KNOSSOS IS A THOUSAND YEARS IN THE MAKING.

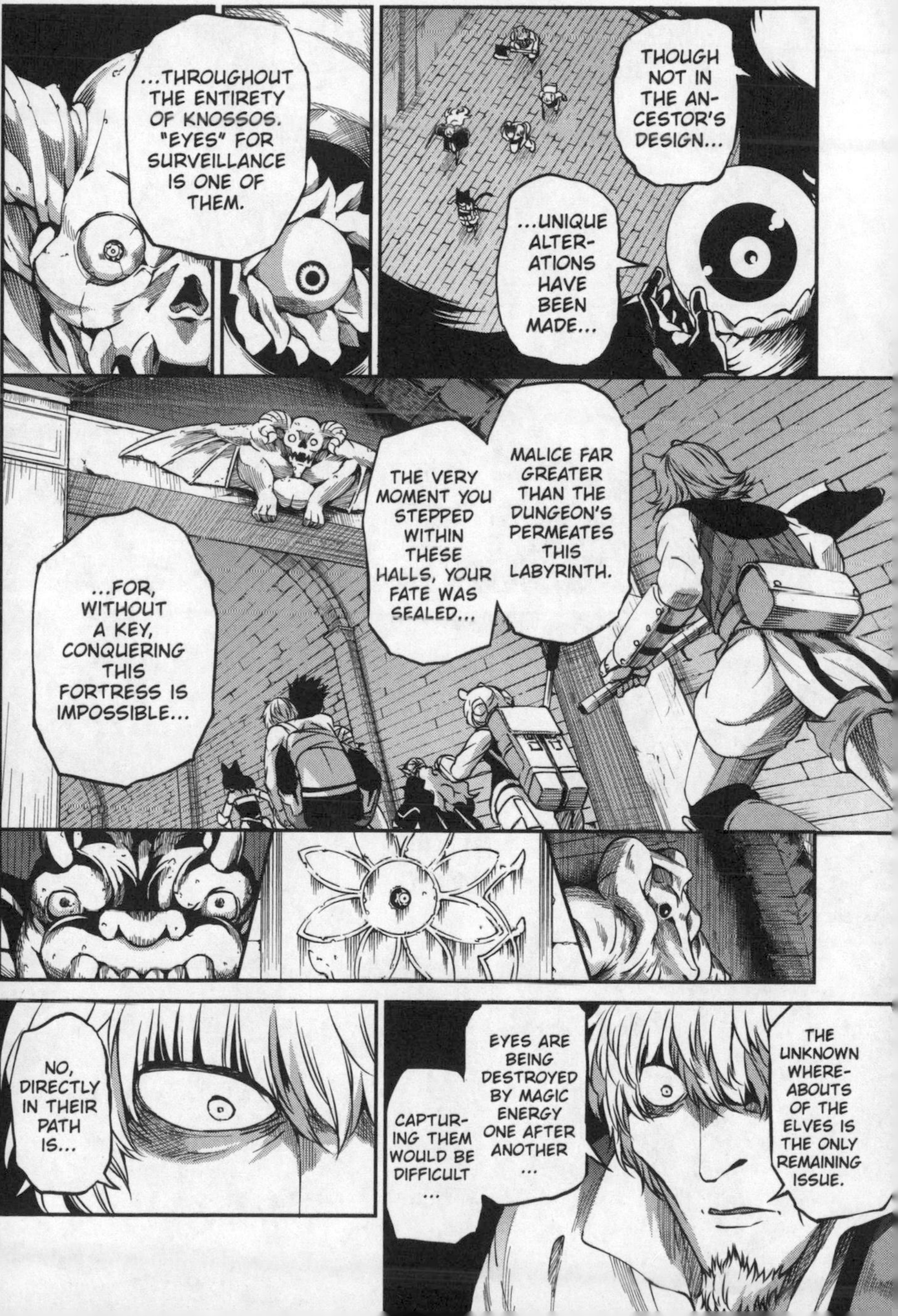
THOUGH NOT IN THE ANCESTOR'S DESIGN...
...UNIQUE ALTERATIONS HAVE BEEN MADE...
...THROUGHOUT THE ENTIRETY OF KNOSSOS. "EYES" FOR SURVEILLANCE IS ONE OF THEM.
MALICE FAR GREATER THAN THE DUNGEON'S PERMEATES THIS LABYRINTH.
THE VERY MOMENT YOU STEPPED WITHIN THESE HALLS, YOUR FATE WAS SEALED...
...FOR, WITHOUT A KEY, CONQUERING THIS FORTRESS IS IMPOSSIBLE...
THE UNKNOWN WHEREABOUTS OF THE ELVES IS THE ONLY REMAINING ISSUE.
EYES ARE BEING DESTROYED BY MAGIC ENERGY ONE AFTER ANOTHER...
CAPTURING THEM WOULD BE DIFFICULT...
NO, DIRECTLY IN THEIR PATH IS...

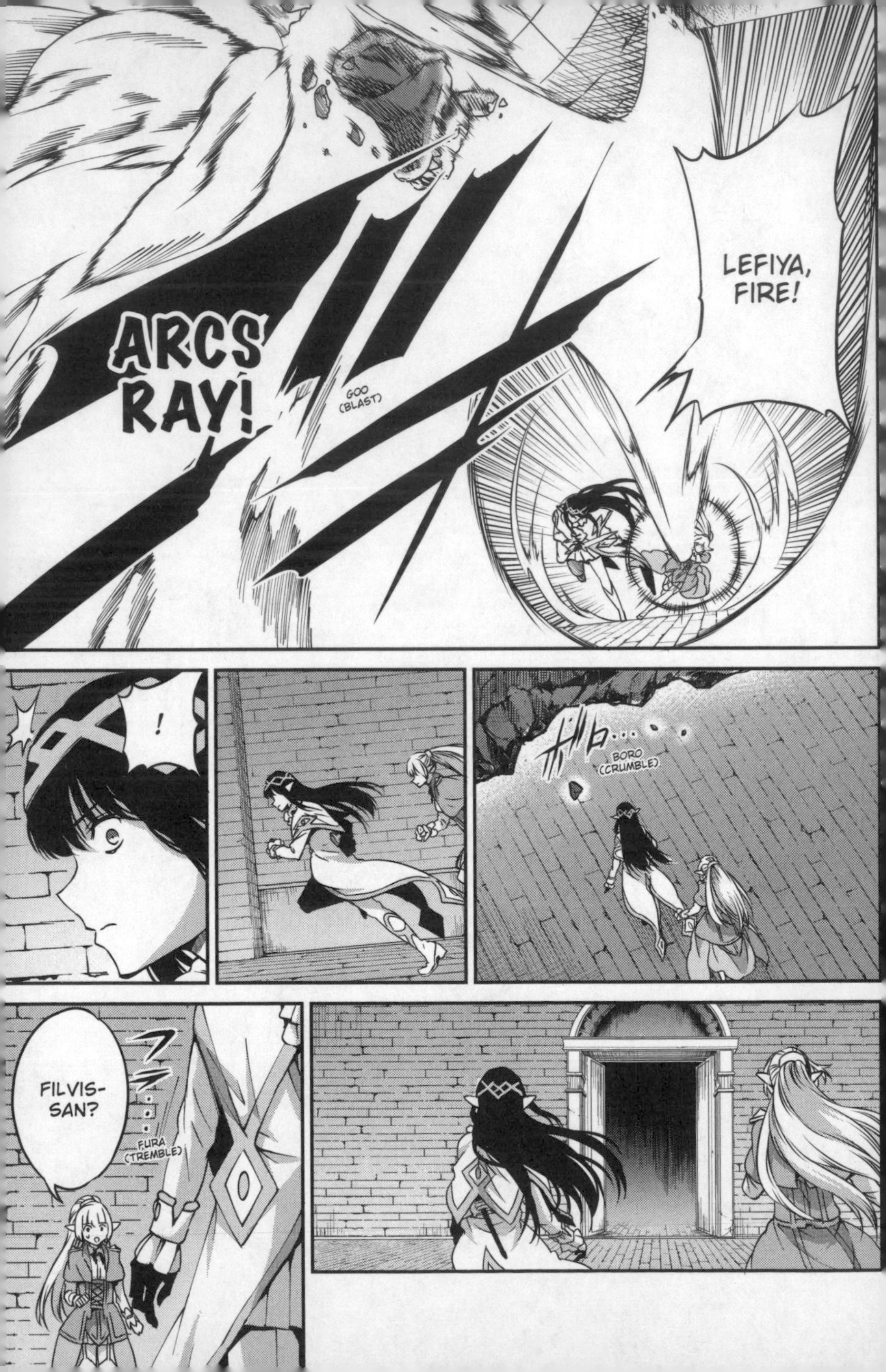
LEFIYA, FIRE!
ARCS RAY!
GOO (BLAST)
BORO (CRUMBLE)
!
FILVIS-SAN?
FURA (TREMBLE)

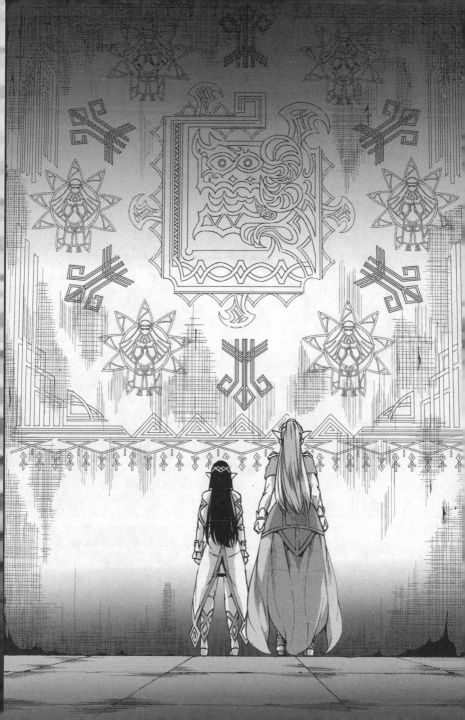

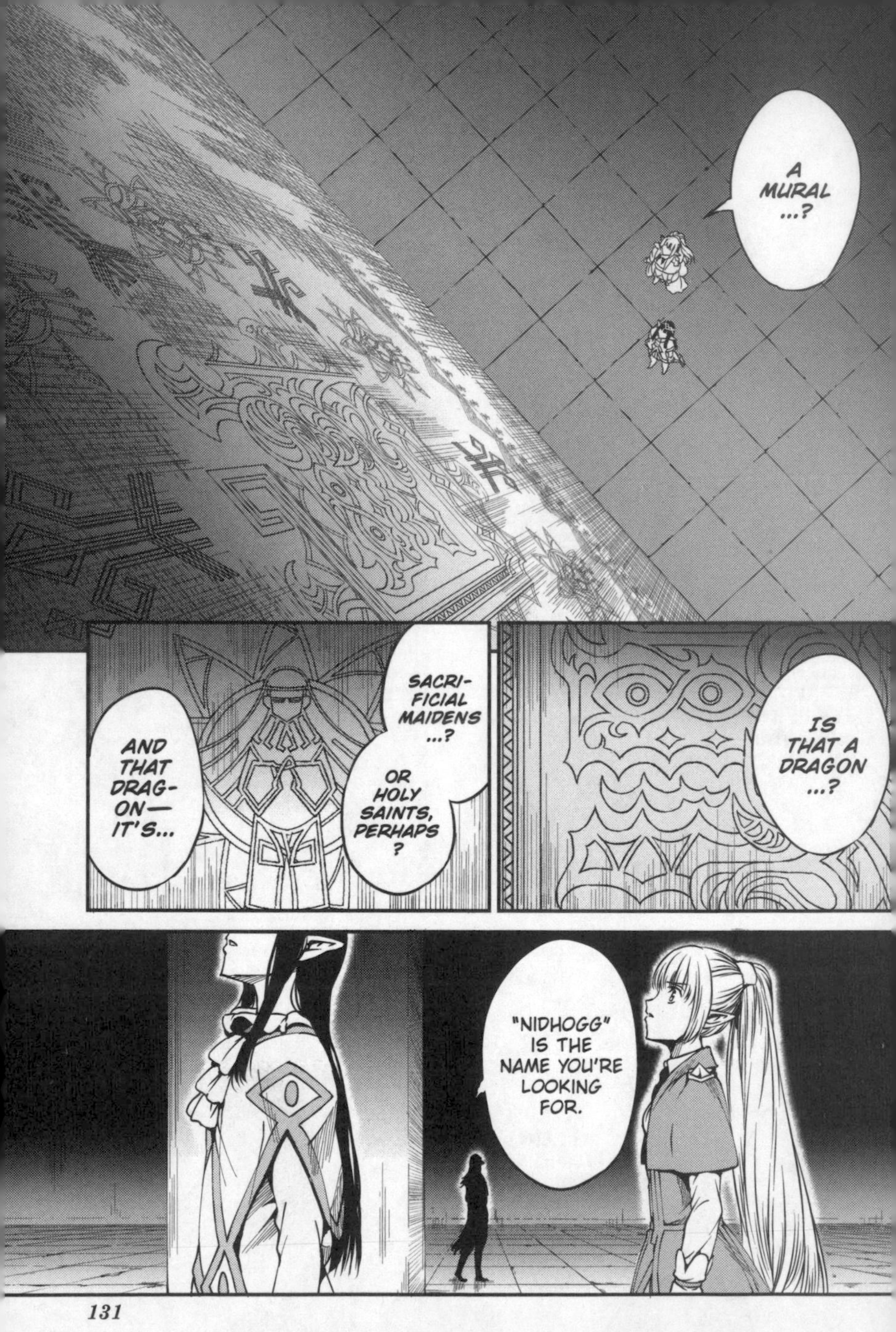
A MURAL...?
IS THAT A DRAGON...?
SACRIFICIAL MAIDENS...?
OR HOLY SAINTS, PERHAPS?
AND THAT DRAGON—IT'S...
"NIDHOGG" IS THE NAME YOU'RE LOOKING FOR.

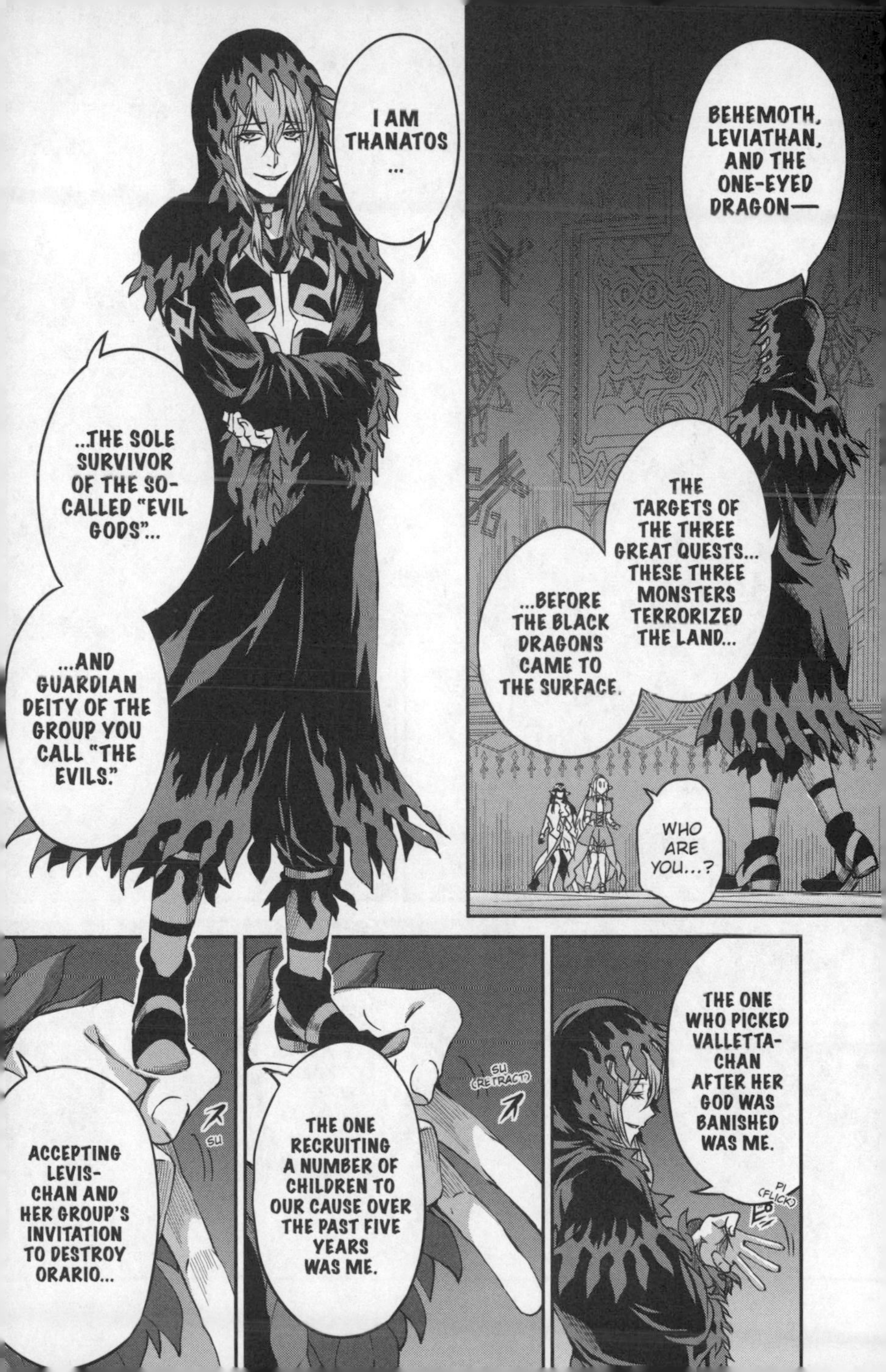
BEHEMOTH, LEVIATHAN, AND THE ONE-EYED DRAGON—
THE TARGETS OF THE THREE GREAT QUESTS... THESE THREE MONSTERS TERRORIZED THE LAND...
...BEFORE THE BLACK DRAGONS CAME TO THE SURFACE.
WHO ARE YOU...?
I AM THANATOS ...
...THE SOLE SURVIVOR OF THE SO-CALLED "EVIL GODS"...
...AND GUARDIAN DEITY OF THE GROUP YOU CALL "THE EVILS."
THE ONE WHO PICKED VALLETTA-CHAN AFTER HER GOD WAS BANISHED WAS ME.
PI (FLICK)
SU (RETRACT)
THE ONE RECRUITING A NUMBER OF CHILDREN TO OUR CAUSE OVER THE PAST FIVE YEARS WAS ME.
SU
ACCEPTING LEVIS-CHAN AND HER GROUP'S INVITATION TO DESTROY ORARIO...

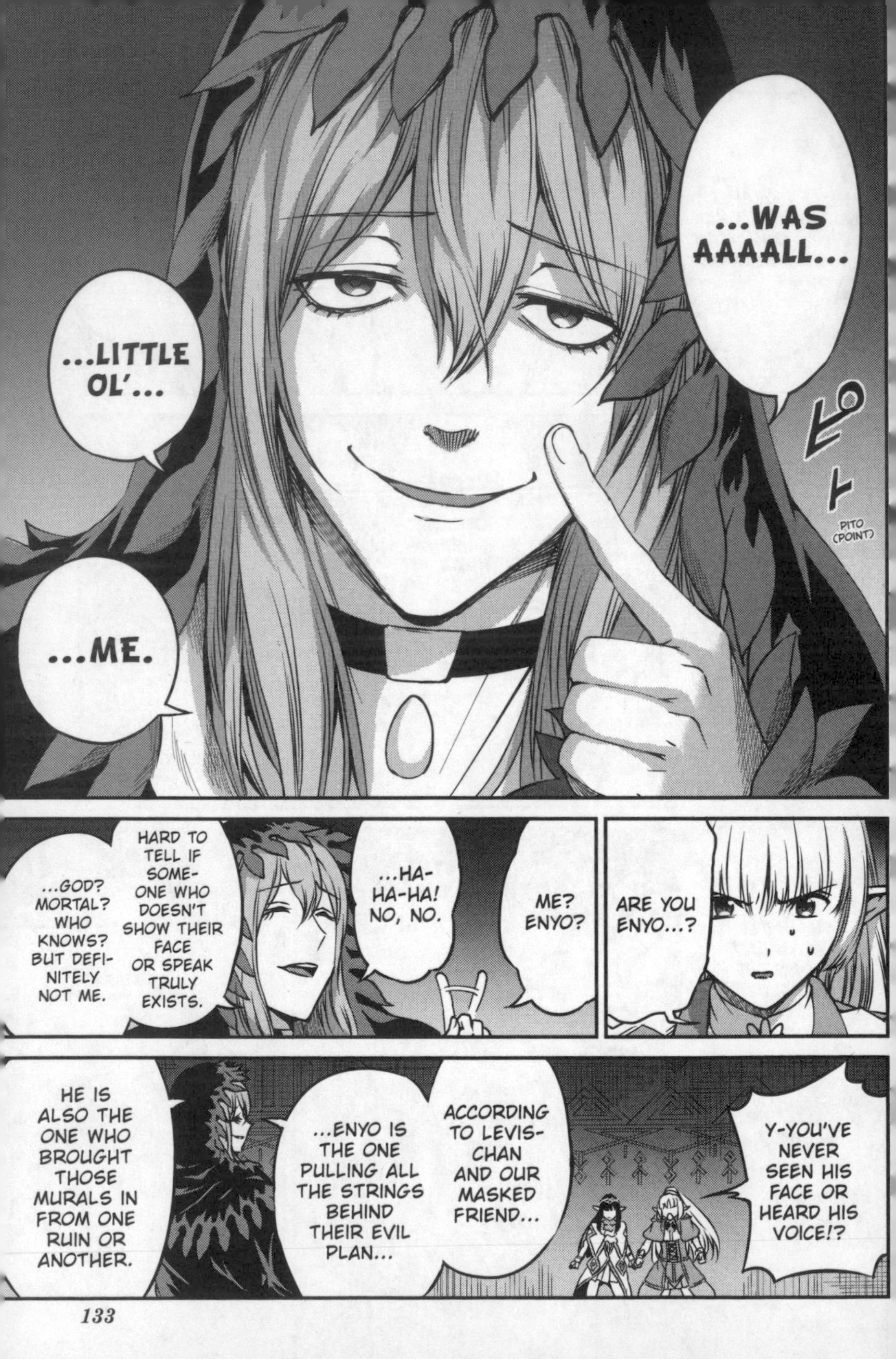
...WAS AAAALL...
ピト
PITO (POINT)
...LITTLE OL'...
...ME.
ARE YOU ENYO...?
ME? ENYO?
...HA-HA-HA! NO, NO.
HARD TO TELL IF SOME-ONE WHO DOESN'T SHOW THEIR FACE OR SPEAK TRULY EXISTS.
...GOD? MORTAL? WHO KNOWS? BUT DEFI-NITELY NOT ME.
Y-YOU'VE NEVER SEEN HIS FACE OR HEARD HIS VOICE!?
ACCORDING TO LEVIS-CHAN AND OUR MASKED FRIEND...
...ENYO IS THE ONE PULLING ALL THE STRINGS BEHIND THEIR EVIL PLAN...
HE IS ALSO THE ONE WHO BROUGHT THOSE MURALS IN FROM ONE RUIN OR ANOTHER.

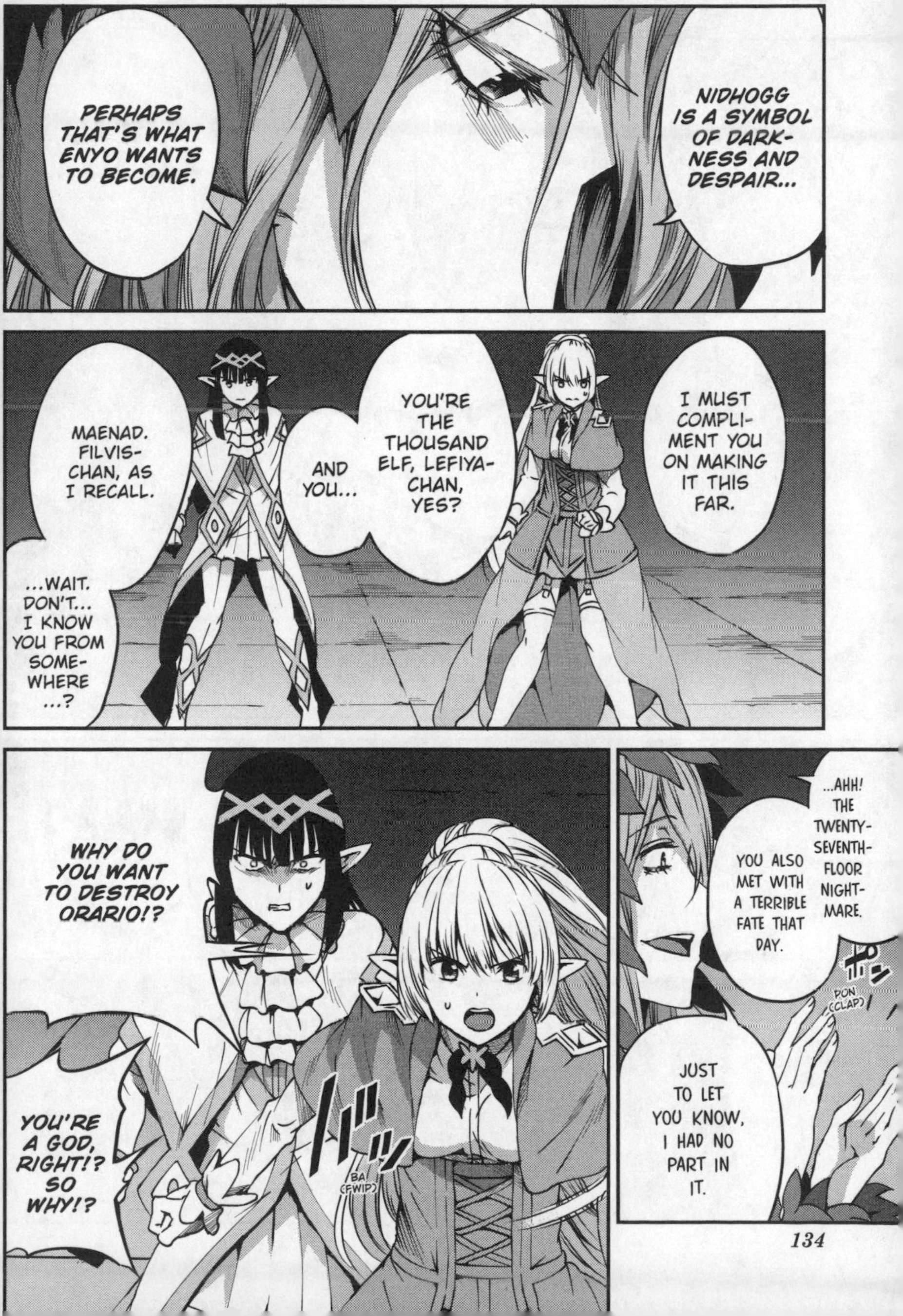
NIDHOGG IS A SYMBOL OF DARKNESS AND DESPAIR...
PERHAPS THAT'S WHAT ENYO WANTS TO BECOME.
I MUST COMPLIMENT YOU ON MAKING IT THIS FAR.
YOU'RE THE THOUSAND ELF, LEFIYA-CHAN, YES?
AND YOU...
MAENAD. FILVIS-CHAN, AS I RECALL.
...WAIT. DON'T... I KNOW YOU FROM SOMEWHERE ...?
...AHH! THE TWENTY-SEVENTH-FLOOR NIGHTMARE.
YOU ALSO MET WITH A TERRIBLE FATE THAT DAY.
PON (CLAP)
JUST TO LET YOU KNOW, I HAD NO PART IN IT.
WHY DO YOU WANT TO DESTROY ORARIO!?
BA (FWIP)
YOU'RE A GOD, RIGHT!? SO WHY!?

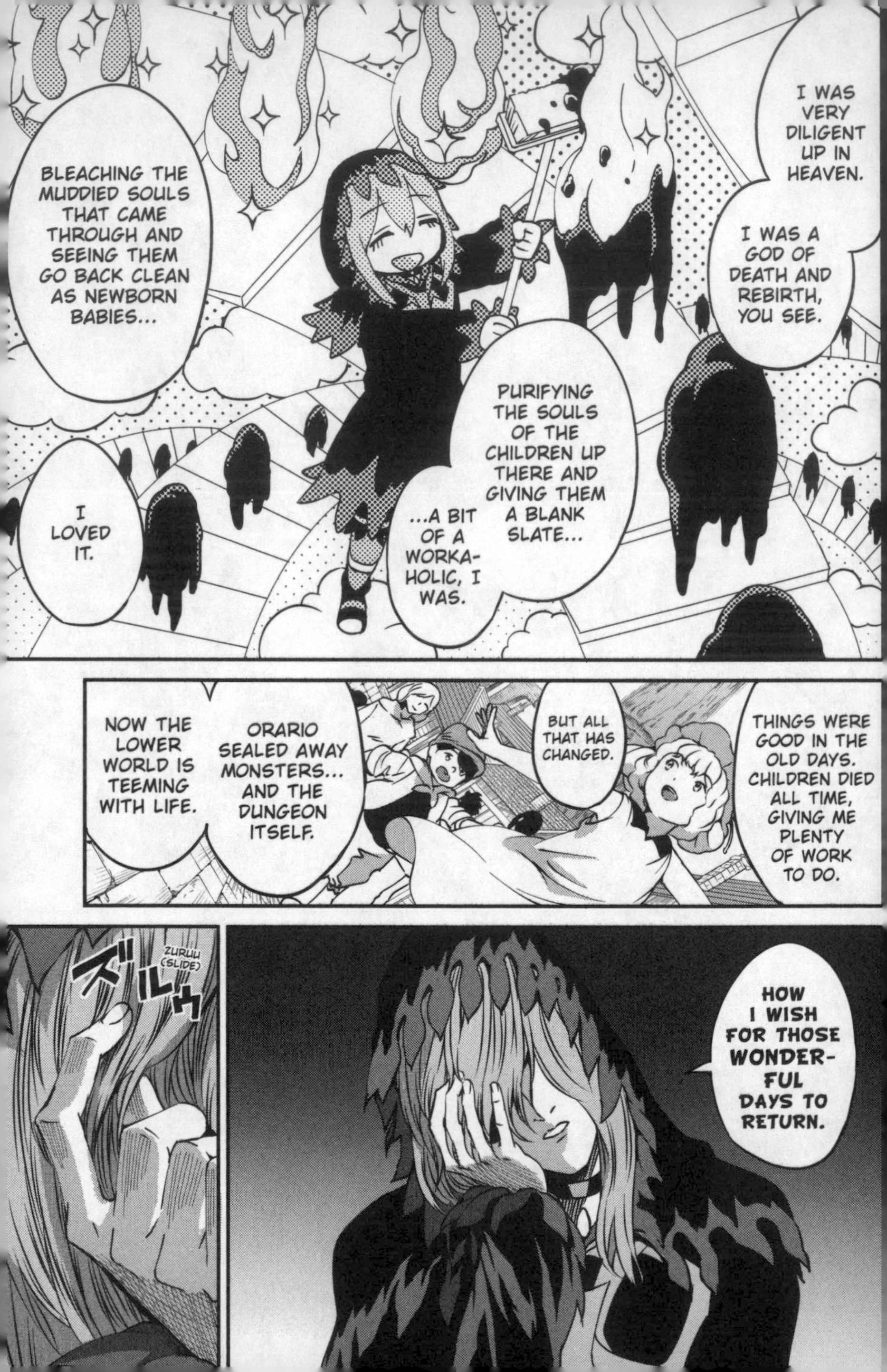
I WAS VERY DILIGENT UP IN HEAVEN.
I WAS A GOD OF DEATH AND REBIRTH, YOU SEE.
BLEACHING THE MUDDIED SOULS THAT CAME THROUGH AND SEEING THEM GO BACK CLEAN AS NEWBORN BABIES...
PURIFYING THE SOULS OF THE CHILDREN UP THERE AND GIVING THEM A BLANK SLATE...
...A BIT OF A WORKA-HOLIC, I WAS.
I LOVED IT.
THINGS WERE GOOD IN THE OLD DAYS. CHILDREN DIED ALL TIME, GIVING ME PLENTY OF WORK TO DO.
BUT ALL THAT HAS CHANGED.
ORARIO SEALED AWAY MONSTERS... AND THE DUNGEON ITSELF.
NOW THE LOWER WORLD IS TEEMING WITH LIFE.
HOW I WISH FOR THOSE WONDER-FUL DAYS TO RETURN.
ズルゥ
ZURUU (SLIDE)

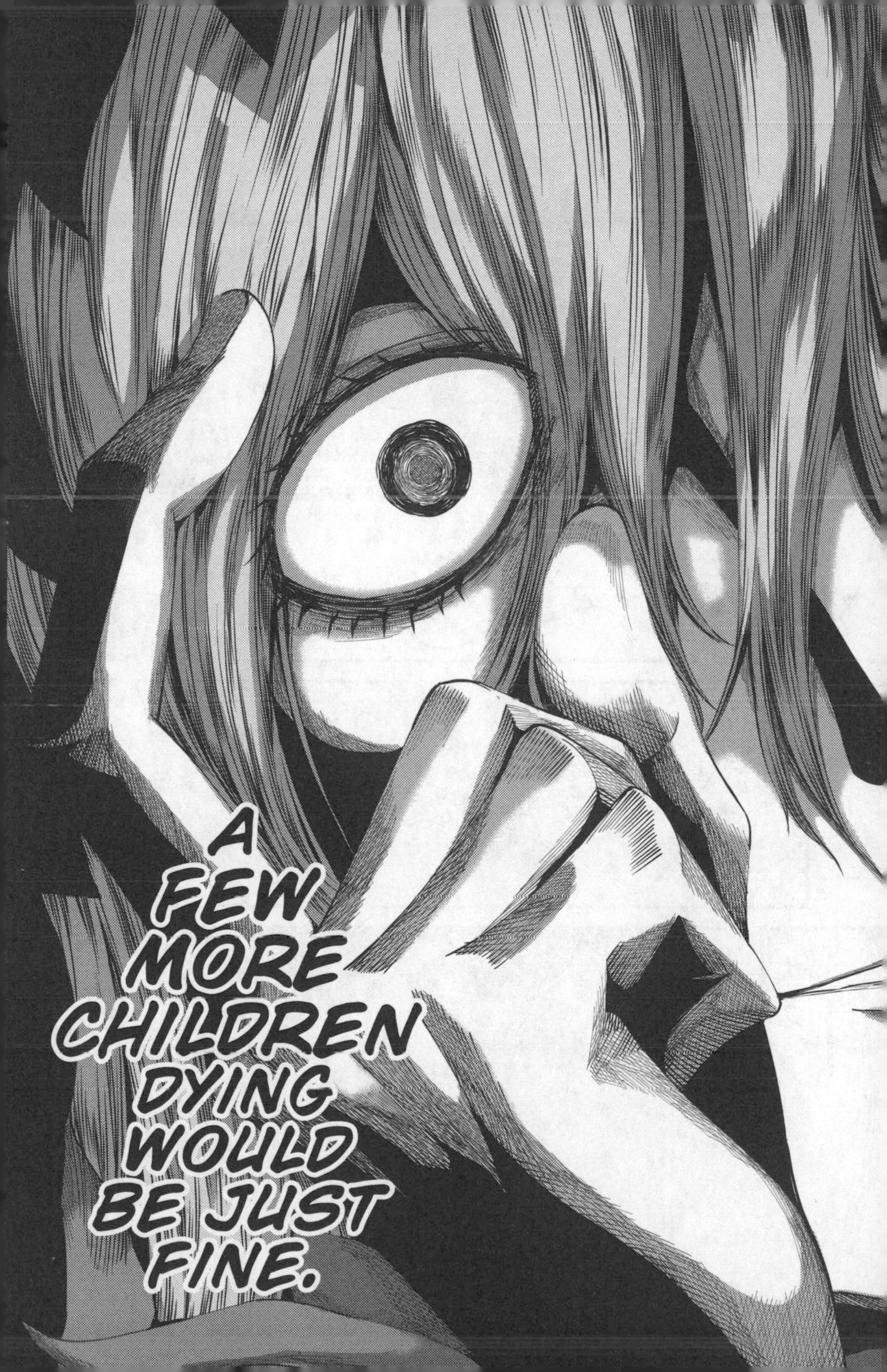
A FEW MORE CHILDREN DYING WOULD BE JUST FINE.

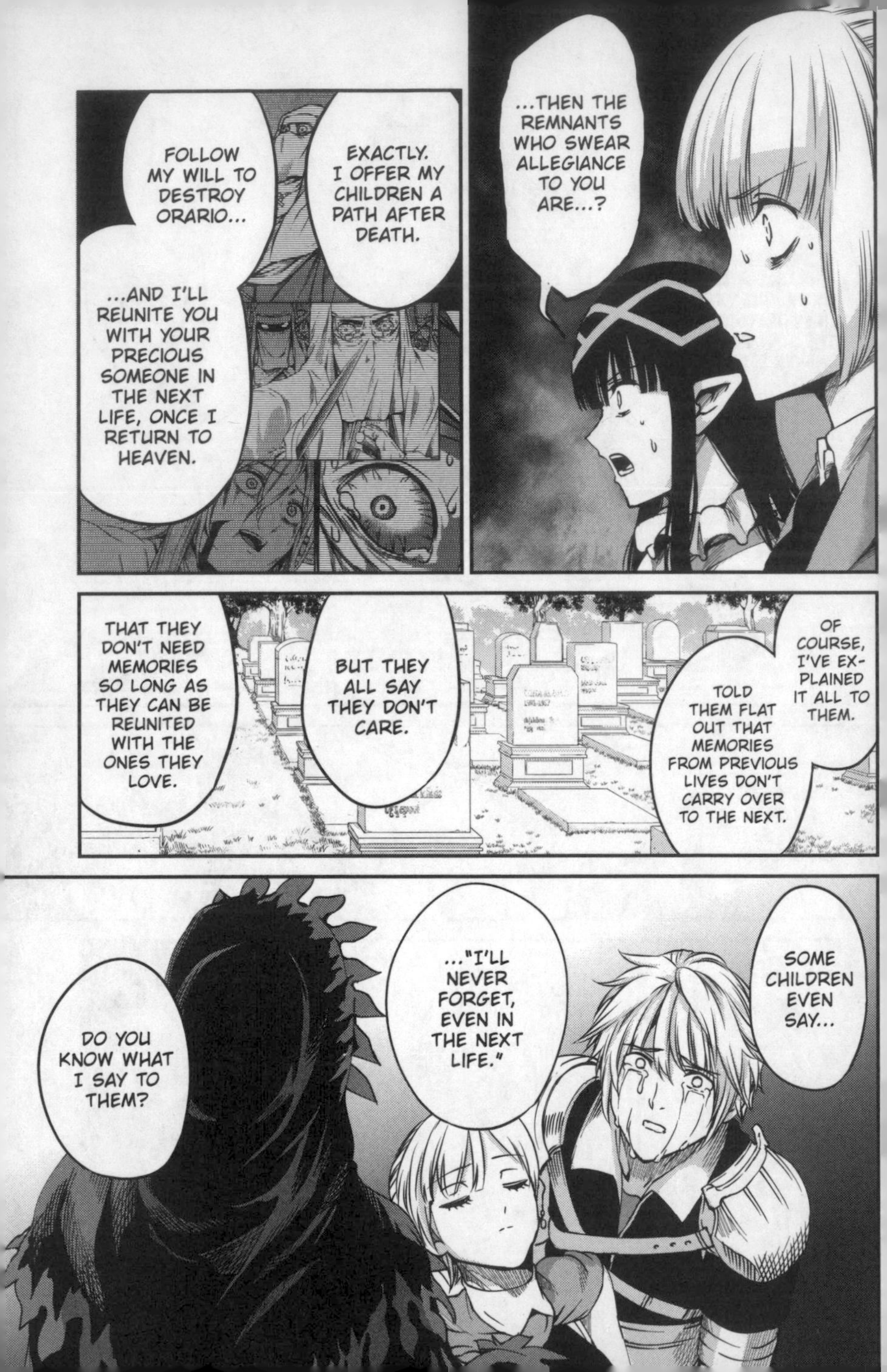
...THEN THE REMNANTS WHO SWEAR ALLEGIANCE TO YOU ARE...?
EXACTLY. I OFFER MY CHILDREN A PATH AFTER DEATH.
FOLLOW MY WILL TO DESTROY ORARIO...
...AND I'LL REUNITE YOU WITH YOUR PRECIOUS SOMEONE IN THE NEXT LIFE, ONCE I RETURN TO HEAVEN.
OF COURSE, I'VE EXPLAINED IT ALL TO THEM.
TOLD THEM FLAT OUT THAT MEMORIES FROM PREVIOUS LIVES DON'T CARRY OVER TO THE NEXT.
BUT THEY ALL SAY THEY DON'T CARE.
THAT THEY DON'T NEED MEMORIES SO LONG AS THEY CAN BE REUNITED WITH THE ONES THEY LOVE.
SOME CHILDREN EVEN SAY...
..."I'LL NEVER FORGET, EVEN IN THE NEXT LIFE."
DO YOU KNOW WHAT I SAY TO THEM?

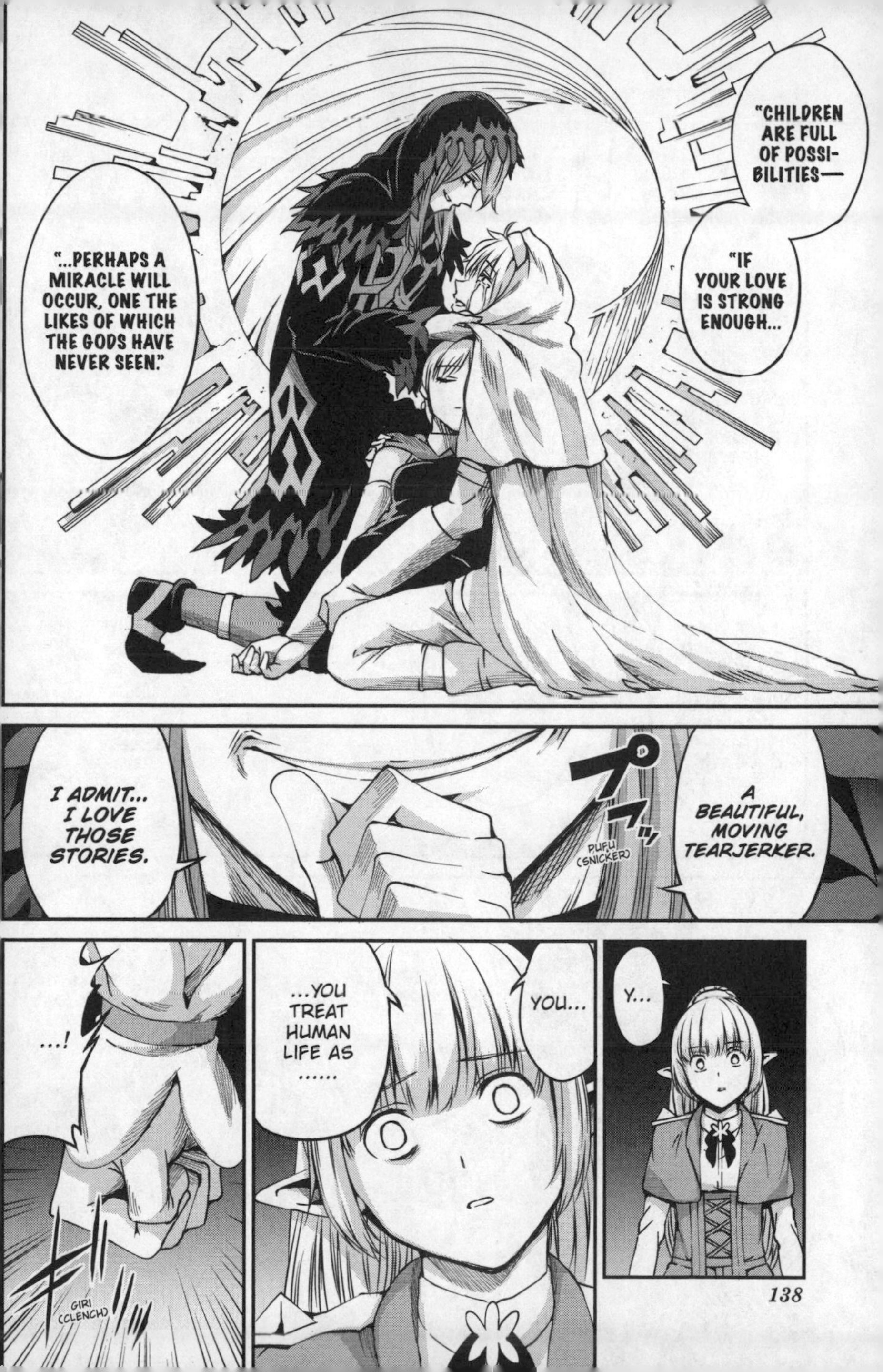
"CHILDREN ARE FULL OF POSSI-BILITIES—
"IF YOUR LOVE IS STRONG ENOUGH...
"...PERHAPS A MIRACLE WILL OCCUR, ONE THE LIKES OF WHICH THE GODS HAVE NEVER SEEN."
A BEAUTIFUL, MOVING TEARJERKER.
PUFU (SNICKER)
I ADMIT... I LOVE THOSE STORIES.
Y...
YOU...
...YOU TREAT HUMAN LIFE AS ......
...!
GIRI (CLENCH)

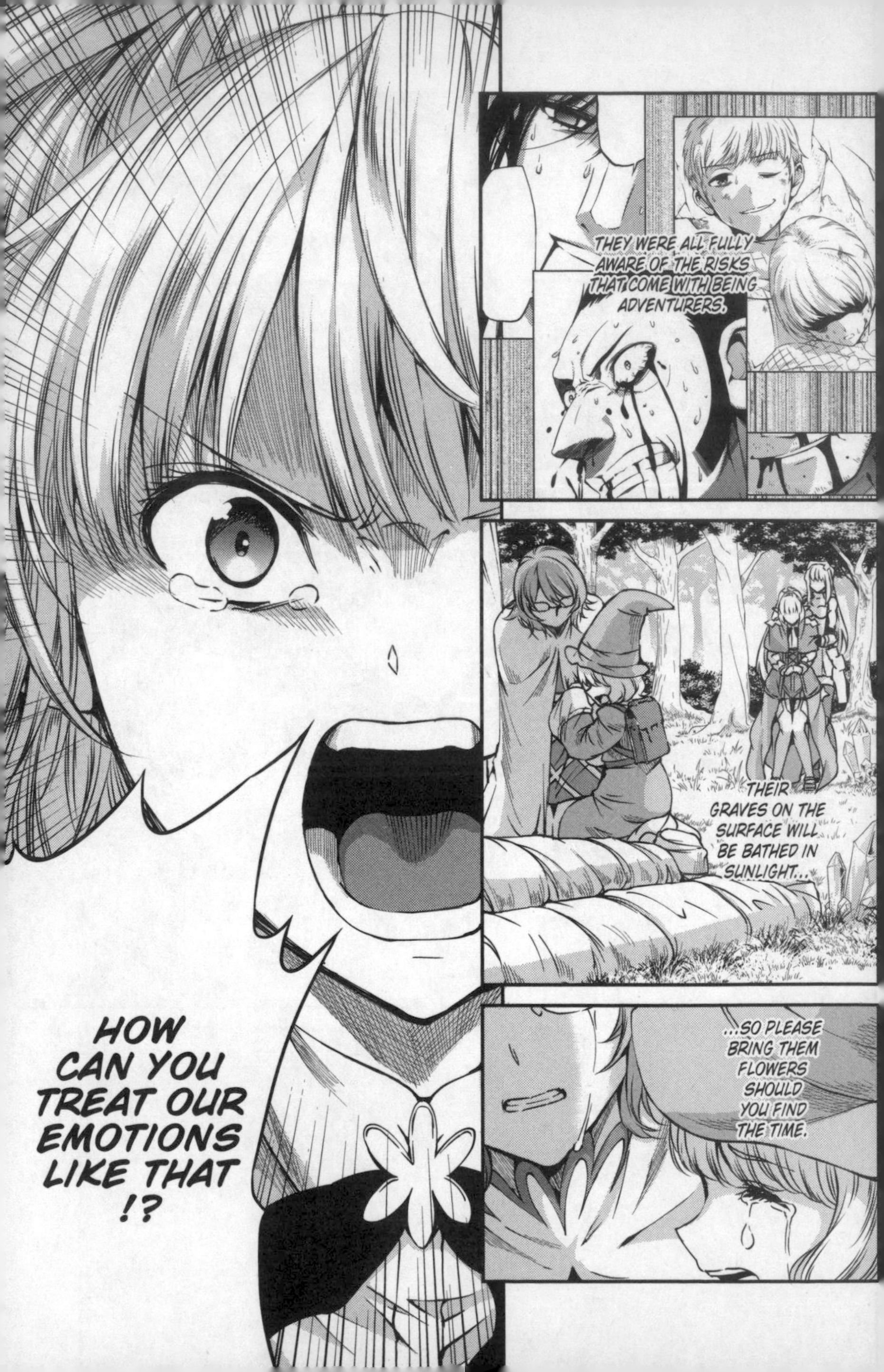
THEY WERE ALL FULLY AWARE OF THE RISKS THAT COME WITH BEING ADVENTURERS.
THEIR GRAVES ON THE SURFACE WILL BE BATHED IN SUNLIGHT...
...SO PLEASE BRING THEM FLOWERS SHOULD YOU FIND THE TIME.
HOW CAN YOU TREAT OUR EMOTIONS LIKE THAT!?

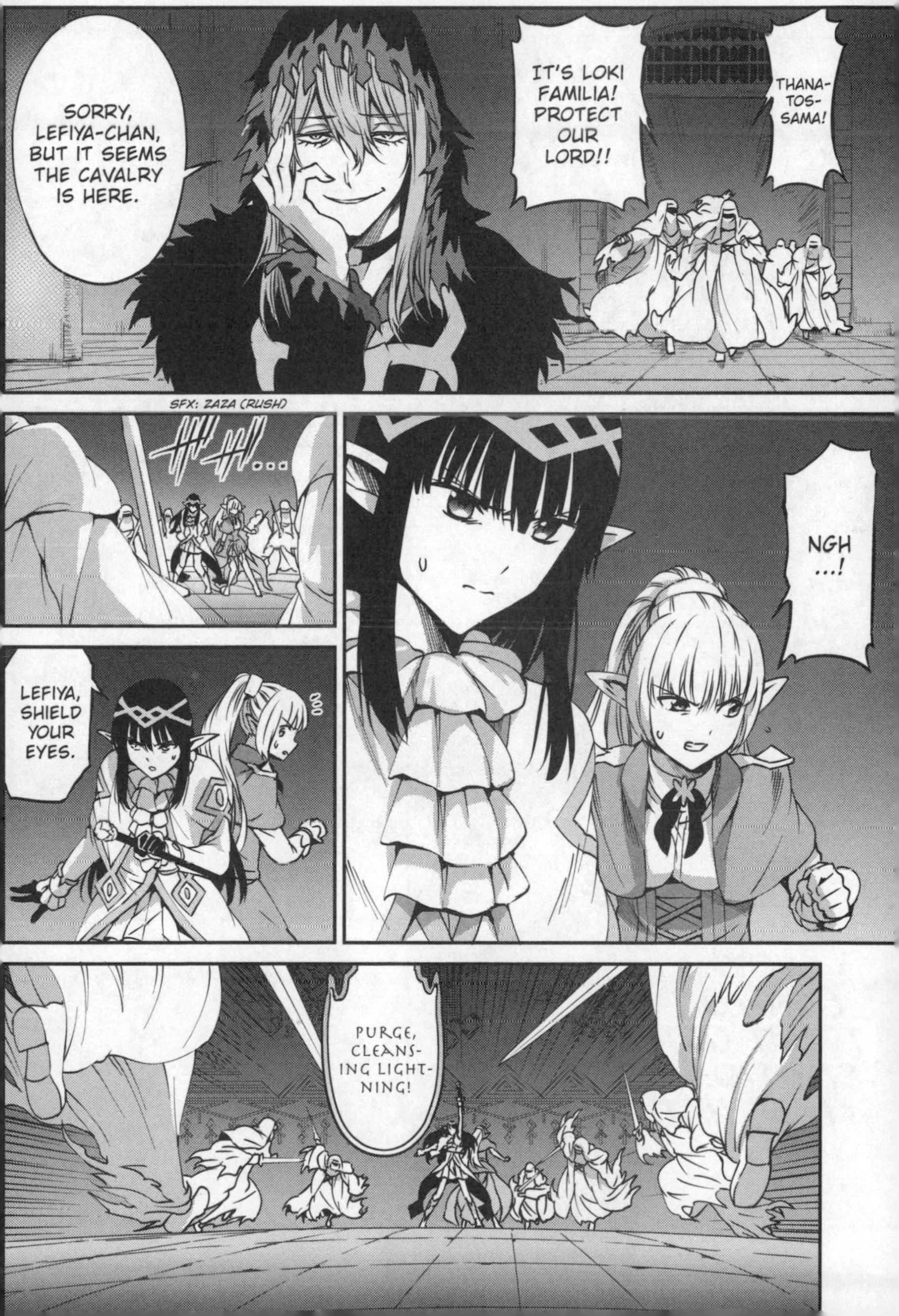
THANA-TOS-SAMA!
IT'S LOKI FAMILIA! PROTECT OUR LORD!!
SORRY, LEFIYA-CHAN, BUT IT SEEMS THE CAVALRY IS HERE.
SFX: ZAZA (RUSH)
NGH ...!
LEFIYA, SHIELD YOUR EYES.
PURGE, CLEANS-ING LIGHT-NING!

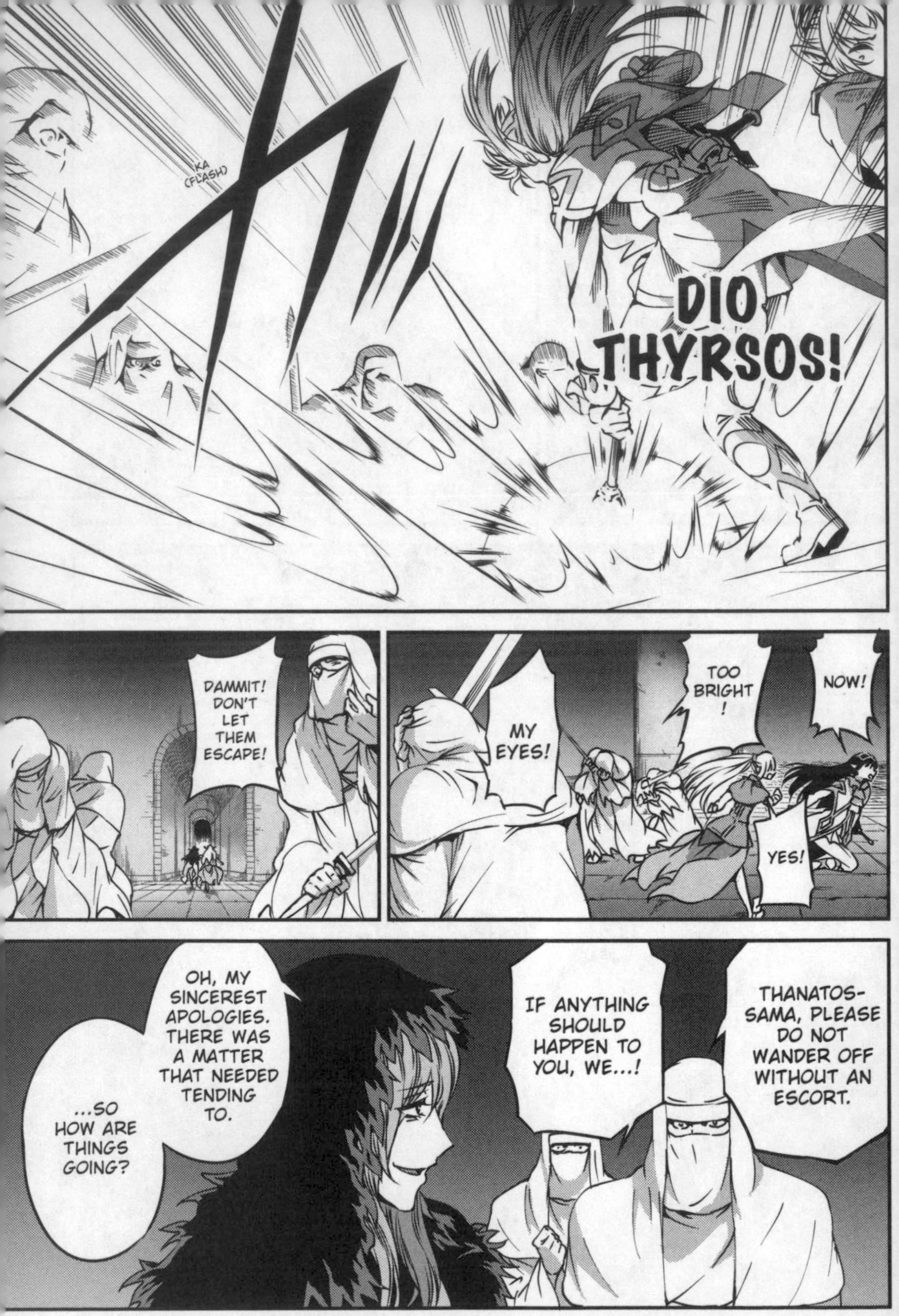
DIO THYRSOS!
KA (FLASH)
NOW!
TOO BRIGHT!
MY EYES!
YES!
DAMMIT! DON'T LET THEM ESCAPE!
THANATOS-SAMA, PLEASE DO NOT WANDER OFF WITHOUT AN ESCORT.
IF ANYTHING SHOULD HAPPEN TO YOU, WE...!
OH, MY SINCEREST APOLOGIES. THERE WAS A MATTER THAT NEEDED TENDING TO.
...SO HOW ARE THINGS GOING?

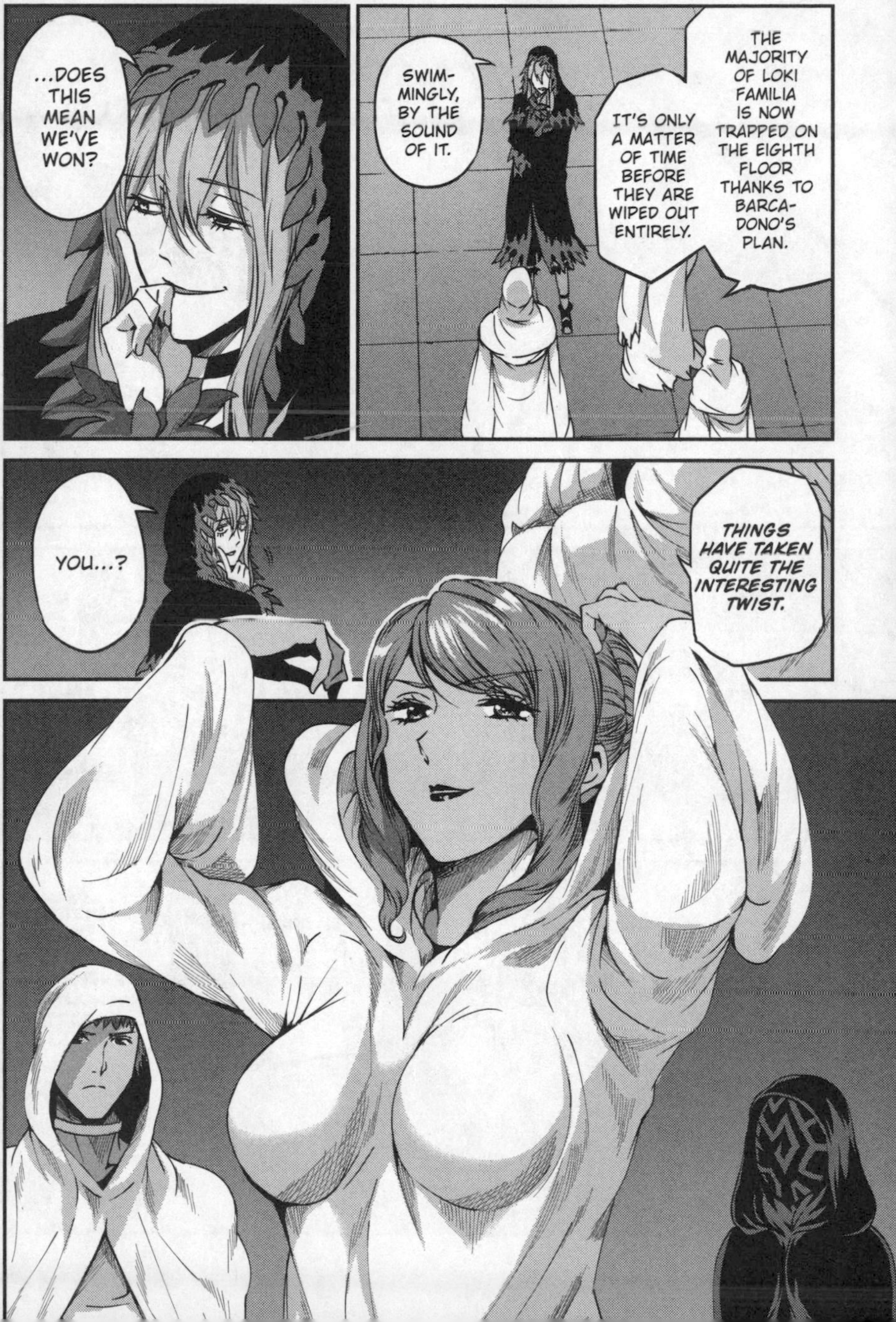
THE MAJORITY OF LOKI FAMILIA IS NOW TRAPPED ON THE EIGHTH FLOOR THANKS TO BARCA-DONO'S PLAN.
IT'S ONLY A MATTER OF TIME BEFORE THEY ARE WIPED OUT ENTIRELY.
SWIM-MINGLY, BY THE SOUND OF IT.
...DOES THIS MEAN WE'VE WON?
THINGS HAVE TAKEN QUITE THE INTERESTING TWIST.
YOU...?

Is it WRONG to TRY to PICK-UP GIRLS IN A DUNGEON? ON THE SIDE

Sword Oratoria

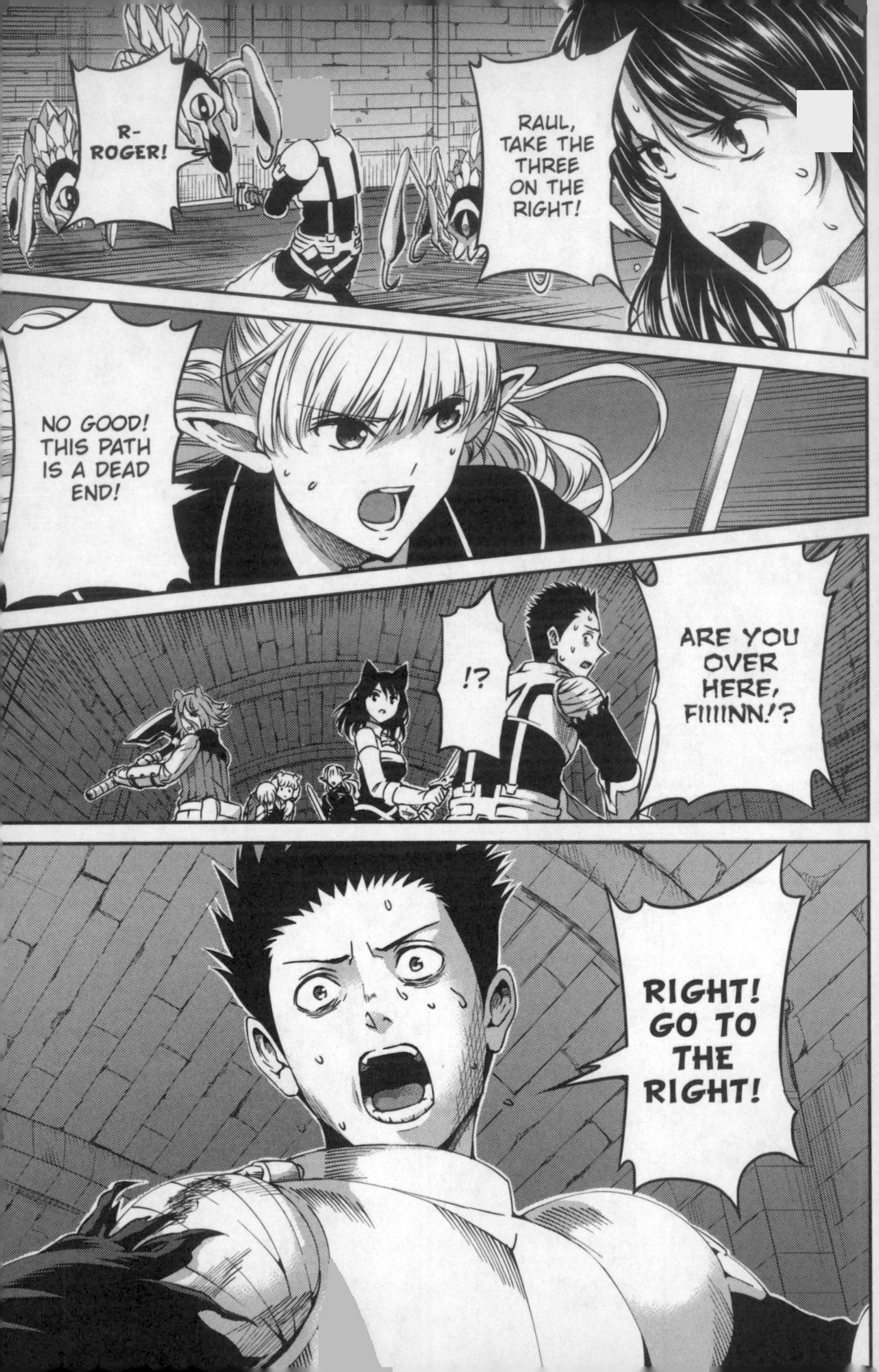
RAUL, TAKE THE THREE ON THE RIGHT!
R- ROGER!
NO GOOD! THIS PATH IS A DEAD END!
ARE YOU OVER HERE, FIIIINN!?
!?
RIGHT! GO TO THE RIGHT!

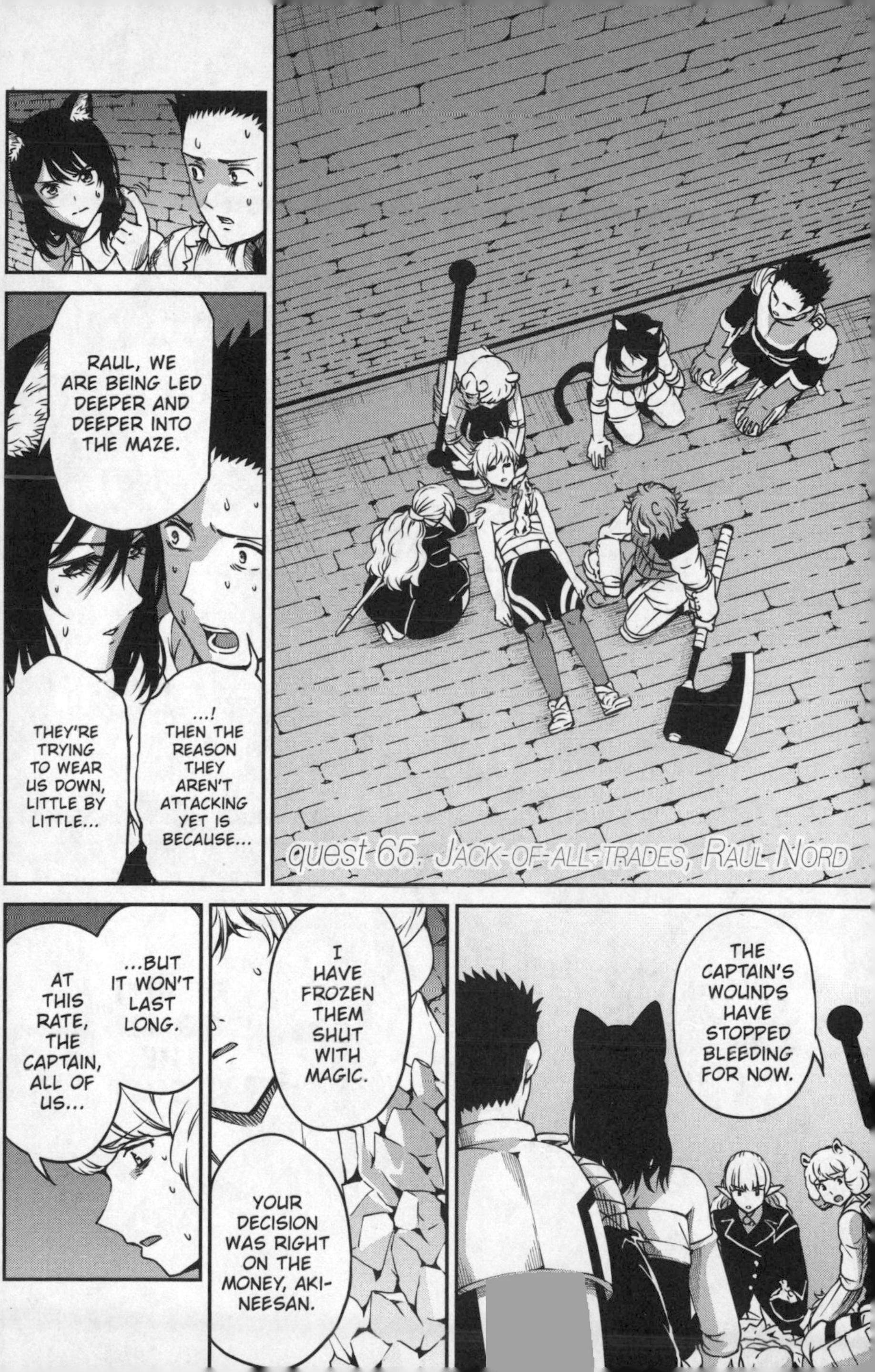
quest 65: Jack-of-all-trades, Raul Nord
RAUL, WE ARE BEING LED DEEPER AND DEEPER INTO THE MAZE.
...! THEN THE REASON THEY AREN'T ATTACKING YET IS BECAUSE...
THEY'RE TRYING TO WEAR US DOWN, LITTLE BY LITTLE...
THE CAPTAIN'S WOUNDS HAVE STOPPED BLEEDING FOR NOW.
I HAVE FROZEN THEM SHUT WITH MAGIC.
YOUR DECISION WAS RIGHT ON THE MONEY, AKI-NEESAN.
...BUT IT WON'T LAST LONG.
AT THIS RATE, THE CAPTAIN, ALL OF US...

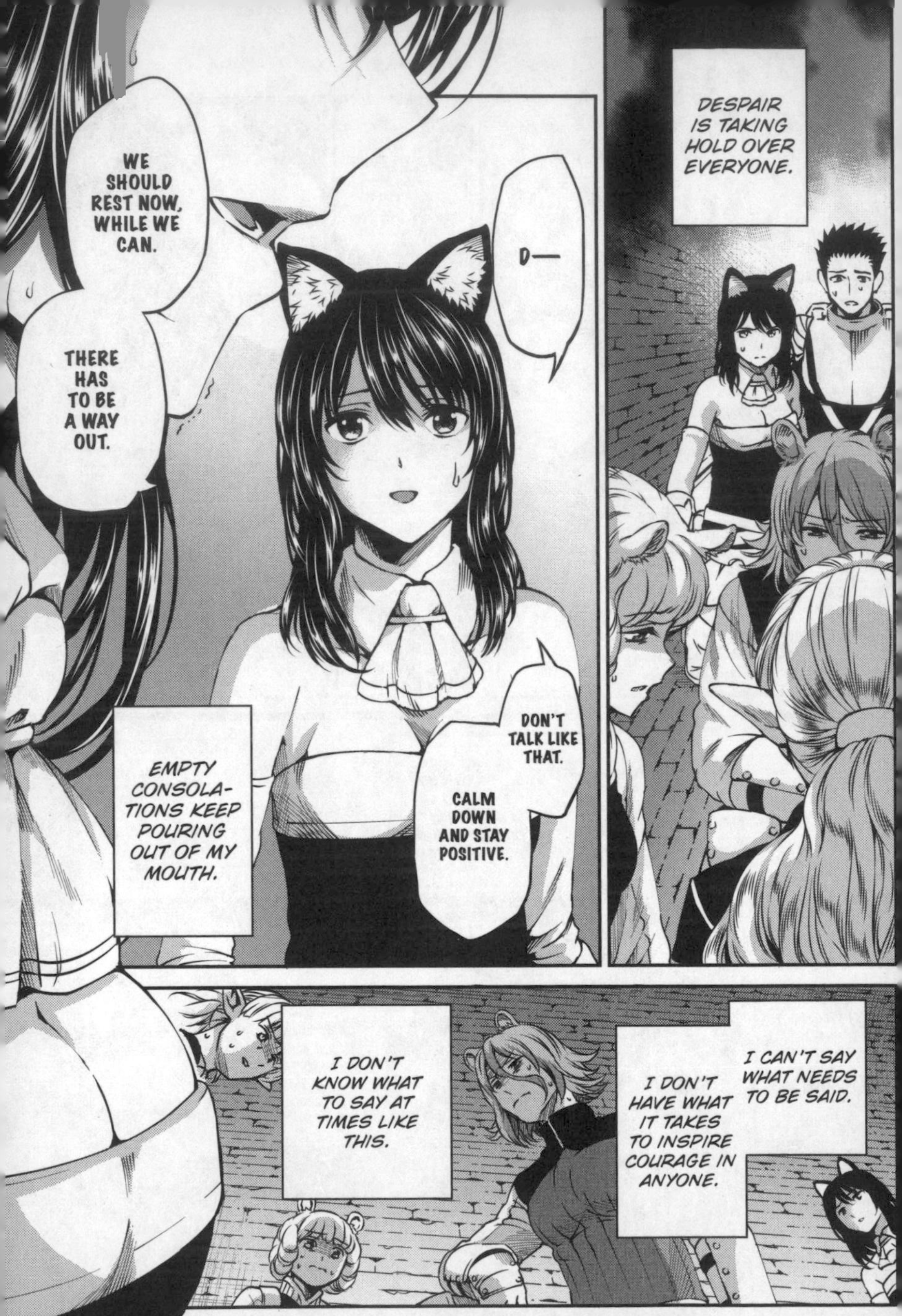
DESPAIR IS TAKING HOLD OVER EVERYONE.
D—
WE SHOULD REST NOW, WHILE WE CAN.
THERE HAS TO BE A WAY OUT.
DON'T TALK LIKE THAT.
CALM DOWN AND STAY POSITIVE.
EMPTY CONSOLATIONS KEEP POURING OUT OF MY MOUTH.
I CAN'T SAY WHAT NEEDS TO BE SAID.
I DON'T HAVE WHAT IT TAKES TO INSPIRE COURAGE IN ANYONE.
I DON'T KNOW WHAT TO SAY AT TIMES LIKE THIS.

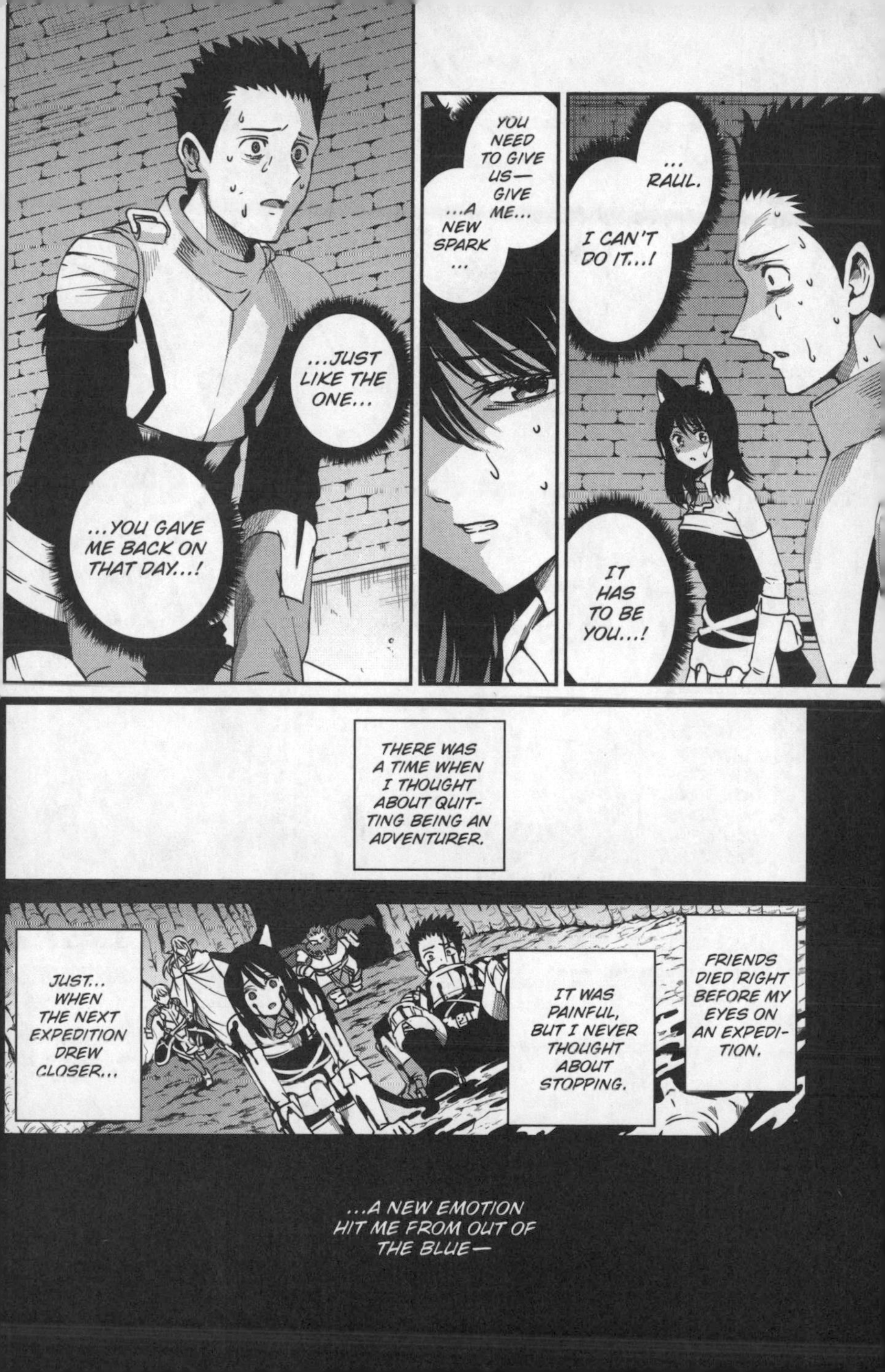
... RAUL.
I CAN'T DO IT...!
IT HAS TO BE YOU...!
YOU NEED TO GIVE US— GIVE ME...
...A NEW SPARK...
...JUST LIKE THE ONE...
...YOU GAVE ME BACK ON THAT DAY...!
THERE WAS A TIME WHEN I THOUGHT ABOUT QUIT-TING BEING AN ADVENTURER.
FRIENDS DIED RIGHT BEFORE MY EYES ON AN EXPEDI-TION.
IT WAS PAINFUL, BUT I NEVER THOUGHT ABOUT STOPPING.
JUST... WHEN THE NEXT EXPEDITION DREW CLOSER...
...A NEW EMOTION HIT ME FROM OUT OF THE BLUE—

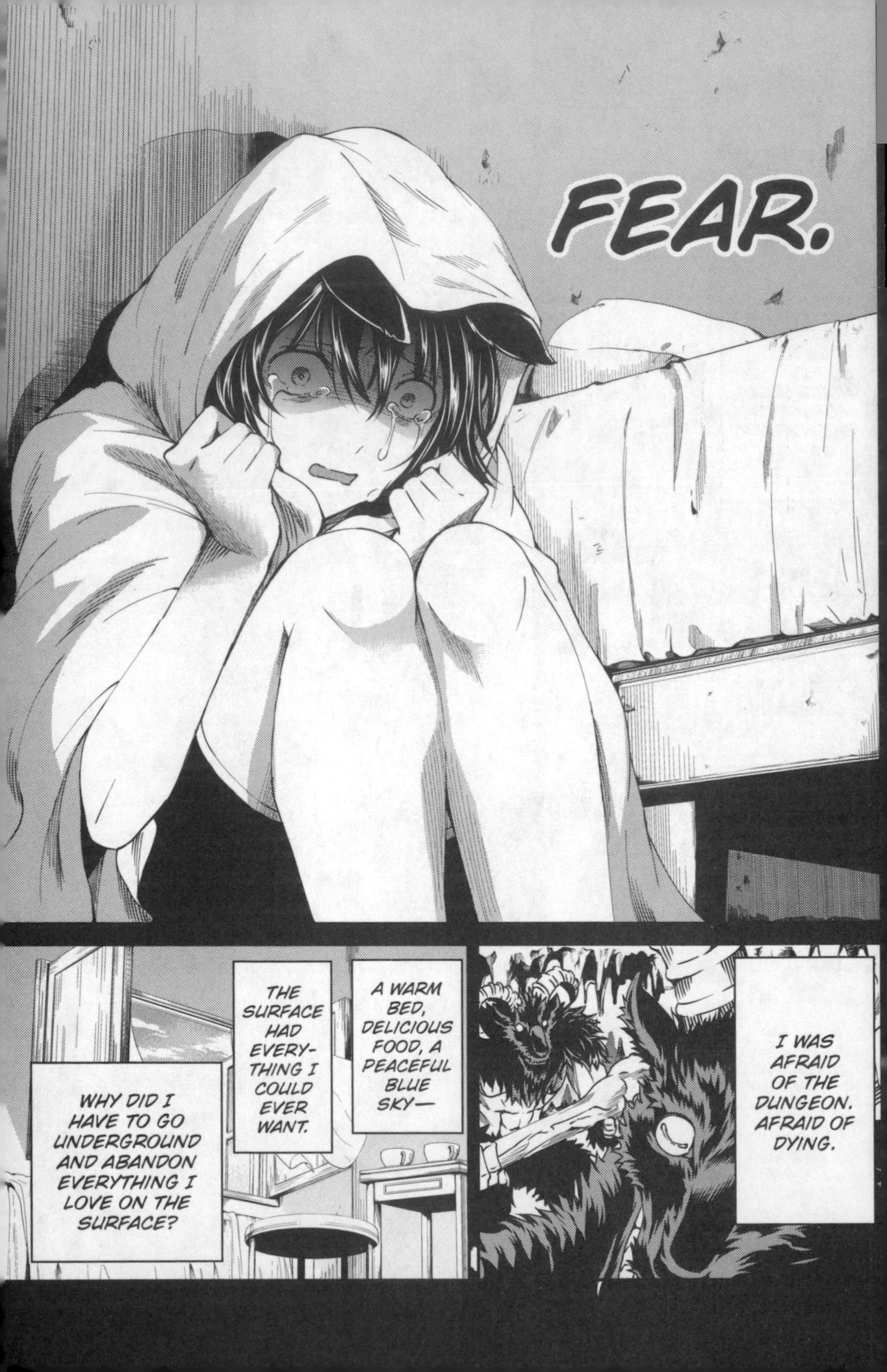
FEAR.
I WAS AFRAID OF THE DUNGEON. AFRAID OF DYING.
A WARM BED, DELICIOUS FOOD, A PEACEFUL BLUE SKY—
THE SURFACE HAD EVERYTHING I COULD EVER WANT.
WHY DID I HAVE TO GO UNDERGROUND AND ABANDON EVERYTHING I LOVE ON THE SURFACE?

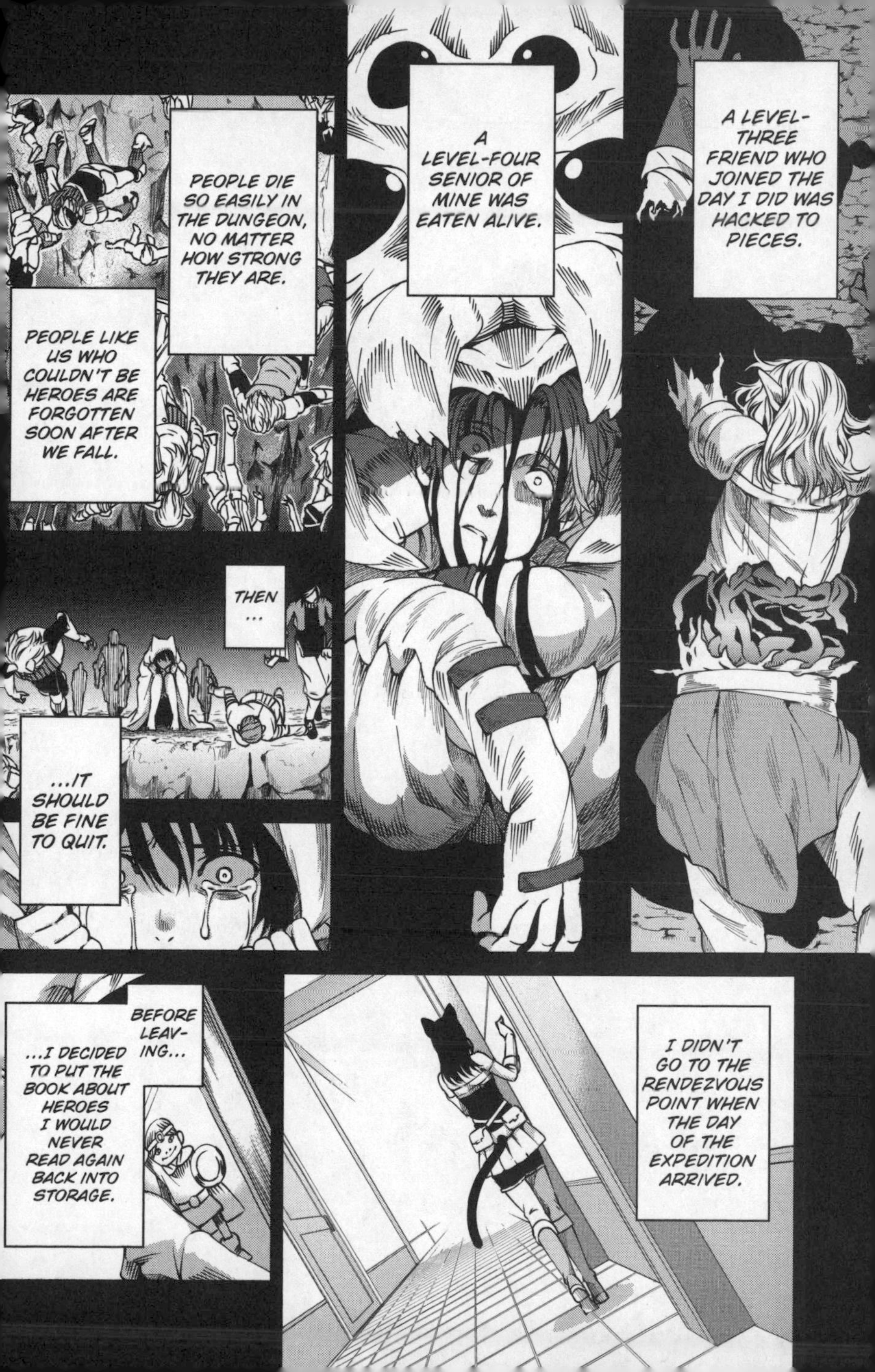
A LEVEL-THREE FRIEND WHO JOINED THE DAY I DID WAS HACKED TO PIECES.
A LEVEL-FOUR SENIOR OF MINE WAS EATEN ALIVE.
PEOPLE DIE SO EASILY IN THE DUNGEON, NO MATTER HOW STRONG THEY ARE.
PEOPLE LIKE US WHO COULDN'T BE HEROES ARE FORGOTTEN SOON AFTER WE FALL.
THEN ...
...IT SHOULD BE FINE TO QUIT.
I DIDN'T GO TO THE RENDEZVOUS POINT WHEN THE DAY OF THE EXPEDITION ARRIVED.
BEFORE LEAVING...
...I DECIDED TO PUT THE BOOK ABOUT HEROES I WOULD NEVER READ AGAIN BACK INTO STORAGE.

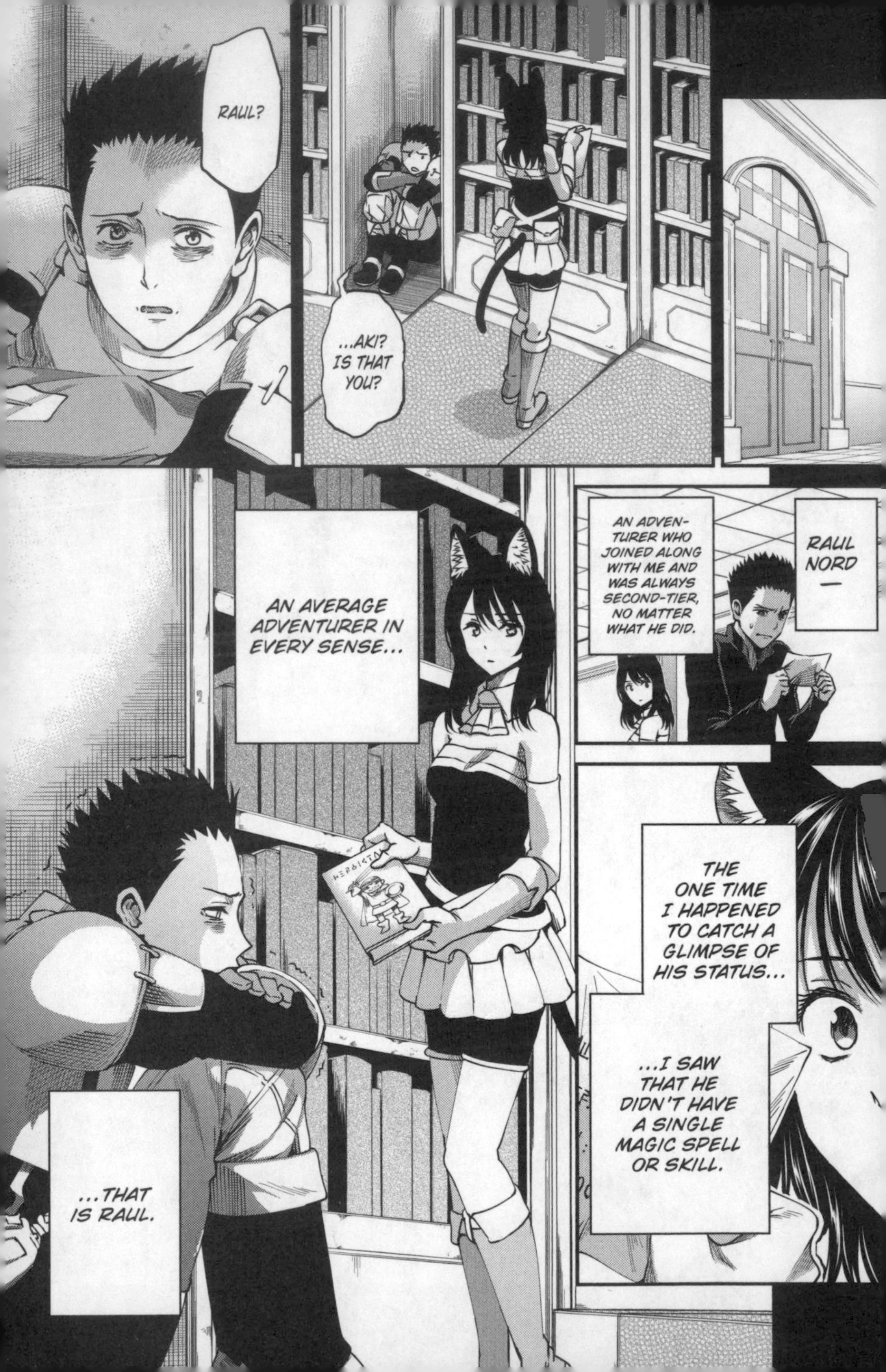
...AKI? IS THAT YOU?
RAUL?
RAUL NORD —
AN ADVENTURER WHO JOINED ALONG WITH ME AND WAS ALWAYS SECOND-TIER, NO MATTER WHAT HE DID.
THE ONE TIME I HAPPENED TO CATCH A GLIMPSE OF HIS STATUS...
...I SAW THAT HE DIDN'T HAVE A SINGLE MAGIC SPELL OR SKILL.
AN AVERAGE ADVENTURER IN EVERY SENSE...
...THAT IS RAUL.

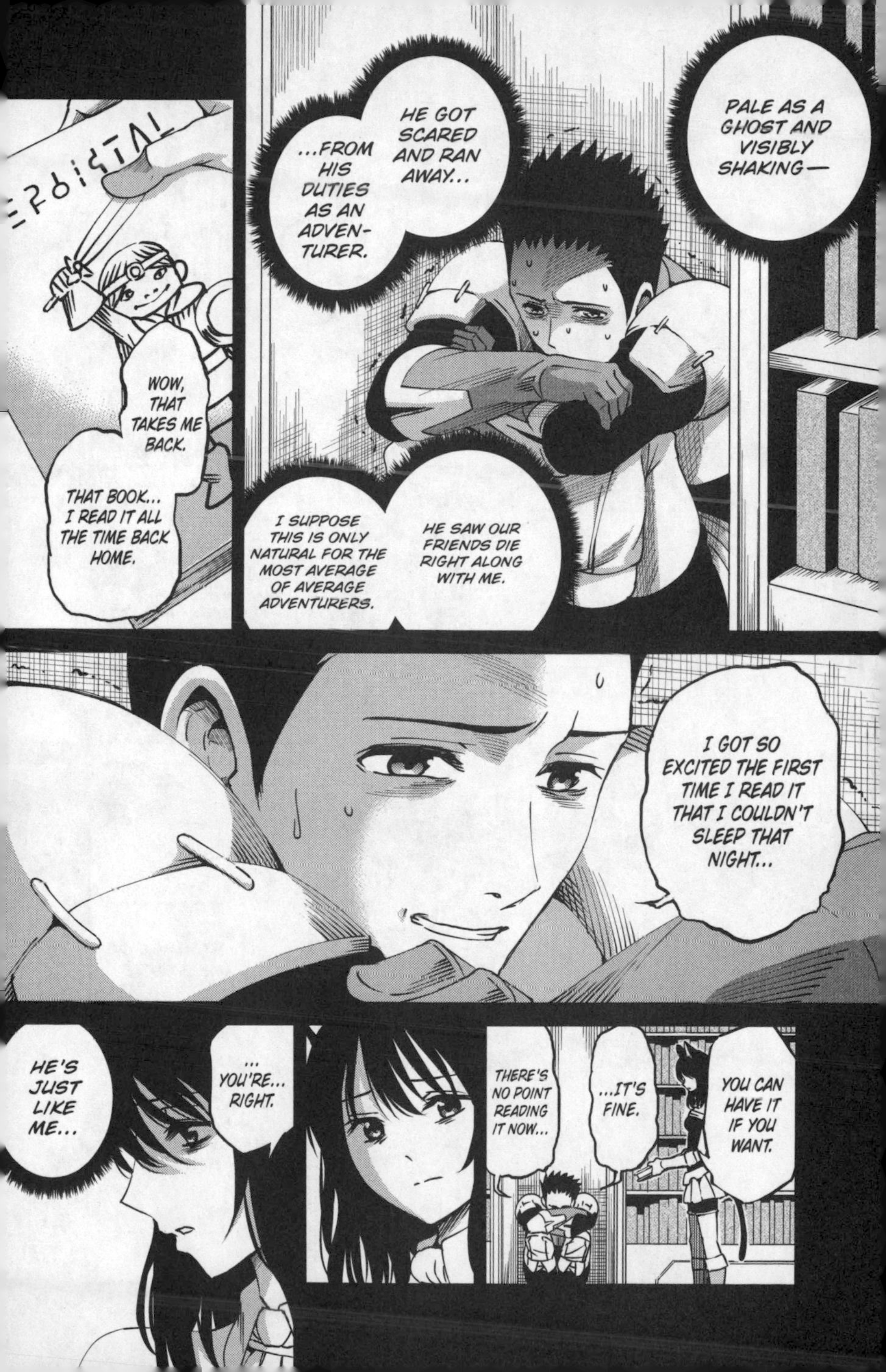
PALE AS A GHOST AND VISIBLY SHAKING—
HE GOT SCARED AND RAN AWAY...
...FROM HIS DUTIES AS AN ADVENTURER.
HE SAW OUR FRIENDS DIE RIGHT ALONG WITH ME.
I SUPPOSE THIS IS ONLY NATURAL FOR THE MOST AVERAGE OF AVERAGE ADVENTURERS.
WOW, THAT TAKES ME BACK.
THAT BOOK... I READ IT ALL THE TIME BACK HOME.
I GOT SO EXCITED THE FIRST TIME I READ IT THAT I COULDN'T SLEEP THAT NIGHT...
YOU CAN HAVE IT IF YOU WANT.
...IT'S FINE.
THERE'S NO POINT READING IT NOW...
... YOU'RE... RIGHT.
HE'S JUST LIKE ME...

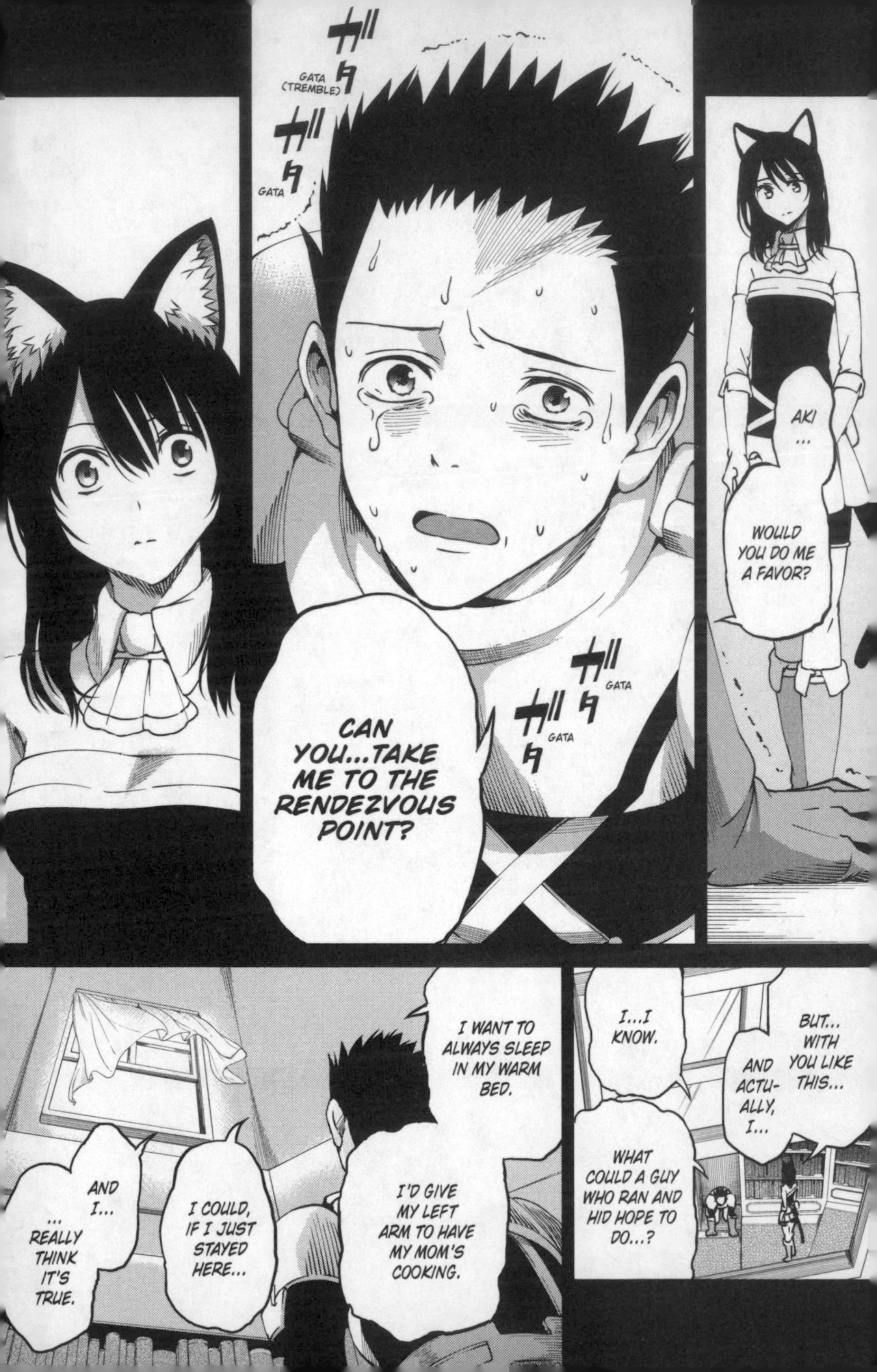
AKI...
WOULD YOU DO ME A FAVOR?
ガタ
GATA (TREMBLE)
ガタ
GATA
ガタ
GATA
ガタ
GATA
CAN YOU...TAKE ME TO THE RENDEZVOUS POINT?
BUT... WITH YOU LIKE THIS...
AND ACTUALLY, I...
I...I KNOW.
WHAT COULD A GUY WHO RAN AND HID HOPE TO DO...?
I WANT TO ALWAYS SLEEP IN MY WARM BED.
I'D GIVE MY LEFT ARM TO HAVE MY MOM'S COOKING.
I COULD, IF I JUST STAYED HERE...
AND I...
...REALLY THINK IT'S TRUE.

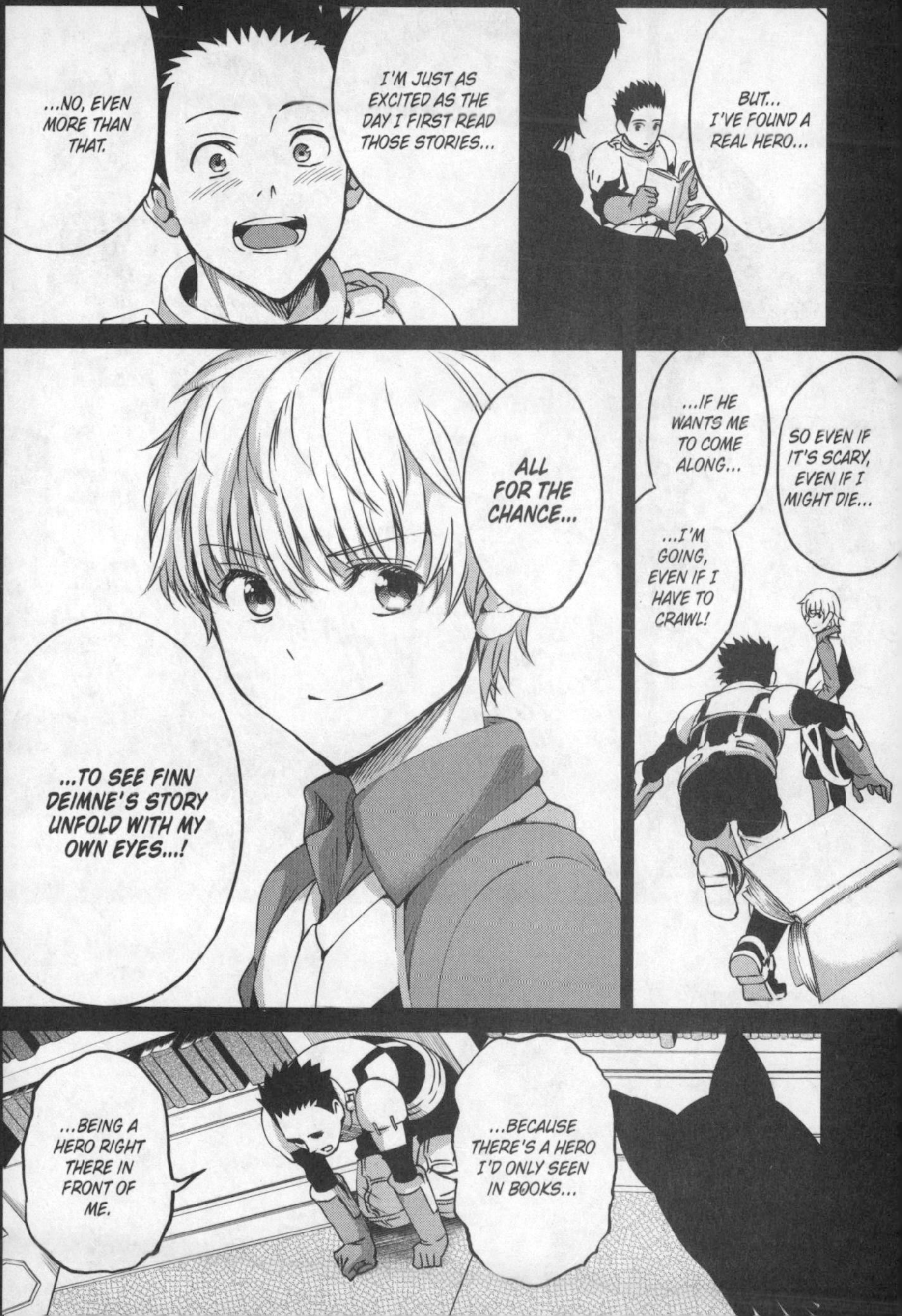
BUT... I'VE FOUND A REAL HERO...
I'M JUST AS EXCITED AS THE DAY I FIRST READ THOSE STORIES...
...NO, EVEN MORE THAN THAT.
SO EVEN IF IT'S SCARY, EVEN IF I MIGHT DIE...
...IF HE WANTS ME TO COME ALONG...
...I'M GOING, EVEN IF I HAVE TO CRAWL!
ALL FOR THE CHANCE...
...TO SEE FINN DEIMNE'S STORY UNFOLD WITH MY OWN EYES...!
...BECAUSE THERE'S A HERO I'D ONLY SEEN IN BOOKS...
...BEING A HERO RIGHT THERE IN FRONT OF ME.

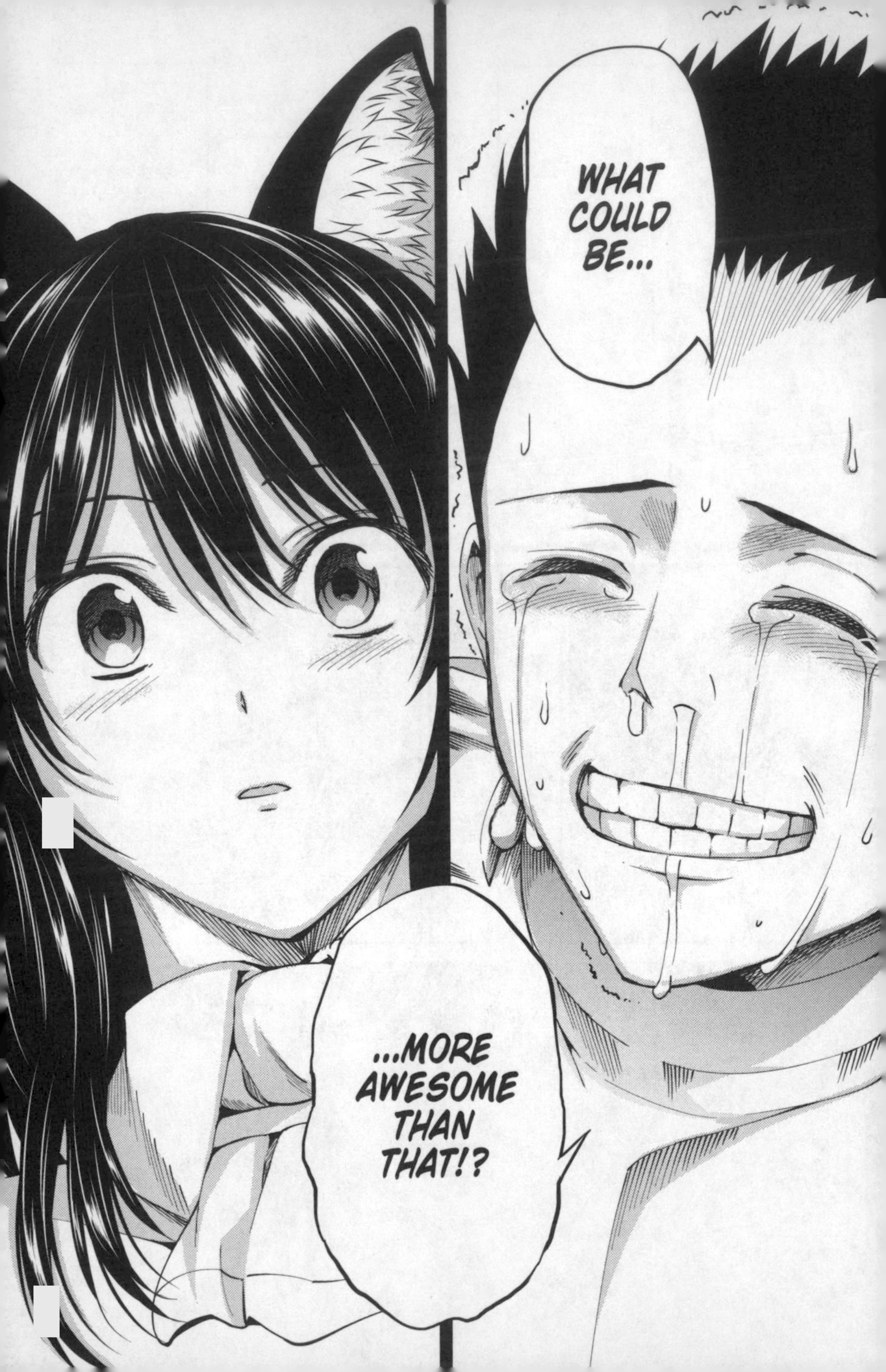
WHAT COULD BE...
...MORE AWESOME THAN THAT!?

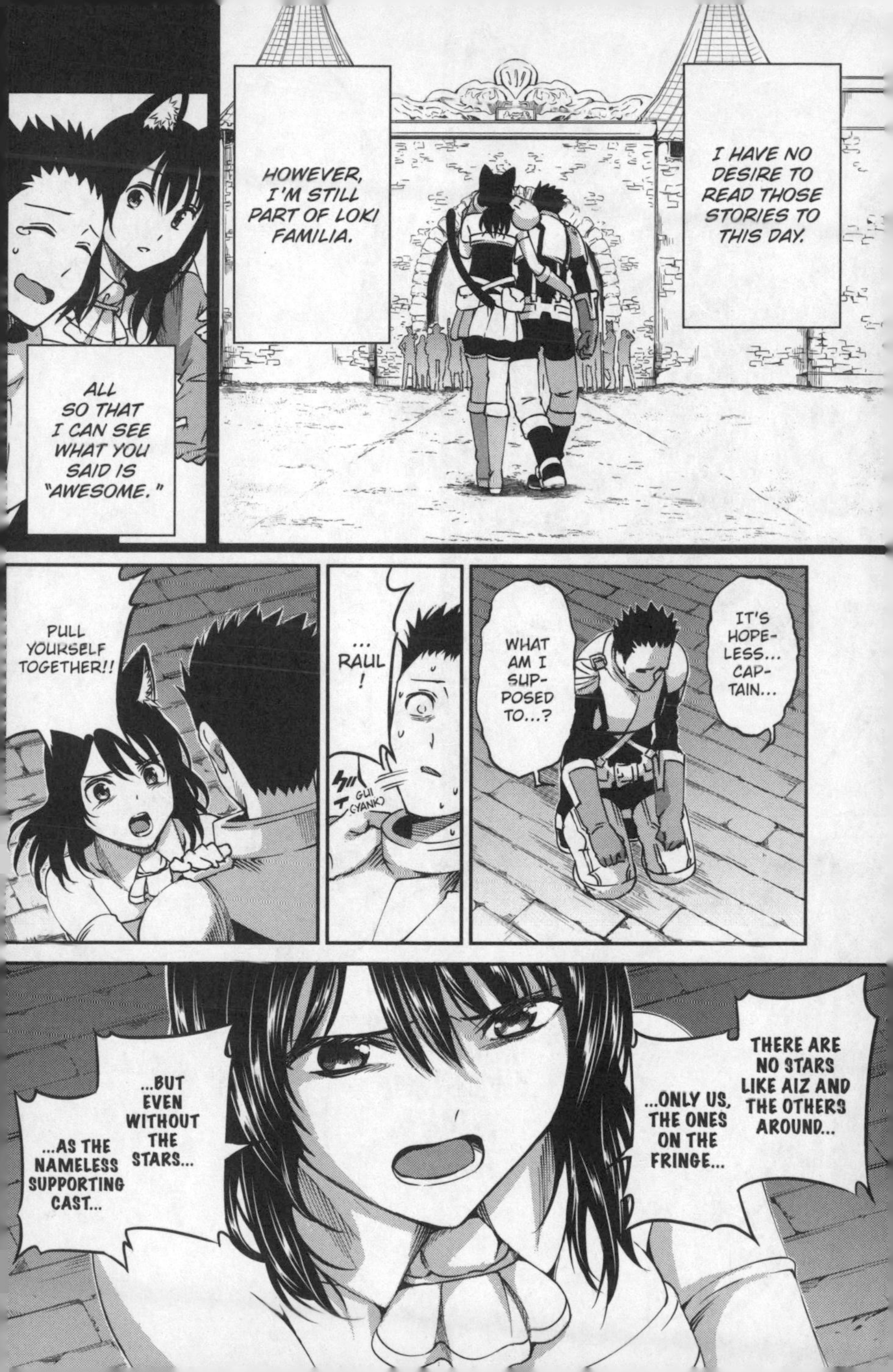
I HAVE NO DESIRE TO READ THOSE STORIES TO THIS DAY.
HOWEVER, I'M STILL PART OF LOKI FAMILIA.
ALL SO THAT I CAN SEE WHAT YOU SAID IS "AWESOME."
IT'S HOPELESS... CAPTAIN...
WHAT AM I SUPPOSED TO...?
...RAUL!
GUI (YANK)
PULL YOURSELF TOGETHER!!
THERE ARE NO STARS LIKE AIZ AND THE OTHERS AROUND...
...ONLY US, THE ONES ON THE FRINGE...
...BUT EVEN WITHOUT THE STARS...
...AS THE NAMELESS SUPPORTING CAST...

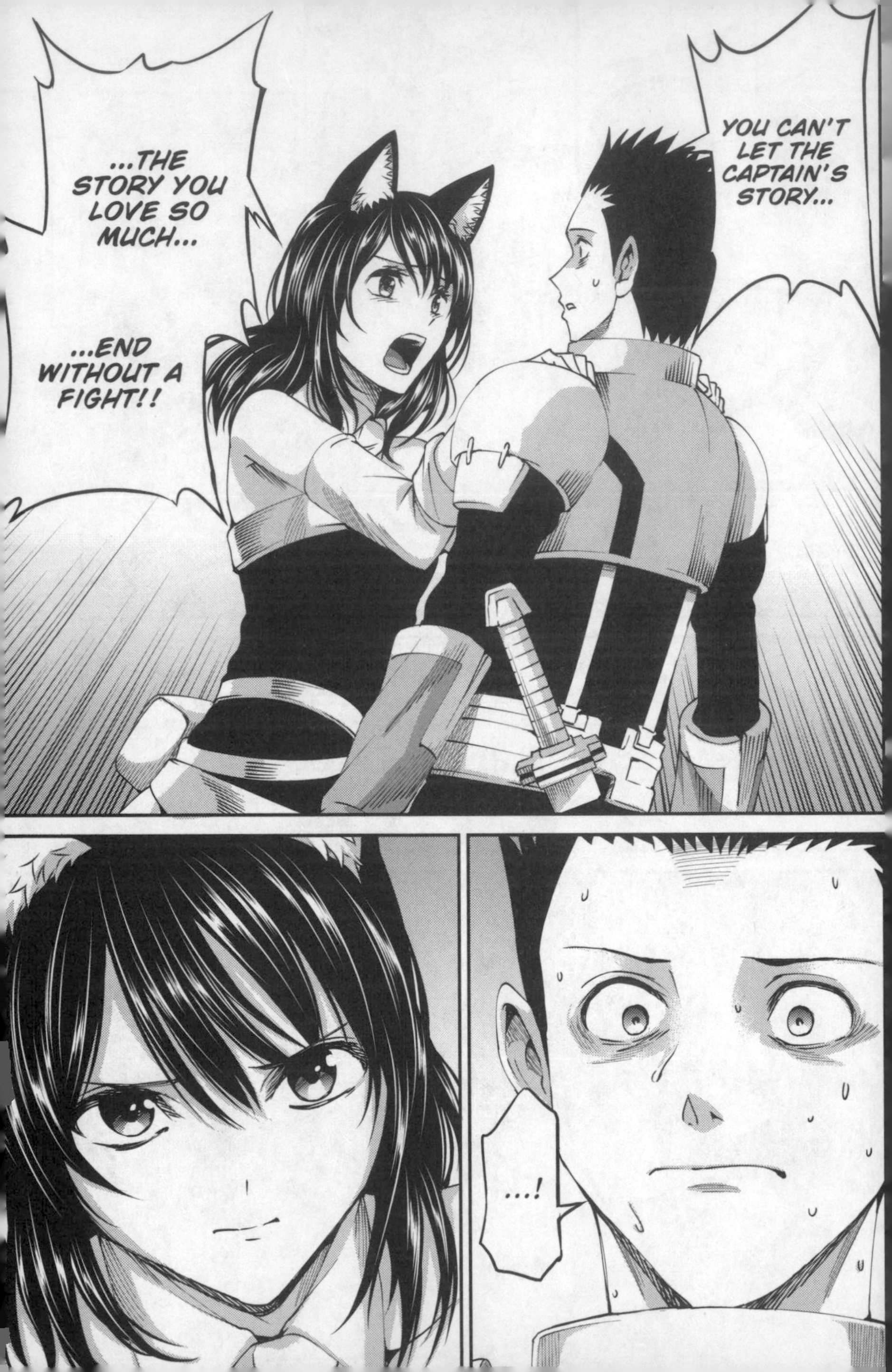
YOU CAN'T LET THE CAPTAIN'S STORY...
...THE STORY YOU LOVE SO MUCH...
...END WITHOUT A FIGHT!!
...!

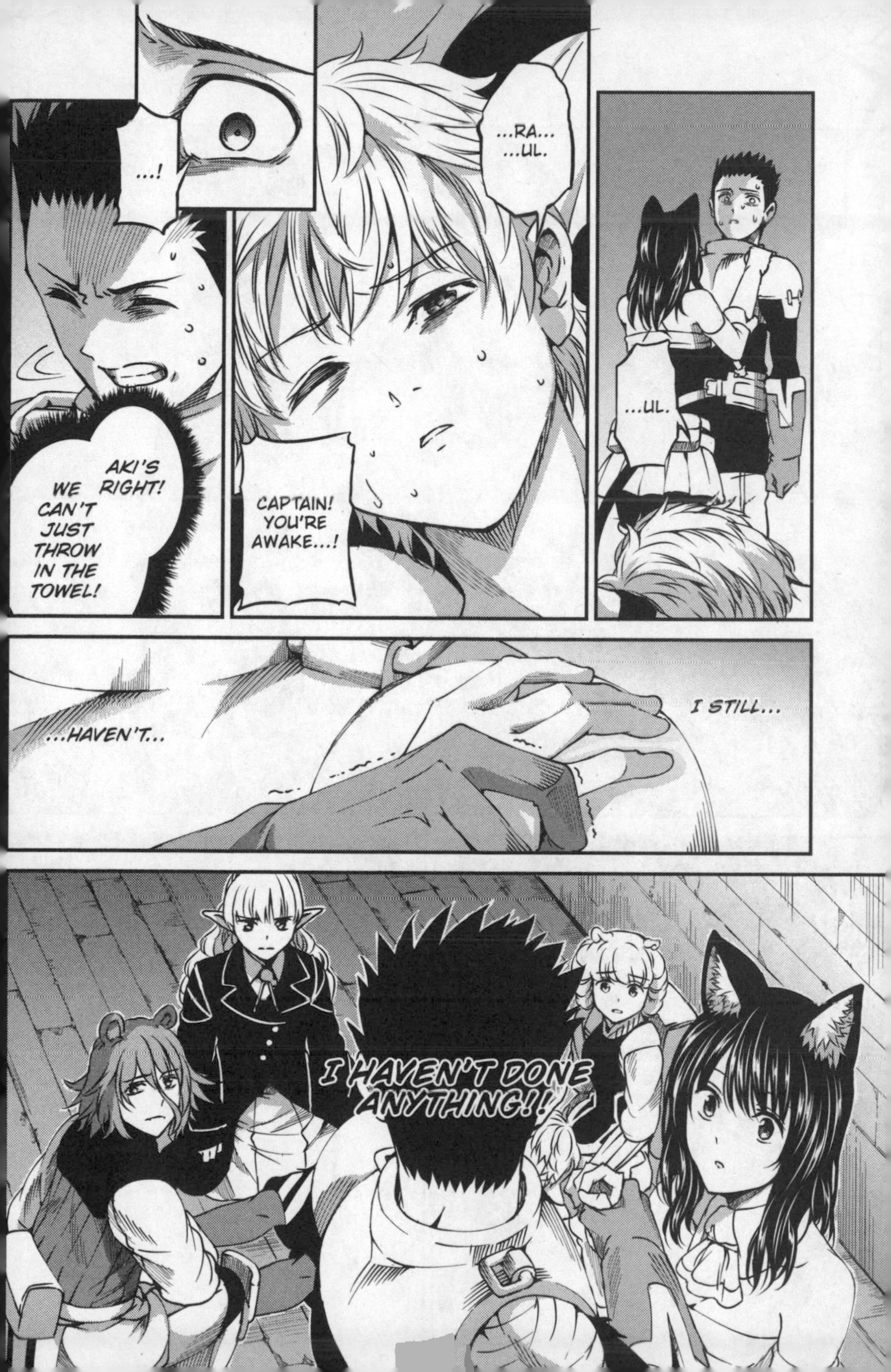
...UL.
...RA...
...UL.
CAPTAIN! YOU'RE AWAKE...!
...!
AKI'S RIGHT! WE CAN'T JUST THROW IN THE TOWEL!
I STILL...
...HAVEN'T...
I HAVEN'T DONE ANYTHING!!

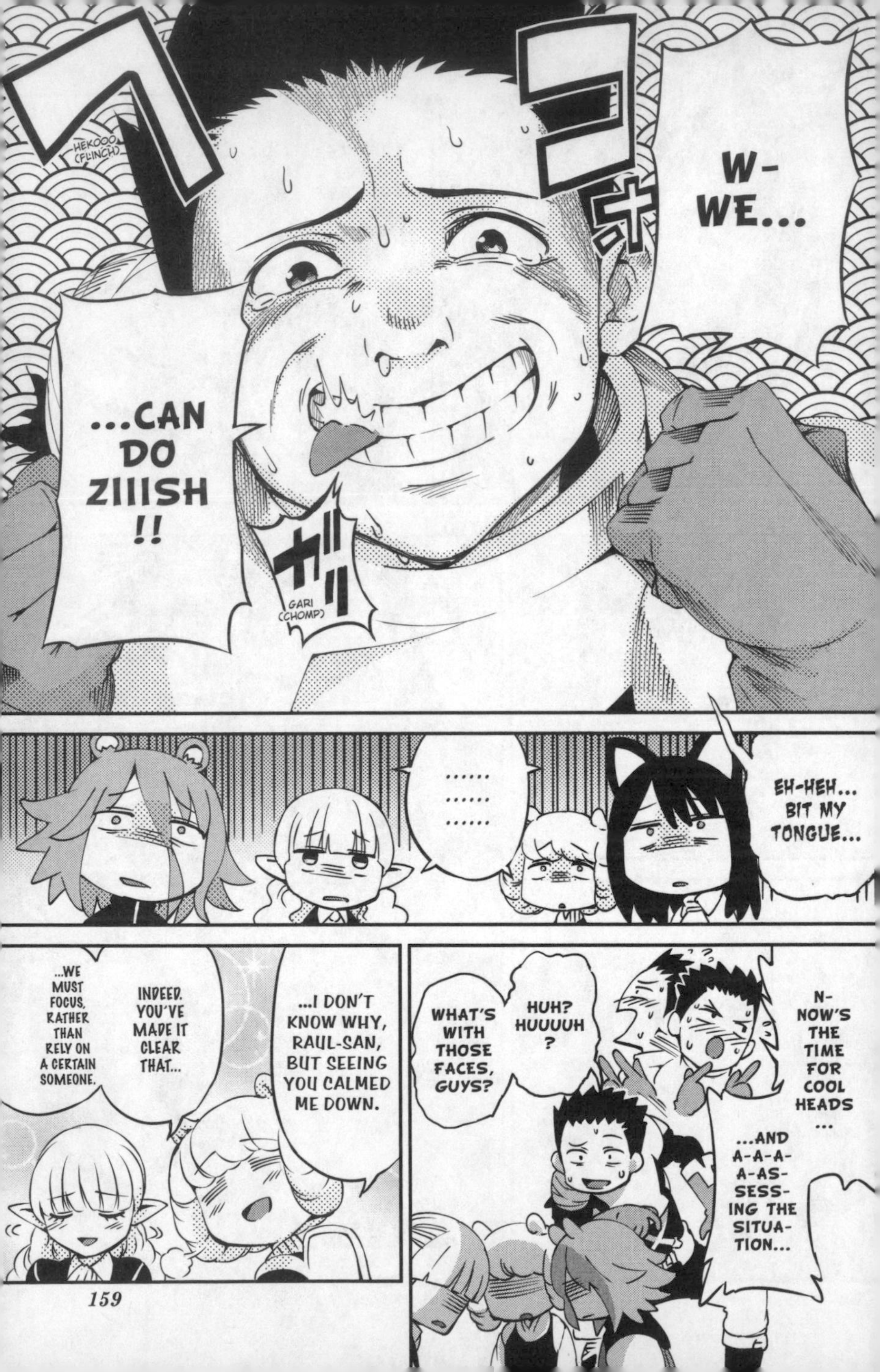
W-WE...
HEKOOO (FLINCH)
...CAN DO ZIIISH !!
GARI (CHOMP)
EH-HEH... BIT MY TONGUE...
....
N-NOW'S THE TIME FOR COOL HEADS...
...AND A-A-A-A-ASSESSING THE SITUATION...
HUH? HUUUUH?
WHAT'S WITH THOSE FACES, GUYS?
...I DON'T KNOW WHY, RAUL-SAN, BUT SEEING YOU CALMED ME DOWN.
INDEED. YOU'VE MADE IT CLEAR THAT...
...WE MUST FOCUS, RATHER THAN RELY ON A CERTAIN SOMEONE.

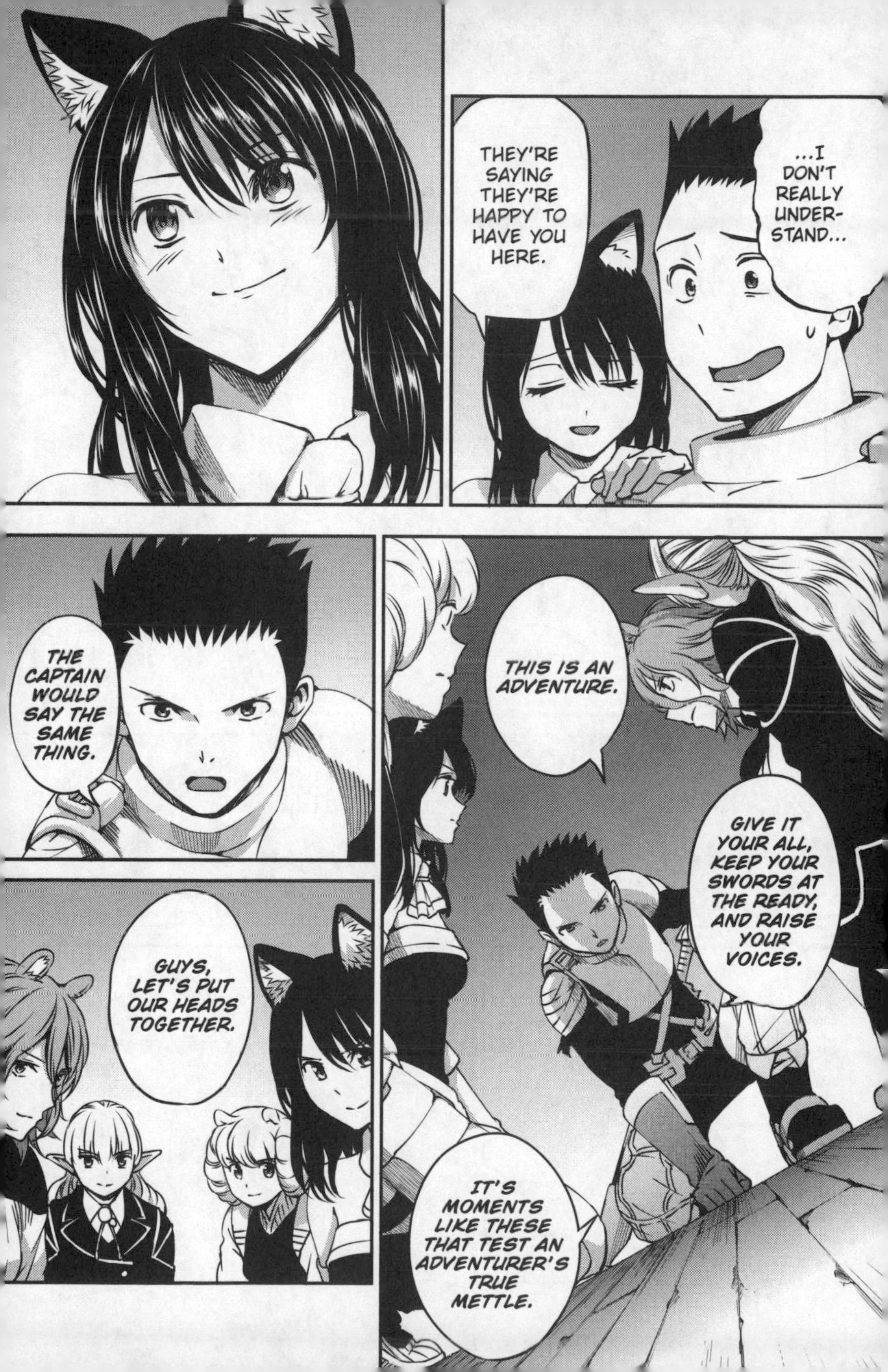
...I DON'T REALLY UNDERSTAND...
THEY'RE SAYING THEY'RE HAPPY TO HAVE YOU HERE.
THIS IS AN ADVENTURE.
GIVE IT YOUR ALL, KEEP YOUR SWORDS AT THE READY, AND RAISE YOUR VOICES.
IT'S MOMENTS LIKE THESE THAT TEST AN ADVENTURER'S TRUE METTLE.
THE CAPTAIN WOULD SAY THE SAME THING.
GUYS, LET'S PUT OUR HEADS TOGETHER.

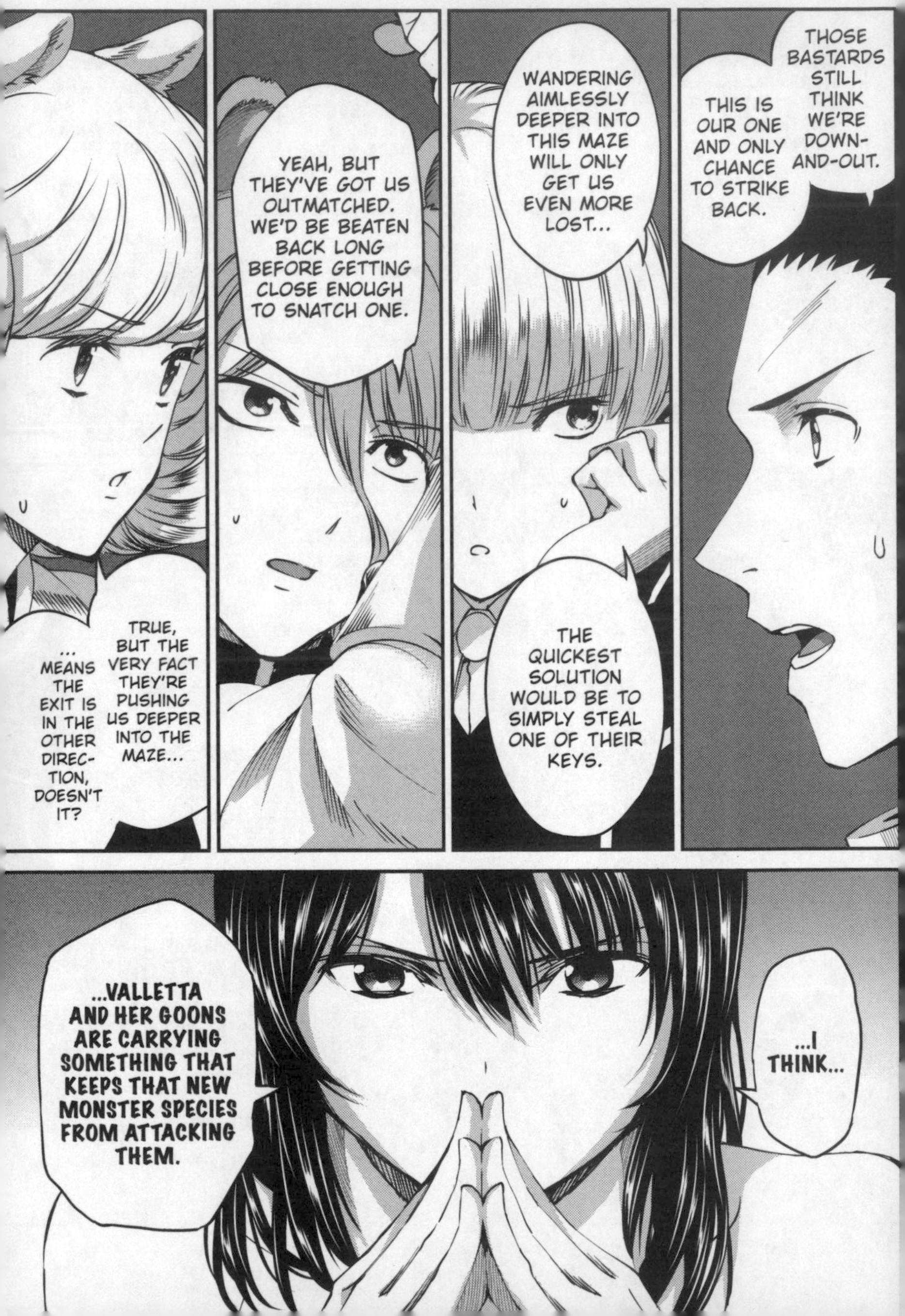
THOSE BASTARDS STILL THINK WE'RE DOWN-AND-OUT.
THIS IS OUR ONE AND ONLY CHANCE TO STRIKE BACK.
THE QUICKEST SOLUTION WOULD BE TO SIMPLY STEAL ONE OF THEIR KEYS.
WANDERING AIMLESSLY DEEPER INTO THIS MAZE WILL ONLY GET US EVEN MORE LOST...
YEAH, BUT THEY'VE GOT US OUTMATCHED. WE'D BE BEATEN BACK LONG BEFORE GETTING CLOSE ENOUGH TO SNATCH ONE.
TRUE, BUT THE VERY FACT THEY'RE PUSHING US DEEPER INTO THE MAZE...
...MEANS THE EXIT IS IN THE OTHER DIRECTION, DOESN'T IT?
...I THINK...
...VALLETTA AND HER GOONS ARE CARRYING SOMETHING THAT KEEPS THAT NEW MONSTER SPECIES FROM ATTACKING THEM.

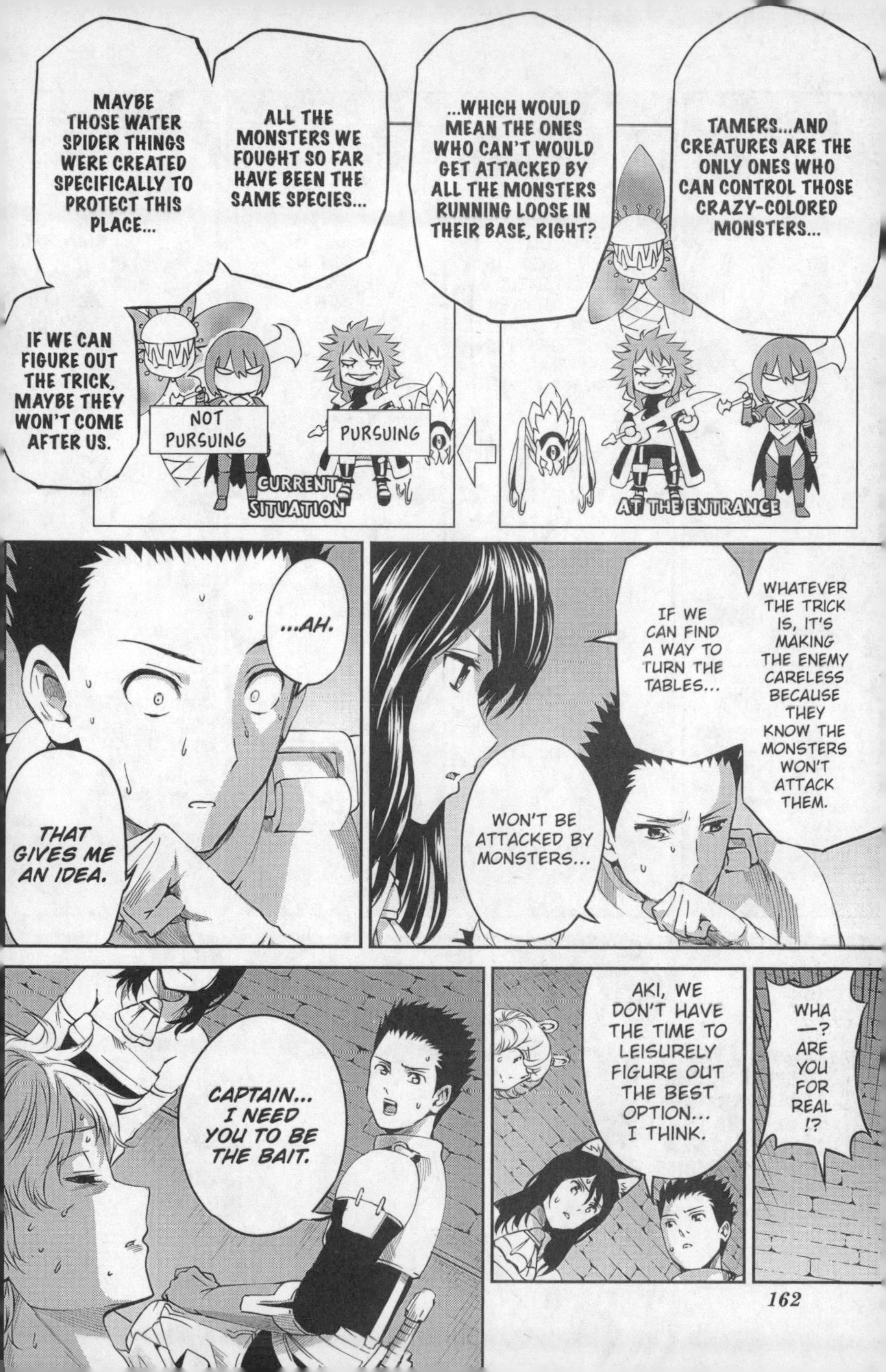
TAMERS...AND CREATURES ARE THE ONLY ONES WHO CAN CONTROL THOSE CRAZY-COLORED MONSTERS...
...WHICH WOULD MEAN THE ONES WHO CAN'T WOULD GET ATTACKED BY ALL THE MONSTERS RUNNING LOOSE IN THEIR BASE, RIGHT?
AT THE ENTRANCE
ALL THE MONSTERS WE FOUGHT SO FAR HAVE BEEN THE SAME SPECIES...
MAYBE THOSE WATER SPIDER THINGS WERE CREATED SPECIFICALLY TO PROTECT THIS PLACE...
IF WE CAN FIGURE OUT THE TRICK, MAYBE THEY WON'T COME AFTER US.
PURSUING
NOT PURSUING
CURRENT SITUATION
WHATEVER THE TRICK IS, IT'S MAKING THE ENEMY CARELESS BECAUSE THEY KNOW THE MONSTERS WON'T ATTACK THEM.
IF WE CAN FIND A WAY TO TURN THE TABLES...
WON'T BE ATTACKED BY MONSTERS...
...AH.
THAT GIVES ME AN IDEA.
WHA—? ARE YOU FOR REAL!?
AKI, WE DON'T HAVE THE TIME TO LEISURELY FIGURE OUT THE BEST OPTION... I THINK.
CAPTAIN... I NEED YOU TO BE THE BAIT.

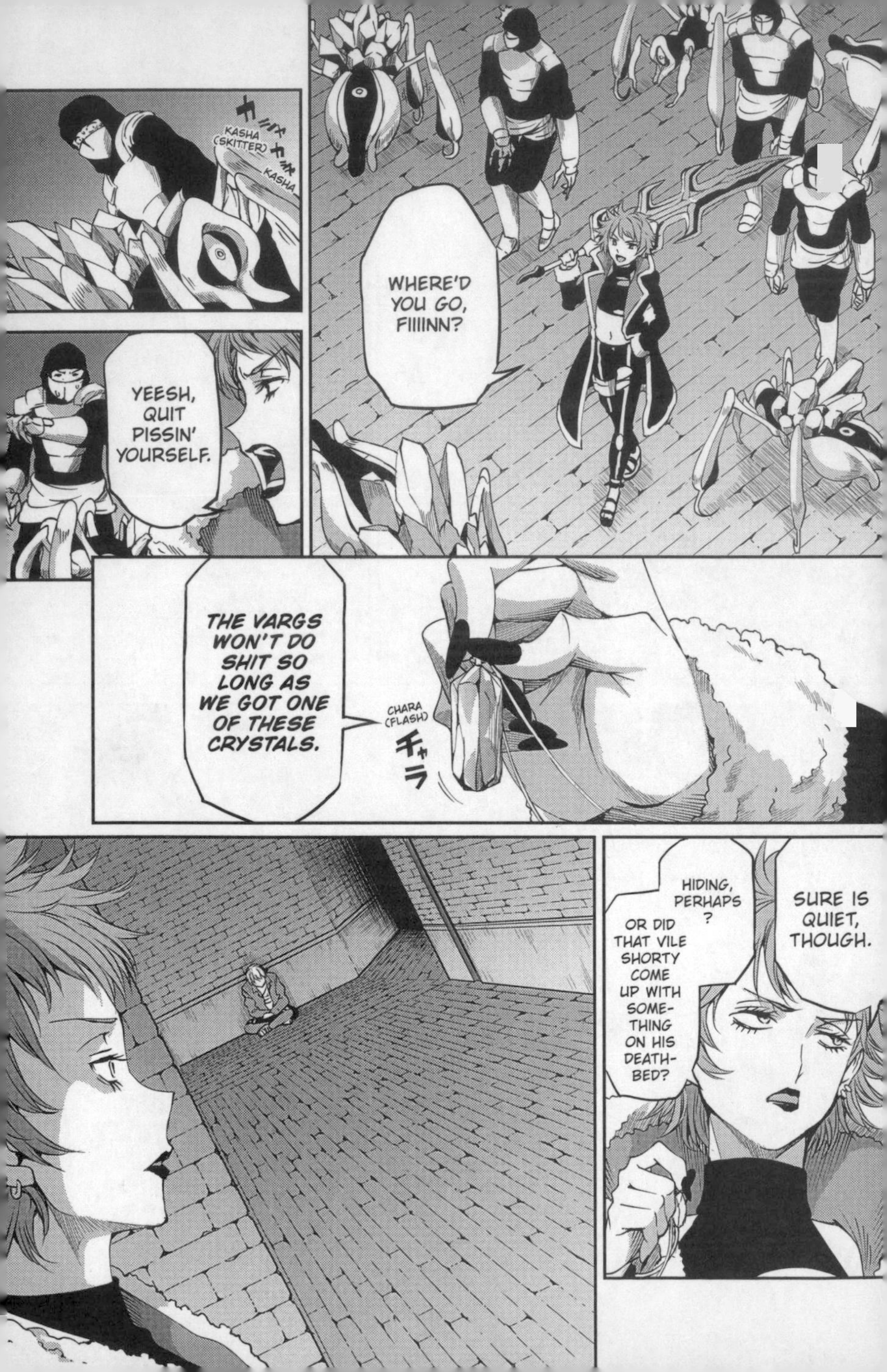
WHERE'D YOU GO, FIIIINN?
KASHA (SKITTER)
KASHA
YEESH, QUIT PISSIN' YOURSELF.
THE VARGS WON'T DO SHIT SO LONG AS WE GOT ONE OF THESE CRYSTALS.
CHARA (FLASH)
チャラ
SURE IS QUIET, THOUGH.
HIDING, PERHAPS?
OR DID THAT VILE SHORTY COME UP WITH SOMETHING ON HIS DEATHBED?

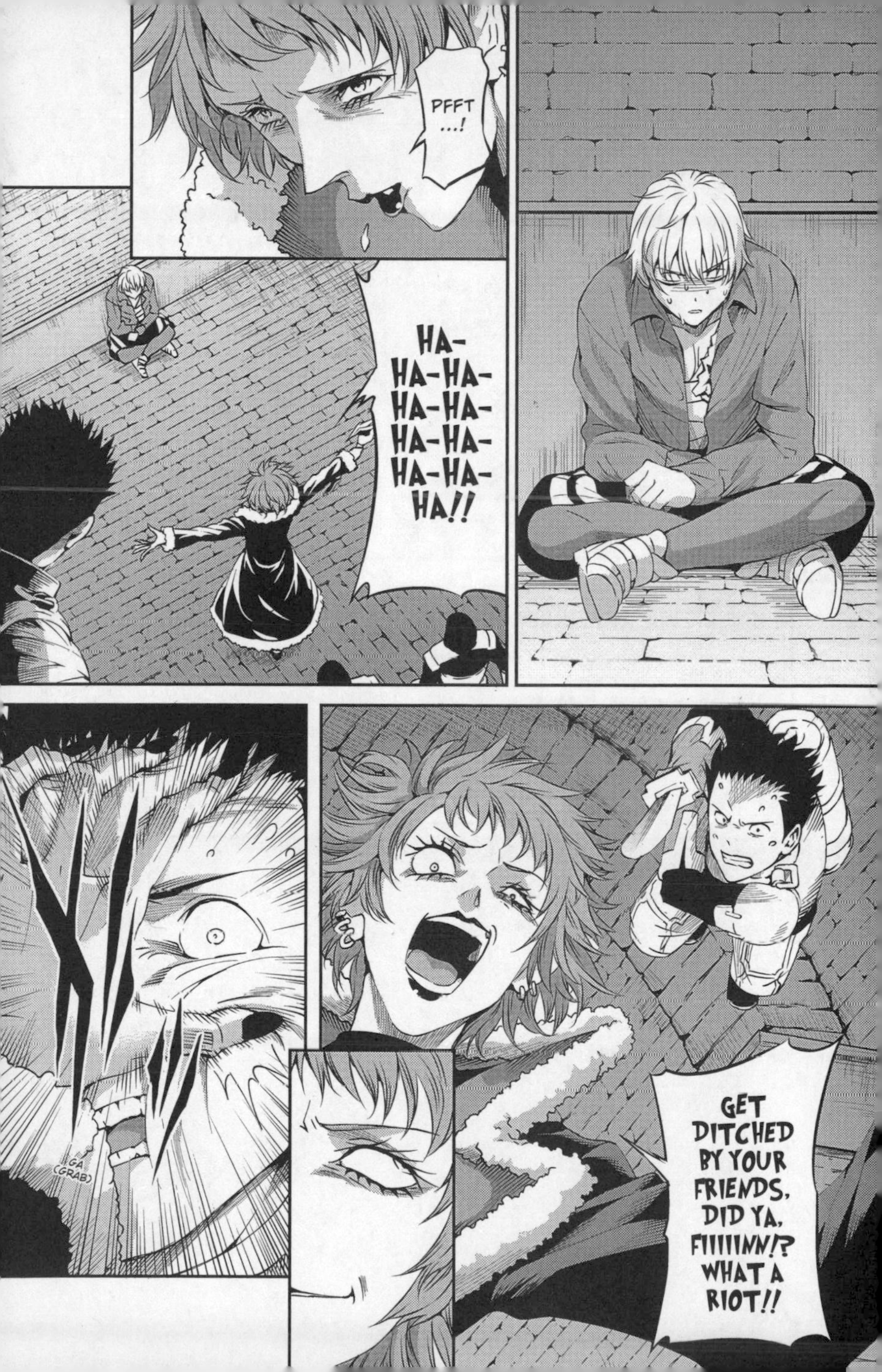
PFFT ...!
HA-HA-HA-HA-HA-HA-HA-HA-HA-HA-HA!!
GET DITCHED BY YOUR FRIENDS, DID YA, FIIIIIINN!? WHAT A RIOT!!
GA (GRAB)

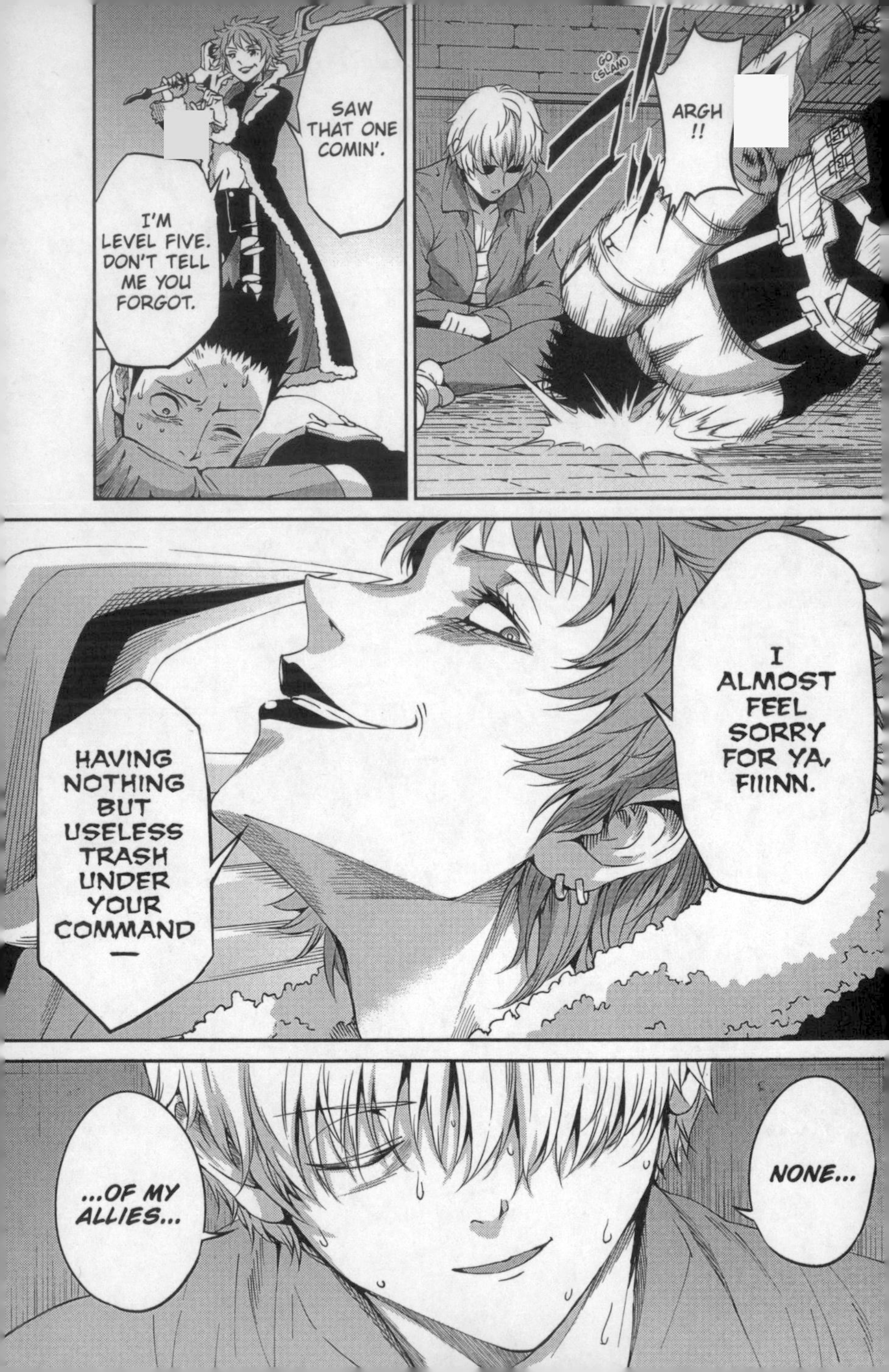
ARGH !!
GO (SLAM)
SAW THAT ONE COMIN'.
I'M LEVEL FIVE. DON'T TELL ME YOU FORGOT.
I ALMOST FEEL SORRY FOR YA, FIIINN.
HAVING NOTHING BUT USELESS TRASH UNDER YOUR COMMAND —
NONE...
...OF MY ALLIES...

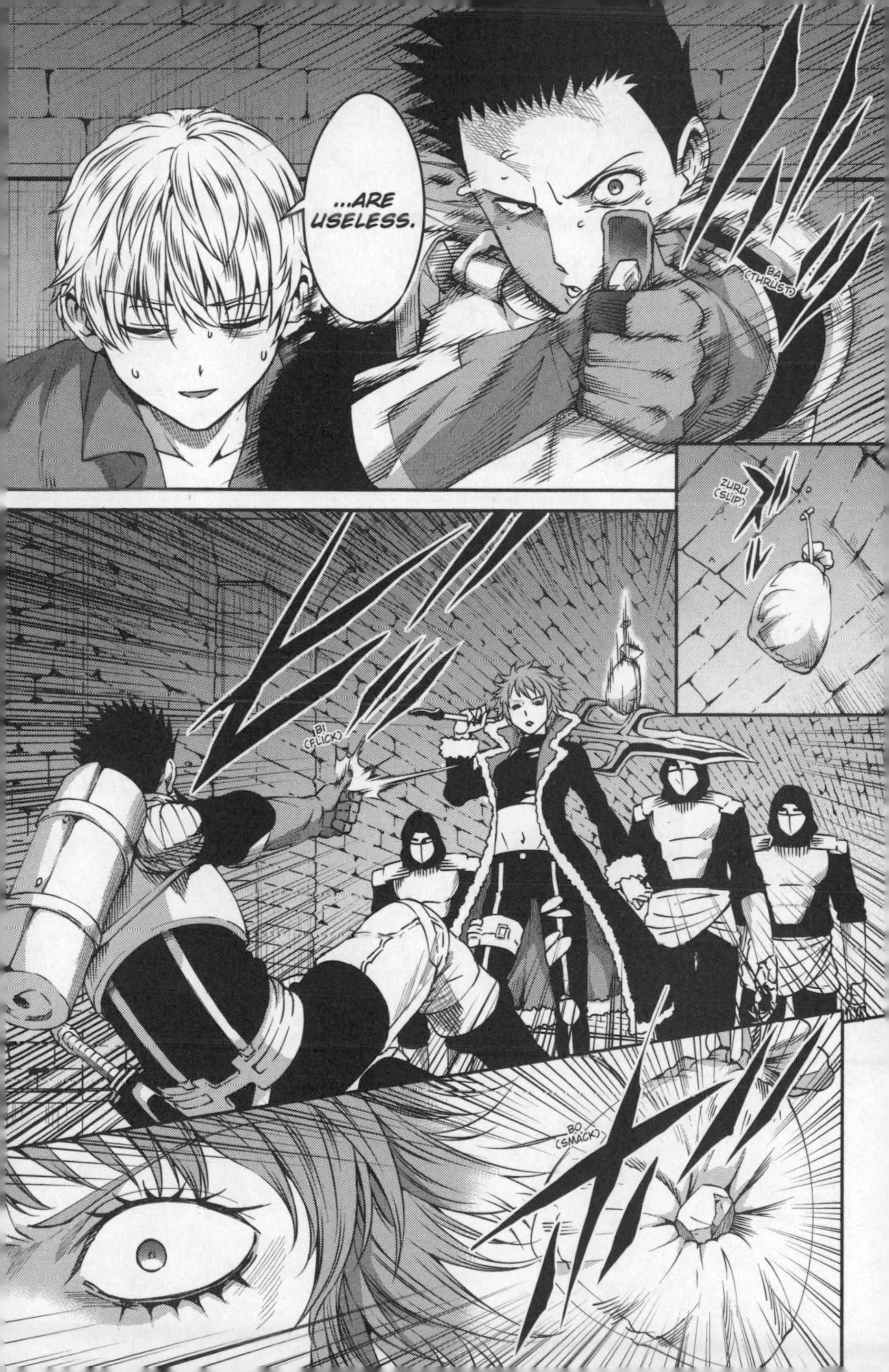
...ARE USELESS.
BA (THRUST)
ZURU (SLIP)
BI (FLICK)
BO (SMACK)

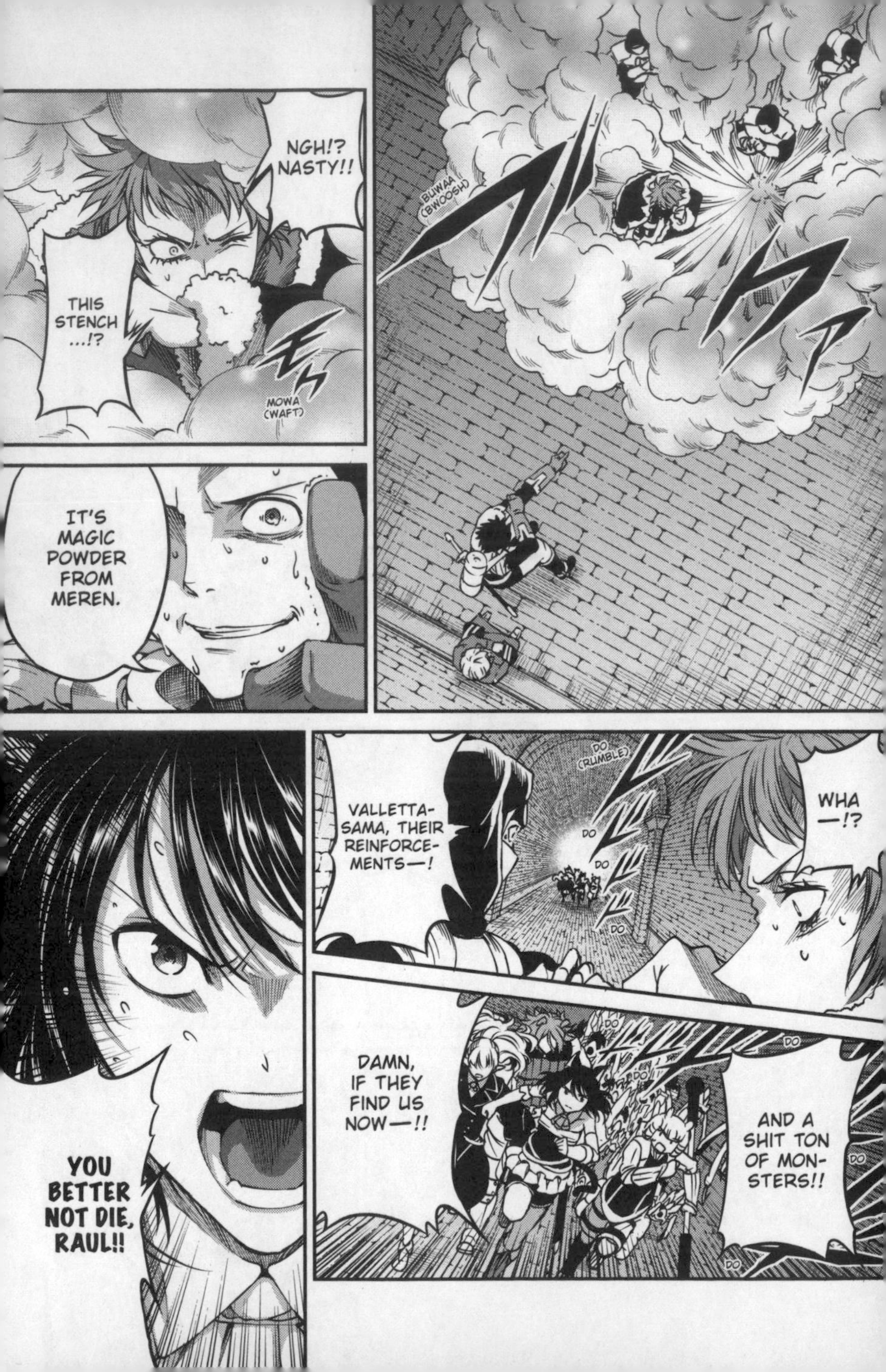
BUWAA (BWOOSH)
NGH!? NASTY!!
THIS STENCH ...!?
MOWA (WAFT)
IT'S MAGIC POWDER FROM MEREN.
WHA —!?
DO (RUMBLE)
DO
DO
DO
VALLETTA-SAMA, THEIR REINFORCEMENTS—!
DO
DO
DO
DO
DO
AND A SHIT TON OF MONSTERS!!
DAMN, IF THEY FIND US NOW—!!
YOU BETTER NOT DIE, RAUL!!

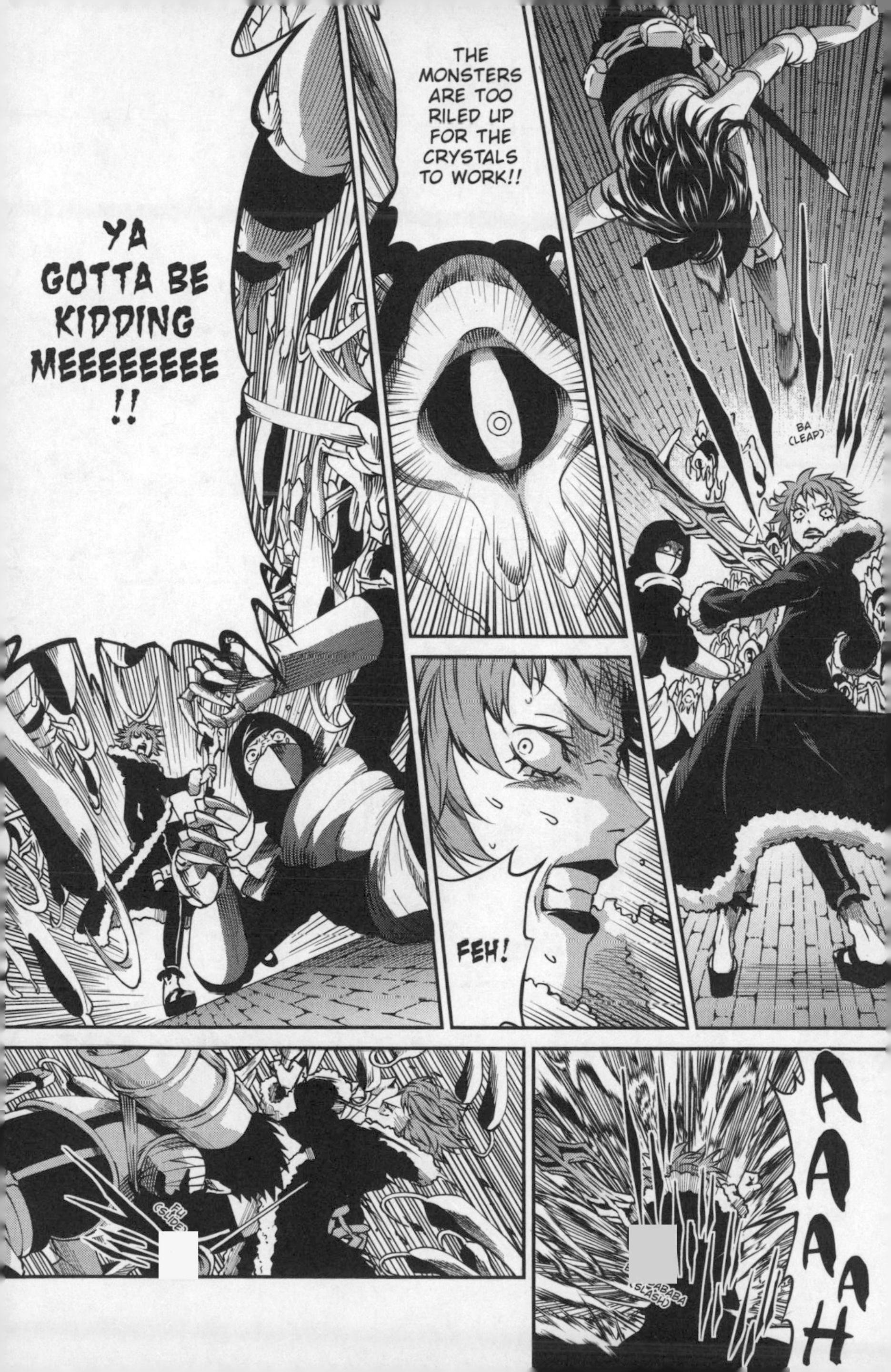
BA (LEAP)
THE MONSTERS ARE TOO RILED UP FOR THE CRYSTALS TO WORK!!
YA GOTTA BE KIDDING MEEEEEEEE!!
FEH!
AAAAAH
(SLASH)
FU (SLIDE)

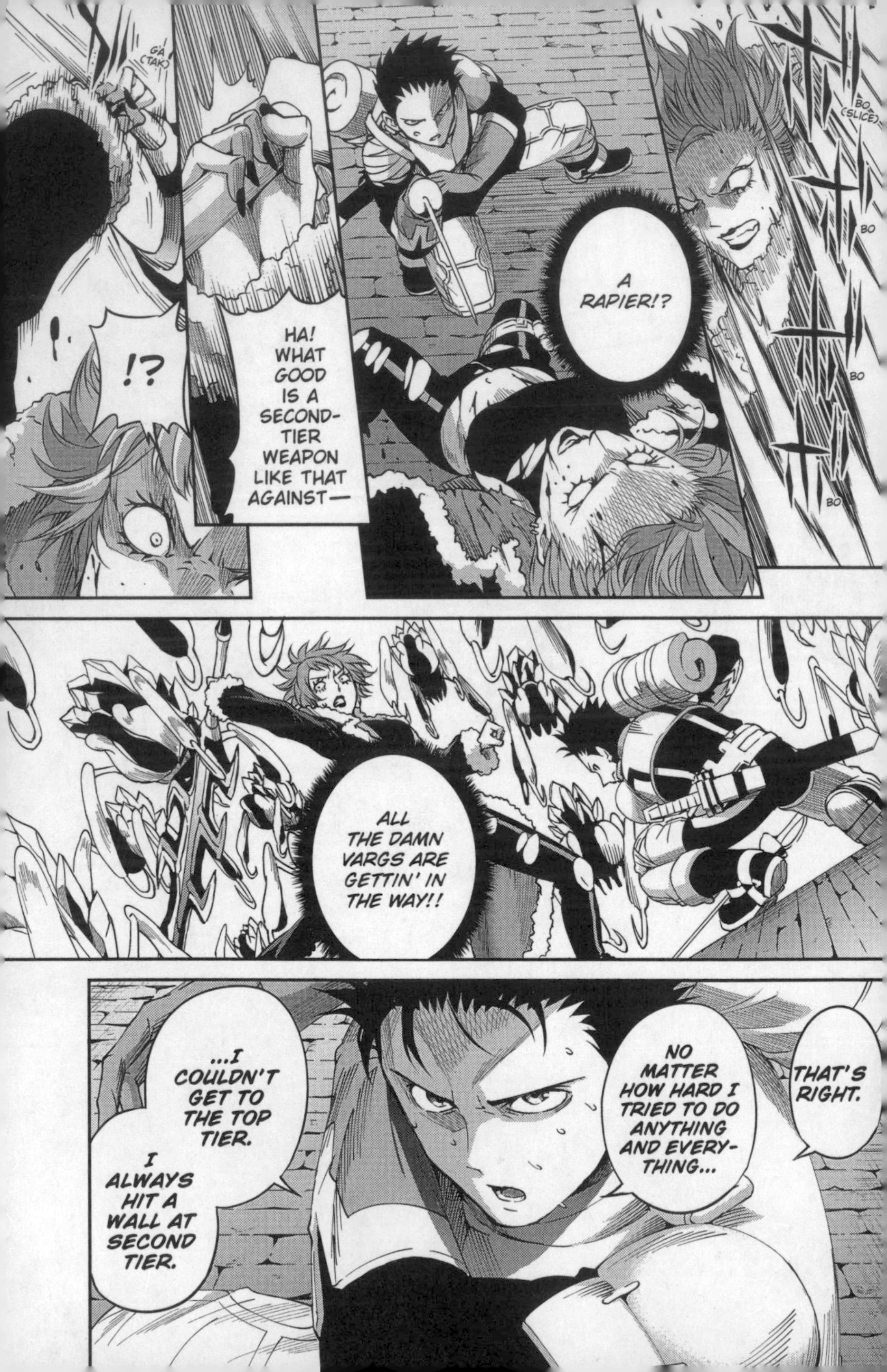
BO (SLICE)
BO
BO
BO
A RAPIER!?
HA! WHAT GOOD IS A SECOND-TIER WEAPON LIKE THAT AGAINST—
GA (TAK)
!?
ALL THE DAMN VARGS ARE GETTIN' IN THE WAY!!
THAT'S RIGHT.
NO MATTER HOW HARD I TRIED TO DO ANYTHING AND EVERY-THING...
...I COULDN'T GET TO THE TOP TIER.
I ALWAYS HIT A WALL AT SECOND TIER.

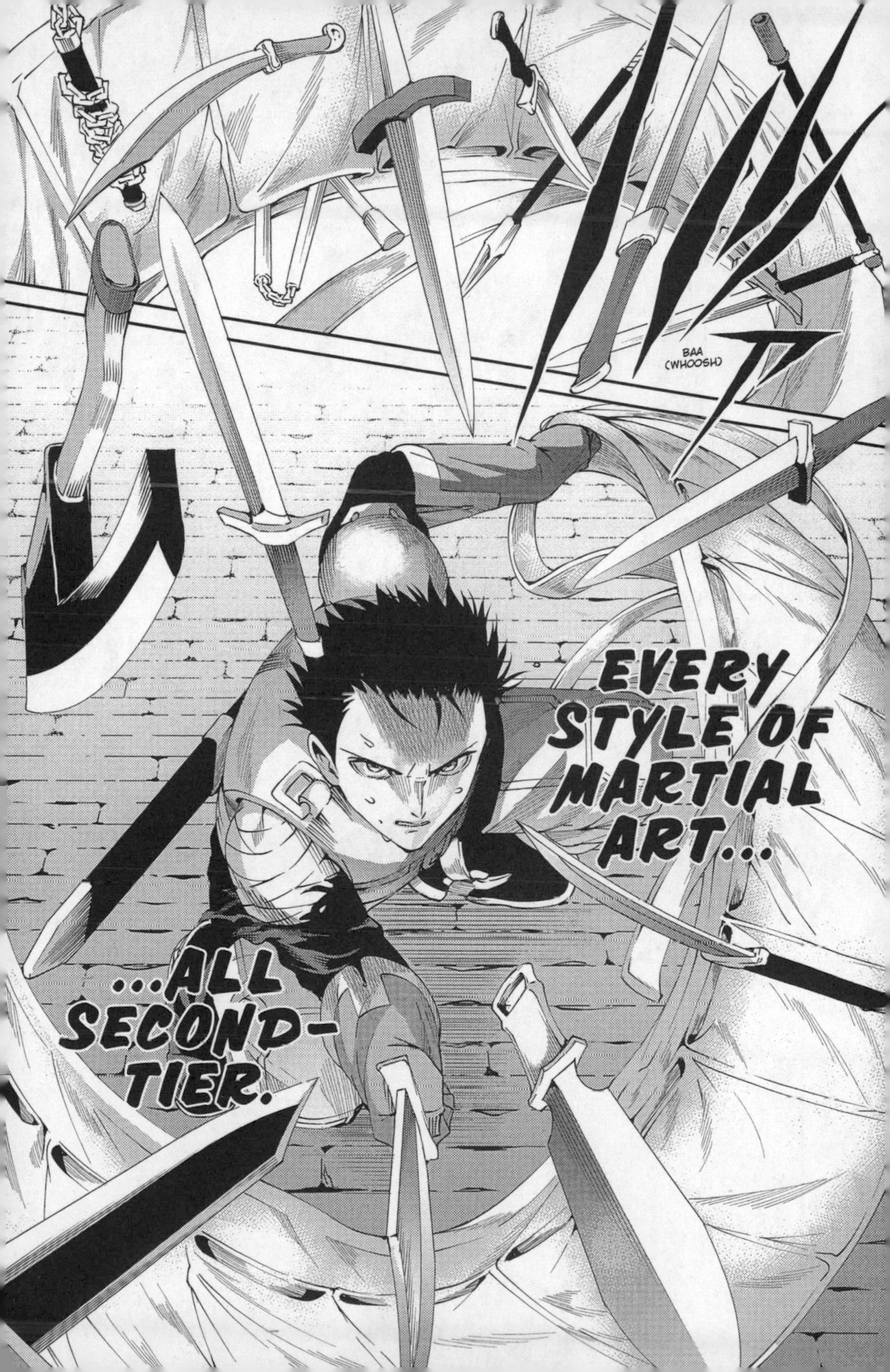
BAA (WHOOSH)
EVERY STYLE OF MARTIAL ART...
...ALL SECOND-TIER.

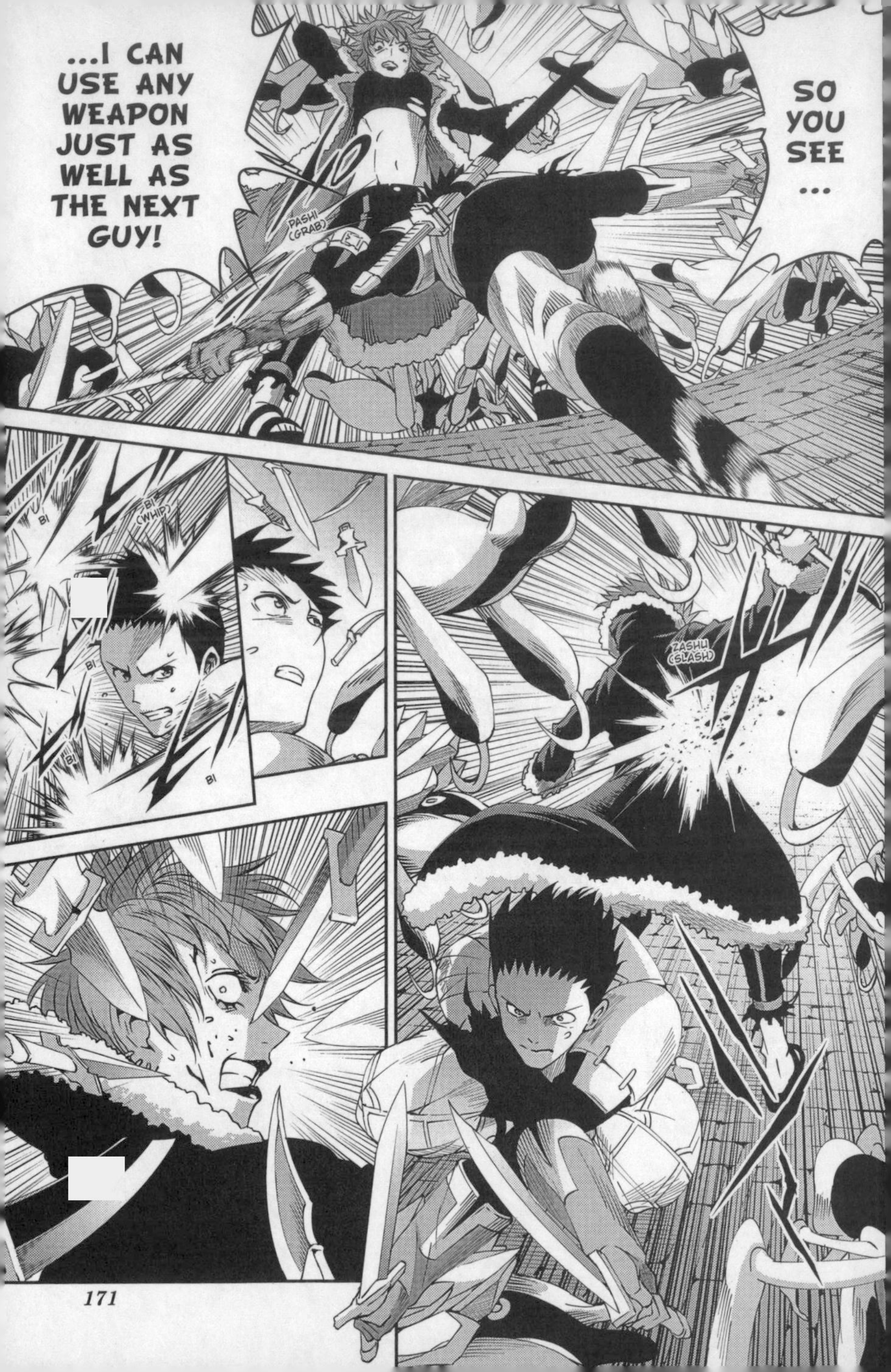

SO YOU SEE ...
...I CAN USE ANY WEAPON JUST AS WELL AS THE NEXT GUY!
PASHI (GRAB)
ZASHU (SLASH)
BI (WHIP)
BI
BI
BI
BI

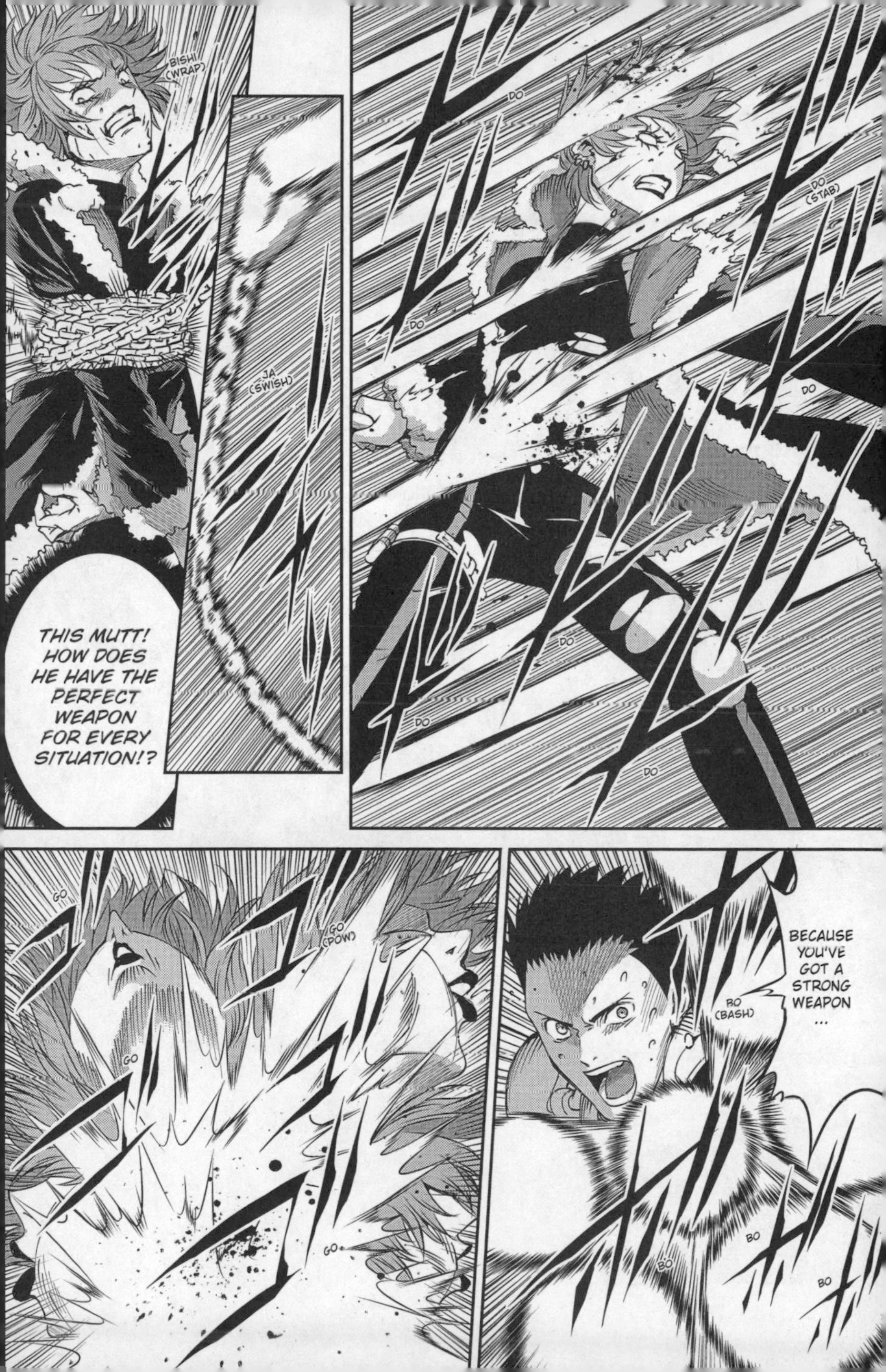
DO
DO (STAB)
DO
DO
DO
DO
DO
JA (SWISH)
BISHI (WRAP)
THIS MUTT! HOW DOES HE HAVE THE PERFECT WEAPON FOR EVERY SITUATION!?
BECAUSE YOU'VE GOT A STRONG WEAPON ...
BO (BASH)
BO
BO
BO
GO (POW)
GO
GO
GO

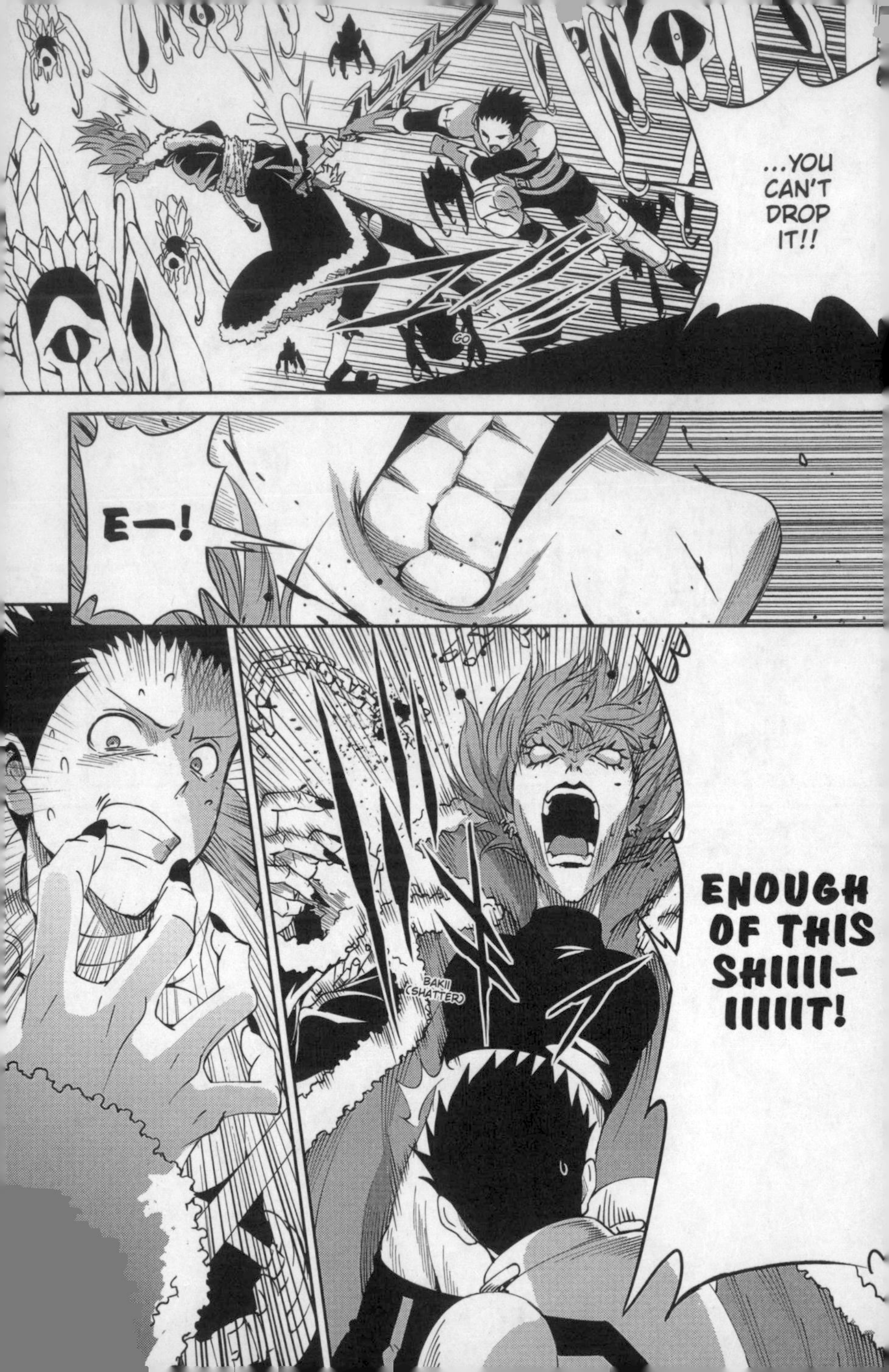
...YOU CAN'T DROP IT!!
GO
E—!
BAKII (SHATTER)
ENOUGH OF THIS SHIIII-IIIIIT!

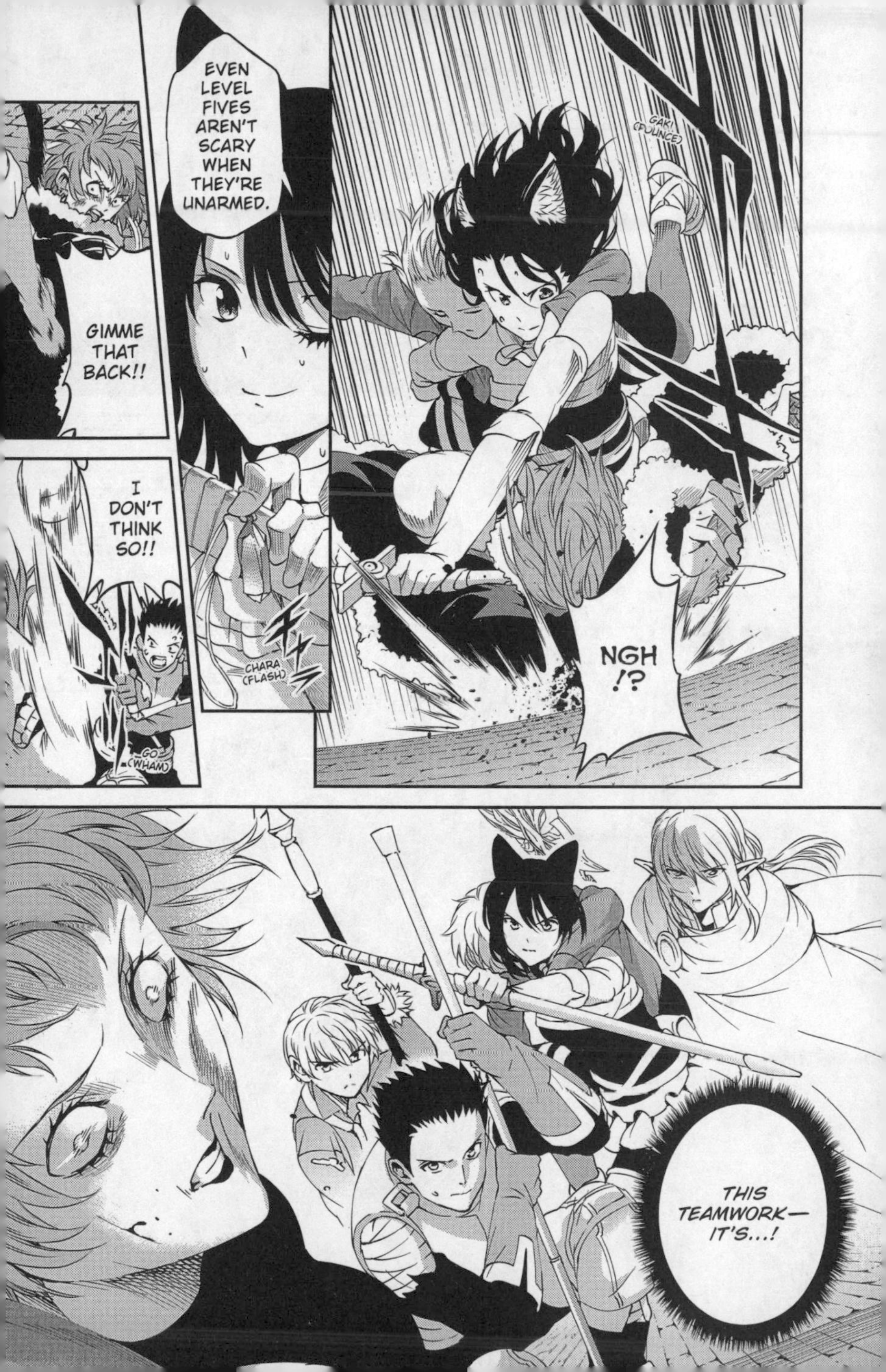
GAK! (POUNCE)
NGH!?
EVEN LEVEL FIVES AREN'T SCARY WHEN THEY'RE UNARMED.
CHARA (FLASH)
GIMME THAT BACK!!
I DON'T THINK SO!!
GO (WHAM)
THIS TEAMWORK—IT'S...!

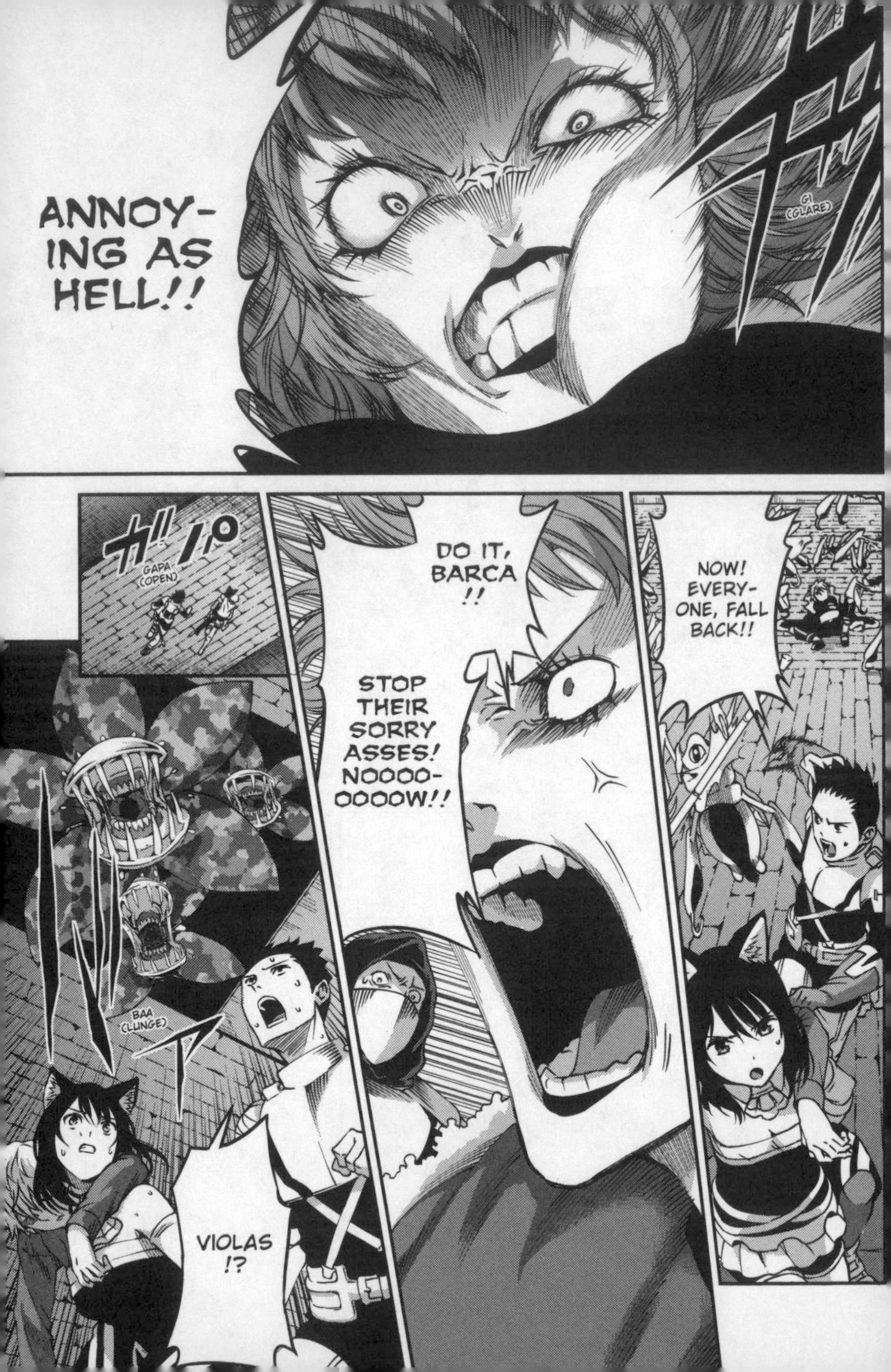
GI (GLARE)
ANNOY-ING AS HELL!!
NOW! EVERY-ONE, FALL BACK!!
DO IT, BARCA!!
STOP THEIR SORRY ASSES! NOOOOOOOOW!!
GAPA (OPEN)
BAA (LUNGE)
VIOLAS!?

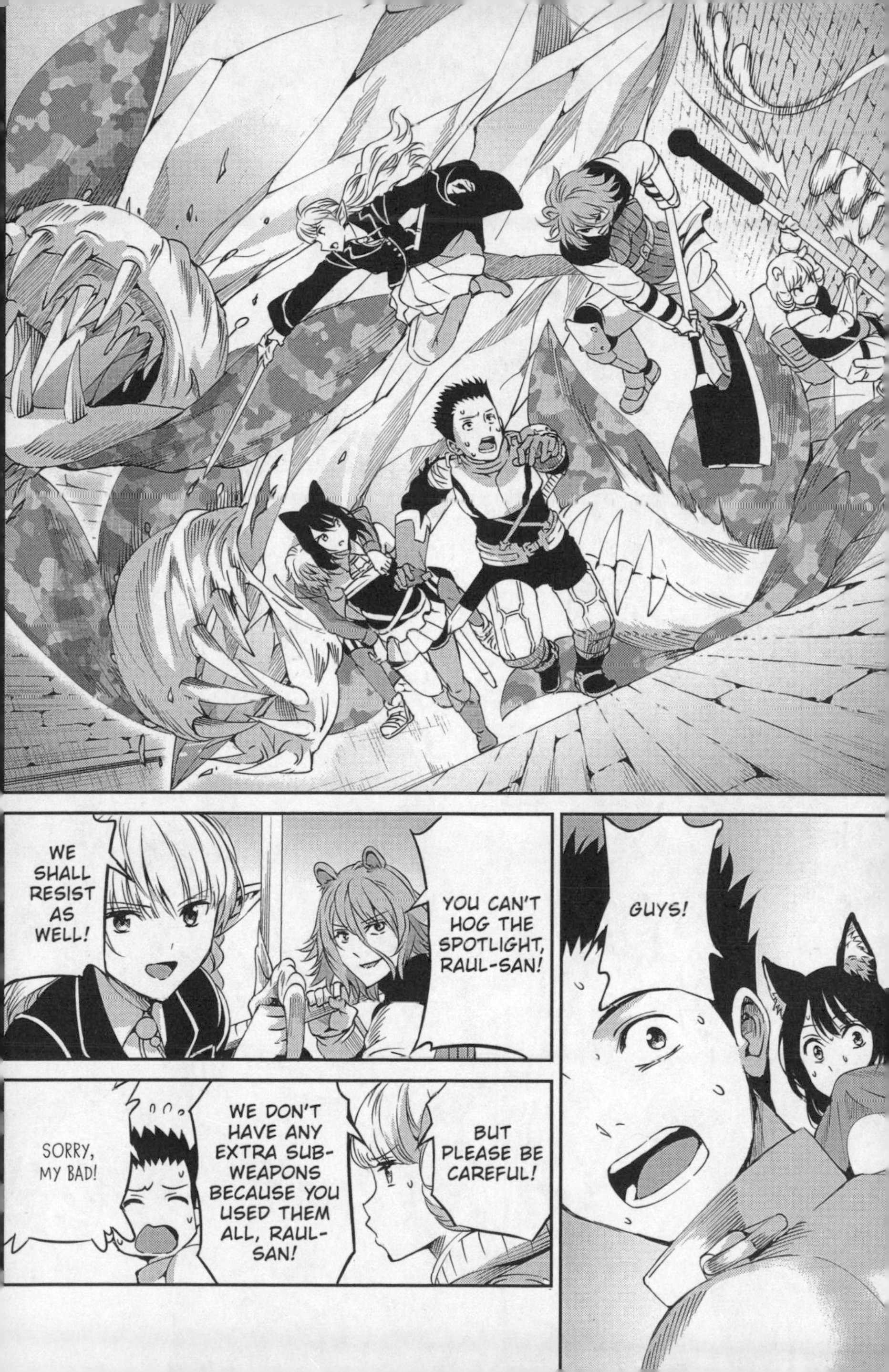
GUYS!
YOU CAN'T HOG THE SPOTLIGHT, RAUL-SAN!
WE SHALL RESIST AS WELL!
BUT PLEASE BE CAREFUL!
WE DON'T HAVE ANY EXTRA SUB-WEAPONS BECAUSE YOU USED THEM ALL, RAUL-SAN!
SORRY, MY BAD!

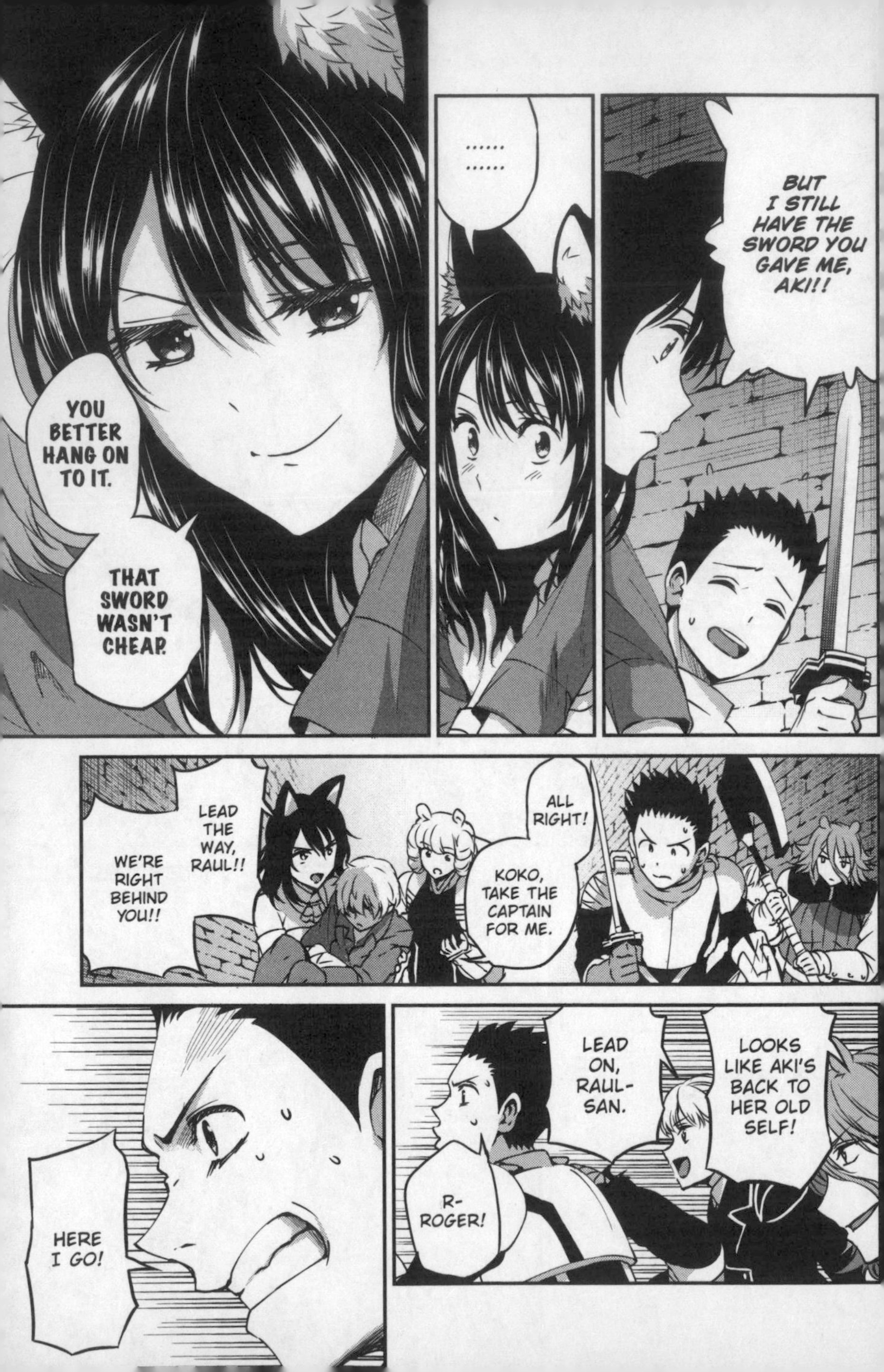
BUT I STILL HAVE THE SWORD YOU GAVE ME, AKI!!
......
......
YOU BETTER HANG ON TO IT.
THAT SWORD WASN'T CHEAP.
ALL RIGHT!
KOKO, TAKE THE CAPTAIN FOR ME.
LEAD THE WAY, RAUL!!
WE'RE RIGHT BEHIND YOU!!
LOOKS LIKE AKI'S BACK TO HER OLD SELF!
LEAD ON, RAUL-SAN.
R-ROGER!
HERE I GO!

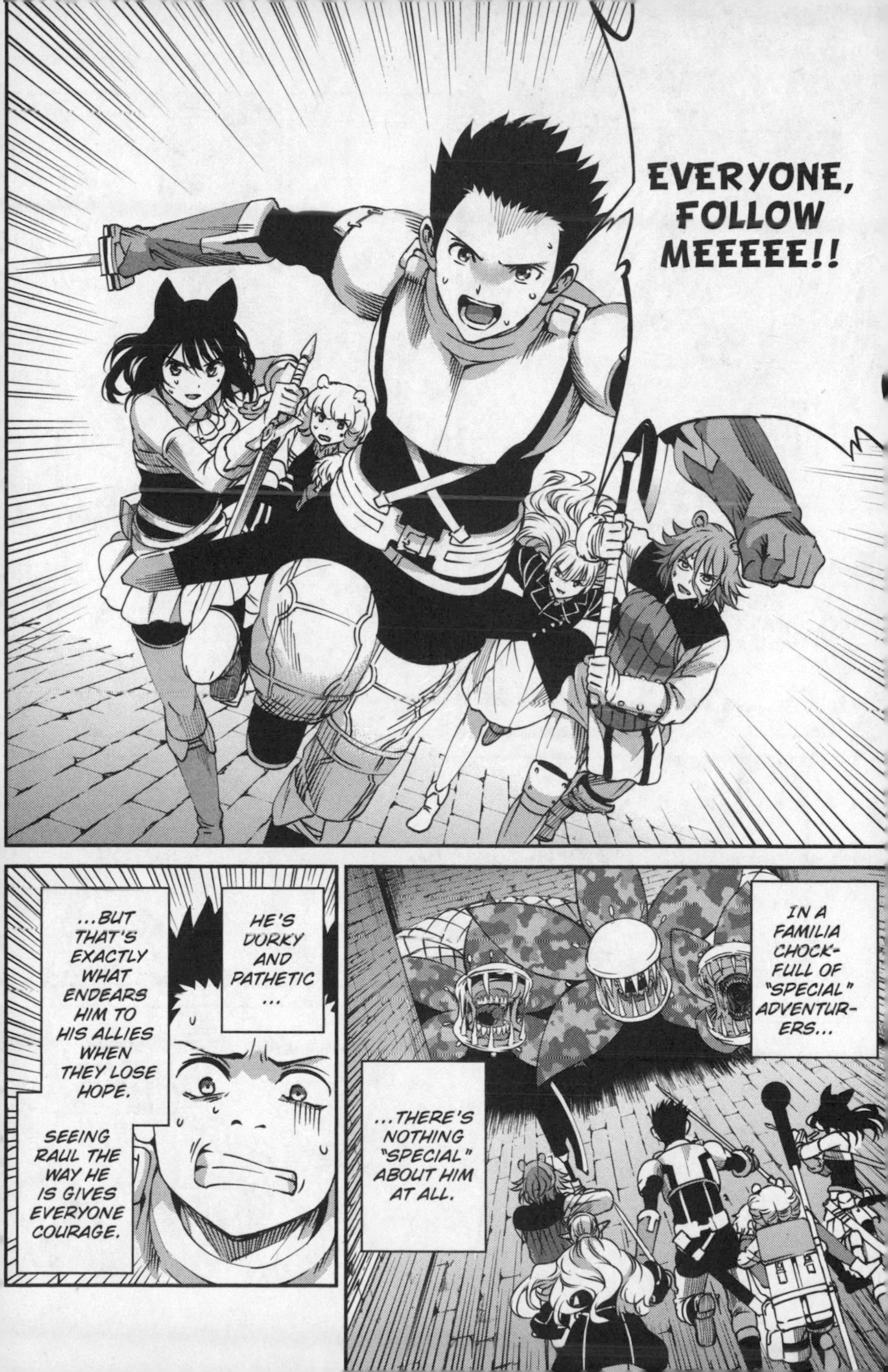
EVERYONE, FOLLOW MEEEEE!!
IN A FAMILIA CHOCK-FULL OF "SPECIAL" ADVENTURERS...
...THERE'S NOTHING "SPECIAL" ABOUT HIM AT ALL.
HE'S DORKY AND PATHETIC...
...BUT THAT'S EXACTLY WHAT ENDEARS HIM TO HIS ALLIES WHEN THEY LOSE HOPE.
SEEING RAUL THE WAY HE IS GIVES EVERYONE COURAGE.

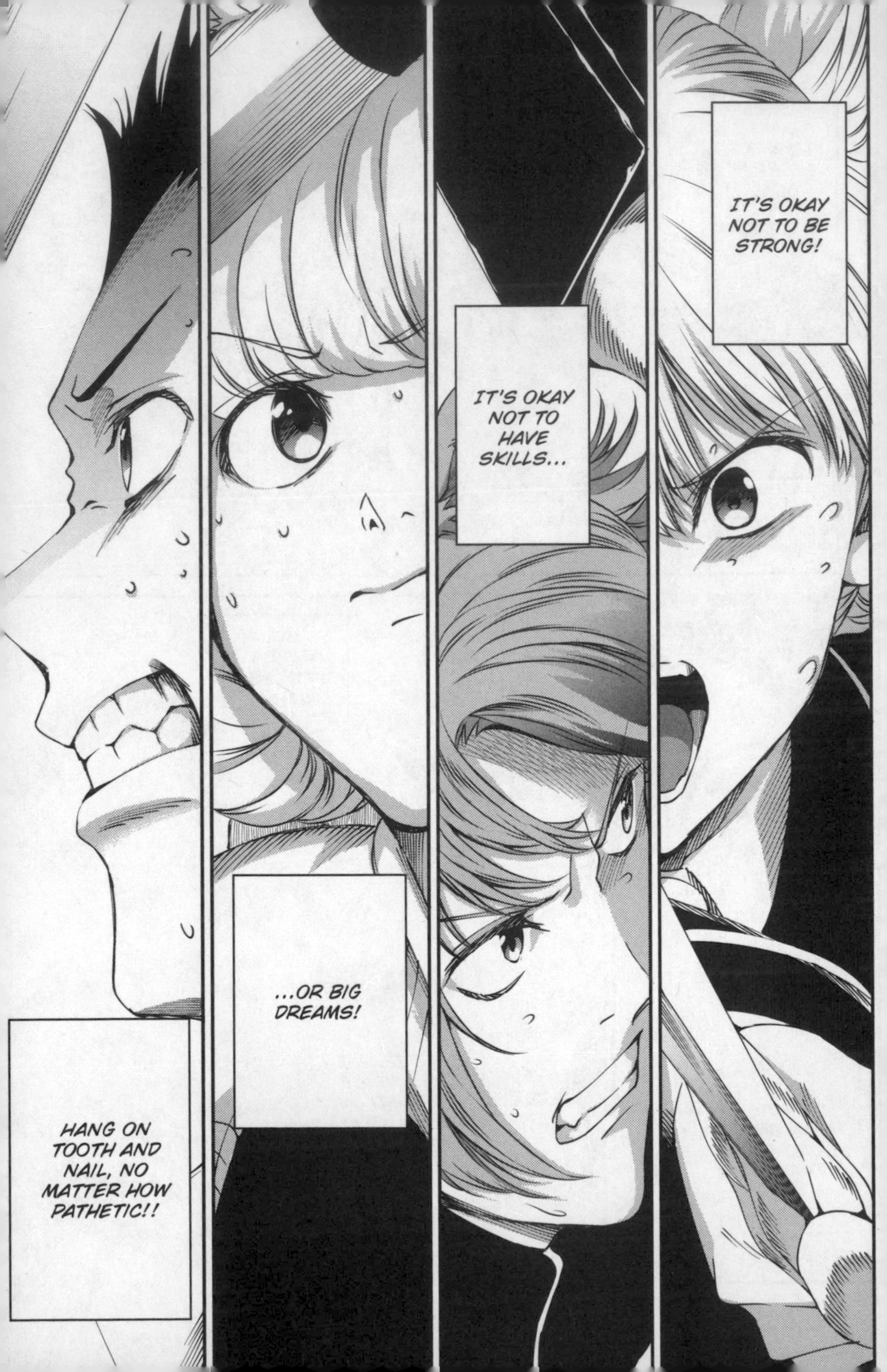
IT'S OKAY NOT TO BE STRONG!
IT'S OKAY NOT TO HAVE SKILLS...
...OR BIG DREAMS!
HANG ON TOOTH AND NAIL, NO MATTER HOW PATHETIC!!

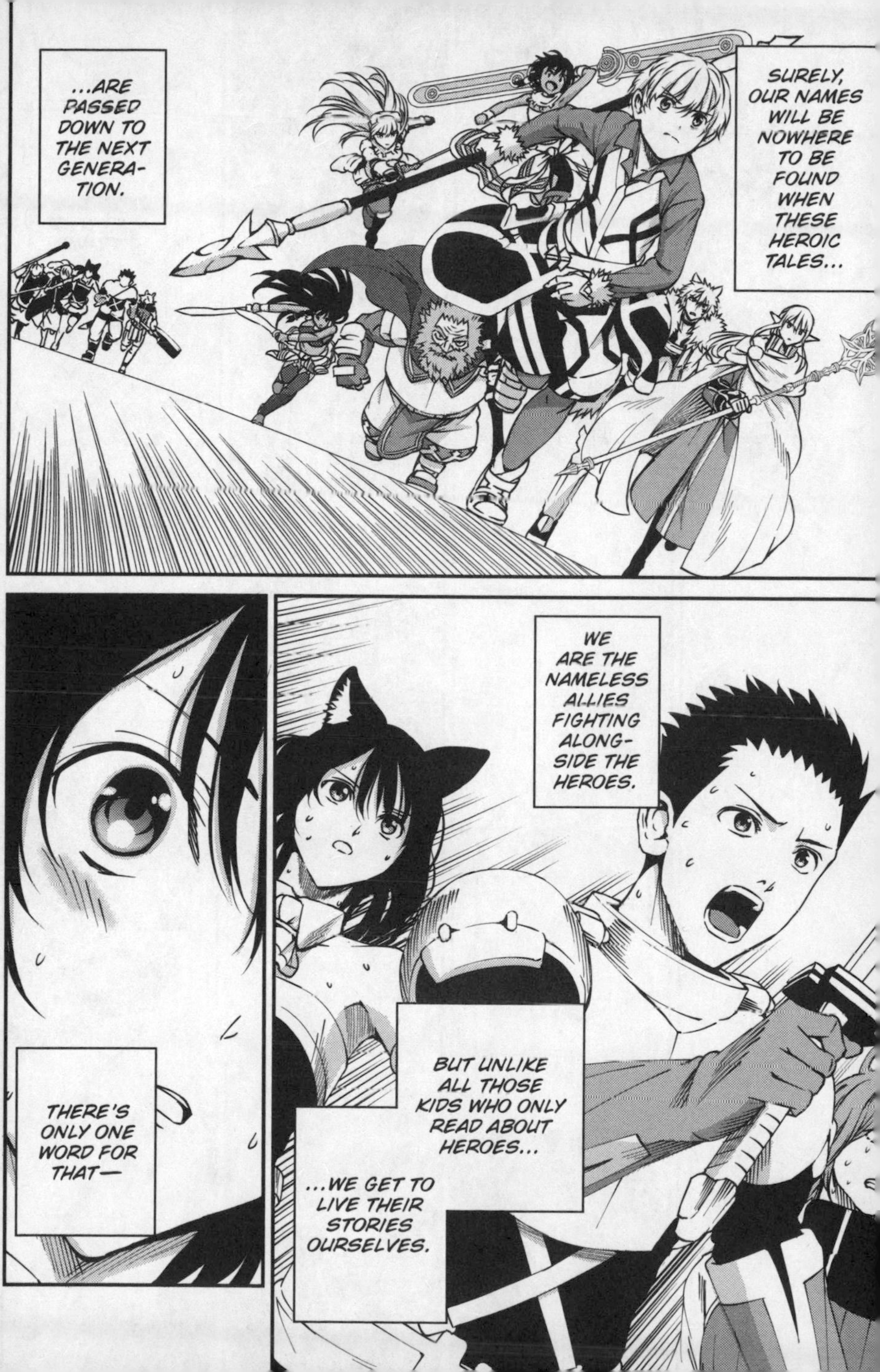
SURELY, OUR NAMES WILL BE NOWHERE TO BE FOUND WHEN THESE HEROIC TALES...
...ARE PASSED DOWN TO THE NEXT GENERATION.
WE ARE THE NAMELESS ALLIES FIGHTING ALONGSIDE THE HEROES.
BUT UNLIKE ALL THOSE KIDS WHO ONLY READ ABOUT HEROES...
...WE GET TO LIVE THEIR STORIES OURSELVES.
THERE'S ONLY ONE WORD FOR THAT—

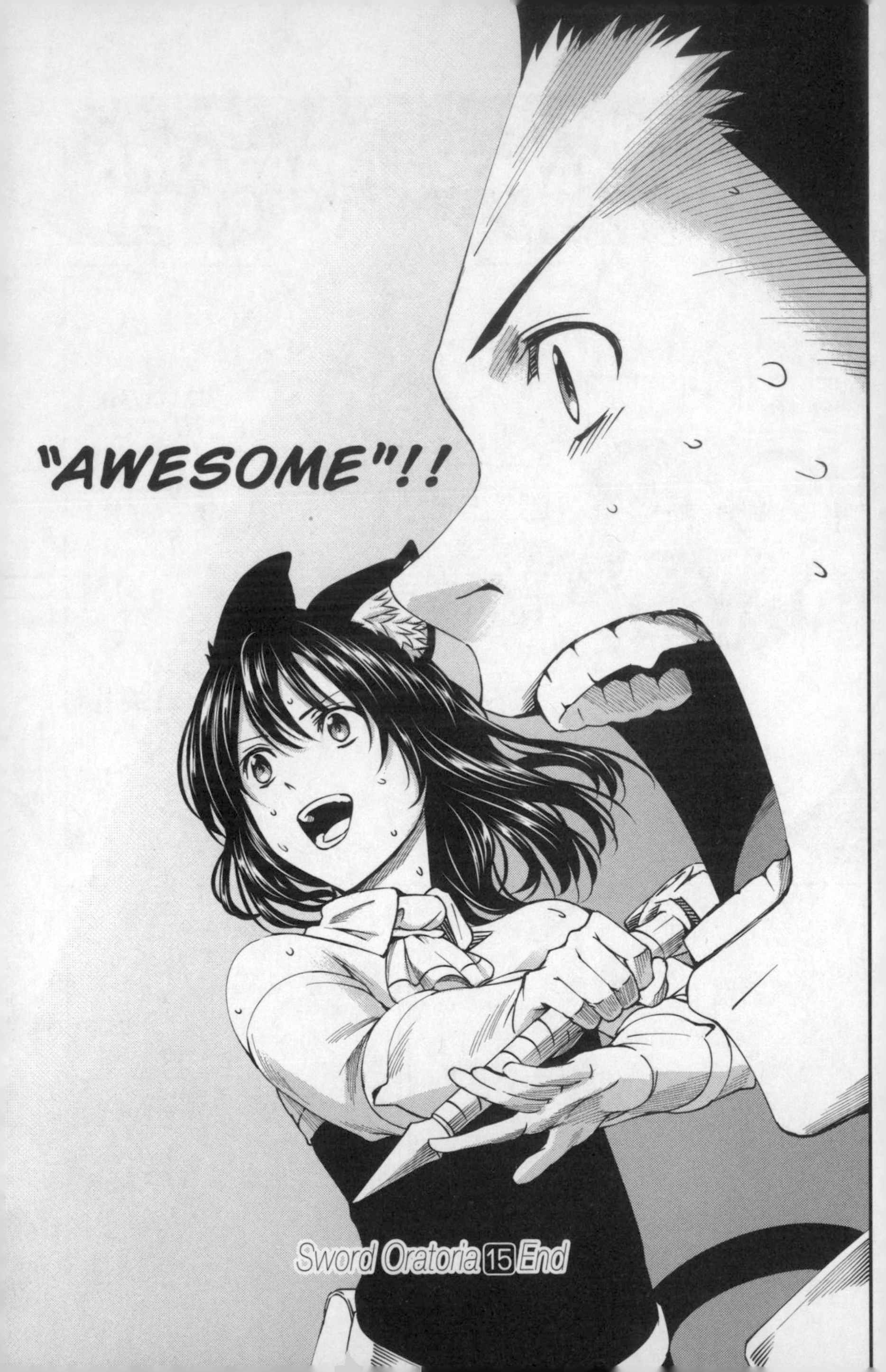
"AWESOME"!!
Sword Oratoria 15 End

THE 2ND ANNUAL LOKI FAMILIA PAJAMA PARTY

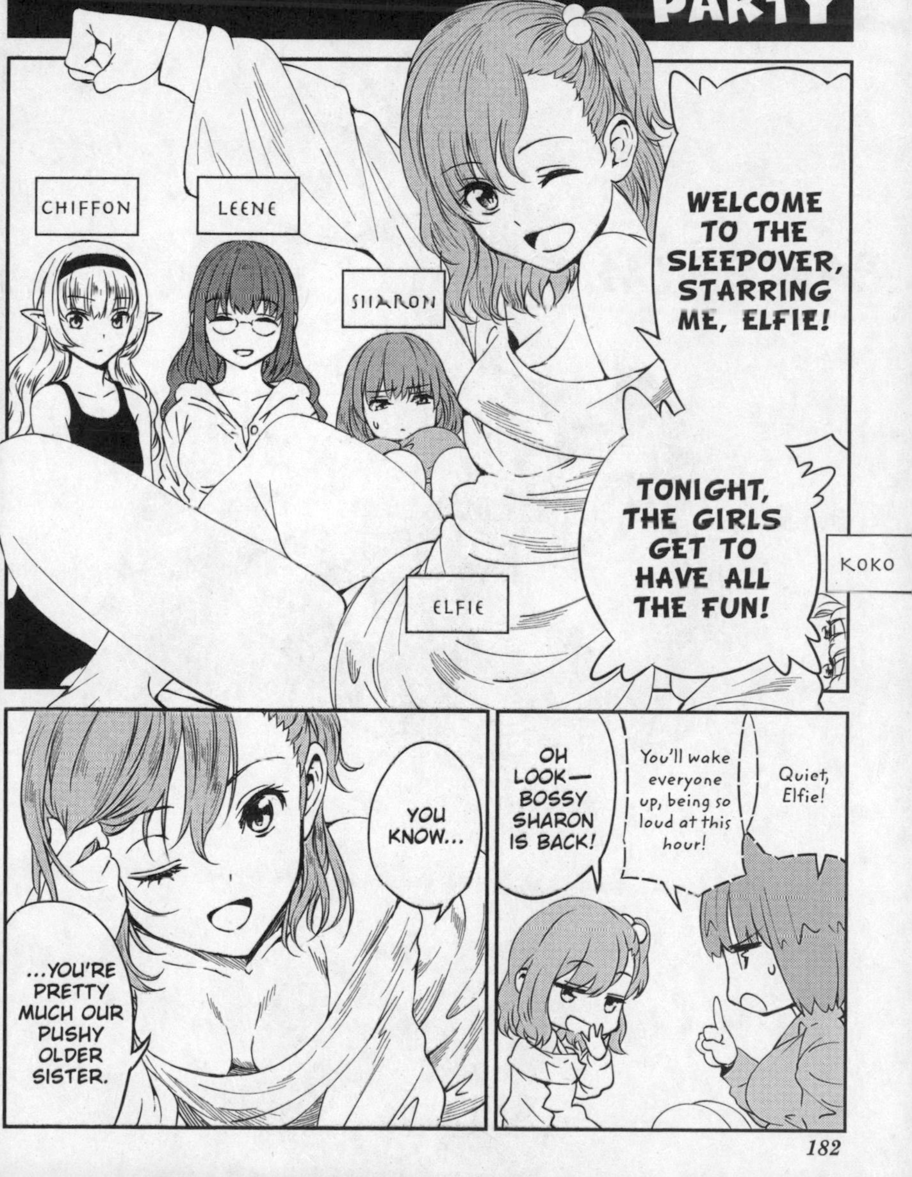
WELCOME TO THE SLEEPOVER, STARRING ME, ELFIE!
TONIGHT, THE GIRLS GET TO HAVE ALL THE FUN!
KOKO
ELFIE
SHARON
LEENE
CHIFFON
Quiet, Elfie!
You'll wake everyone up, being so loud at this hour!
OH LOOK—BOSSY SHARON IS BACK!
YOU KNOW...
...YOU'RE PRETTY MUCH OUR PUSHY OLDER SISTER.

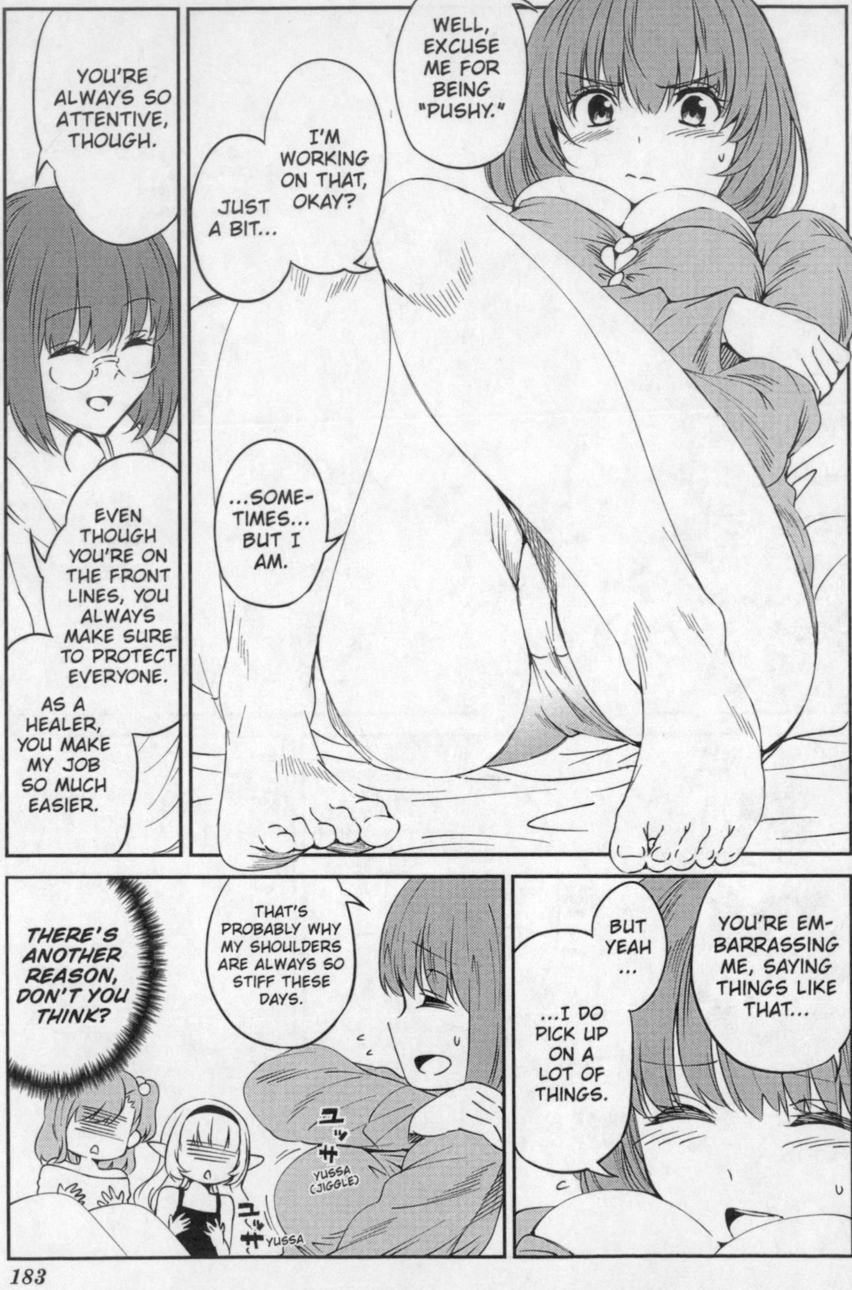
WELL, EXCUSE ME FOR BEING "PUSHY."
I'M WORKING ON THAT, OKAY? JUST A BIT...
...SOME-TIMES... BUT I AM.
YOU'RE ALWAYS SO ATTENTIVE, THOUGH.
EVEN THOUGH YOU'RE ON THE FRONT LINES, YOU ALWAYS MAKE SURE TO PROTECT EVERYONE.
AS A HEALER, YOU MAKE MY JOB SO MUCH EASIER.
YOU'RE EM-BARRASSING ME, SAYING THINGS LIKE THAT...
BUT YEAH ...
...I DO PICK UP ON A LOT OF THINGS.
THAT'S PROBABLY WHY MY SHOULDERS ARE ALWAYS SO STIFF THESE DAYS.
ユッサ
YUSSA (JIGGLE)
ユッサ
YUSSA
THERE'S ANOTHER REASON, DON'T YOU THINK?

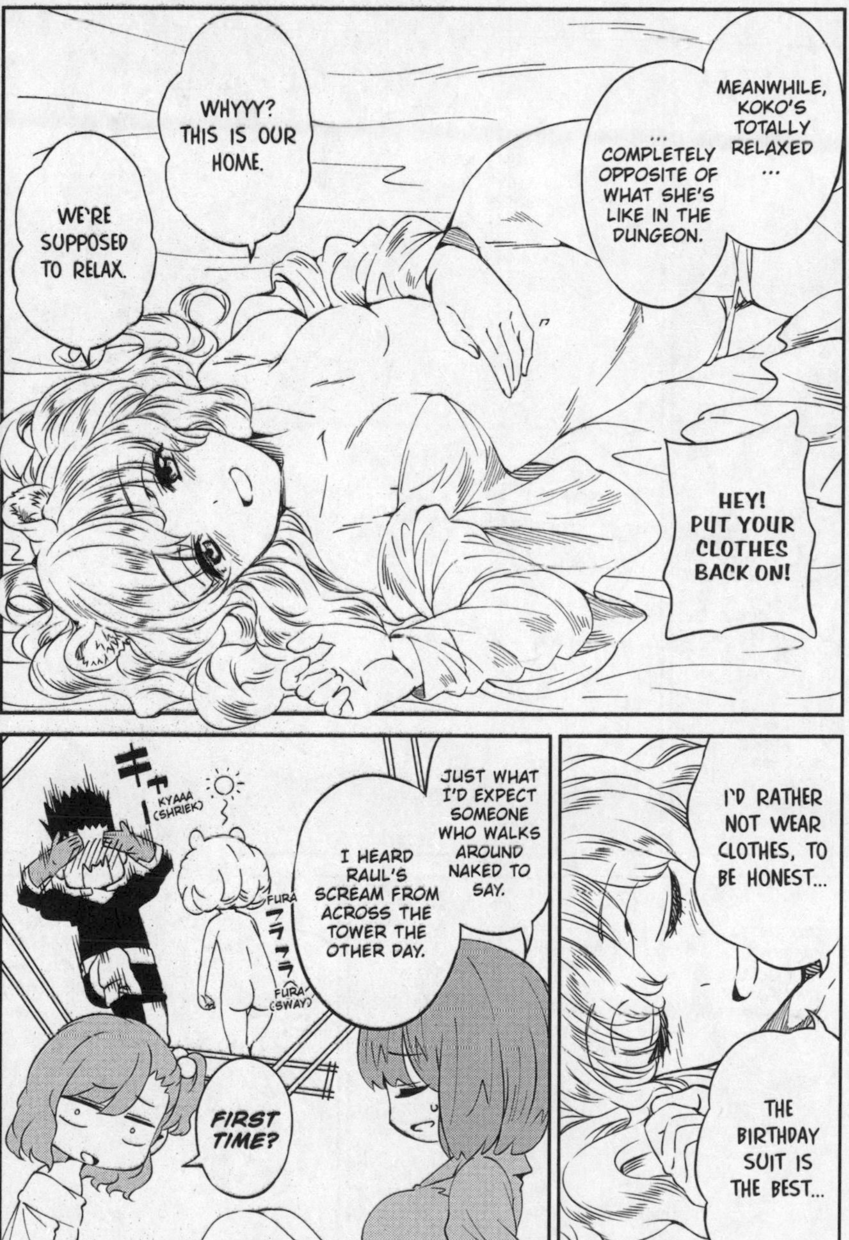
MEANWHILE, KOKO'S TOTALLY RELAXED...
...COMPLETELY OPPOSITE OF WHAT SHE'S LIKE IN THE DUNGEON.
HEY! PUT YOUR CLOTHES BACK ON!
WHYYY? THIS IS OUR HOME.
WE'RE SUPPOSED TO RELAX.
I'D RATHER NOT WEAR CLOTHES, TO BE HONEST...
THE BIRTHDAY SUIT IS THE BEST...
JUST WHAT I'D EXPECT SOMEONE WHO WALKS AROUND NAKED TO SAY.
I HEARD RAUL'S SCREAM FROM ACROSS THE TOWER THE OTHER DAY.
キャー
KYAAA (SHRIEK)
フラフラ
FURA FURA (SWAY)
FIRST TIME?

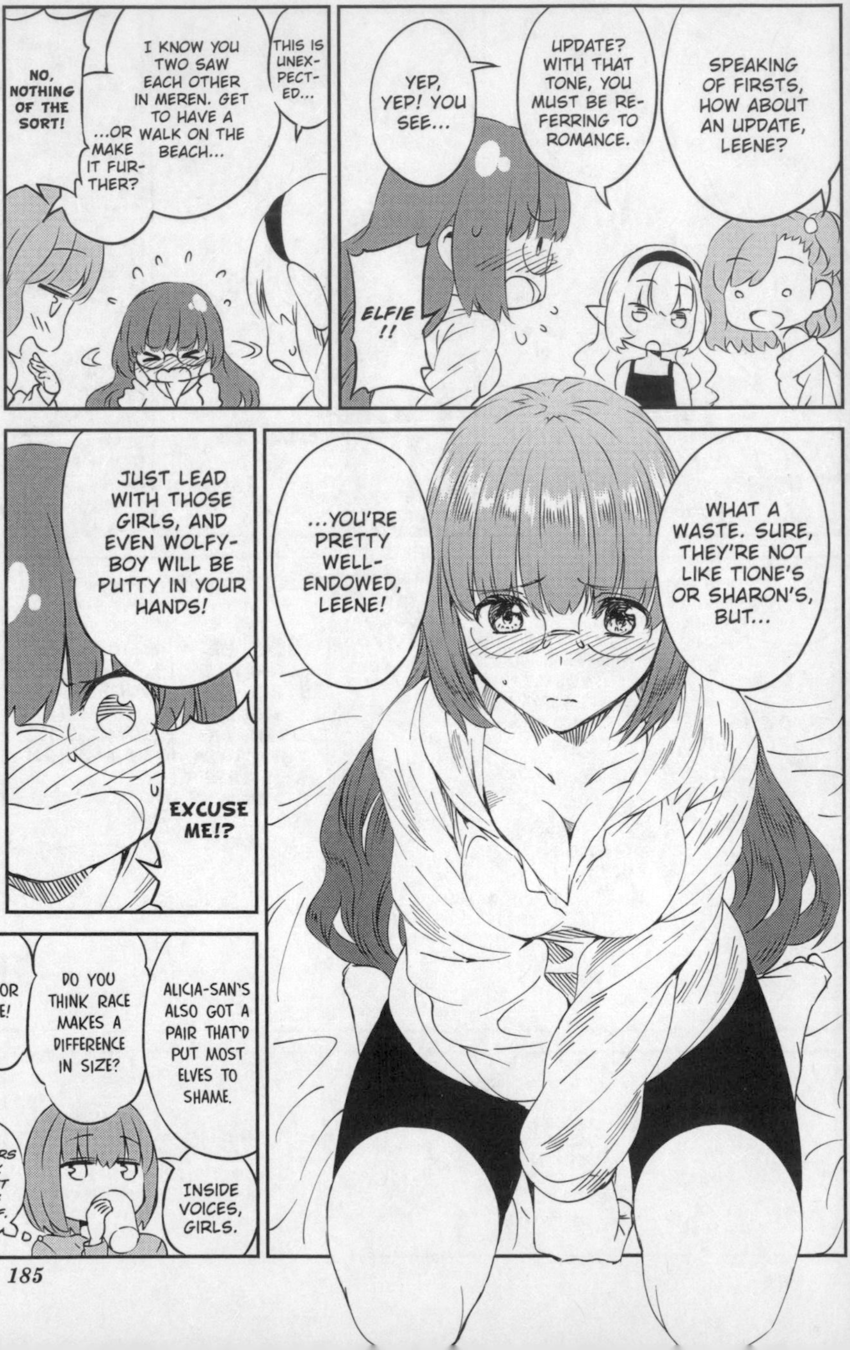
SPEAKING OF FIRSTS, HOW ABOUT AN UPDATE, LEENE?
UPDATE? WITH THAT TONE, YOU MUST BE REFERRING TO ROMANCE.
YEP, YEP! YOU SEE...
ELFIE!!
THIS IS UNEXPECTED...
I KNOW YOU TWO SAW EACH OTHER IN MEREN. GET TO HAVE A WALK ON THE BEACH...
...OR MAKE IT FURTHER?
NO, NOTHING OF THE SORT!
WHAT A WASTE. SURE, THEY'RE NOT LIKE TIONE'S OR SHARON'S, BUT...
...YOU'RE PRETTY WELL-ENDOWED, LEENE!
JUST LEAD WITH THOSE GIRLS, AND EVEN WOLFY-BOY WILL BE PUTTY IN YOUR HANDS!
EXCUSE ME!?
ALICIA-SAN'S ALSO GOT A PAIR THAT'D PUT MOST ELVES TO SHAME.
DO YOU THINK RACE MAKES A DIFFERENCE IN SIZE?
OH, FOR SURE!
INSIDE VOICES, GIRLS.
GEEZERS TALK ABOUT THIS STUFF.

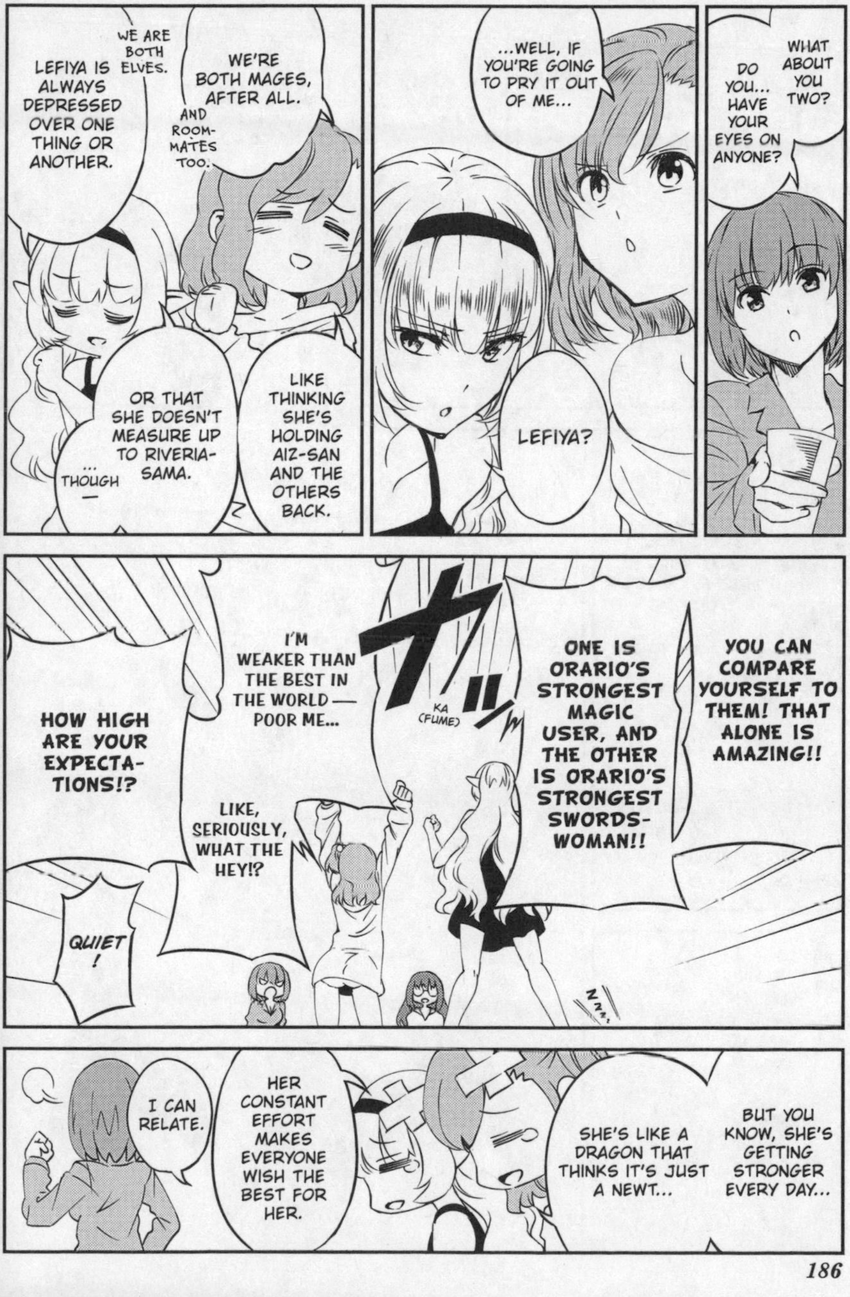
WHAT ABOUT YOU TWO?
DO YOU... HAVE YOUR EYES ON ANYONE?
...WELL, IF YOU'RE GOING TO PRY IT OUT OF ME...
LEFIYA?
WE'RE BOTH MAGES, AFTER ALL.
WE ARE BOTH ELVES.
AND ROOM-MATES TOO.
LEFIYA IS ALWAYS DEPRESSED OVER ONE THING OR ANOTHER.
LIKE THINKING SHE'S HOLDING AIZ-SAN AND THE OTHERS BACK.
OR THAT SHE DOESN'T MEASURE UP TO RIVERIA-SAMA.
...THOUGH—
YOU CAN COMPARE YOURSELF TO THEM! THAT ALONE IS AMAZING!!
ONE IS ORARIO'S STRONGEST MAGIC USER, AND THE OTHER IS ORARIO'S STRONGEST SWORDS-WOMAN!!
KA (FUME)
I'M WEAKER THAN THE BEST IN THE WORLD—POOR ME...
LIKE, SERIOUSLY, WHAT THE HEY!?
HOW HIGH ARE YOUR EXPECTA-TIONS!?
QUIET!
BUT YOU KNOW, SHE'S GETTING STRONGER EVERY DAY...
SHE'S LIKE A DRAGON THAT THINKS IT'S JUST A NEWT...
HER CONSTANT EFFORT MAKES EVERYONE WISH THE BEST FOR HER.
I CAN RELATE.

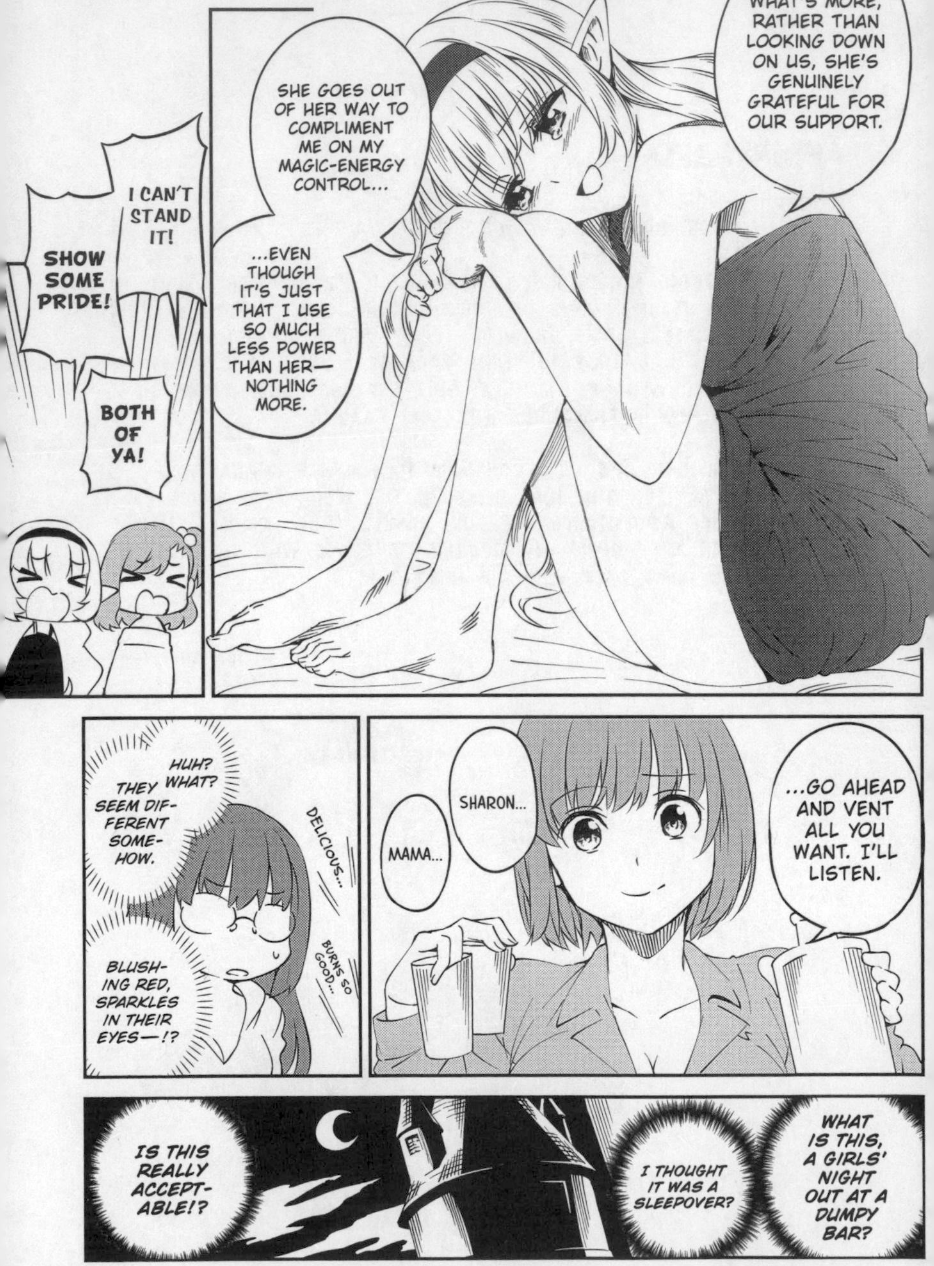
WHAT'S MORE, RATHER THAN LOOKING DOWN ON US, SHE'S GENUINELY GRATEFUL FOR OUR SUPPORT.
SHE GOES OUT OF HER WAY TO COMPLIMENT ME ON MY MAGIC-ENERGY CONTROL...
...EVEN THOUGH IT'S JUST THAT I USE SO MUCH LESS POWER THAN HER—NOTHING MORE.
I CAN'T STAND IT!
SHOW SOME PRIDE!
BOTH OF YA!
...GO AHEAD AND VENT ALL YOU WANT. I'LL LISTEN.
SHARON...
MAMA...
HUH? WHAT?
THEY SEEM DIF-FERENT SOME-HOW.
DELICIOUS...
BURNS SO GOOD...
BLUSH-ING RED, SPARKLES IN THEIR EYES—!?
WHAT IS THIS, A GIRLS' NIGHT OUT AT A DUMPY BAR?
I THOUGHT IT WAS A SLEEPOVER?
IS THIS REALLY ACCEPT-ABLE!?

AFTERWORD

THANK YOU FOR PURCHASING *SWORD ORATORIA* 15!

I STARTED ADDING NAMES FOR LOKI FAMILIA'S SECOND-TIER SQUAD IN THE PREVIOUS VOLUME. SOME OF THEIR DESIGNS COME DIRECTLY FROM THE ANIME, WHILE I CAME UP WITH OTHERS FROM SCRATCH. THEY WON'T ALL GET A CHANCE TO SHINE BECAUSE I ONLY HAVE SO MANY PAGES TO WORK WITH, BUT I HOPE THAT READING THESE BOOKS HAS GIVEN YOU A NEW APPRECIATION FOR LOKI FAMILIA.

ORATORIA'S SECOND ARC WILL CONTINUE TO FEATURE CHARACTERS OTHER THAN AIZ FOR THE TIME BEING, BUT I DECIDED TO FOCUS ON THE LOWER-TIER ADVENTURERS OF LOKI FAMILIA THIS VOLUME. I'LL KEEP DRAWING THE HOPES AND DREAMS OF THOSE WHO WILL NEVER BE STARS, SO COME BACK FOR THE NEXT ONE!

TAKASHI YAGI

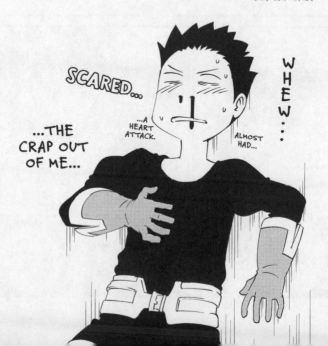

WHEW...
ALMOST HAD...
...A HEART ATTACK.
SCARED...
...THE CRAP OUT OF ME...

Coming up...

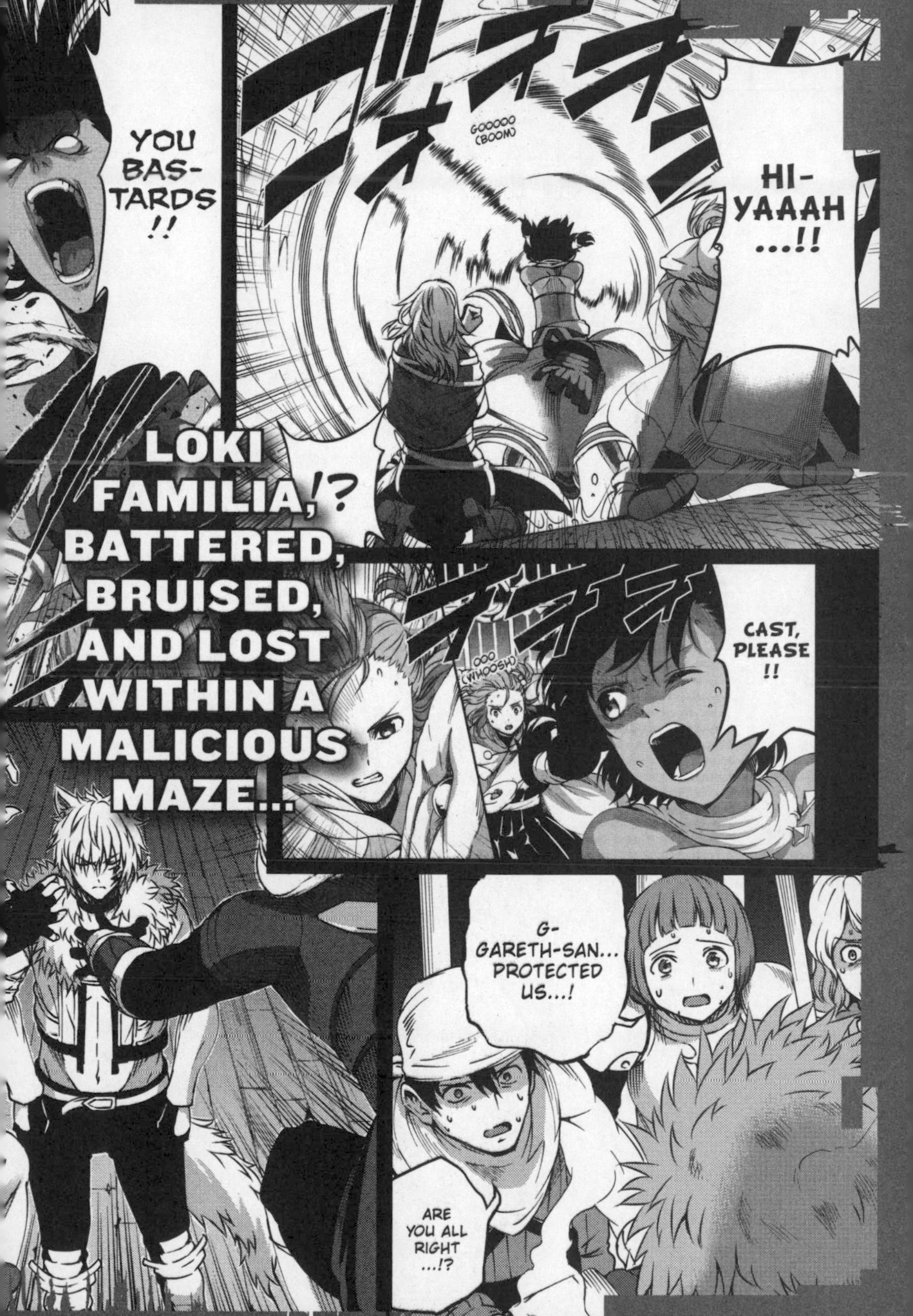
HI-YAAAH...!!
GOOOOO (BOOM)
YOU BASTARDS!!
LOKI FAMILIA!? BATTERED, BRUISED, AND LOST WITHIN A MALICIOUS MAZE...
CAST, PLEASE!!
OOO (WHOOSH)
G-GARETH-SAN... PROTECTED US...!
ARE YOU ALL RIGHT...!?

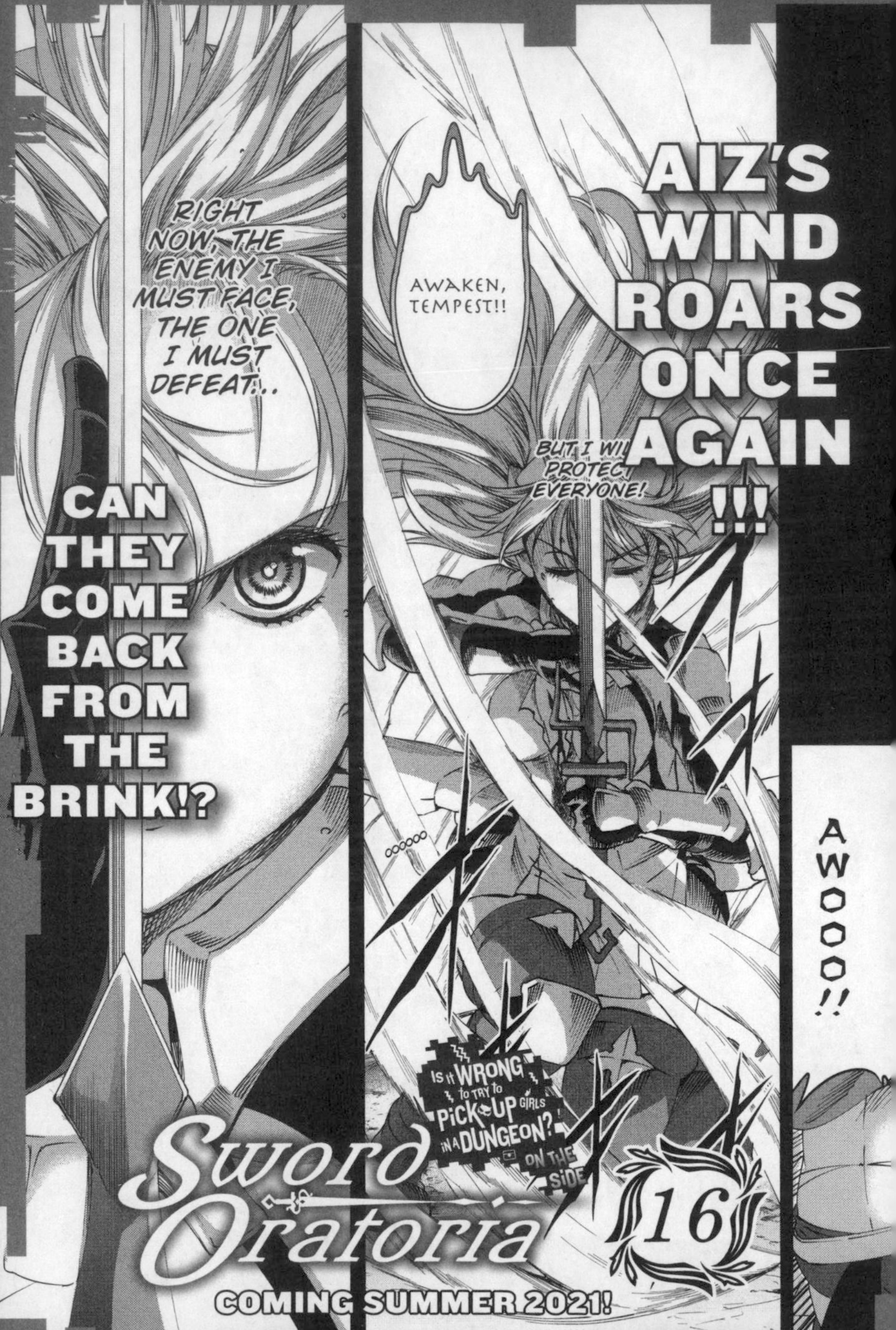
AIZ'S WIND ROARS ONCE AGAIN!!!
AWOOOO!!
AWAKEN, TEMPEST!!
BUT I WI PROTEC EVERYONE!
RIGHT NOW, THE ENEMY I MUST FACE, THE ONE I MUST DEFEAT...
CAN THEY COME BACK FROM THE BRINK!?
IS IT WRONG TO TRY TO PICK UP GIRLS IN A DUNGEON? ON THE SIDE
Sword Oratoria
16
COMING SUMMER 2021!

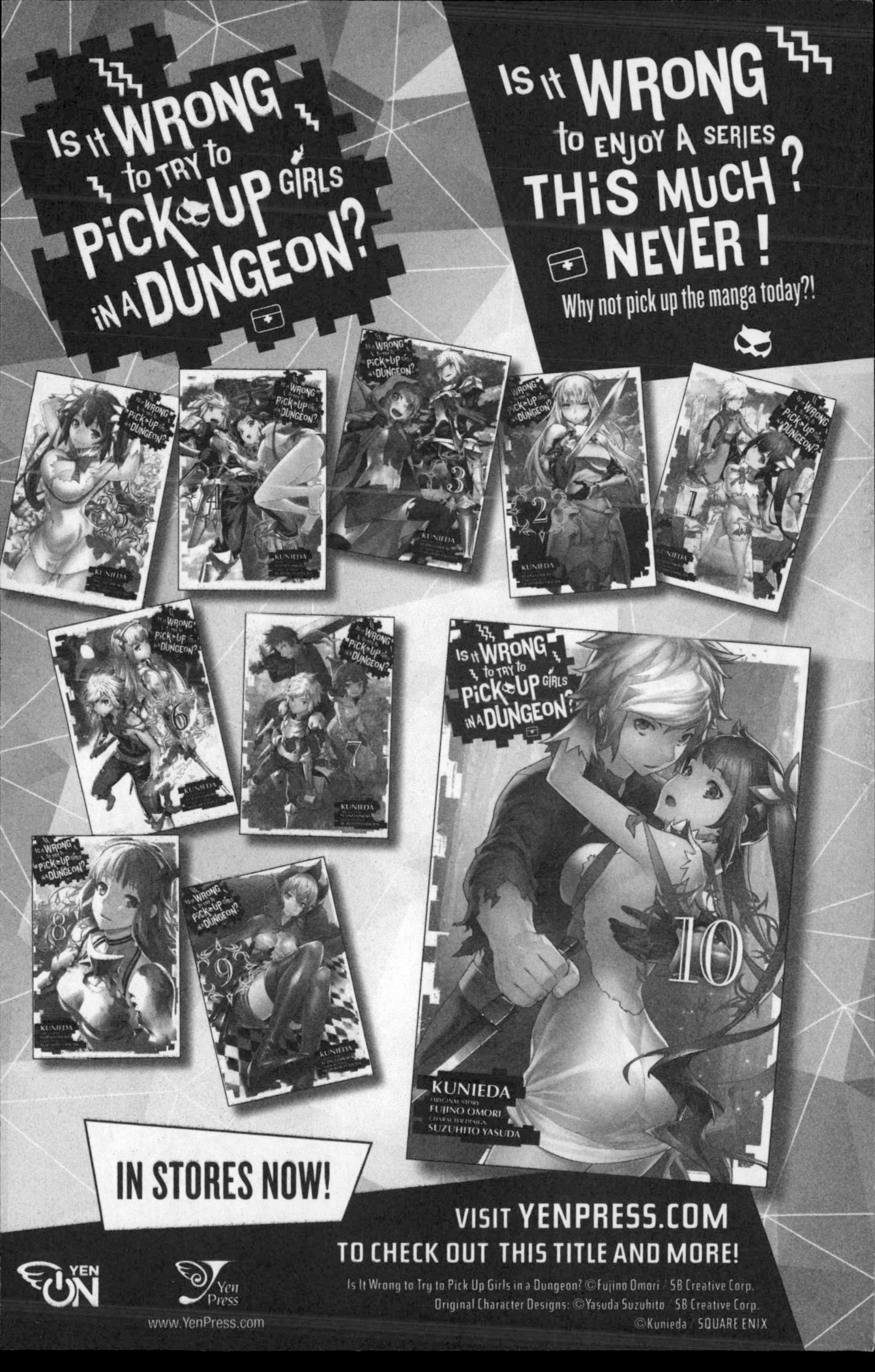

Is it WRONG to TRY to PICK UP GIRLS in a DUNGEON?
Is it WRONG to ENJOY A SERIES THIS MUCH?
NEVER!
Why not pick up the manga today?!
KUNIEDA
ORIGINAL STORY FUJINO OMORI
CHARACTER DESIGN SUZUHITO YASUDA
IN STORES NOW!
VISIT YENPRESS.COM
TO CHECK OUT THIS TITLE AND MORE!
YEN ON
Yen Press
www.YenPress.com
Is It Wrong to Try to Pick Up Girls in a Dungeon? ©Fujino Omori / SB Creative Corp.
Original Character Designs: ©Yasuda Suzuhito / SB Creative Corp.
©Kunieda / SQUARE ENIX

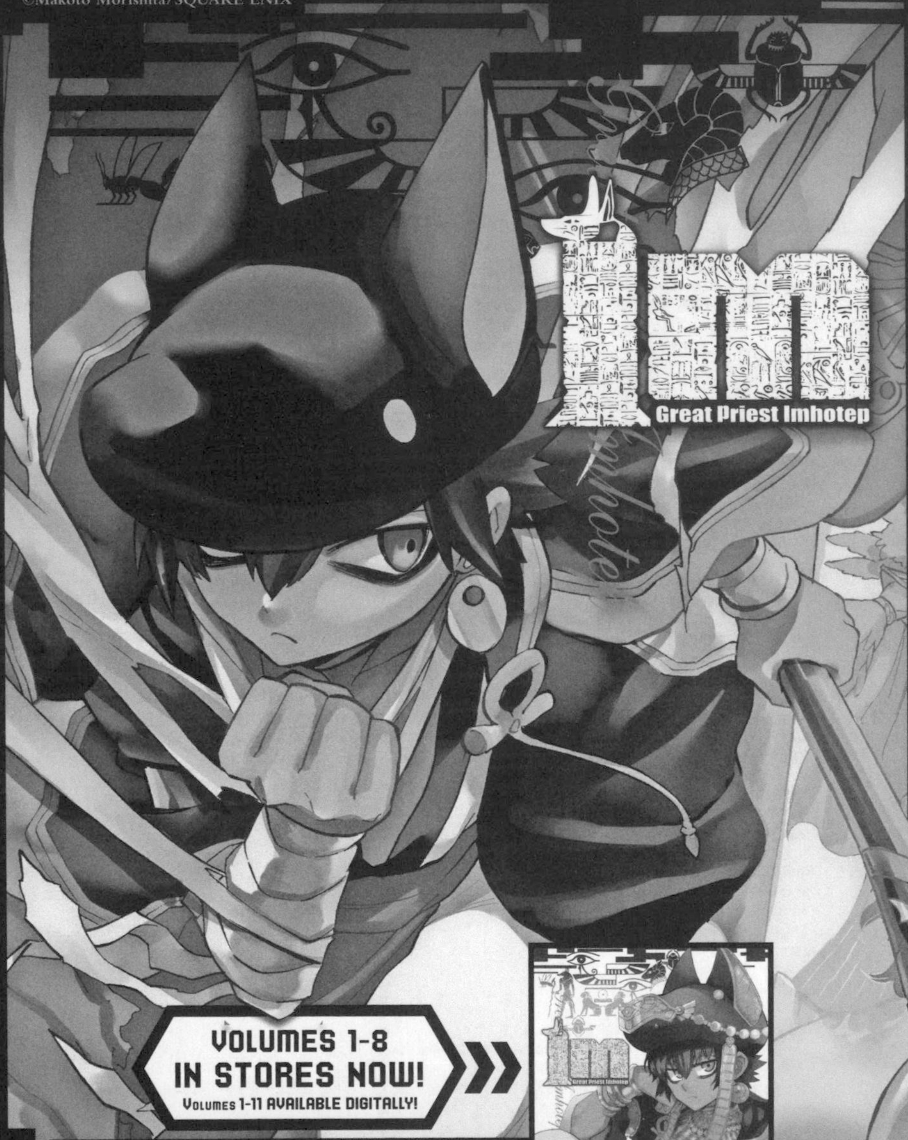

IM
Great Priest Imhotep
VOLUMES 1-8
IN STORES NOW!
VOLUMES 1-11 AVAILABLE DIGITALLY!
IM
Great Priest Imhotep
1 MAKOTO MORISHITA

From the sands of ancient Egypt to the streets of modern Japan, being displaced by thousands of miles and years won't distract the newly resurrected Great Priest Imhotep from his hunt for the Magai, devious beings who impersonate the gods and have an appetite for destruction! When schoolgirl Hinome crosses paths with this illustrious ancient, is her loner lifestyle about to change for the better...or the worse?!

For more information
visit www.yenpress.com

Yen Press

IS IT WRONG TO TRY TO PICK UP GIRLS IN A DUNGEON? ON THE SIDE: SWORD ORATORIA

Haimura Kiyotaka, Yasuda Suzuhito

Translation: Andrew Gaippe • Lettering: Barri Shrager

DUNGEON NI DEAI WO MOTOMERU NO WA MACHIGATTEIRUDAROUKA GAIDEN SWORD ORATORIA vol. 15
©Fujino Omori/SB Creative Corp.
Original Character Designs:©Kiyotaka Haimura/SB Creative Corp.
Original Character Designs:©Suzuhito Yasuda/SB Creative Corp.
© 2019 Takashi Yagi/SQUARE ENIX
First published in Japan in 2019 by SQUARE ENIX CO., LTD.
English translation rights arranged with SQUARE ENIX CO., LTD. and Yen Press, LLC through Tuttle-Mori Agency, Inc.

English translation © 2021 by SQUARE ENIX CO., LTD.

Yen Press
150 West 30th Street, 19th Floor
New York, NY 10001

Visit us at yenpress.com
facebook.com/yenpress
twitter.com/yenpress
yenpress.tumblr.com
instagram.com/yenpress

First Yen Press Edition: April 2021

Yen Press is an imprint of Yen Press, LLC.
The Yen Press name and logo are trademarks of Yen Press, LLC.

Library of Congress Control Number: 2016946068

ISBNs: 978-1-9753-1507-8 (paperback)
       978-1-9753-1506-1 (ebook)

10 9 8 7 6 5 4 3 2 1

BVG

Printed in the United States of America